Contemporary Spanish Cultural Studies

Edited by

BARRY JORDAN

Professor of Hispanic Studies,
De Montfort University

and

RIKKI MORGAN-TAMOSUNAS

Dean, School of Languages and Social Sciences,
Anglia Polytechnic University

A member of the Hodder Headline Group
LONDON
Co-published in the United States of America by
Oxford University Press Inc., New York

First published in Great Britain in 2000 by
Arnold, a member of the Hodder Headline Group,
338 Euston Road, London NW1 3BH

http://www.arnoldpublishers.com

Co-published in the United States of America by
Oxford University Press Inc.,
198 Madison Avenue, New York 10016

British Library Cataloguing in Publication Data
A catalogue entry for this book is available from the British Library

Library of Congress Cataloging-in-Publication Data
A catalog record for this book is available from the Library of Congress

ISBN 0 340 73121 4 (hb)
ISBN 0 340 73122 2 (pb)

1 2 3 4 5 6 7 8 9 10

Production Editor: Anke Ueberberg
Production Controller: Priya Gohil
Cover Design: Terry Griffiths

Typeset in 10/12pt Sabon by Phoenix Photosetting, Chatham, Kent
Printed and bound in Great Britain by MPG Books Ltd, Bodmin, Cornwall

What do you think about this book? Or any other Arnold title?
Please send your comments to feedback.arnold@hodder.co.uk

Contents

Contributors

Mark Allinson is Head of Hispanic Studies at Royal Holloway College, University of London. His interests are in modern and contemporary Spanish culture, particularly drama, cinema and subcultures. He has published articles on Lorca, Pirandello, violence in contemporary Spanish cinema and an essay on the films of Pilar Miró. Forthcoming publications include essays on gay identity, youth culture and punk in Spain. He is currently writing a book on the films of Pedro Almodóvar and a language textbook, *Negotiating Spanish*, in collaboration with Richard Pym.

Margaret Andrews is a research student in Hispanic Cultural Studies at Nottingham Trent University where she is working on women and social change in Spain with particular reference to women's contemporary constructions of the city in Barcelona. Her research interests also include cultural distinctions in the production and consumption of flamenco.

Elvira Antón is Lecturer in Hispanic Studies at Thames Valley University. Her research interests are Spanish and Latin American cultural studies, particularly in relation to literature, advertising and popular culture. She has published articles on contemporary Spanish literature and race and identity in Cuba. She is currently working on issues of race and identity in nineteenth-century Cuba.

Anny Brooksbank Jones is Senior Lecturer in Hispanic Studies at the University of Leeds. She has published widely on Spanish and Latin American culture and socio-cultural theory. Recent publications include her book *Women in Contemporary Spain* (1997), and a volume of essays co-edited with Catherine Davies: *Latin American Women's Writing: Feminist Readings in Theory and Crisis* (1996). She has recently completed two edited volumes: *Culture and Politics in Latin America* and a special issue of *Latin American Perspectives* on the politics of postmodernism in Latin

America, both with R. Munck. She is also preparing a reader on hybridity with R. Bromley and J. Tomlinson, and writing a single-authored book, *In Love and War*, on Spanish and Latin American cultural studies.

Jacky Collins is Lecturer in Hispanic Studies at the University of Northumbria at Newcastle. Her main areas of research are lesbian cultures in Spain and women in the Spanish Civil War.

Madeline Conway is a research student at Birkbeck College, University of London where she is writing her doctoral thesis on 'The Representation of Disability in Contemporary Spanish Culture'.

David Corkill is Reader in Iberian Studies at Manchester Metropolitan University. He has written numerous articles on the economy and politics of both Spain and Portugal. Recent publications include *The Development of the Portuguese Economy. A Case of Europeanization* (Routledge, 1999). He is currently writing (with Joseph Harrison of Manchester University) *Spain: a Modern European Economy* as well as researching a volume on the economies of Spain's autonomous communities.

Liz Crolley is Senior Lecturer in Spanish at Manchester Metropolitan University. She has published widely on the history, politics and sociology of football and issues of nationalism and identity, particularly in relation to Spain, Italy and Argentina. She also has a research interest in Spanish linguistics and gender. Her recent publications include *Football, Nationality and the State* (1996) with V. Duke, and she is currently completing *Image and Identity in European Football Writing* (working title) with D. Hand and R. Jeutter.

Philip Deacon is Senior Lecturer in Hispanic Studies at the University of Sheffield. He has published widely on eighteenth- and twentieth-century Spanish culture, including an edition of Leandro Moratín's *El sí de las niñas* (1995) and articles on the Spanish media. His current research involves a book on Nicolás Moratín and a study of eighteenth-century erotic poetry. He is Editorial Advisor for the *British Journal for Eighteenth Century Studies* and member of the Editorial Board of *Dieciocho*.

Carrie Hamilton is Lecturer in Spanish Social and Political Studies at Southampton University. Her main research interests are modern history, especially oral history, memory and women's activism in contemporary Spain. She is currently preparing her recently completed Ph.D. on *The Gender Politics of ETA and Radical Basque Nationalism 1959–1982* for publication.

Barry Jordan is Professor of Hispanic Studies and Head of Spanish at De Montfort University, Leicester. He has published five books including

Writing and Politics in Franco's Spain (1990), *Carmen Laforet: Nada* (1993), and *Contemporary Spanish Cinema* (1998) with Rikki Morgan-Tamosunas. He has also published numerous articles on post-war Spanish fiction, drama, media, intellectual and cultural history as well as on literary and critical theory. He is currently writing a volume on Spanish cinema.

Dorothy Kelly is Principal Lecturer in the Department of Translation and Interpreting at the University of Granada. She has researched mainly in the field of translator training and translation as inter-cultural mediation; she has also written on print representations of Spanish national identity and the role of the translator in the marketing and advertising of Spanish goods in English-speaking markets.

Alex Longhurst is Professor of Hispanic Studies at the University of Leeds. He is the author of six books and numerous articles on modern and contemporary Spanish literature and social history. He is currently working on naturalism and modernism in the writings of the Generation of 1898 as well as aspects of social change in contemporary Spain. He is Visiting Professor at the University of Glasgow and Editor of the *Bulletin of Hispanic Studies*.

Trinidad Manchado is Senior Lecturer in Spanish and Curriculum Leader for Peninsular Spanish at Middlesex University. Her main research interest is in Spanish cultural memory, particularly in relation to heritage, cinema and literature. Forthcoming publications include essays on documentary films in Spain.

Richard Maxwell, having taught Radio, TV and Film Studies at NorthWestern University, is currently Associate Professor in the Department of Media Studies at Queens College–City University of New York. He has published widely on Spanish media. His writings include *The Spectacle of Democracy: Spanish Television, Nationalism and Political Transition* (1995).

Alberto Mira is Reader in Spanish at Oxford Brookes University, having recently held the Queen Sofía Research Fellowship at Exeter College, Oxford. His research interests are homosexuality and Spanish and Latin American culture (especially gay identities in history and homosexual/gay writing), Spanish cinema, theatre, and translation as cultural practice. He has recently published *De silencios y espejos: hacia una estética del teatro español contemporáneo* (1996), a Spanish translation of Albee's *Who's Afraid of Virginia Woolf* (1997) and *Para entendernos* (1999), an encyclopedia of homosexual and lesbian culture within the Hispanic world.

Cristina Moreiras Menor is an Assistant Professor in Modern Spanish at Yale University, USA. Her main research interests are nineteenth- and twentieth-century modern Spanish literature, contemporary Spanish cultural studies, Spanish film and cultural theory. She has published various articles in Spain and the USA and is currently writing a book, *Historia y síntoma: cultura herida y escritura traumática en la España contemporánea* (working title), focusing on Spanish literature and film of the last two decades in relation to the social and political events of the post-dictatorship period.

Tony Morgan is Senior Lecturer and Head of Spanish at Anglia Polytechnic University in Cambridge. His research interests include regional cultures in Spain and Europe, the politics of devolution in Spain, and the Spanish labour market on which he has published widely. Recent publications include *Pay and Conditions in Spain* (1998) and *Recruitment and Termination of Contract in Spain* (1999). He has also researched and written on popular cultures and customs in the early industrialization of Mexico, and his current research interests are focused on traditional cultures in peripheral European regions, and language and national dominance.

Rikki Morgan-Tamosunas is Dean of Languages and Social Sciences at Anglia Polytechnic University in Cambridge. Her research interests include Spanish and Latin American film and cultural studies. She has published widely on Spanish cinema, particularly in relation to gender and sexuality, postmodernism, and representation of the past. Recent publications include *Contemporary Spanish Cinema* (1998) co-authored with Barry Jordan. She continues to work on contemporary Spanish cinema, but is also preparing articles on cinema and the Spanish Civil War, and contemporary Latin American cinema.

Hugh O'Donnell is Reader in Language and Media at Glasgow Caledonian University. His research has been concerned with the comparative analysis of popular culture in Western Europe, particularly in relation to sport, soap operas and representations of monarchy. In addition to many articles, he has also published *Good Times, Bad Times: Soap Operas and Society in Western Europe* (1999) and, with N. Blain and R. Boyle, *Sport and National Identity in the European Media* (1993). He is currently working on modernism and postmodernism in Western European television.

Chris Perriam is Professor and Head of the Department of Spanish, Portuguese and Latin American Studies, and Postgraduate Sub-Dean of the Faculty of Arts at the University of Newcastle. His research areas are modern Spanish writing and cinema and Queer Studies. His publications include *The Late Poetry of Pablo Neruda* (1989) and *Desire and Dissent: an Introduction to Luis Antonio de Villena* (1995). He is currently completing a co-authored book entitled *A New History of Spanish Writing: 1939 to the 1990s*, and working on a future volume on stars and masculinities in

Spanish cinema, as well as a series of articles on male same-sex Spanish writing. He is a member of the Editorial Advisory Board for the *Journal of Spanish Cultural Studies*.

Ryan Prout is currently Junior Research Fellow in Spanish at Christ Church, Oxford. His main areas of research are contemporary Spanish language cinema and literature and his current work has an emphasis on popular culture. His work on film has included articles on the work of Almodóvar, Calparsoro, Mendiola, Arcand and Palmero. He has also written on the Mexican novel and has forthcoming a monograph on phobia and reproduction in the work of Juan Goytisolo. He reviews films and literature for the *Gay and Lesbian Review*.

Michael Richards lectures in European History at the University of the West of England, Bristol. He is the author of *A Time of Silence: Civil War and the Culture of Repression in Franco's Spain, 1936–45* (1998). He is currently writing a social history of contemporary Spain.

Antonio Sánchez is Lecturer in Spanish at Birkbeck College, University of London. His main research interests are cinema, literature and theatre on which he has published a number of articles.

Núria Triana Toribio teaches Spanish Film and History at the University of Liverpool. Since completing her Ph.D. on *Subculture and Popular Culture in the Films of Pedro Almodóvar* (1994), she has published articles on Almodóvar, Ana Marisical and Pilar Miró. She is currently working on a book on Spanish National Cinema and a further project on women film directors.

Iñaki Zabaleta is Professor of Communication Studies in the Department of Journalism at the University of the Basque Country. He has written several books on technological and programming changes in Spanish and global radio and television including *El factor humano en radio y television* (1995). He has also worked as a journalist and documentary maker for Basque television and CNN as well as having published novels, short stories and poetry.

Introduction

Spanish cultural studies constitutes an exciting and newly emerging area, which is still establishing itself as a field of academic enquiry and as a set of teaching and learning practices. Given its adoption of the term 'cultural studies', the Spanish variant is still in the process of defining itself in relation to other modern languages variants and to its more established mainstream cousins. In this connection, the discipline of cultural studies in general has been in formation since the 1970s and exists in a number of different forms and traditions, in various institutional settings and countries, most notably the UK, USA, Canada and Australia. Cultural studies developed from the interaction between various academic disciplines (initially literary studies, history and sociology and subsequently linguistics, anthropology, psychology, etc.) and sought to combine and bring to bear on the study of 'culture' the various approaches characteristic of these disciplines. This legitimized the claim of cultural studies to interdisciplinarity – a feature which has traditionally been lacking in Spanish studies (Graham and Labanyi, 1995, p. v). Of course, in a lot of ways, interdisciplinarity makes it more not less difficult to define exactly what cultural studies is and to develop a language through which teachers and students can talk meaningfully to each other about culture. And even after nearly 30 years of development and debate, cultural studies is by no means a wholly settled area, with commonly accepted scholarly agendas, curricula, theoretical paradigms, protocols, methodological approaches, and so on (Hall, 1986, pp. 33–8). Indeed, debates continue to rage over what we mean by such terms as meaning, identity, representation, knowledge and social agency (Thwaites, Davis and Mules, 1994). In a sense, this is exactly how it should be. After all, cultural studies came into being motivated precisely by the commitment to demystify and extend the meaning of the word 'culture' beyond the notion of a narrowly defined 'canon' of great works of art or the preserve of social elites towards those institutional activities, behaviours and beliefs which define the 'way of life' of particular social groups (Williams, 1993, pp. 5–6). No wonder then that as relative newcomers to the field of cultural studies, students and teachers of Spanish studies might feel slightly concerned at its rather amorphous nature, its view of cultural artefacts as 'texts' which are always symptomatic of wider social contexts, its unfamiliar and often intimidating concepts and terms, and so on. Yet, the difficulty we have in defining cultural studies is arguably a strength, a positive advantage, since it allows us to combine together the ideas, insights and resources of many disciplines. These can allow us to develop different ways of understanding, which we can then apply to diverse aspects of our own field of Spanish studies.

Before describing in more detail Spanish cultural studies and indicating how our readers might use our book, we thought it might be useful if we offered to those relatively unfamiliar with the field in general a brief overview of some of the main concepts and issues which we believe lie at the heart of a modern cultural studies approach and of which Spanish and other forms of cultural studies are increasingly taking account. What follows is by no means a comprehensive summary but a selection of key ideas and positions which inform the essays in this volume and which offer a foothold in the field as well as a basis for discussion.

Culture, identity, meaning, cultural studies

In recent decades, there is no doubt that the domain of the 'cultural' and the meanings we attach to the idea of 'culture' have expanded and changed out of all recognition. Culture is not simply the sphere of art, literature, aesthetics and moral values but, as Barthes explained way back in the 1950s (*Mythologies*, 1957), a wide-ranging set of practices (including French wine, the Michelin Guide, Garbo's face, professional wrestling) whose meanings and conventions are not natural or given but historically contingent, ideologically loaded and amenable to demystification. In the same period, while Williams and Hoggart sought to recuperate the lost traditions of 'working class' culture, European Marxism talked of the oppressive nature of capitalism's 'mass culture' (as opposed to 'popular culture') and its ideological manipulations of passive consumers (Hall, 1986, p. 45). Under the impact of world-wide independence movements and decolonization processes since the 1960s, the notion of culture has expanded to include the 'cultures' of hitherto neglected groups, including various movements in feminism and multiculturalism as well as groups (especially youth subcultures) who resist their subordination through the creative use of the products of mass culture (Hall, 1976). Culture thus becomes a site where different groups struggle to establish their presence, their identities and through which they secure the domination of subordinate groups or, using Gramsci's term, impose their hegemony (Bennett, 1986, p. xiii). Moreover, with the explosion of new media technologies, the means of producing, distributing, exchanging and refashioning cultural artefacts and 'flows' of cultural information have been revolutionized. We now live in a world in which the technological compression of time and space has led to the rapid globalization of this cultural revolution and has given us the opportunity to inhabit multiple and indeed virtual (cyber) worlds. Such transformations have undoubtedly led to a high degree of cultural homogenization, the global Coca Cola/Pepsi/McDonalds syndrome, increasingly eroding local features and peculiarities. Yet such potentially negative effects are by no means uniform or predictable; moreover, they are very unevenly spread across the world and in many places are subject to countervailing forces and forms of resistance, which counteract such Western-inspired uniformity (as in the resurgence of Islam and various forms of religious fundamentalism). As we argue in this book, global culture thrives (and does its business) not on the basis of sameness, but on the strength of creating user differences and thus by incorporating and harnessing local tastes, preferences and habits. Indeed, as a result of cultural mixing across national boundaries, rather than wiping out old cultural forms with new ones, global culture tends to create saleable hybrid alternatives. Thus, particularly potent and widely used forms of global culture (e.g. the Sony Walkman; *see* Hall, 1997), may well form part of a dominant Western cultural tide, but the uses to which they are put or the meanings and values attached to them may differ radically, according to the societies and local cultures in which they circulate.

From another perspective, it is difficult to deny that while certainly eroding and destabilizing forms of national identity and culture, globalization gives (some of) us access to different worlds, cultures and ways of life we would otherwise not be aware of. Such new worlds are crucially mediated, however, by representations (images) and messages produced by the culture industries. Cultural forms are predominantly manufactured and seem to seep into the very fabric of social life, mediating our encounters with those worlds. Cultural changes have probably had the deepest impact on our sense of who we are, since culture plays such a crucial role in shaping our own subjectivities, identities and images of self as individual and social agents. Here, the sort of stories we pick up and tell each other about who we are and how we regard our lives are important in shaping our attitudes and attachments. Such stories or narratives tend to contain a mixture of sound and unsound information, hearsay, cliché, stereotype and myth but we use them to construct not only our view of self but also of community and nation. While these stories might offer us a convincing account of who we are and where we stand (and thus be 'true' for us), they are far from complete since they are continually being redefined. However, one story more than others may well catch our attention, appeal to us and get us to invest emotionally in its meanings, provisionally locking into place our allegiance to a certain idea, view or outlook. Here, quite possibly, through our responding repeatedly to this or that mode of address, a local or national identity comes into being. Identity thus emerges in the interplay between what we call a 'discourse', a sort of language or mode of language use (e.g.

medical, legal, advertising discourse, etc.) and our willingness to be called upon, to be 'hailed' by that discourse (or another) and step into the slot or subject position it constructs for us. The process of identity construction, of getting us to merge at least some of our own identity with that of another person, idea or set of images, is not fixed or immutable, however; our views and allegiances can and do change, all the time. From a cultural studies perspective, the main point is that identities, i.e. positions made available for us in various discourses, are culturally formed and (re-)presented to us through various sets of meanings (signifying practices) which are also culturally produced. Cultural studies thus tends to ask how far we are shaped by cultural forces and how far we are responsible for moulding our own cultural identity.

Any and every social activity generates its own world of social relations, meanings and practices – its own culture. In a sense, we belong to this or that culture when we buy into and operate within certain meaning systems and not others. Of course, what we do not tend to notice very much is the fact that the links between social divisions (racial, sexual, ethnic, class, etc.) and economic inequalities are often obscured, naturalized and taken for granted. In this sense, social activity is not formless, nor does it operate in a vacuum; in fact, it is highly regulated according to all sorts of norms, rules, regulations and possible sanctions. Culture allows us, at least to some extent, to be active and creative, offering areas where we can and do show who we are by our own particular use and transformation of cultural materials (e.g. Spain's punk movements of the 1980s). Yet, culture also governs us, shapes us, bears down upon us and regulates our conduct. Our social activity also takes place against a background of knowledge, sedimented into a set of taken for granteds, a 'common sense', which we are called upon to share and not to question. This faciltitates our willingness to work within certain cultural norms and allows us to mark out who belongs where (do they act like us, according to our rules?) and who is seen as 'other', different, acting outside normative limits, that is, outside our discourse or our ways of doing things. Culture thus draws upon and channels our creative energies, allowing us opportunities to express ourselves through those languages and cultural materials we have available to us and which we creatively reshape. In many senses, culture also 'makes' us; it produces us as individual and collective subjects, it sets the normative frame in which we are offered a set of limited and finite choices and possibilities as subjects. In short, culture constructs us and has power over us. Culture is thus determined by power (be it economic, political, institutional, social, familial) and by whatever and whomever can influence the general and particular shape of cultural life at all levels of society. For this reason, we should be vitally aware of who or what determines culture since in the end we are determined by it and its purveyors. To conclude this section, our understanding of the term 'culture' has moved radically over the years to a point where, just as we tend to regard the economy or political system as foundational, culture is now seen as fully enmeshed in and constitutive of the social world and the individual identities we inhabit.

Spanish cultural studies

Spanish cultural studies is arguably bringing to bear on the discipline of Spanish studies a range of issues and debates which have been helping to redefine the content, approaches and agendas of the discipline over last decade (*see* Jordan, 1990). These debates are also gradually having the effect of moving Spanish studies from minority to more mainstream and cross-disciplinary curricula and helping us engage in issues which more adequately reflect Spain's complex international positioning in the world today. Indeed, as noted above, contemporary Spanish cultural studies acknowledges the impact of globalization on Spanish cultural forms, the many struggles between the forces of homogenization and resistance and the emergence of new, hybridized cultural artefacts. We thus recognize the need to study Spanish culture within the modern, indeed postmodern framework of the de-legitimation of knowledges, the challenge to fixed identities and at the same time the resurgence of local identities and ethnic nationalisms. Spanish cultural studies thus takes a profound interest in identities and their construction, particularly the ways in which various forms of discourse (including those of class, race, ethnicity, sexuality, gender, nation, etc.) traverse and inflect their formation and affect their transmission. This is particularly relevant to the contemporary, post-Franco period of unstable cultures and newly forming cultural identities arising from the new autonomies, multiculturalism, immigration, and so on. Such an interest is crucial at a time when it is becoming increasingly difficult to talk confidently any more of a singular Spanish identity as such, as Spain becomes both globalized and internally fragmented through processes of political devolution. How do we get a handle on such issues? One obvious form of representation is textual and the reader will find within this volume numerous instances of textual analysis which deal with such questions. However, Spanish cultural studies is also interested in exploring a much wider range of cultural materials and deals with the signifying functions of film, video, television, museums, galleries, new technologies, etc. – all are forms of signification which play a key role in the mediation and construction of Spanish identities and experience. In brief, we hope to bring increasingly to the mainstream of Spanish studies areas of work which have been previously ignored or marginalized or which only recently have begun to receive more sustained attention (identities, new ethnicities, as well as media, sexualities, aspects of popular culture, heritage, etc.).

What is the relationship between cultural and literary studies? Cultural studies had its origins in linguistic and literary analysis and in the application of literary study techniques to other cultural artefacts. Over the years, however, this heritage has been radically problematized; the literary text is now seen as but one artefact, one signifying practice among others, to be read as a form of cultural practice. Also, common sense notions of literary canons and their boundaries have been seriously eroded, with canons being extended to take into account writings by previously marginalized groups (women, ethnic minorities, post-colonial cultures) as examples of their 'cultural experience'. Such changes raise issues such as the extent to which literary forms exist as textual forms 'in themselves' and how far they create or construct the cultures and realities they are said to 'represent' (Culler, 1997, p. 49). As for Spanish studies, given the discipline's massive accumulated investments in literary scholarship and study over decades if not centuries, what provisions do we make for literary study, what forms of study do we favour and why? In principle, cultural studies would appear to be an all-embracing category allowing us to combine Cervantes and *bakalao* (Spain's house/techno music), Pereda and Spanish punk, high and low, past and present cultural forms. Yet, the fact that Spanish cultural studies arose in part out of a series of dissatisfactions with Spanish literary studies (*see* Jordan, 1990) perhaps suggests a reticence towards a certain form of literary studies. This would be one traditionally conceived of in terms of reaffirming through criticism a self-selecting canon of great works, whose beauty, complexity, universality and subtlety of meaning simply inhere in the 'text' itself. There again, it could be argued that Spanish literary studies has never been wholly unified around one single notion of what it was doing. Also, since the arrival of literary theory, many Spanish teachers and academics have been quick to take up new theoretical insights and ideas, leading to a contestation of the discipline where all kinds of new work, literary and non-literary, are demanding recognition and in many cases getting it. This suggests that, in some ways, Spanish literary studies now takes a much more flexible approach to its object of analysis, an approach or set of approaches which cultural studies need not reject out of hand or take fundamental issue with. Moreover, and in any case, much of the work done in cultural studies is based on treating cultural objects and artefacts as texts to be read 'closely'; at the same time, literary studies can be fundamentally energized and renewed when literary texts are studied as particular forms of social practice and related to other forms of signification. So, in principle, a cultural studies approach, by examing the sorts of meanings, uses and functions with which the literary text has been inscribed over time, could in fact regenerate the study of literature as a complex and rewarding intertextual process (Culler, 1997, p. 48).

In light of the above, how should we deal with approaches which still seem to rest on apparently 'high culture' definitions of Spanish culture? As the editor of a recent compendium on modern Spanish culture argues: ' "Culture" will be used here in a restricted sense, one referring to "the general body of the arts" and to "the intellectual side of civilisation" ' (Gies, 1999, p. 4). Though openly proclaiming its narrower focus and more traditional view of culture, this appears to be a perfectly legitimate approach to take and is arguably a major advance on even more traditional definitions of Spanish culture, based on a highly restrictive notion of a self-selecting literary 'canon'. Yet, the definition of culture in terms of the 'arts' arguably rests on an evaluation of Spanish 'culture' which is assumed rather than analysed. A modern cultural studies approach might suggest, in principle, that Spanish culture can and should be viewed in a rather more inclusive, plural and wide-ranging fashion. But, the inclusion of a wider range of cultural forms in the equation is insufficient in itself. We would also need to explore the rationale behind the inclusion of the selected material. In relation to the so-called 'arts', this would mean problematizing the notion of the 'arts' as well as acknowledging the existence of various forms of elite, popular and mass culture (as Gies in fact does, 1999, p. 4). But then, we could take the further step of explaining how these areas become defined and positioned as such, what is included in them and why. And of course, who or what makes those selections? Moreover, a cultural studies 'take' on Spanish 'intellectual' culture might then wish to look at how such concepts, definitions and their meanings arise historically and, crucially, how the boundaries between the various cultural forms/fields proposed are drawn and redrawn and how these demarcations are negotiated and change over time. In other words, our notion of Spanish 'intellectual' culture is immediately unfixed, relativized and set in motion; we thus become aware that definitions are provisional and change over time and that they change because such definitions are continually being contested and challenged from other points of view. We also become aware that Spanish culture is a much wider and more complex field, encompassing not only the arts (in their many fascinating forms), but also, as noted above, the many ways in which Spanish people live their lives and define who they are.

For example, like anywhere else in Europe or the USA, Spaniards at work are increasingly aware of attempts made by their employers to promote certain forms of 'culture' at the workplace in order to ensure success of one kind or another. Here, the notion of 'culture' is given significant importance since it is seen as a way of achieving organizational efficiency and profitability by maximizing the contribution and commitment of the workforce to the aims of the enterprise. In this sense, 'culture' – i.e. the meanings, norms, values and behaviours produced at the workplace and circulated through work practices and their associated 'languages' or 'discourses' – is crucially regarded as the means of shaping and structuring the way people think, feel and behave in their respective organizations. The 'cultural' is thus intimately connected to the 'economic'; managers of companies are anxiously seeking to create the proper organizational 'cultures' because these are seen as crucial to success and to creating the appropriate forms of subjectivity and commitment in the workforce. In this light, our definitions of 'culture' have again been radically extended: no longer is the cultural side of life seen simply as the soft, second order, 'intellectual' expression of an economic 'base', but both are intimately connected and contribute to the way in which people behave and see themselves in work and in many other areas (Du Gay, 1997, p. 4).

In this sense, and taking into account not only the workplace in Spain, but leisure activities, consumption, politics, heritage, family relationships, sexuality, and so on, Spanish cultural studies is crucially concerned with how the self-definitions or identities of people and what they do come into being and with how people interact with the material cultural forms which help to shape these identities. In short, we wish to focus on how people shape their lives and in turn how people are shaped and moulded into individual and collective subjects through the 'cultures' they inhabit, how such identities are ordered, regulated and contested over time and indeed how these then relate to social divisions and economic and political inequalities.

This volume

Up until recently, Spanish cultural studies suffered from a serious dearth of appropriate, useful and accessible materials, with both teachers and students often obliged to scour more specialist books and scholarly journals for relevant background. Here, we offer the present volume as a way of helping to rebalance and rectify this situation and overcome some of the more obvious obstacles, gaps and absences occasioned by the lack of materials. At the same time, we are bound to acknowledge that over the last five years, several important publishing initiatives in this and contiguous fields have emerged, notably works by Chris Ross, Marsha Kinder, David Gies, Eamonn Rodgers and the pioneering volume edited by Helen Graham and Jo Labanyi, *Spanish Cultural Studies: An Introduction* (1995).

In our case, we approach Spanish cultural studies as a significant new field concerned primarily with the study of how cultural meanings and thus identities get sedimented and organized through cultural practices and relations of power. These processes and practices inhabit many different areas of experience and, as noted above, are intersected by complex relations of class, race, gender, ethnicity, regional identity, etc. So, we go beyond a conception of Spanish culture as a set of finished texts, forms, symbols, and so on, to a study of how such features (also including tastes, values and behaviours) get generated and structured, are laid down and positioned and how they work to create meaning and identity. In short, we begin to look at how such features are 'represented' in the relevant mode of language use or 'discourse' and how this affects the way in which Spanish people see themselves and are seen by others. 'Culture' is not a one-way process, however; as outlined above, culture also bears down upon and regulates the options people have available in the process of identity construction.

We continue to acknowledge in this volume the importance of a long-range historical framework for Spanish cultural studies, already established by Graham and Labanyi, taking account as they do of the bitter struggles for modernization/modernity, the role of culture(s) in both promoting as well as resisting these often conflictive processes and the need of modern Spain and its communities to come to terms with that still troubling historical legacy. With that in mind, the main historical frame and starting point for the present study is the 1960s. From here, we begin to focus more closely on Spain as an evolving, proto-consumer society, still enmeshed in the contradictions arising out of its uneven economic development while also anticipating the clash with postmodernity in the political, cultural and communications revolutions of the later 1970s and 1980s. Hence our overall focus on the contemporary period, which is deliberately incorporated into the title of the volume.

The main contribution of this volume to the emerging discipline of Spanish cultural studies comes from the 28 essays themselves, which offer a deliberately wide range of topic areas and viewpoints including: (1) national and regional identities (in relation to the development of Spain as a consumer society, the cultural impact of economic change since the 1960s, the role of collective memory on versions of 'Spanishness', tourism and the marketing of Spanish 'difference', Spanish cinema and national identity, conflictive readings of Spain's 1992 celebrations); (2) race and ethnicity (in terms of the shift from mono- to multiculturalism, traditional and new ethnicities, immigration policy, internal and external migrations, Spain's role as gatekeeper on Europe's southern flank); (3) representations of the past (coming to terms with Spain's multiple 'pasts', redefining postmodernism and the avant-garde, 'theming' the past in literature, art, film, political discourse, etc.); (4) gendered identities (in television advertising, fiction and film, feminist and gay activisms, in radical Basque nationalism) and the representation of disability; (5) youth and popular cultures (punk and popular music, popular cinema, television sitcoms and serials, football and fandom); (6) media (television systems, struggles between public and private domains, the impact of new technologies (including digitial and cable television), the politics of television news, the renewal of the Spanish film industry, Spain as a transnational consumer society).

Conscious of the fact that Spanish cultural studies is still an evolving field, we decided to commission a fairly large number of essays ranging over a wide spectrum of topic areas and issues. However, we were anxious to allow our contributors sufficient space to develop their arguments and analyses in some depth and thus to help the reader come to terms with some of the more challenging issues involved in the field. The essays presented here have been commissioned from a wide spectrum of specialists working in the UK, Spain and the USA. Many of our contributors are recognized and established experts in their own respective fields of study and their names will no doubt be familiar to many of our readers. However, we have also made an effort to attract to the project less well-known researchers, as we are aware of the fact that more and more of the younger generation of scholars are developing valuable work informed by cultural studies perspectives. All the essays for the volume have been specially commissioned by the editors to represent the best and most up-to-date work taking place in the field.

In keeping with the more generous word limit for the essays, we have allowed contributors space for notes and references. We have also placed all quotations in English, with Spanish originals in the form of endnotes where appropriate. Translations have been provided by the individual contributors unless otherwise indicated. Suggestions for further reading are found in a separate section (p. 317) and here we limit ourselves to works available mainly written in English. Apart from the references relating to each individual essay, readers should find sufficient guidance here in order to help them broach new or unfamiliar topic areas. For readers who are unfamilar with twentieth-century Spain, we also provide a glossary giving brief explanations of mainly Spanish terms which arise in the text and which may require elucidation.

The volume is divided into five parts, each part being headed by a key thematic marker, which signals a major field of work developing within Spanish cultural studies. The essays in each part are preceded by an editorial introduction which seeks not to summarize or gloss each essay in turn but to outline the main issues arising in the area in question and the sorts of approaches broadly adopted by the essays contained therein. As they work through the volume, readers will find a significant degree of overlap and interconnection between essays and parts given the ways in which, for example, matters of identity raised in Part I re-emerge and inform the sort of issues dealt with in differing contexts in, say, Part IV. In broad terms, our volume seeks to satisfy the reader's requirements on two broad fronts: for those looking for the more long-range, overview-type of essay, readers will find a number of such pieces, which seek to critically reappraise received wisdom as well as to open up new questions around the topic area; at the same time, the volume offers a number of new and challenging case-study pieces, essays focusing closely on specific texts (both written and visual) or authors/auteurs, seeking to expose conventional assumptions while setting the text in an appropriate context. However, we also find that the above distinction between overview and more closely argued case study invariably breaks down given that many of the case studies illustrate the connection between detailed scrutiny of cultural production and wider discursive processes and cultural trends.

The essays in the present volume range widely across questions of economic and political devleopments, reception and consumption, lifestyles, media, sexuality and gender, as well as ethnicity and identities. Given the sheer range of topic areas, it would be surprising if the views of the contributors fully coincided with those of the editors. Where differences of approach and point of view emerge, these have been respected and retained. Also, we believe we have produced a volume which is theoretically well-informed though, it is to be hoped, jargon-light and thereby as accessible as possible as a textbook and sourcebook for our mainly undergraduate readership. We have also quite deliberately avoided the temptation to allow ourselves or our contributors to make a fetish out of cultural theory. Whilst the essays in the present volume have not been commissioned for their engagement in matters of high theoretical debate, we believe that they can and do provide significant theoretical gains in the on-going construction of the discipline. This is so, not in the sense of making linear advances but in terms of achieving a set of positive, open-ended shifts from one problematic to another where we gain some substantive, fresh understanding by thinking anew a set of problems. In fact, this sort of work need not involve a new theory or theories at all, but a cool and considered rethink of old positions. And while the gains might not result in a systematic, well-ordered sense of progress from one issue to another, such work can raise enough questions in order to shed new light on the ways we think about Spanish culture. And this is precisely what we are aiming for. One of the less widely publicized points about cultural studies in general, leaving aside its interdisciplinarity, plurality and frequently political and interventionist motivation, is that it increasingly exists, not so much as a set of theoretical arguments or metalanguages, but more as a set of localized and contested knowledges, to do with the analysis of what Raymond Williams regarded as broadly practical, day-to-day experiences and how these are 'culturally' ordered (1993, p. 7). We are confident that the present volume can make a serious contribution to just such a project in helping to develop Spanish cultural studies as a discipline.

References

BARTHES, R. 1957: *Mythologies*. Paris: Editions du Seuil.

BENNETT, T. 1986: Introduction: popular culture and 'the turn to Gramsci'. In Bennett, T. *et al.*, *Popular culture and social relations,* Milton Keynes: Open University Press, v–xv.

CULLER, J. 1997: *Literary theory. A very short introduction.* Oxford: Oxford University Press.

DU GAY, P. (ED.) 1997: *Production of culture/Cultures of production.* London: Sage/The Open University.

DU GAY, P., HALL, S., JANES, L., MACKAY, H. and NEGUS, K. 1997: *Doing cultural studies: the story of the Sony Walkman.* London: Sage/The Open University.

GIES, D. T. (ED.) 1999: *The Cambridge companion to modern Spanish culture,* Cambridge: Cambridge University Press.

GRAHAM, H. and LABANYI, J. (EDS) 1995: *Spanish cultural studies. An introduction.* Oxford: Oxford University Press.

HALL, S. 1976: *Resistance through rituals.* London: Hutchinson.

—— 1986: Cultural studies: two paradigms. In Collins, R. *et al.*, *Media, culture and society. A reader.* London: Sage, 33–48.

—— (ED.) 1997: *Representation. Cultural representation and signifying practices.* London: Sage/The Open University.

JORDAN, B. 1990: *British Hispanism and the challenge of literary theory.*
    Warminster: Aris and Phillips.
THWAITES, D., DAVIS, L. and MULES, W. 1994: *Tools for cultural studies. An
    introduction.* Melbourne: Macmillan.
WILLIAMS, R. 1993: Culture is ordinary. In Gray, A. and McGuigan, J. (eds),
    Studying culture. An introductory reader. London: Arnold, 5–14.

PART

I

REDEFINING NATIONAL IDENTITIES

Introduction

Spain may be a very old state, but historically the political and cultural processes required to modernize and weld together its various peoples and cultures into a nation were highly uneven, asynchronous and incomplete. There was thus a failure to construct the nation as a modern, integrative, pluralist entity with a common collective identity, able to incorporate and tolerate various communities, with their linguistic and cultural differences. Partly through circumstance, partly through their own political inadequacies, Spain's experiments with democratic Republican politics (1873–74 and 1931–36) were too short-lived and too lacking in resources to give shape to a collective project aimed at the economic and political modernization of the country. Out of the failures of economic development, democratic politicians and indeed the political classes as a whole were unable to articulate and sediment sufficiently within the popular imagination notions of community, common identity, tolerance, pluralism and the legitimacy of differences and otherness. Waiting in the wings was a hostile, reactionary, messianic tradition which, underpinned by the close ties between Spain's traditional land-owning elites and the Roman Catholic Church, gave ideological legitimation to the Spanish right and a particularly virulent form of nationalist reaffirmation.

The Civil War in Spain and the military regime to which it gave rise under General Franco (1939–75) merely served to reinforce divisions, hatreds and social fragmentation. Franco's Spain was initially forged from a mixture of violence, brutality and hatred. It was ideologically driven by an antiquated, anti-modern model of nationalist identity, based on the doubtful legitimacy derived from military victory, the refusal to countenance any form of national reconciliation and the flamboyant rhetoric of Castilian nationalism. The latter demonized Spain's 'enemy within' (the Republican parties, trade unions, the working classes, the liberal middle classes, supporters of regional political and cultural self-determination) and projected the regime's 'organic democracy' as morally superior to the decadent, inorganic, liberal politics of an undesirable Europe. Yet, fortress Spain still failed to unite the nation, preferring to exacerbate and then mythologize divisions, thus reinforcing them. Hence the relative weakness of the Francoist state, unable to achieve any deep or long-lasting social legitimacy. By the 1960s, and despite the faddish rhetoric of economic development, the regime only slowly acceded to economic liberalization. Ordinary (mainly working class) Spaniards, by contrast, were already on the move; their migrations gave rise to massive population shifts, internally and externally, as they sought to improve their economic and social conditions of existence. This they did, in spite of rather than because of the regime's desultory interest in indicative planning and 'development poles'. Yet, by the 1970s, even if Spain was now economically more developed, it was still officially promoted as 'different', as Europe's exotic other and thus still widely perceived as being at the margins of modernity. Such external prejudices gave the impression of a country strangely free of its own internal forms of racism, social exclusionism and intolerance.

Once Franco died, notions of Francoist legitimacy and national unity collapsed virtually overnight. And since 1975, Spain's national identity has been fundamentally transformed in line with the country's rapid political and economic modernization, the transition to democracy and the reintegration into the European and international political arena, through membership of the EU and NATO. At the same time, Spain has become radically regionalized, experiencing a breathtaking process of political devolution in little over five years (1978–83) and moving ever more quickly towards a form of federal state. Modernization, however, has also brought with it new and unfamiliar challenges, including those of dealing with the effects of multiculturalism and new ethnicities. As part of Europe's southern flank, Spain is now charged by the EU with regulating and policing inflows of migrant labour and coping with new forms of racism, intolerance and social marginalization. Notions of national identity are thus undergoing dramatic change, most graphically illustrated perhaps in the early 1990s by Spain's role as host to the Olympic Games and the Seville Expo. How did the organization of these major international, public events seek to portray modern Spain and how were such representations perceived in different quarters? Indeed, what does it mean to be Spanish these days? In a world of globalized media and decentralized politics, where do Spaniards believe they belong? Are they becoming increasingly detached from their 'homeland', whatever that might be? Are they on the way to constructing new identities, ethnicities and affiliations? Are such indentities inevitably interconnected and hybridized? The essays in this part seek to engage with some of these questions.

1

Culture and development: the impact of 1960s 'desarrollismo'

ALEX LONGHURST

Introduction

Between 1960 and 1975, Spain underwent an intense process of socio-economic change. After two decades of stagnation, the 1960s witnessed the transformation of Spain from a predominantly rural economy to an indus-trialized nation well on the way to becoming the world's sixth-largest car manufacturer. Per capita income, which had barely changed in the previous 30 years, went up nearly two-and-a-half times. In 1960, the percentage of households with electrodomestic appliances was below the 5 per cent mark, as it was for car ownership. By 1976, the vast majority of Spanish house-holds had fridges and television sets, and half had cars (see Table 1.1). In 1960, 42 per cent of the working population was employed in agriculture,

Table 1.1 Proportion of households with consumer durables in 1960 and 1976

Type of consumer durable	1960	1976
	% of households	% of households
Television set	1	90
Refrigerator	4	87
Bath and/or shower	44	86
Car	4	49
Telephone	12	44
Electric food mixer	4	44
Record player	3	39

Sources: FOESSA; Banesto; Francisco A. Orizo, *Las bases sociales del consumo y del ahorro en España* (1977)

30 per cent in industry and construction and 28 per cent in services. By 1976 the figures were respectively 21 per cent, 36 per cent, and 42 per cent. The far-reaching changes in the pattern of employment were accompanied by a massive transfer of population from a rural to an urban environment. Despite persisting inequalities of wealth and very uneven industrial development, a newly prosperous, largely urban society was unlikely to retain the attitudes and habits of a stagnant rural society for very long.

The nature of *desarrollismo*

On the whole, it can be said that economic development came to Spain despite Franco's economic planners rather than because of them. Indeed regional economic planning, which was a keystone of Francoist economic policy in the 1960s, was by and large a failure, with substantial sums of regional development aid going largely to waste. Development occurred almost ahead of the planners and in a spontaneous, sometimes haphazard, way. The textbook statistic of the 7 per cent average yearly growth in the Spanish economy between 1960 and 1974 to which economic historians have accustomed us suggests that development was purely a matter of economic growth. While impressive, such a measure is but a crude indicator of the transformation of Spain. *Desarrollismo* was not a purely economic phenomenon. The rapid economic development of Spain in the 1960s was more than an 'economic miracle' brought about by the Opus Dei economic mandarins of the 1959 Stabilization Plan. Indeed the 1957 change of orientation of the Franco regime with the introduction of the 'technocrats' into the government was largely a response to the serious social disturbances of 1956 promoted by striking workers and demonstrating students, in itself an indication that Spanish society was on the move *before* the economic redirection of the regime. The great leap forward of post-1960 Spain was a collective, if instinctive, enterprise. Shunned by Western democracies, cut off from Marshall Aid, and subjected to a policy of self-sufficiency which merely led to a developmental cul-de-sac, the Spanish people in their millions had endured economic deprivation, political suppression and social immobilism. Emerging by the end of the 1950s from 20 years of stagnation and ideological stultification, Spanish society was ripe for change; political life, by contrast, was to lag behind, though not wholly unaffected by the changes that were occurring in the socio-economic sphere. Economic and social change went hand in hand. To see the latter as merely a consequence of the former is an oversimplification.

By 1960, the working and middle classes of Spain were abandoning their attitudes of passive acceptance and retrenchment, and were showing clear signs of restlessness, renewed expectations, and endeavour. The most obvious indication of this awakening is the vastly increased disposition among Spaniards to emigrate as a first step in their efforts to better themselves. Nor is this just a matter of foreign emigration, crucial as such emigration was to be. Migration within the Peninsula was even more crucial, since several million rural families flocked to larger towns and cities, often in quite different regions and generally with a south-to-north or west-to-east direction of migratory flow. The willingness to sacrifice the attachment to the *patria chica* in order to work long hours in factories, hotels, ports, airports, and other urban environments is a clear manifestation of the decision of many Spaniards to improve their lot at the cost of abandoning their roots. To Andalusian peasants, Barcelona in the 1960s must have seemed almost as foreign as Wolfburg or Lille. The rapid process of urbanization, despite the severe pressure put on the still inadequate social, educational and sanitary facilities, and the hideous if temporary appearance of shanty towns, was a key step in the cultural transformation of Spanish society, since the concentration of population hugely facilitated education and social homogenization. External migration, though not as pronounced as internal, was also culturally important. It is often forgotten that worker emigration to other countries of Europe was a temporary affair. Although nearly one-and-a-half million Spaniards (of whom a majority were Galicians and Andalusians) left their country to go and work abroad, most of these returned after just a few years. The contact of these returnees with a foreign culture (especially French, German and Swiss) helped to encourage more liberal, tolerant and permissive attitudes than those traditionally found in a clerically influenced Spain. The arrival of foreign tourists in large numbers, with the consequent influx of Spanish workers, including many women, to the Mediterranean resorts, also affected the cultural reorientation of ordinary Spaniards.

Rural exodus, foreign contacts, a developing urban consumerism, and rapid technological progress made possible by access to foreign currency and therefore imports, went hand in hand with an explosion in school enrolments. Between 1960 and 1975 the number of secondary school pupils went up sevenfold, a spectacular increase in school enrolments which shadowed very closely the process of urban concentration. This did of course require a major, although belated, investment by the state, an investment made possible by the dynamism of the Spanish economy. But if the expansion of education in the 1960s and 1970s was consequent on urbanization and economic growth, it was also a reflection of the aspiration of many working-class families to ensure better opportunities for their children. Thus the poor urban immigrant of one generation became the educated white-collar employee of the next. Illiteracy, still relatively widespread at the start of the period of development, was by the early 1970s confined to an older unschooled generation and some remaining pockets of rural deprivation.

Industrialization and foreign investment were the engines of economic growth in the 1960s, but the parallel growth in the number of family businesses says something about the Spaniards' readiness to exploit the opportunities afforded by the new economic climate. Many of the firms that were eventually to emerge as major players started off as family enterprises in the late fifties and early sixties. Furthermore, many workers in dependent employment who had no chance of starting their own businesses did not fight shy of pressurizing their employers, by strikes if need be, for better working conditions and a fairer share of the economic cake. Despite the state-controlled unions and the illegality of strikes, industrial relations during the last 20 years of the Franco regime were characterized by recurrent labour unrest and illicit but intense trade union activity. All of which suggests that the unprecedented economic expansion of the 1960s was due to a confluence of factors that may be broadly summarized as: (1) greatly increased investment, (2) a favourable international climate, (3) a new determination among Spaniards to improve their living conditions.

Socio-cultural developments

If the third of these factors is an important one, it follows then that *desarrollismo* was as much an attitude of mind as an economic event. As such it cannot be easily divorced from the social and cultural developments that accompanied it. Among the most significant socio-cultural developments of contemporary Spain whose roots can be traced back to the 1960s, the following are arguably the most influential: (1) decline in the birth rate, (2) mesocratization of the population, (3) changes in moral and religious attitudes.

With an average of 1.2 children per woman of child-bearing age, Spain today has one of the lowest birth rates in the world. The beginnings of the decline can be observed in the 1960s, although the trend was to accelerate in the 1970s and 1980s. Since the marriage indices did not fall until the 1980s, it follows that married couples were quite deliberately choosing to limit the size of their families. This went against both Francoist encouragement of *familias numerosas* through welfare inducements and the Roman Catholic Church's marital doctrine. The importance of this is that it tells us something about the changing attitudes and independence of mind of many Spaniards. What made better family planning possible was the increasing availability of hormonal contraceptives. Although such contraceptives were only supposed to be legally available for the treatment of relatively rare hormonal disorders, the fact is that according to the Spanish Department of Health, by 1975 more than half-a-million women allegedly had hormonal disorders requiring treatment with the pill, to say nothing of those who bought theirs illegally or abroad. The four- and five-child family, very common in the 1950s, had become on average a 2.5-child family by the end of the Franco regime.

The mesocratization of the population (not just according to the classification of sociologists but just as importantly through self-placement in a given social class) implies a massive reclassification of the *clase obrera* or working classes. Most sociological measures of class put the working classes at 60 to 65 per cent of the population in the 1950s. By the 1970s such measures were down to 45 per cent, with the sharpest decline occurring between 1965 and 1975. Since these estimates tend to be based on occupation, what they tell us is that an increasingly large proportion of working Spaniards were employed in jobs traditionally perceived as middle class. The explanation for the new pattern of employment lies in the tertiarization of the Spanish economy, that is, the shift towards an economy based principally on services, which is a characteristic of all advanced societies. Even during the 1960s phase of industrial expansion, the average yearly growth in jobs was higher in services than in industry; and when recession hit in 1975 it was the industrial sector that shrank remorselessly and the services sector that continued to grow. This is not the full picture, however, for the changing pattern of employment has also resulted in greater equality of income. Despite huge disparities of income between the poorest 10 per cent and the richest 10 per cent of the population, by 1973 the bulk of Spanish households had moved closer to the centre of the income distribution, a trend that was to continue, though not as strongly, in the 1980s, as can be deduced from the FOESSA reports published in the 1970s and 1980s. The expenditure surveys of the Instituto Nacional de Estadística confirm this greater homogeneity: the differences in average annual expenditure on food and drink, clothing and footwear, housing, household goods and services and health narrowed very considerably. Only in transport and leisure (which include car purchase and holidays) were there major disparities. Such surveys help to show that the process of socio-economic change begun in the 1960s has resulted in a population whose lifestyle and living standards are reasonably homogeneous.

Changes in moral and religious attitudes during the 1960s are more difficult to specify with certainty since sociological surveys were rare and subject to political controls. Nevertheless a few points do emerge. In 1970, only 3 per cent of Spaniards called themselves atheists or agnostics; by the end of the 1980s this had grown to 26 per cent. The proportion of those who referred to themselves as practising Catholics moved in the opposite direction: from 64 per cent to 27 per cent. This astonishing reversal in religious attitude may no doubt be ascribed in part to increasing materialism, but the gulf between Francoist and post-Francoist Spain is almost certainly exaggerated by the reluctance, even in 1970, to admit to irreligiosity in a society in which the Catholic Church still held sway. With the advent of democracy the church's influence waned sharply, but it is in any case an established fact that during the twentieth century, before, during, and after Franco, the Spanish working classes showed little allegiance to the church. What is also clear is that, from being a predominantly social phenomenon during the 1960s, religion has become a predominantly private matter. Once the social constraint was removed decline was inevitable. It is not so much basic beliefs that have changed – belief in God has remained relatively strong – as allegiance to the church and its doctrines. The other point to emerge with equal clarity from both earlier and more recent surveys is that it is precisely those who were born and brought up between 1960 and 1975 who were to swell the ranks of the indifferent. A male youth survey of 1960 yielded a 91 per cent figure for those who called themselves practising Catholics. A similar survey in 1975 (this time of males and females) yielded a figure of 62 per cent for young practising Catholics and 38 per cent for non-practising and indifferent. The decline of religion, which was to be consolidated in the 1980s, was clearly under way. In terms of moral, rather than purely religious, attitudes, the trend, timid during the 1960s but increasingly apparent in the 1970s, was towards a greater relativism in judging personal relationships, sexual matters, drug consumption, and Social Security fraud, although the vast majority of Spaniards outside the Basque Country maintained a hardline attitude towards the terrorist problem that emerged strongly in the 1970s. The far more rapid change in the attitude towards divorce and abortion, which went from majority disapproval in the late 1970s to majority approval in the mid-1980s, must to some extent at least be attributed to the lead given by left-wing politicians as well as the strong public support of feminist organizations, for the change of attitude was more marked in the case of women than of men, in itself an indication of the impact of the increasing access of women to higher education and to jobs.

Desarrollismo and intellectual life

The visible signs of economic and social development were quickly followed by a noticeable change in the political rhetoric of the Franco regime, with previous pseudo-historicist clichés that appealed to an imagined Spanish tradition now increasingly being replaced by the equally vacuous but more progressive-sounding language of technocracy. Both in the economic and cultural spheres, the regime tended to be reactive rather than anticipatory, but its adaptability was limited by the unwillingness of a hard core of influential Francoists to yield, or be seen to yield, to changing attitudes and habits among the population. The new rhetoric of *desarrollismo* was very largely just that; the real changes were surging ahead of government policy and creating a challenge not just for economic planners but for the regime's propagandists and those whose job it was to exercise vigilance over the media and public forms of expression. The new language of technocratic bureaucracy, meant to convince and reassure that the government was fully in control of economic and social change, could not hide increasing tensions at the very heart of the regime as it tried to retain its hegemony and monolithic ideology with no genuine political concessions. These tensions became increasingly obvious as the 1960s decade wore on and are well illustrated by the debate within the pages of the monarchist newspaper *ABC* in 1970 between the liberal-conservative José María de Areilza, one of Franco's most prominent diplomats in the the 1950s and early 1960s, and Franco's trusted and devoted right-hand man, Admiral Luis Carrero Blanco. Whereas Areilza believed that the new Spain rendered old-style Francoism anachronistic, Carrero insisted that the institutions created by the regime around the sanctity of family and workplace and enshrined in the new Organic Law of the State (Ley Orgánica del Estado) could not possibly be altered. Carrero, the victim in 1973 of ETA's most notorious act of terrorism, was not to live long enough to witness the inevitable and wholesale abandonment of the Francoist state. For despite spatial inequalities of wealth that have always been marked in a regionally diverse country, by the time of Franco's death in November 1975, Spain as a whole was a modern consumer society little different from others in Western Europe. First, the process of integration of the Spanish economy into the international, especially European, economy, which was to culminate in Spain's formal incorporation into the EC in 1986, was already under way, with the concomitant interchange of goods and services. Second, the foreign perception of Spain as a semi-European exotic leftover of the nineteenth century may have been encouraged by the 'Spain is different' slogan of the Ministry of Tourism, but it was wholly out of tune with the economic and social realities of the day. Third, it was by now apparent to all but the tiny minority that came to be known as Franco's 'bunker' that the regime's hopes of achieving economic development with minimal social emancipation had been both unreasonable and illusory. The fabric of ideas perforce had to change, was indeed already changing.

The impact of social and economic change on the intellectual and artistic life of Spain, although by its very nature unquantifiable, is nevertheless susceptible of descriptive treatment. That there was some small degree of political relaxation is not in doubt, but this was forced on the government by changing circumstances. Liberals and left-wing intellectuals scored a major victory in 1962 after their well-publicized meeting in Munich quashed whatever chance the Spanish government might have had of persuading the EEC to accept its application for membership. The angry frustration of the government, which reacted by punishing the Munich delegates with internal and external exile, only served to confirm the views of its opponents. Conscious of its poor image, the regime cautiously began to examine ways in which it could be made to look more Western and less characterized by a siege mentality. Another external pressure on the regime was the new social orientation given to the Catholic Church by Pope John XXIII and particularly his 1963 encyclical *Pacem in Terris*, which appealed for understanding and mutual respect among peoples of different religious and political persuasions, supported freedom of conscience, and defended the right freely to elect one's representatives in government. The effect of such social doctrines was to give an important boost to Spanish dissidents, making them seem politically respectable. Pope Paul VI put further pressure on the Franco regime by criticizing it in the course of his address to the College of

Cardinals in 1969. By this time, the divergence of church and regime, impelled by the attitudes of younger clergy who had, after years of protests, police persecution and denunciations, finally persuaded the hierarchy to abandon its support of the regime and openly contest the latter's social policies and violent suppression of workers' rights to peaceful protest, was becoming increasingly apparent. Thus by 1970 we have the extraordinary spectacle in Spain of anticlerical outbursts coming not from the left but from the extreme right.

The most frequently cited attempt of the Spanish government to make itself appear what it was patently not is the new press law of 1966, which has often been seen as the clearest manifestation of *aperturismo* or cautious political relaxation which characterized the later 1960s. But the much trumpeted alterations to the censorship laws changed little in practice. In fact the new law making pre-publication submission to the censors optional was a clever piece of bureaucratic manipulation that certainly did not confer greater freedom of expression to writers, dramatists and journalists. Few publishers were prepared to risk confiscation of an entire print run. What the law of 1966 did was to put the onus for staying on the narrow political path on writers and publishers even more so than before. In other words it encouraged self-censorship. There is no detectable change in political audacity between pre- and post-1966 publications. On the other hand, taking a longer-term view, there was undoubtedly a relaxation in the moral outlook of the censors: what was morally acceptable in the 1960s would not have been tolerated in the 1940s or even the 1950s; but this is no more than a reflection of a changing social outlook, for no matter how ideologically orthodox, the readers employed by the censors in the 1960s were not those employed 20 years earlier.

There were more important developments than the press law of 1966. Although censorship continued, albeit in modified form, there was a more relaxed attitude to writers considered unsympathetic to the regime such as Juan Goytisolo; and more importantly perhaps, there was a vastly increased importation of foreign books which fed the intellectual and literary appetites of an increasing university population and even of a better educated general reading public. New or resurrected journals of a liberal-intellectual disposition such as *Cuadernos para el Diálogo* or *Revista de Occidente* served to enrich the intellectual climate, although their circulation was naturally very limited. The real significance of these ventures lies in the fact that their pluralist outlook ran counter to the narrowly conservative ideology promoted hitherto by the regime's propaganda machine. Alongside new publications and increased availability of foreign books official approval was given for the introduction of new degree courses in the social sciences, although there were also a number of suspensions of university professors who overstepped the mark or sided with demonstrating students. Indeed the lack of any coherent long-term socio-cultural policy on the part of the regime is patent: it was a constant but inconsistent game of loosening and tightening which depended on the cabinet personalities of the moment. In fact, the progressive nature of Spanish cultural development was becoming increasingly manifest and could no longer be easily controlled without seeming heavy-handed and repressive, and it is the conflict between image and authority that the regime failed to solve.

By and large, Spanish literature of the 1940s had been strongly ideologized and had more of a propaganda value than an artistic one. In the 1950s, there was a much clearer social commitment expressed, as far as permissible, through documentary realism, which at its best was sober and revealing. Although commendable in its attempt to 'tell the truth' about contemporary Spain, the literary arts of the 1950s seemed, retrospectively, naive in their assumptions, particularly in believing that their implied critique of Spain's sociopolitical ideology and structures could have a reformist impact. Neither the objectivist novel, nor the social poetry, nor indeed the political theatre of the 1950s appears to have had any such effect, in the case of the theatre because it was seldom cleared for performance by the censors. The mid-1960s witnessed a pronounced shift in literary orientation and the appearance of a remarkable series of experimental novels, starting with Luis Martín Santos's *Tiempo de silencio* (1962) and followed by now canonic titles such as Miguel Delibes's *Cinco horas con Mario* (1966) and *Parábola del náufrago* (1969), Juan Marsé's *Ultimas tardes con Teresa* (1966), Juan Goytisolo's *Señas de identidad* (1966) and *Reivindicación del Conde don Julián* (1970), Camilo José Cela's *San Camilo 1936* (1969), Juan Benet's *Volverás a Región* (1968), and slightly later, one of the most astonishingly original of all, Gonzalo Torrente Ballester's *La saga/fuga de J.B.* (1972). What these novels have in common is the search for new non-mimetic forms, in itself an implicit recognition that the stark realism of the 1950s and early 1960s was no longer adequate for a new more complicated world in which ideologies were no longer black and white. While the critical attitude to political and social realities tended to persist in these new works, there was now a complex and often richly ironic vision as well as a formal experimentalism which was to continue throughout the 1970s with the arrival on the scene of a wholly new wave of writers.

The appearance of new literary styles is never easily explainable but one can reasonably speculate that changes in fictional narrative in 1960s Spain were conditioned by an admixture of literary and social factors. The European success of the Latin American boom novel, which was ensured not just by the undoubted talent of many Latin American writers but even more by the self-interested collaboration between these writers and their literary agents on the one hand and commercial publishing houses on the other, encouraged Spanish writers to emulate their transatlantic cousins. For the Latin American boom novel was every bit as much a European phenomenon as a Latin American one. Written with a European audience in mind, an audience eager for a 'different' product originating in a 'different' culture, and cleverly promoted by leading Spanish publishers (Mario Vargas

Llosa was even awarded the Seix Barral Biblioteca Breve prize in 1962), the Latin American novel with its magic–realist trappings may be ranked alongside Coca-Cola as one of the greatest marketing ploys of the century; but it had the immediate effect of persuading Spanish writers that they too could benefit from the newly-created market for exotic products. Ironically demonstrating perhaps that the political manipulation carried out by the Franco regime could be profitably applied elsewhere, the manipulation of the literary market by certain leading publishing houses and a handful of influential critics is one of the marks of the age, as witnessed by the development of a substantial cult-following for the esoteric products emanating from the pen of Juan Benet, many of whose readers probably failed to decipher his deliberately abstruse narratives. Yet, at the same time, this literary manipulation could only have taken place among a developing readership rapidly gaining in sophistication and with expectations stretching beyond the often well-crafted but always predictable accounts of the realist novel. In a word, Spanish readers too were becoming 'developed'.

The new or more sophisticated readership of novels had its parallels in the new or more sophisticated audiences for the stage. The ideologically committed and politically confrontational stance adopted by one of the two major dramatists of the 1950s and 1960s, such as Alfonso Sastre, meant that such works seldom made it to the stage. The theatre of the time was thus dominated by a bland and conventional bourgeois comedy of manners or by the more subtle but purely humorous works of long-established writers such as Enrique Jardiel Poncela and Miguel Mihura. The other major dramatist, Antonio Buero Vallejo, evinces a more interesting approach. Both he and Sastre shared the same determination to confront the realities of contemporary Spain, and during the summer of 1960, in the pages of the theatre magazine *Primer Acto,* the two dramatists engaged in debate about how a playwright should proceed in the face of the severe constraints imposed by the regime's censorship laws. Sastre's position was uncompromising: to negotiate with the censors was tantamount to collaborationism; the dramatist owed his responsibility to the authority of truth and not to that of the political masters of the moment. Buero Vallejo on the other hand argued that if the dramatist was to reach his audience he had to work within the bounds of what was possible and adapt his style accordingly. Even while conceding the inherent respectability of both positions, there can be little doubt that Buero's was subsequently shown to be the more intelligent and successful. Adapting his earlier critical realism to offer a far more symbolic and allegorical interpretation of the reality of Spain and of contemporary humanity, Buero's oblique approach succeeded on three fronts: i) it worked in getting past the censors plays which would have been rejected if written in a more starkly realist style; ii) it responded to the theatre-going public's aspiration to a more challenging style of theatre and indeed helped to educate that public; and iii) it greatly enriched the theatrical literature of a Spain in full economic and social development while pointing the way to a new generation of playwrights of the *nuevo teatro* that was to come to the fore in the 1970s. While it would still be true to say that the typical theatre of a developing Spain was a conventional one (epitomized by the plays of that most prolific of modern playwrights Alfonso Paso who had totally dominated the Spanish stage for three decades), there can be no doubt that the more sophisticated and challenging works of Buero Vallejo found a powerful echo in a significant minority of the theatre-going public, professional critics, and academic scholars.

Conclusion

The cause and effect relationship between economic and cultural development is less clear than one would wish. The seventeenth-century Golden Age of Spanish literature and painting occurred at a time when economic decline had already set in. The Silver Age of the late nineteenth and early twentieth centuries occurred at a time of limited economic progress, political corruption and upheaval, and social conflict. The cultural resurgence of the 1960s, though scarcely comparable to those two other periods, nevertheless represented an interesting departure from the stultifying 1940s and the timid 1950s. Rather than say that the cultural enrichment of the 1960s and beyond was the consequence of increased economic wealth and social emancipation, I would be more inclined to suggest that the socio-economic and the cultural dimensions went hand in hand. There is of course little doubt that greater wealth generates greater cultural possibilities, but the widened horizons of the 1960s, despite the extreme nervousness of the political authorities, was very obviously the result of an instinctive collaboration between increasingly audacious purveyors and increasingly sophisticated consumers. By the end of the Franco regime in 1975, Spain had transformed itself economically and socially; political modernization was to follow swiftly and consensually. As I proposed at the beginning of this essay, to ascribe these profound and far-reaching changes to a variety of macro-economic indicators would be less than satisfactory. It was the people who transformed their economic situation, not the other way round. *Desarrollismo* was as much a state of mind, a determination to succeed, as a question of increasing foreign earnings, increasing investments, and increasing wages. The determination of writers and readers, of teachers and students, of entrepreneurs and trade union leaders to pursue their artistic, intellectual and professional aspirations and not be deterred by an anachronistic and immobile political ideology is what lay at the root of Spain's leap forward in the 1960s. The severe economic retrenchment induced by the energy crisis that followed in the later 1970s and early 1980s could not hold back the tide of cultural emancipation that had begun some 15 years earlier. By the time of the emergence of the new democratic Spain of the late 1970s, the country was already manifesting the sociological features by which developed societies are recognized: lowered birth rate, higher life expectancy, urbanization, technological advances in the home and at work, improved communications, greatly increased social mobility, and much more complex organizational structures whether economic, political, or cultural.

References

ABELLAN, J. L. 1976: *La industria cultural en España*. Barcelona: Ediciones Península.

ABELLAN, M. L. 1980: *Censura y creación literaria en España (1939–1976)*. Barcelona: Ediciones Península.

CARR, R. and FUSI, J. P. 1979 (2nd edn 1981): *Spain: dictatorship to democracy*. London: Allen and Unwin.

DE MIGUEL, A. 1975: *Sociología del franquismo*. Barcelona: Euros.

DIAZ, E. 1978: *Notas para una historia del pensamiento español actual*. Segunda edición corregida. Madrid: Cuadernos para el Diálogo.

DIAZ, E. 1983: *Pensamiento español en la era de Franco (1939–1975)*. Madrid: Tecnos.

FONTANA, J. 1986: *España bajo el franquismo*. Barcelona: Editorial Crítica.

FUNDACION FOESSA. 1970: *Informe sociológico sobre la situación social de España*. Madrid: Euramérica.

FUNDACION FOESSA. 1975: *Estudios sociológicos sobre la situación social de España*. Madrid: Euramérica.

FUNDACION FOESSA. 1983: *Informe sociológico sobre el cambio social en España, 1975–1983*. Madrid: Euramérica.

GARCIA DELGADO, J. L. (ED.) 1990: *Economía española de la transición y la democracia, 1973–1986*. Madrid: Centro de Investigaciones Sociológicas.

GIES, D. T. (ED.) 1999: *The Cambridge companion to modern Spanish culture*. Cambridge: Cambridge University Press.

GRAHAM, H. and LABANYI, J. 1995: *Spanish cultural studies: an introduction*. Oxford: Oxford University Press.

HARRISON, J. 1993: *The Spanish economy. From the Civil War to the European Community*. London: Macmillan.

JACKSON, G. 1976: The Franco era in historical perspective. *The Centennial Review* (Spring), 103–27.

LIEBERMANN, S. 1982: *The contemporary Spanish economy. A historical perspective*. London: Allen and Unwin.

MARAVALL, J. M. 1978: *Dictatorship and political dissent: workers and students in Franco's Spain*. London: Tavistock.

PAYNE, S. G. 1987: *The Franco regime, 1936–1975*. Madison, Wis.: University of Wisconsin Press.

SANZ VILLANUEVA, S. 1984: *El siglo XX. Literatura actual*. Vol. 6.2 of *Historia de la literatura española*. Barcelona: Ariel.

WRIGHT, A. 1977: *The Spanish economy, 1959–1976*. London: Macmillan.

|2|

Selling Spanish 'otherness' since the 1960s

Introduction

In this essay, I shall address the issue of images of Spain produced internally, consciously or otherwise, by the authorities and other opinion-formers (politicians, trade unionists, the print and audiovisual media, etc.) for both internal and external consumption. I shall take as my starting point the 'Spain is different' tourist promotion campaign of the 1960s and attempt to trace the evolution of different and sometimes contradictory constructions of Spain through the transition to democracy up to the present day, paying particular attention to the official discourse of 1992 as a watershed development. To conclude, I shall describe what I believe is an identifiable, if complex, tendency within Spain's current official discourses. This trend seeks to recuperate traditional cultural stereotypes after years of embarrassed rejection.

In a short essay of this kind, it is impossible to go into detail regarding the sort of discourses which have been developed over a period of almost 40 years. References are given where appropriate to more detailed studies of individual aspects of the discourses discussed. There is also a certain risk of oversimplifying what are in fact very complex representations of Spain and Spanish identity/ies. In what follows, my main intention is to describe over-all tendencies rather than to offer exhaustive analyses of the discourses dealt with. In my analysis, I understand that constructions of identity are not always, nor even usually, deliberate or conscious, but rather (re-)produce, often subconsciously, dominant or desired, 'common sense' images, which are in turn accepted in varying degrees by different readers or receivers. The discussion of such discourses in texts of all kinds produced by a society at a particular point in time is therefore a powerful tool in social and cultural analysis.

'Spain is different'

When in the 1960s the tourist slogan 'Spain is different' was launched, the intention was to attract tourists to an 'exotic' destination, with interesting local customs and traditions differing from the European norm. The fact that this slogan played precisely on Spain's otherness fits in well with the Franco regime's deliberate effort to promote, both internally and externally, positive constructions of Spanishness as opposed to negative versions of foreign otherness. In this process, the construction of self both affects and is affected by the construction of the other: Spain's ills were blamed on the corrupting influence of foreign ideas imported by the internal 'other': the left, the working classes and other opposition groups. The slogan is also, significantly, an example of how the regime's attempts to establish such clear-cut distinctions backfired on occasion, provoking what Hall refers to as 'oppositional readings' (1980, p. 138). The slogan, which was designed to encourage tourism from abroad and doubtless also to reinforce the regime's particular construction of reality at home, rapidly became a byword for both internal and external criticism of the reality of Franco's Spain. So much so, in fact, that over 30 years later the same expression is often to be heard to sum up many of the ills still portrayed as endemic to Spanish society today.

Spain's difference was notoriously symbolized under Franco by some of the popular customs, rituals and traditions found in certain parts of the country, notably Castile and Andalusia: religious festivals, bullfighting, flamenco, and so on. These were glorified by the regime and appropriated as examples of Spain's very own 'national' culture, to be defended and promoted in the face of undesirable foreign imports. One of the essential underlying macropropositions in this message was, of course, that of national unity and uniformity. This constituted for the various (and silenced) nationalities and regions of Spain a denial of that very same right to be different which the regime constructed for Spain as opposed to the rest of Europe. This Spanish nationalist discourse clearly fulfilled the role of constructing a unity intended as a denial of, and hence defence against, Basque and Catalan nationalism, two of the main nuclei of opposition to the regime after their experience of a degree of autonomy under the Second Republic (1931–36).

Other macropropositions linked to the discourse of 'bullfighting and flamenco' include deeply conservative patriarchal values, a resigned acceptance of deep social inequalities, the exaltation of rural life as opposed to the supposed moral degradation of (working class) urban communities and the spiritual authority of the Catholic Church as an institution, amongst others. This Manichean vision of Spain was thus a deliberate attempt to make internal opposition invisible and to eliminate any trace of the reasons behind its existence. It also served, in this case unintentionally, to promote abroad a stereotyped image of a folkloric, inefficient and backward Spain, which permeated collective awareness to such an extent throughout much of Europe that it rapidly replaced the romantic view of the country of the late nineteenth and early twentieth centuries, present even in accounts of the Civil War, the so-called 'last romantic war'. The folkloric stereotype has indeed outlived the dictator, and is alive and well in many current accounts of Spain today, as witnessed constantly, for example, in the British press (see Kelly, 1997).

Moving forward/Catching up with Europe

Other authors (Graham and Labanyi, 1995, pp. 311–13) have analysed the parallel and often contradictory discourses which characterize officialdom and indeed society in contemporary Spain. They emphasize the vertiginous speed at which change has been effected in the country since the death of Franco, which has led to the coexistence of a deeply traditional, often rural society alongside a modern, mainly urban Spain. The contradictions inherent in this kind of development are one of the most complex aspects of contemporary Spain and will be present in the various discourses which I will analyse here as indicative of dominant official discourses throughout the period under discussion.

The vastly oversimplified folkloric construction of Spain gave way during the transition to democracy (1975–82) to the construction of a Spain on the road to modernity, embodied often in the notion of Europe as a desirable objective and political imperative. It is true that both during the dictatorship and afterwards, many of the opposition forces saw Europe not only as a model to follow, but as a form of insurance policy against any return to authoritarian rule. This construction of Europe as an unconditional guarantee of hard-won freedoms was too often made in a totally uncritical manner. It reflected a blanket rejection of all that had been constructed for so many years as 'typically Spanish' as shameful evidence of the backwardness engendered and perpetuated by the Franco regime. Excellent examples of this modernizing new discourse can be found in some of the electoral campaign materials of the Partido Socialista Obrero Español (PSOE) in the early 1980s, where Felipe González, the socialist candidate for prime minister, was portrayed as smiling benignly on blond, blue-eyed children playing in green Alpine meadows. Spain, according to the PSOE, was destined to become a modern Germanic paradise, 'Mitteleuropa on the Med', as *The Economist* put it some years later (1992, p. 25). Change (*el cambio* in the 1982 Socialist electoral campaign literature), modernization for modernization's sake, Europe for Europe's sake, became bywords in Spanish politics, and unfavourable comparisons of Spain's circumstances with those of the country's neighbours ('north of the Pyrenees') were frequent in political speeches, press editorials and trade union demands, amongst other forms of discourse. This deep desire to 'move forward' is interestingly shared by political rivals: *por buen camino* (in the right direction) the 1986 PSOE electoral slogan, is mirrored in *salir adelante*, (moving forward/ahead), the slogan of the right-wing Coalición Popular (Popular Alliance Party) at the same elections. Similarly, 'Europeanization' was the main selling point for Felipe González's astonishing U-turn over the issue of continuing NATO membership in the mid-1980s, when he was already firmly installed as prime minister (*see* Arceo Vacas *et al.*, 1993).

Spain was, then, in official discourse, no longer entirely 'different', but well on the way to becoming the same as, and hence equal to, the rest of Europe. 'Catching up' virtually became a national obsession and permeated all spheres of public and private life. Negative criticism of the social model of Western Europe (the Europe of 'catching up' never included countries on the 'wrong' side of the Berlin Wall), was scarce and given very little publicity. Virtually no comment was made on the negative effects of membership of the then EEC, which Spain formally joined in January 1986. One result is that the Spanish population is today one of the most pro-European of European Union member states.

'Everything under the sun'

Still heavily dependent on tourist income, official Spain during this period addressed potential tourists (and thus the outside world in general) through a revamped promotion campaign incorporating a new, modern image of a Europeanized Spain. Gone were the bullfights and the flamenco dancers: Spain was now 'Everything under the sun', symbolised by a Miroian sun and illustrated by photographs of spectacular natural vistas and monumental sights throughout the country. This shift to a more diversified construction of the country reflected a growing recognition of and respect for regional difference, essential to a peaceful political transition, and indicated a strong desire no longer to be portrayed as one massive seaside resort for northern Europe. Spain was attempting to reposition itself as a country with a rich and diverse multicultural history. All of that, however, under a sun which still retained very profitable and recognizable traces of the previous imagery.

On a rather different note, this same period can also be seen as one heralding a search for a new set of identities, after long years of imposed Francoist constructions of what 'Spain' was supposed to signify. Yet, the lack of a clear idea of exactly what Spain was, so palpable in the parliamentary debates over the Constitution in 1978, and the lexical gymnastics surrounding the concepts of nation, nationalities and regions (*see* Fernández Laguinilla, 1986), are arguably also contained in the slogan 'Everything under the sun'. There was and there remains, without any doubt, a clear lack of definition of what it means to be Spanish and this is felt in so many sectors of Spanish society (Imbert, 1990). Of course, the nationalists in the

Basque Country and Catalonia have had little problem in casting off the old imposed 'Spanish' identity in favour of their own national and regional identities. They have made, and make, extensive use of oppositional discourses when promoting themselves abroad. Indeed, the promotion of Euskadi and Catalonia internationally (mainly for foreign investors) began studiously to avoid the use of any terms relating to Spain, preferring to refer to themselves as 'European', or 'Mediterranean'. They even began to make use of the old cultural stereotypes of inefficiency and backwardness often linked to Spain in order to construct a positive and heavily differentiated self-image of extreme efficiency and modernity (Sangrador, 1981).

An obvious point of inflection with regard to the transition to democracy, and arguably also for this very process of constructing a new set of identities in this period, was the attempted *coup d'état* of 23 February 1981. Much has been written regarding the effects of this event on the subsequent evolution of Spanish politics, but perhaps most interesting for the issues analysed here is the recuperation (analysed at length by Imbert (1990)) by the political parties, most noticeably in those on the left, of national colours and symbols. Official discourse was once more to incorporate and refigure these signs of national identity, for too long associated exclusively with the extreme right.

During this period and as part of the modernization process, Spanish politicians and opinion-makers gradually adopted standard European discourse on questions such as immigration, which had in fact not been issues in pre-1975 Spain, or rather had been perceived from a very different point of view. The use of the term *inmigración* itself is a recent addition to the language of a society which, until the 1970s, had been a net exporter of cheap emigrant labour to other European countries. Once the country had 'caught up', it did not take long for the authorities at different levels of government to adopt the dominant discourse of Western Europe regarding those migrants who aspired to basic human living conditions in our opulent societies. As a signatory to the Schengen agreement, Spain became the 'gateway to Europe', the guardian of 'Europe's southern border'. At the same time, Spanish politicians rapidly and very avidly took on their new role as custodians of Europe's considerable privileges by endorsing the control as well as the expulsion of illegal migrants (*see* Martin Rojo and Van Dijk, 1997, pp. 523–66).

1992: 'discovery', 'encounter of cultures', 'coming of age'

The culmination of the modernization process for Spanish official discourse was arguably in 1992. The fifth centenary of the 'discovery' of America, or the 'encounter of cultures' (as the authorities finally agreed to describe the event) offered a perfect opportunity for Spanish politicians to proclaim internally and externally that the transition had come to an end, that Spain had 'caught up' and was now the 'very model of a modern European democracy'. The celebrations of this 'coming of age' centred on the Expo '92 World Fair in Seville, together with the Barcelona summer Olympics. Alongside these two events, Madrid was designated European City of Culture. The three vertices of this celebratory triangle were of course a statement of Spain's new diversity, although the authorities were visibly less pleased with Catalan attempts to capitalize on the event in Barcelona by publicizing their very own 'difference' both spontaneously and individually during the various ceremonies, and institutionally in the international press.

1992 is a watershed in post-transitional official discourse. The self-congratulatory tone of the mainly Socialist construction of these events provoked a certain degree of internal dissent and rejection. The government of the time was accused of reproducing the Franco regime's taste for 'Pharaonic works', substituting the Expo's national pavilions and the new, high-speed train (the AVE) for Franco's dams and reservoirs. Critics pointed to alternative and far more deserving uses for the tremendous expenditure lavished on the Expo, while sceptics both at home and abroad questioned the capacity of the country to live up to such a vast organizational challenge. The event was, however, constructed officially by Socialist politicians, the King, and others as a great success, a return for Spain to her rightful place in the world arena, in a delicate balancing act between delusions of neo-imperial grandeur and recognition of the country's really quite minor position and role in world politics.

Interestingly, this official Spanish discourse met with the practically unanimous determination of the British press (reminiscing perhaps about another lost empire) to decry all these efforts to re-figure Spain as a modern, efficient democracy. Constant reminders were made of the delays in building work, the accidents and fires on the sites, highly symbolic disasters such as the sinking on its launch of the replica of the Victoria sailing ship, or of the violent repression by police of demonstrations against the Expo at the opening ceremony, news of which, claimed the British press, was (self-)censored in Spain itself. Spain, in short, was portrayed as a backward, inefficient and authoritarian state, unworthy of equal status with other European states, particularly in relation to the UK. There is little doubt that this portrayal formed part of the official British anti-European discourse of the time, but the virulence of the criticism is perhaps worthy of note.

'Passion for life'

After years of seemingly rejecting, through a mixture of a desire for change and collective embarrassment, the stereotypes promoted by the previous regime (though see Imbert, 1990, on how the Spanish left used national symbols immediately after the 1981 attempted *coup d'état*), 1992 also marks the beginning of a process of recuperation by official discourse of more of the 'national' values associated with the old stereotypes. The official tourist campaign of this period, for example, adopts as its central slogan 'Passion for life', deliberately playing on and reinforcing a Latin or Mediterranean stereotype, using advertisements extolling such supposedly Spanish national (and uniformly distributed) virtues and concepts as 'soul', 'spirit' and 'olé'.

In contrast to this rather risky deployment for external consumption of what are sometimes conceived in other cultures as negative images, some authors have noted the reticence of the private and commercial sectors in Spain to use any images at all of national identity in their publicity (Cannon, 1997; Fuentes and Kelly, forthcoming). It has been pointed out that, whilst many companies of countries such as Germany, France and Italy make extensive use of the positive values associated with their national traits to sell their products (German efficiency for engineering products, French 'class' for luxury items such as perfumes, Italian elegance and design for fashion and accessories), Spain's private companies, unlike their public counterparts, shy away from any direct association with Spain, and tend to insist on the individual virtues of their products themselves. This link with 'Spain' has been seen to be something of a handicap for the marketing of products abroad, and is undoubtedly related to the use of excessively stereotyped images associated with negative values outside Spain by official discourse over the years.

'España va bien', 'Bravo España'

The messy end to the long period of Socialist government, after an embarrassing string of corruption scandals and the arrival of the right-wing Popular Party (Partido Popular) in power in March 1996, has undoubtedly also influenced the change in official constructions of Spain for internal consumption. Most noticeable, perhaps, is the change in state television. Under the PP, considerations of quality apart, there has been a distinct move to include much more coverage of the monarchy (for further analysis of the construction of the monarchy since the transition, see O'Donnell and Blain, 1994; O'Donnell, 1996), the church, the jet set, together with some of the more folkloric aspects of Spanish life. The macropropositions of this discourse are evident and are, amongst other things, part of the heated debate over the future of regional autonomy, particularly in the Basque Country and Catalonia, despite the minority government's dependence on votes from Catalan nationalists.

Shortly after the PP took office, Deputy Prime Minister Francisco Alvarez Cascos declared football to be an issue of national interest, again reminiscent of the Franco regime's use of the sport to take the public's mind off the serious economic and political problems of the time. For the 1998 World Cup, *Televisión Española* (official sponsors of the Spanish team) broadcast an advertisement in which the players were stereotypically represented as bulls rushing into the ring, images which unwittingly and ironically predicted the fate of the team, which was subsequently eliminated in the first round. Conveniently for many commentators, the Basque (nationalist) team manager was there to take the brunt of the blame for the failure of the national team, or the team representing the Spanish state, as it is referred to in Basque and Catalan nationalist terms (León Solís, 1996; Crolley, 1997).

One telling illustration of what I see as a return to openly Spanish nationalist values in official discourse (stigmatized for a period during and after the transition) is the huge broadcasting operation by state television of the recent (October 1998) wedding of the daughter of the Duchess of Alba, Eugenia Martínez de Irujo, to the young bullfighter ('son and grandson of bullfighters') Fran Rivera. The televised event, billed as 'the wedding of the year', was attended by the heterogeneous mix of aristocrats, show-business personalities and professional jetsetters who constitute Spain's beautiful people today, and was widely compared in sectors of the Spanish press to a royal wedding. Its televising at state expense was justified by the director-general of *Televisión Española* on the basis of the enormous public interest in the event, and the honour it apparently constituted that the families of the bride and groom should have chosen the state channel in preference to one of the private ones to relay the nuptials. What is more, descriptions of the event on television, radio and in Spain's many and very profitable gossip magazines referred to it repeatedly as a representation of the 'real Spain'. This description is at the very least disconcerting, especially if we bear in mind that the wedding took place in Seville, a province with one of the highest unemployment and poverty rates in Europe.

The combination of football, bullfighting and members of the aristocracy parading in traditional dress, is undoubtedly a part of the official PP construction of contemporary Spain, widely parodied as 'España va bien' (Spain is doing well). Let us point out here also that the current tourist campaign for Spain abroad uses the self-congratulatory slogan 'Bravo', incorporating very modern images of Spanish culture in the 1990s, such as the new Guggenheim Museum in Bilbao. It is difficult to avoid the conclusion that the governing party is making use of a revamped version of the old, clichéd discourse of Spanish national identity, firstly to help create a climate favourable to its position in dealing with the increasingly complex issues of autonomy for the nationalities and regions, and secondly to create a sense of wealth and well-being which is not necessarily in keeping with real lives lived by many millions of Spaniards.

References

ARCEO VACAS, J. L. *et al.* (EDS) 1993: *Campañas electorales y 'Publicidad Política' en España (1976–1991)*. Barcelona: Promociones y Publicaciones Universitarias.

CANNON, J. 1997: Spain as a marketing tool: an examination of perceptions of Spanish products. *International Journal of Iberian Studies*, 11(2), 112–22.

CROLLEY, L. 1997: Real Madrid v Barcelona: the state against a nation? The changing role of football in Spain, *International Journal of Iberian Studies* 10 (1), 33–43.

Economist, The 1992: After the fiesta: A survey of Spain, 25 April.

FERNANDEZ LAGUINILLA, M. 1986: Stéreotypes discursifs de la droite contemporaine espagnole autour de la Nation. In Tournier, M. *et al.* (eds) *Nationalisme en Espagne. Du Franquisme a la démocratie.* Paris: Klincksieck.

FUENTES, A. and KELLY, D. forthcoming: The translator as mediator in international advertising: the case of Spanish products in English-speaking markets. In Beeby, Allison *et al.* (eds), *Investigating Translation.* Amsterdam: John Benjamins.

GRAHAM, H. and LABANYI, J. 1995. Democracy and Europeanization: continuity and change 1975–1992. In Graham, H. and Labanyi, J (eds): *Spanish cultural studies: an introduction.* Oxford: Oxford University Press, 311–13.

HALL, S. 1980: Encoding/decoding. In Hall *et al.* (eds), *Culture, media, language.* London: Routledge, 128–38.

IMBERT, G. 1990: *Los discursos del cambio. Imágenes e imaginarios sociales en la España de la transición (1976–1982).* Madrid: Akal.

KELLY, D. 1997: *Prensa e identidad nacional: la imagen de España en la prensa británica.* Granada: Universidad de Granada (doctoral thesis on microfilm).

LEON SOLIS, F. 1996: El juego de las nacionalidades: Discursos de identidad nacional española en los Mundiales de Fútbol. *International Journal of Iberian Studies* 9 (1), 28–45.

MARTIN ROJO, L. and VAN DIJK, T. A. 1997: There was a problem and it was solved!: legitimating the expulsion of 'illegal' migrants in Spanish parliamentary discourse. *Discourse and Society* 8 (4), 523–66.

O'DONNELL, H. 1996: Constructing the citizen-king: monarchy, media and myth in contemporary Spain, *International Journal of Iberian Studies* 9 (3), 143–54.

O'DONNELL, H. and BLAIN, N. 1994: Royalty, modernity and postmodernity: monarchy in the British and Spanish presses. *ACIS Journal* 7 (1), 42–53.

SANGRADOR, J. L. 1981: *Estereotipos de las nacionalidades y regiones de España.* Madrid: CIS.

|3|

Collective memory, the nation-state and post-Franco society

MICHAEL RICHARDS

Introduction

The challenge facing Spaniards in the period after the death of General Franco was nothing less than the reinvention of Spain as a state and as a nation. The new democracy had to be capable of absorbing possible competing nationalist sentiments which might have destabilized the country and ended in violent conflict. Any territorial settlement contributing to this absorption of nationalisms was above all to be decentralizing, allowing political parties not governing at the level of the Spanish state to have a voice where they had most support. The aim was to avoid the ever-radicalizing pendulum swing from left to right politically which was a feature of the descent of the democratic Second Republic of the 1930s into the Civil War (1936–39). Judged by these criteria, Spain's transition to democracy was a success. Violent Basque separatism, in the shape of the activities of ETA, meant that the process was not entirely peaceful. But, fortunately the country did not fall back into the internecine divisions of the past. For a population which had been ruled by dictatorship for nearly 40 years, the transition revealed considerable political maturity. However, part of this maturity was an unspoken agreement to leave certain fundamental issues unresolved. Was Spain to be considered a nation or merely a state formed by a group of nations, for example (Mercadé, 1986)? Behind this problem lay centuries of complex history.

Constructing the Spanish state

Spain is, of course, a very old state. Its centralized national administration was one of the first in Europe. The expulsion of the Moors and the Jews in the fifteenth century and Spain's isolation from Europe during the Counter-Reformation were accompaniments to the construction of this centralized state. Its power was linked to a Castile-oriented army which resisted professionalization and saw part of its historic destiny as preventing the fragmentation of the *patria*, and a Roman Catholic Church which was economically and politically privileged and fiercely resistant to social change. By the nineteenth-century, the Spanish political class had become peculiarly restricted in size and increasingly divided. The contemporary history of the authority of this weak oligarchical state over Spain's geographic periphery is problematic and bloody. Formal authority resided mainly in the geographic centre of Spain. 'Spanishness' (*hispanidad*) was measured according to idealized (and gendered) religious and militarist models: the austerity, stoicism, and crusading mentality of warrior-monks and the interiorized sensibilities of Holy Sisters. The socially more advanced localities of the coast, often industrial and more liberal – Barcelona, the Basque Country, Valencia, Málaga, etc. – were seen as heterodox and dangerous.

In previous centuries, the army and the church were sources of warrior-like crusading strength, a legacy of the long and uneven process of the Reconquest of Spain in the Middle Ages. But, in the latter part of the nineteenth century, by which time most of Spain's empire had been dissipated, they became symptomatic of a crisis of the nation-state. Spain had declined from the metropolitan centre of a seaborn empire to a relatively inconsequential power on the periphery of Europe. By the last third of the nineteenth century, liberal reforms, secularization and the rationalization of state institutions headed the Europeanist political and social agenda. Catholicism in Spain was slowly on the wane, though its control of most of the country's educational establishments was tenacious. It would not be long before modern political parties and movements began to call for an end to electoral falsification and governmental corruption and for a better way of life through the actions of the state. The Second Republic in the 1930s tried and failed to answer this call, democratically.

Liberal governments of the mid-nineteenth century instituted reforms, seeking to restrict the economic power of the church and attempting to make civic national institutions work. But, the restoration of the monarchy in the mid-1870s perpetuated clerical and military power somewhat artificially and kept politics as the exclusive reserve of elite society, controlled from Madrid. Mass schooling was fragmented, inadequate and dominated by Catholic doctrine (Boyd, 1997). Crucially, the education system failed to play the role of agent of cultural homogenization. Overall, the liberal revolution of the last century was a very passive one. Consequently there was a great deal of resistance to the authority of the state and the process by which people in Spain were 'made national' was truncated.

Since the beginning of the present century, regional nationalist sentiment, culture and politics have been particularly pronounced in the north-eastern region of Catalonia and the northern coastal areas of the Basque Country and Galicia. The expression of these differences, and claims for political autonomy to articulate them, were met by obstructionism and resistance from the Restoration state (1874–1931). The response, especially of the political right, to the autonomy provisions of the 1931 constitutional pro-gramme of the democratic Second Republic, was bellicose and threatening. The Republic was granted insufficient time to take up what was liberal of the nineteenth-century legacy and to popularize a modern sense of common identity and community in Spain. The governments of the Republic were unable to reoccupy the territory of Spain's history as civil ideology.[1]

In contrast, the army and political conservatives revealed the depth of their hatred of 'separatism' by claiming that even an 'España Roja' (a 'Red Spain') would be preferable to an 'España Rota' (a 'Broken Spain'). The response of unitary nationalism to this regionalism therefore became a sig-nificant contributory factor in the onset of the Civil War in Spain in 1936. Autonomy, in the 1930s, entailed a major challenge to existing power which would not be tolerated. These claims of difference were washed away in a torrent of blood during the war and in its aftermath and were suppressed and denied during the reign of the centralized authority in the Franco years.

The nineteenth-century 'nationalization' of state and society, through the liberal juridical revolution, had been resisted right up to the Civil War years, just as resistance after the Civil War to the centralism of Franco was later sustained throughout the years of dictatorship and beyond. The pre-Civil War struggle was ideological and economic, but also, in part, based on a sense of locality. Two sets of tensions are of interest here. First, there had long been a conflict between the state and urban modernizers (especially in Catalonia) who wanted to go much further than Madrid-based liberals in rationalizing authority. After the disastrous loss of the remnants of the American empire in 1898, some of them appeared to want to take direct hold of the reins of power themselves, virtually by 'catalanizing' the Spanish state. Second, another long-standing tension existed between the state and largely rural, anti-liberal dissenters in the provinces who had not benefited materially from the liberal land reforms of the previous century, and wanted only to safeguard religion, monarchy and local (*pueblo*) lifestyles or institu-tions, in areas such as Navarre, Zaragoza, Soria, La Rioja and the Basque Country. In a sense, the experience of Francoism dissolved both of these ten-sions.

Francoism: the fantasy of 'nation'

The Francoist state was, above all, a centralizing power. Faced with Franco's victory, a substantial number of 'realists' within the Catalan social elite underwent a voluntary process of *'españolización'* (hispanicization) in the aftermath of the Civil War. The hope of securing leadership of the

Spanish state was given up in return for maintaining the basis of their hold on the local economy and diversifying nationally through financial investments. The lesser objective of gaining some measure of regional autonomy remained, however, an ultimate desire, in the post-Franco period.

By contrast, rank-and-file, provincial, anti-liberal dissent suffered a different fate. Francoism might have been expected faithfully to represent this particular social constituency, but the heartlands of social conservatism lost out much more than the Catalan elite in the wake of Franco's victory. In the immediate post-Civil War decades, the Francoist state favoured monopolistic economic forces and put resources behind grandiose industrializing projects. Spanish family agriculture was treated to rhetorical and ideological eulogization while suffering virtually total material neglect.

In addition, broader social change did little to favour the perpetuation of a social consensus based on a so-called 'Francoist nationalism'. Almost in spite of itself, in its later phase, Francoism was economically modernizing, coinciding with the great social upheavals of the 1960s and the dramatic urbanization and economic growth of these years. Paradoxically, the heart was torn from communities which historically had engendered politically non-subversive *pueblo* culture and had supported Catholic, anti-liberal, *Spanish* nationalism through its daily habits, customs and economic way of life. While Catalanism could be reborn after 1975, it is not surprising that there was little sign of a renaissance of Castilian nationalism after Franco.

Other developments further afield, on which Francoist Spain was dependent, tended to militate against an internally coherent unitary nationalism. Full incorporation into all of the most important international institutions was denied to Spain while Franco reigned. Spain could not occupy a place by the side of other democratic European states as an equal and did not become a member of the European Union until 1986. The inability, indeed unwillingness, of Franco to incorporate the country into Europe had been an isolationist tendency which it was feared threatened definitively to detach Spain from the rest of the developed world.[2] Franco preferred to maintain the 'purity' of 'organic democracy', maintaining his own violent rule, rather than open the country to the considerable benefits of integration into such bodies.

However, from the early 1950s the Franco regime, in spite of its rhetoric of self-sufficiency, was obliged to form political associations with transnational bodies, like the United Nations Organization, and to make far-reaching bilateral agreements with the international powers, especially the United States.[3] The purity of Francoism's version of Spanish culture was diluted years before the dictator's demise. Since Franco, the Spanish regions have often turned their backs on Madrid and looked outwards to Europe and beyond. After the 1950s, economic growth depended hugely on the tourist boom. Therefore, by the 1960s, the formal Spanish nation-state, despite its rhetoric of powerful nationhood, functioned upon a rather weak foundation. Although Franco would not admit it, Spain existed within a European and world system on which the country depended. The apparently exclusivist Francoist state imposed itself in a context of institutional diversity in international terms, and a reality of social and cultural fragmentation in Spain. The Francoist nation, meanwhile, remained a fantasy.

Mobilizing historical memory

The regime was marginalized by Europe because of the past, and yet, Francoism depended on memory to maintain itself. While the social base of Francoist nationalism, such as it was, has essentially disappeared and Spanish sovereignty has been partially usurped by transnational arrangements, the painful legacy of Franco and the Civil War remains. The legitimation of the Franco regime, of course, rested on its military victory, its violence, and its construction of the Civil War as a religious 'crusade'. Franco's nationalism was therefore inevitably highly divisive. Particularly during the first two decades, the regime sought constantly to remind Spaniards of its capacity for violence in defence of its vision of the nation. The manipulation of history mingled with memories of blood and sacrifice. Franco called for 'a pact of the future with the past'. The Civil War 'imposed a duty to cultivate memory' (Richards, 1998, p. 7).

Catalonia, the Basque Country and Galicia were especially prey to discrimination, providing the regime with images of dangerous internal enemies. A struggle over collective memory has been waged in these places, as in the rest of Spain. In these areas particularly, and not surprisingly, regional identity has been in the foreground of opposition. The Nationalist war effort, and the repression in its aftermath, was intentionally brutal. As Franco proclaimed at the height of the Civil War in 1938: 'The cruel war sustained today, and the sterile sacrifice made to their regions by the Basque and Catalan leaders, are so hard a lesson that they will never be able to forget it' (Franco, 1938, p. 202). In areas of the country with a distinct regional identity, the rebels attempted a form of cultural genocide, affecting language, customs and freedoms, of the type carried out in the 1930s and 1940s against other European nationalities: Czechs, Slovaks, Albanians, Poles, Lithuanians.

This vengeance was only slightly mitigated, first, by the nature of regional conflict in Spain and, secondly, by the way in which social memory functions. The cultural 'cleansing' of the Civil War, though wrapped in the language of Castilian ultranationalism, was not essentially an ethnic phenomenon, despite the retrospective attempts of some regional nationalists to depict it in such terms. Also, although anti-clericalism was important, there was no conflict between different religions in Spain which could be portrayed in terms of 'ethnic' difference. The categories of class and morality, and, above all, a desire on the part of the Francoist authorities to prevent the 'break-up of Spain', ideologically, culturally, spiritually and juridically, were more significant to Francoism than ethnicity. Much of Spain, by the time of Franco's death in 1975, was left with a legacy of repression and systematic discrimination against the regions, and a memory of fearful violence. However, the Spanish Civil War did not encompass specific ethnic destruction as such, comparable to the Second World War memories of Serbs and Croats, for example.

Memory does not exist in a social vacuum and Spanish society since the 1940s has done anything but stand still. The decline in the social and political influence of the Catholic Church meant that anti-clericalism no longer weighed heavily upon the mentality of the left and its social constituencies. Although the ownership of land still remained concentrated a in few hands, for the most part, agricultural production no longer depended on the exploitation of masses of poorly paid rural workers. Many people in the rural south, in Andalusia, for example, continue to express a kind of regional identity in determinedly voting for the Spanish Socialist Workers' Party (PSOE) – the governing party in Spain from October 1982 until March 1996 – since the establishment of democracy, because they associate the party with attempted land reforms in the 1930s and the extreme economic exploitation of Andalusia with Franco and his regime. But Spain was a very different society in 1975 to that of the 1930s. There was a dramatic contrast between the enormous hardship of the first post-Civil War decade and the rampant consumerism of the 1970s. Moreover, at a personal level, there were good psychological reasons for forgetting the sheer awfulness of the conflicts of earlier years.

In this changing environment, the effort of keeping alive a submerged memory of the days of hope of the early 1930s was an enterprise of diminishing practical and psychological returns. As the Spanish economy and society experienced modern development in the 1960s, the past, in some ways, seemed irrelevant. The objectives of most progressive political activity inevitably shifted from 1940s' strategies aimed at the violent overthrow of the regime to more mundane, everyday concerns. The Francoist state, in many senses, had to run just to keep up with society and ultimately, by the late 1960s, lagged far behind. Subtle though they were, changes of emphasis can be traced in the pronouncements of the dictatorship in order to adapt. Examination of the sources of political socialisation employed by the regime – documentaries, speeches, commemorative monuments, political institutions – show that the balance between the 'legitimacy of origin' of Francoism (the Civil War), and its 'legitimacy of office', or tenure (*ejercicio*) was a shifting one. There was a dialectical relationship between a narration of war and triumph, on the one hand, and a discourse of peace, security and even reconciliation, on the other (Aguilar Fernández, 1996).

Recuperation of difference

These 'messages' from the state were not, as we have seen, devised in isolation, for consumption by a passive society, but partly as a response to social pressures. By the 1960s, the Francoist state could not control all information or even all schooling. This 'slippage' of the totalitarian state permitted some degree of articulation of difference. Recovering regional identity was part of the rebuilding of civil social relations (Pérez Díaz, 1987). In recent years, there have been many examples of political transitions with varying degrees of success or failure: Argentina, Portugal, Chile, South Africa, the Soviet bloc, the Balkans. In all these cases, the role of history and collective memory have been undeniably significant whether in a positive or negative way. Democratization has been based on claims from below – recapturing regionalist, ethnic or national cultures, employing the symbols of long liberation struggles and on concessions granted from above. Those transitions where conflicting ideas of 'the nation' have played a part have often experienced more difficulties than others, occasionally with tragic consequences. An element of 'forgetting' was intrinsic to Spain's peaceful transition to democracy after Franco, becoming an example to other countries in this sense. But 'forgetting' had to be supplemented (even compensated for) by political and ideological representation, especially of the 'historic regions'. Here, the devolution of administration and decision-making through the so-called 'state of autonomies', in spite of its imperfections, is crucial.

State, nation, nationalities

It was inevitable, as society began to contemplate life after Franco by the early 1970s, that the question of regional representation and the relationship of state to nation and nationalities would again rise to the surface of political debate surrounding the new Constitution approved in 1978. Plurality demanded the renunciation of the centralizing mission of the state. The existence of other nationalities became a primary focus of attention. Although the Constitution was based on 'the indivisible unity of the Spanish Nation' and Castilian remained the official language of the state, the right to autonomy of the nationalities within the state was guaranteed and other languages were to be official in their respective Autonomous Communities. Spain now has a semi-federal structure in which the powers of the state are shared with the 17 autonomous regions (Newton and Donaghy, 1997). Basque and Catalan statutes of autonomy were approved in October 1979, shortly after the second democratic elections in Spain since the death of Franco. Both regions also secured their own parliaments. Galicia followed suit in April 1981.[4]

In spite of the challenges posed by ETA and the bunker mentality still discernible within the army in the early 1980s, democratic institutions have since been consolidated. As a 1985 editorial in the much respected Spanish national daily *El País* claimed, celebrating the progress made in the 10 years since Franco's death, 'the State of the autonomies has opened up practicable ways for the solution of the historic disputes with Catalonia and the Basque

Country'.[5] In spite of the unanswered questions, the new territorial distribution of powers appears to go from strength to strength, constituting, certainly in terms of distributing finance, the greatest decentralization process of the modern era.[6]

1992: reappropriating *hispanidad*

By the 1990s, the generation for which the Franco dictatorship, which it hardly knew, had been simply an anachronistic vestige of inter-war Fascism, had reached adulthood and was now incorporated into society. In contrast to the interiorism of Francoism, Spain's democratic governments have followed the younger generation in stressing openness to the outside world, constructing Spain as a stage for the performance of international events, for example. This is demonstrated in Spain's relations with Europe and America and her growing role in world affairs. Some of this, like membership of NATO in May 1982, has been forced through, apparently against the popular mood, though protest was based on a pacifist rationale and the idea of non-alignment rather than on a belief in Spanish isolationism.[7] The Spanish government's hosting of the First Middle East Peace Conference in November 1991 was a symbol of the 'arrival' of Spain onto the world stage as a politically significant player. The following year saw the rapid and impressive consummation of this arrival when, simultaneously, Madrid was named European Cultural Capital for 1992, the Universal Exhibition (Expo) was held in Seville, and the Olympic Games staged in Barcelona. Although these two latter events were really occasions to celebrate regional success (Andalusian and Catalan, respectively), an attempt was made by the Madrid-dominated state to draw a broad historical circle linking these 'Spanish' achievements with 'Spanish' history, especially the discovery of the Americas 500 years earlier, in 1492. Christopher Columbus was reappropriated for Spain, as he had been by the highly conservative creators of *hispanidad* in the lead-up to the Civil War in the 1930s. Not very much was said officially about the expulsion of the Moors and the Jews from Spain which also coincided in 1492 with what some in Spain thought of as a genocide in America but what officially in 1992 became, very ambiguously, '*el encuentro*' (the encounter).

Beyond the 'nation-state'

An irony in referring to Spain as the 'nation of the nations' is that regional nationalist sentiments began to be institutionally recognized at a moment when conditions, especially economic conditions, were making possible, for the first time, the construction of a coherent, rational and unitary administration.[8] The economic development of the 1960s was the basis of a modernization producing a state less encumbered by elite divisions than ever before, with financial power able to provide services and use authority for the benefit of the entirety of Spain. The long crisis of the nation-state in Spain could perhaps have been overcome. The growth of Spanish capitalism within an increasingly globalized system produced a uniformity in habits of consumption familiar to modern states post-1945. To an extent, the market has overtaken concerns with locality and the nation. Rampant consumerism has inevitably partly filled the vacuum left by older cultural forms and society, even in the regions, appears uncertain about its own history, stressing the positive and obsessive about the idea of 'progress'.

However, there are significant reasons why regional sentiment will not disappear. First, it is deeply entrenched and based on real and valuable cultural differences like language. Second, sharing an experience of personal consumption in the market place does not necessarily dilute other differences, although an obsession with consumption may well relegate or distort historical memory. Nationalism can be linked to consumerism quite easily, but not always so easily to historical truth. During the autumn holiday in Spain, in October 1992, in a double celebration of Spain's 'National Day' and the quincentenary of '*el encuentro*', customers were invited by one department store chain with branches throughout Spain to make their own 'great discovery', just like Columbus, by collecting a discount cheque for 1492 pesetas. It was 'something else to be thankful to Columbus for'.[9] But, third, it seems that the debts of history do sometimes have to be paid. However much collective or social memory might be submerged, Francoism as a highly destructive and repressive cultural force, will not be merely forgotten in Catalonia, the Basque Country, Galicia or elsewhere. Fourth, Spain has shown other states how regional devolution and recognition of difference are part of modern democracy, a fact understood by many other governments of the European Union. Perhaps the advantages of a fragmentation of identities outweigh the disadvantages and dangers. Finally, although in European terms, Spain's experience of industrial modernity has been a relatively short one, the country is as much a part of globalization as other European states. In a sense, Spain has been plunged into the uncertainties of *post*-modernity without knowing much of modernity at all. The grand narrative of the nation-state – Spain's great historical problem – can perhaps be side-stepped after all.

Notes

1. M. A. Bastenier, 'España y el uso del pasado', *El País*, 3 August 1992, p.10.
2. The Spanish government first requested associate membership of the EEC as early as 1962. Full membership was applied for in July 1977, virtually as soon as the first post-Franco democratic elections were held. The Treaty of Accession was finally signed in Madrid in June 1985.
3. Spain signed military and economic agreements with the US in September 1953.

During the dictatorship, Spain was admitted to the following international bodies: UNO (1955), ILO (International Labour Organization) (1956), IMF (International Monetary Fund) and IBRD (International Bank for Reconstruction and Development) (1958), OECD (Organization for European Co-operation and Development) (1961).
4. 61 per cent of voters participated in the referendum on the Catalan statute, of which 88 per cent were in support. The figures for the Basque referendum are almost identical in both respects. The other regions of Spain had statutes approved in the period December 1981 to February 1983.
5. *El País*, 20 November 1985, p. 10.
6. In 1979, the state and its central institutions administered 90 per cent of public spending. By 1986, this was down to below 70 per cent. In 1990, more than 40 per cent of expenditure was regulated by the Autonomous Communities or local town halls *(ayuntamientos)*.
7. A referendum in March 1986 confirmed Spain's membership.
8. See the article by Antonio Elorza, *El País, Extra*, 28 December 1990, p. 31.
9. *El País*, 10 October 1992, p. 23.

References

AGUILAR FERNANDEZ, P. 1996: *Memoria y olvido de la Guerra Civil Española*. Madrid: Alianza.
BOYD, C. 1997: *Historia patria: politics, history, and national identity in Spain, 1875–1975*. Princeton, N.J.: Princeton University Press.
FRANCO, F. 1938: *Palabras del Caudillo*. Barcelona.
MERCADÉ, F.1986: El marco ideológico de los nacionalismos en España (siglos XIX, XX). In Dupláa, C. and Barnes, G., *Las nacionalidades del estado Español: una problemática cultural*. Minneapolis, Minn.: University of Minnesota.
NEWTON, M. and DONAGHY, P. 1997: *Institutions of modern Spain: a political and economic guide*. Cambridge: Cambridge University Press.
PÉREZ DIAZ, V. 1987: *El retorno de la sociedad civil*. Madrid: Instituto de Estudios Económicos.
RICHARDS, M. 1998: *A time of silence: civil war and the culture of repression in Franco's Spain, 1936–1945*. Cambridge: Cambridge University Press.

|4|

Race, immigration and multiculturalism in Spain

DAVID CORKILL

Introduction

Immigration, racism and the problems these can generate have, until recently, been a marginal concern in Spain. However, the twin processes of democratization and European integration undertaken by Spain since 1975 have demanded a reassessment of national self-perceptions and led to a reformulation of national identity as constructed under the Franco regime. An interesting, and sometimes controversial, aspect of the modernizing 'Europeanization' process has been Spain's transformation from a dominant monoculturalism and its replacement by a new emergent multiculturalism. This process has caused difficulties as the social visibility of immigrant and minority groups has increased and their numbers and composition have changed. The sudden influx of migrants from the Muslim world during the 1990s forced the Spanish authorities to confront the problem of ethnic, cultural and religious differentiation and the potential for social disharmony such immigrant insertions can cause. As a consequence, immigration is no longer a marginal public concern but has become an issue of some importance surrounded by prejudice, distortion and misunderstanding.

The aim of this essay is to examine how existing notions of identity, nationality and citizenship are being challenged in Spain today by changing political, demographic and social realities. The essay places the treatment of Spain's ethnic minorities – a term embracing both the resident gypsy population and *inmigrantes* from South America and North Africa – in its historical context by tracing the evolution of notions of national identity from the dominant monoculturalism imposed under the Franco regime to the pluralist society proclaimed in the modern, democratic Spain. An assessment will be made of the integration of ethnic and racial minorities against a background of Spain's rapid, if uneven, economic development over the past three decades.

Spain is a particularly interesting case because the country, so recently renowned as a major labour exporter, has now acquired the status of a 'new immigration centre'. This reversal of roles has inevitably foregrounded issues such as integration and rejection. The extremely rapid socio-economic development experienced by Spain since accession to the European Community in 1986 rekindled traditional immigrant patterns from the former colonies in South America and proved to be a magnet for would-be entrants from the Maghreb in particular. The surge in immigration occurred at a time when Spain was suffering from the highest levels of unemployment in the European Union, creating the potential for a backlash among the jobless.

At the level of legislation, by signing the Schengen[1] agreement, Spain moved more into line with the restrictive stance towards immigration adopted in northern Europe. By so doing, Spain took on the role as a 'guardian state' on the EU's southern flank, involved in the practice of exclusion. It will be argued that, despite the frequently confirmed self-perception that Spaniards are still an open and tolerant people, this aspect of Spain's 'Europeanization' is problematic and challenges long-held assumptions.

Francoism and post-Francoism

Franco's authoritarian regime launched a crusade to 'purify' Spanish society. It sought, with only partial success, to construct a centralist, autarkic, anti-liberal, and isolated state. This was to be achieved by political repression and the imposition of ideological conformity. Its key element was retribution against opponents who fought the Nationalists during the Civil War. Above all, the Francoist state was intolerant, predicated on vengeance against the vanquished rather than national reconciliation – the latter being a task delayed until the transition to democracy in the late 1970s.

Franco attempted to construct an integrative national identity that was Castilian, centralist, inward-looking and based on a highly partisan interpretation of Spanish history. In this connection, for example, the regime instigated numerous 'war holidays' (Day of the Uprising, Day of the Fallen, etc.) and built countless monuments commemorating its victory in the Civil War. Symbols of Spain's imperial past were key components in the dominant ideology; nostalgia for past glories was also assiduously cultivated and enforced (Edles, 1998, p. 32).

The ideological apparatus erected by Franco contained two key components: *hispanidad* and National Catholicism. Both served a purpose – the former because it blended the idea of a community of hispanic nations with a shared history and religion, and the latter because the close relationship with the Roman Catholic Church bestowed legitimacy on the regime. On the far right, *hispanidad* took on a xenophobic character and sought to legitimate the rejection of all things considered to be 'foreign'. Embedded in *hispanidad* was a concept of racial distinctiveness, conveniently ignoring that many Spanish communities had at least partial Moorish and Semitic origins.

National Catholicism is associated with the early 'isolationist' phase of the Franco regime and gradually declined as Spain became more integrated into the broader international community. The Catholic Church's role was more significant as it was given the responsibility of imposing uniformity on a divided nation. This was achieved through control over the education system and the cultural apparatus, including censorship, morals, etc. Tasked with 're-Spanishification', the church became one of the pillars of the dictatorship. Above all, it legitimized a social order based on social inequality, deprivation and repression.

In establishing its legitimacy, nationalist propaganda relied heavily on drawing attention to and demonising various forms of otherness. It rejected everything associated with the previous democratic governments of the 1930s and constructed an 'anti-España' that was variously communist, republican, socialist, liberal, etc. To this way of thinking, everything not Spanish had to be anti-national and all things European were also rejected on these grounds (Boyd, 1997, p. 126). Overt hostility to foreign influences was reinforced by reviving the language and symbols of the *Reconquista*. Inevitably, this bred intolerance towards nonconformity and outsiders. Under Franco, the 'other' was not just limited to the regime's opponents, but embraced any manifestation of cultural pluralism and difference. Hence, all aspects of regional identity (linguistic, cultural and political) were ruthlessly repressed by the Madrid-based central authorities who regarded Spain's essential character as Castilian.

Ultimately, the Francoist state failed to develop mechanisms that could achieve political, social and cultural integration. The authoritarian nationalists promoted a project based on an outmoded concept of national identity that was divisive and ultimately became an obstacle to political and cultural modernization. They conspicuously failed in their efforts to impose conformity and uniformity, in part because localism remained a powerful influence and a large, but overbureaucratic and weak, state continued to have limited reach and impact.

It is important to note that some of the contradictions in the regime's ideological underpinnings remained unexposed simply because the role of the 'other' was already assigned to the defeated Republicans. Moreover, the dominant monoculturalism remained unchallenged because there were so few foreigners living in Spain. In late Francoism, less was made of this oppositional element when the economy had became more open and legitimacy was increasingly founded on economic success and the delivery of continually rising living standards. Such a reliance created a divide between a rapidly modernizing society and an antiquated, anachronistic state.

Inevitably economic growth involved closer links with Europe and exposed the absence of freedoms and attitudes normally associated with a pluralist society.

The transition to democracy

The transition to democracy required changes both to the political *modus operandi* of the regime and to the constructions of Spanish identity it had encouraged. In a reaction to the authoritarian era, the emphasis was now placed on national reconciliation and *convivencia*, or living together (Edles, 1998, pp. 50–1). Although deliberately ambiguous and imprecise, the 1978 constitution did recognize diversity, cultural pluralism and heterogeneity. This provided the signal for the development of separate identities based on historic, cultural and linguistic differentiation to begin. Implicit in this redefinition was the acceptance that incompatible cultural forms may be equally Spanish.

The first test of the new cultural pluralism came in the 1980s. Although the process was initiated in the 1960s, a full-blown, modern consumer society only arrived after the successful consolidation of democracy and Spain's formal entry into the European Community in 1986. While generally welcomed, consumerism was accompanied by a number of unwanted features, including unemployment (the highest percentage in the EU), the erosion of social solidarity, and 'emergent forms of social prejudice' (Graham and Sánchez, 1995, p. 414). One particular form this prejudice took was a mounting hostility towards the growing number of migrant workers.

Migrant labour in Spain

By the 1980s, Spain had begun to earn a reputation as 'Europe's sluicegate'. Substantial numbers of North Africans, principally from Morocco, but also from Equatorial Guinea, Senegal and Gambia, entered the country. They were attracted by the job opportunities generated by high economic growth and the wider possibilities available once immigrants enter the European Union labour market. Although 'push' factors played a part (war, famine, overpopulation, etc.), it was changes in demand for labour in the receptor economy that largely explains the influx. In the increasingly competitive market-place, employers sought sources of cheap, temporary and unprotected labour. As a result, the informal sector expanded and the immigrants became ghettoized and reliant on precarious employment. They endured poor working conditions and were subject to ever tighter controls – all factors which militated against social inclusion.

Spain's immigrants remain very much a minority, constituting only about 2 per cent of the total population (Barberet and García-España, 1997,

p. 176). Typically, their presence is tolerated during periods of economic expansion, but attitudes harden during an economic downturn. A survey among young Spaniards conducted by the *Centro de Investigaciones Sociológicas* (Centre for Sociological Research) in 1999 revealed that almost half of those questioned believed that immigrants competed directly with Spaniards for jobs and believed that by accepting the lowest wages, foreign workers forced down overall wage levels. However, three-quarters believed that immigrants from poorer countries took the jobs that Spaniards no longer wanted to do (*El País*, 1999a). Unsurprisingly, immigrants are normally the first to be laid off in recessionary times, and often become the focus for resentment and frustration. As for their origins, the largest component consists of those born in Ceuta and Melilla. There is also small number from sub-Saharan Africa, particularly Senegal.

Relegated to the margins of Spanish society, the immigrant has become the focus of restrictive legislation. In 1985, a Ley de Extranjería (Foreigners Law) regulated the rights of foreigners to enter and work in the country. A year later the first *centros de internamento* (detention centres) were set up for illegal immigrants awaiting expulsion. Such measures reflect the influence of EU directives which frame immigration issues within a law and order discourse. Spain, along with other countries in Southern Europe, has been tasked with restricting immigration into the EU by the Schengen and Trevi treaties, as noted above.

In popular mythology, immigrants are increasingly portrayed as threatening and unassimilable. Economic hardship has forced them into ethnic enclaves which has reinforced a perception that they are resistant to integration. Centuries-old prejudices against 'Africans' and 'Moors' have been revived and touch a nerve as immigrants from the Maghreb make the often perilous journey across the Straits of Gibraltar. It is now generally accepted that, while anti-immigrant violence is isolated and limited to marginal groups, the potential for racism exists and discrimination is indeed practised in terms of the housing market and police harrassment (Carr, 1993, p. 74). In the popular mind, immigrants have taken the blame for the rising crime rate, the drugs problem and are dismissed in some quarters as parasites on society. A recent study conducted by the *Observatorio Permanente para la Inmigración* (Permanent Survey on Immigration) found that Moroccans and other Arabs aroused the least sympathy among Spaniards (*El País*, 1999b).

Gypsies: 'the foreigners within'

There has been a gypsy population in Spain since the early fifteenth century. Long the butt of prejudice, official persecution and legal action under the Vagrancy and Social Dangerousness Laws, gypsies have been seen as social outcasts and linked to criminal behaviour. During the 1940s the Franco regime ordered the *Guardia Civil* to monitor and investigate gypsy behaviour. This clearly indicates that the regime regarded them as different from mainstream society, forming part of that realm of 'otherness' of popular discourse.

The 1978 Constitution forbade racial and ethnic discrimination. Since then the government has adopted a more integrationist approach. Although hampered by a lack of information and research, the Ministry of Social Affairs launched a special development plan aimed at ensuring that gypsies have access to social benefits and improved housing conditions (Barberet and García-España, 1997, p. 177). There are signs that the gypsy population, which numbered some 330–350 000 according to estimates for 1993 (Arayici, 1998, p. 254), is responding to encouragement from local, regional and European authorities by establishing associations to represent this minority group. Encouragingly, the gypsy leader, Juan de Dios Ramírez Heredia, obtained a seat in the European Parliament. However, there is still a wide gap to bridge if educational, health, employment and general living conditions are to be brought closer to those enjoyed by the majority population. Widespread stereotyping is still common and overt discrimination continues. Gypsies are portrayed as work-shy and inveterate thieves. Such prejudices have been stoked further by attempts to blame Spain's drug problem on the gypsy community.

Illegals and the labour market

Immigrants have played a key role in the changing patterns of labour demand that has been a feature of the Spanish economy since the 1980s. Many employers (some of them immigrants themselves) have resorted to employing low-wage, seasonal, unprotected and nonunionized workers as part of the drive to restructure and retain competitiveness. As a result, immigrants have been subject to exploitation and economic subordination.

The illegal or irregular work-force grew substantially during the 1980s as demand expanded, particularly in agriculture and the construction industry. Employers came to rely on this pool of cheap, nonunionized labour. Meanwhile, organized networks found work for female immigrants, many from Latin America, as domestics or as employees in the service sector. Although small as a percentage of the total work-force, it cannot be disputed that illegal workers now make a significant contribution to the Spanish economy. In some areas, such as Almería, immigrants comprise up to 80 per cent of the agricultural work-force.

As the informal sector and the demand for casual labour expanded, immigrants became victims of illegal employment contracts and sub-standard working conditions Yet, when the authorities do take action, it is the illegal immigrant workers who are often deported, whereas the employers often escape punishment or are fined a derisory amount.

Immigration and the law

Despite their undoubted contribution to Spain's economic well-being, the authorities are intent on controlling the inflow of immigrants. They have instituted a two-pronged approach. One is preventative. This involves policing the frontier and co-operating closely with the Moroccan government in an attempt to prevent Spain's North African enclaves, Ceuta and Melilla, becoming a major staging post. The most dramatic indication that the Spanish were losing patience came in 1998 when high fences and control towers were erected to stem what threatened to become a flood. The other is based on legal enforcement. The 1985 Foreigners Law made it very difficult for immigrants to enter Spain, while thousands of illegal immigrants failed to respond to an amnesty. For critics of the Law, the overriding concern appeared to be 'public safety', the terrorist threat, and the drugs menace rather than immigrant welfare. In the Spanish case, tighter controls have done little to stop an increase in the number of clandestine entrants. Efforts to encourage legalization have had patchy results. During the 1991 legalization campaign, 132 934 foreigners applied for registration. Others, however, mistrusted the process or were unaware of its existence.

Migrants and crime

Given their social marginalization, immigrants are frequently associated with crime. It is all too easily assumed that their poverty predisposes them to adopt survival strategies that involve drug trafficking, prostitution, begging, or general criminality. Clearly, their deprivation as regards employment, housing, access to social security and generally poor socio-economic conditions does make them vulnerable. In addition, the migratory experience uproots and divorces the immigrant from social solidarity mechanisms. While these pressures are undeniably at work, the official figures do not fully support the connection between immigrants and crime. Caution must be exercised when evaluating the crime statistics, which indicate that immigrants constitute approximately 8.5 per cent of the total number of those arrested. As there is a high proportion of young males (the group most likely to be involved in crime) among immigrants, this is not to be entirely unexpected.

Nor should it be forgotten that many immigrants are victimised. Skinhead and other groups do target ethnic groups and perpetrate racially motivated assaults. Fortunately anti-immigrant feeling has not, as yet, found a political outlet. This can be explained in part by the weakness of the far right, but also because the Socialist administration clamped down so hard on immigrants. Nevertheless, while still not as common as elsewhere in the EU, there has been an increase in racially motivated violence. Anti-latino racist attacks targeted at immigrants from the Dominican Republic and other Latin America countries have been widely reported (Carr, 1993, p. 72).

Muslim communities and economic immigrants

It is important to remember that, although its growth is relatively recent, the Muslim community can trace its roots back into Spanish history. Until the expulsions in the late fifteenth century there were sizeable Muslim and Jewish communities in Spain (Boyd, 1997, p. 125). Their influence did not disappear and centuries later, when seeking explanations for Spain's humiliating loss of empire in 1898, the regenerationist, Joaquín Costa referred accusingly to 'the Africa that has invaded us'. It was not until the 1970s that a new wave of immigrants from the Middle East began to arrive in Spain. The inflow occurred at a time when identities, both national and regional, were undergoing reconfiguration during the democratic transition.

Until the 1980s, the Muslim community remained a minority among the immigrant population. Europeans comprised the majority among the legally resident foreigner population, but as they more than doubled between 1980–90 from just under 200 000 to over 400 000 changes occurred in their country of origin and socio-economic status (Solé et al., 1998, p. 333). Calculations are complicated by the large number of clandestines but estimates made in the early 1990s put the numbers at between 111 000 and 175 000 (del Olmo Vicén, 1996, p. 306). This substantial influx lies behind the perception that strict immigration controls have failed to prevent an 'avalanche' of Arab immigrants.

Assimilation is not an easy process for the Arab immigrant in Spain. There are a clutch of reasons for this, the most prominent being their precarious living conditions and cultural–religious practices. The new arrivals are sometimes even rejected by the established (largely convert) Muslim community which, being superior in social status and economic and educational attainment, feels little affinity to new arrivals. As is so often the case with recent immigrant groups, Muslim immigrants establish only primary solidarity ties with kin and local community. When associations are set up, they are limited to subsistence advice and legal support and tend to be nationally based.

Moroccans constitute by far the largest numbers. Economic migration flows from North Africa began in the 1980s and they constitute the largest Muslim community in Spain today. The majority of the new arrivals, who find work as rural labourers, construction workers and domestic servants, have settled in Catalonia, Madrid, Andalusia, Valencia and the Canary Islands. The likelihood is that the numbers will continue to grow as immigrants decide to stay and consolidate their families.

The lack of support organizations is mirrored by the relative absence of mechanisms to promote racial harmony. As already mentioned, the community's recent formation means that there is no strong associational network to promote common interests among newer immigrants. However, some steps have been taken to assist integration. In the wake of the Foreigners Law, a regularization process took place during 1985–86 which allowed some 23 000 immigrants to adopt Spanish nationality. A further opportunity was provided in 1991 which accorded regular status to over 100 000 foreign workers (40 per cent from Morocco).

Organizations representing immigrants are of fairly recent origin and have concentrated on immediate concerns such as employment and social issues. In 1992, a co-operation agreement was signed between the Spanish government and the Islamic Commission of Spain relating to religious observance and conditions of work. North African immigrant workers are represented by associations such as ATIME, the Moroccan Immigrant Workers Association in Spain *(Asociación de Trabajadores Inmigrantes Marroquinos en España)*, which has taken an increasingly militant stance in defence of its members. However, it is the politically active Moroccans who fled from domestic repression in the mid-1980s rather than the more recent arrivals from the rural areas who engage in political activism (Danese, 1998, p. 728).

Conclusion

By the late 1990s, hardly a day passed without a story in the media concerning police mistreatment of illegal immigrants and asylum seekers or protests by Moroccan workers. It has to be recognized that coming to terms with the existence of increasing numbers of Arabs and the role of policing Europe's southern frontier are hard to reconcile. It is no easy task to achieve the correct balance between humane treatment, recognition of their economic and cultural value, and the requirement to keep down the numbers entering the country. In one sense, of course, the emergence of race relations and ethnic minority issues are an indication that Spain is becoming politically mature in the wake of democratic consolidation and European integration. However, modernizing Spain's immigration policy and presenting it in terms of security, control and 'management' to bring it into line with the rest of Europe carries inherent dangers. As Baldwin-Edwards warns, synchronization in immigration policies may have been achieved 'at the cost of dehumanising it' (Baldwin-Edwards, 1997, p. 513). There is an obvious danger that taking a tough line may provoke a backlash among immigrant groups and cause social unrest.

Spain's enthusiasm to incorporate a European identity into its plural (local, regional, national) identities has been a notable feature of the post-Franco era. However, in some spheres, it has engendered Eurocentrist attitudes and a hostility to marginal groups. As Graham and Sánchez observed:

'It is almost as if constructing and adopting the same 'others' or outgroups as the rest were considered the hallmark of Spain's membership of the "club"' (1995, p. 415). Socio-economic realities dictate a different approach. Given the steep projected population decline caused by the falling birth rate, immigration is becoming the only means to ensure population replacement and that the economy continues to function and services are maintained. So there are compelling economic reasons for accepting that multiculturalism is an inevitable feature of the modern Spain.

Note

1. The Schengen Agreement, which Spain signed in 1991, is an EU accord allowing for the free movement of people among the signatory countries. Spain also belongs to the TREVI Group, a forum for joint action on immigration, terrorism and drug trafficking, which has put pressure on Spain to tighten its border controls.

References

ARAYICI, A. 1998: The gypsy minority in Europe: some considerations. *International Social Science Journal* 156, 253–62.

BALDWIN-EDWARDS, M. 1997: The emerging European immigration regime: some reflections on implications for Southern Europe. *Journal of Common Market Studies* 35 (4), 497–519.

BARBERET, R. and GARCIA-ESPANA, E. 1997: Minorities, crime and criminal justice in Spain. In Marshall, I. H. (ed.), *Minorities, migrants, and crime. Diversity and similarity*. London: Sage Publications, 175–97.

BOYD, C. 1997: *Historia Patria. Politics, History and National Identity in Spain, 1975–1995*. Princeton, N.J.: Princeton University Press.

CARR, M. 1993: The year of Spain. *Race and Class* 34, 71–7.

DANESE, G. 1998: Transnational collective action in Europe: the case of migrants in Italy and Spain. *Journal of Ethnic and Migration Studies* 24, 4, 715–33.

EDLES, L. D. 1998: *Symbol and ritual in the new Spain. The transition to democracy after Franco*. Cambridge: Cambridge University Press.

El País, 1999a: El 45% de los jovenes teme la competencia de los inmigrantes. 6 April.

El País, 1999b: 16 cuidades españolas celebran el Día contra el Racismo. 22 March.

GRAHAM. H. and SANCHEZ, A. 1995: The politics of 1992. In Graham, H. and Labanyi, J. (eds), *Spanish cultural studies: an introduction*, Oxford: Oxford University Press, 406–18.

del OLMO VICEN, N. 1996: The Muslim community in Spain. In Nonneman, G., Niblock, T. and Szajkowski, B. (eds) *Muslim communities in the new Europe*. New York: Ithaca Press, 303–14.

SOLE, C. *et al.* 1998: Irregular employment amongst migrants in Spanish cities. *Journal of Ethnic & Migration Studies* 24, 2, 333–46.

|5|

1992: memories and modernities

TONY MORGAN

In 1992, a century after its inauguration, Madrid's newly renovated Atocha station welcomed the Alta Velocidad Española (AVE), latest train technology of the twenty-first century, linking the capital with Seville in 150 minutes. Inside the restored great passenger hall, tall palm trees and luxuriant shrubs, permanently moistened by fine steam, created illusions of the south – or even the Tropics. Atocha was a metaphor for Spain's 1992 experience: leap-frogging technological backwardness, it joined its northern European partners in a post-Maastricht future; it also recalled the southern Andalusian and American adventures of 1492. Multiple identities were exhumed, re-examined, and explored in the year of the *Quinto Centenario*. This essay evaluates the debate in Spain and Latin America over the symbolic significance of 1992 and the events which celebrated 'Spain's Year'.

The Fifth Centenary of Columbus' discovery of the Americas, 1992 also commemorated the fall of Granada to the Catholic Kings, the expulsion of the Jews from Spain and the publication of Nebrija's Castilian Grammar – the first modern European grammar. 1992 was the year of the Maastricht Treaty, binding Spain into Europe, and it was also the culmination of the Socialist decade, in which much of Spain's economic and social infrastructure was transformed. Three major events were staged as showcases of Spain's modern transformation – the Expo in Seville, the Olympic Games in Barcelona and Madrid as Cultural Capital of Europe.

1992 was also the centenary of the Bases de Manresa, the first embryonic declaration of modern Catalanism, and a pointer to late-twentieth-century devolution. That the centenary of the birth of (arch-centralist) Francisco Franco passed so relatively unremarked at the time spoke eloquently of the democratic transformation of the country since 1975.

The nature and organization of the Fifth Centenary itself provoked wide disagreement. While the Spanish authorities promoted the commemoration in terms of a '*Descubrimiento*' ('Discovery'), Latin American opinion largely preferred the term '*Reencuentro*' ('Re-encounter'). The absence of any post-imperial organization similar to the British Commonwealth betrayed the frailty of relations between Spain and her former colonies. 1992 offered an opportunity to examine and fill this gap, with Iberoamerican heads of state holding two 'summit meetings' in Guadalajara, Mexico in July 1991 and in Madrid in July 1992. One tangible legacy of this effort to reappropriate colonial and indigenous heritage was a programme to restore 28 significant monuments in 13 Latin American countries, ranging from the Jesuit Missions in Argentina and Paraguay to the Casa de Sucre in Bolivia and Guatemala's main Tikal temple. Spain contributed 1 100 000 000 pesetas to the cost – more than the 900 000 000 pesetas raised collectively by all the Latin American nations put together; moreover, Spain's National Employment Institute (Instituto Nacional de Empleo or INEM) trained 1200 artisans in restoration skills in those countries. Co-operation since 1992 includes the Iberoamerican Association of National Libraries (Asociación de Bibliotecas Nacionales de Iberoamérica), educational TV ventures via the new Hispasat satellite, the Programa pro Andes and the Regional Investment Plan in Health and the Environment (Plan Regional de Inversiones en Ambiente y Salud). Madrid's Palacio de Linares was refurbished as the Casa de América, a permanent venue for Iberoamerican intercultural activities. These are 'slow, concrete manifestations of interdependence that have given the historical and cultural ties real significance' (Wiarda, 1996, p. 71). The Spanish administration and monarchy were, at the very least, displaying a renewed interest in restoring as well as undertaking new cultural links with Latin America.

Nevertheless, intellectual and political opinion regarding the virtue of commemorating the Discovery varied considerably. Peruvian writer and politician Mario Vargas Llosa believed it was the most important event in world history and argued that the transmission of the Spanish language and culture to the Americas outweighed the bloody downside of the Conquest. He praised Spanish culture for 'criticizing itself to the core, and creating sovereign individuals, pluralism, tolerance and freedom'. Resurrecting the old polemics between *Hispanistas* and *Indigenistas*, he argued, would obscure the causes of Latin America's contemporary problems.[1] Colombian Gabriel García Márquez lauded the Iberoamerican summits for transforming 1992 from a '*fiesta española*' ('Spanish party') into a '*punto de partida de la integración iberoamericana*' ('starting-point for Iberoamerican integration'), and Mexican Carlos Fuentes valued 500 years of a culture 'in which the Indian, the European and the African converged'. While for Paraguayan Ernesto Sábato, *mestizaje* ('racial mixing') demonstrated that Spaniards were not racist, unlike other colonizing groups, the Women United Against the Fifth Centenary (*Mujeres Unidas Contra el V*

Centenario) condemned the origins of the event in terms of the rape of Indian women and African slaves.[2] Mexican Homero Aridjis, acknowledging the oft-repeated contribution the new world made to the old – through such products as maize, chocolate, tomatoes, chillis, potatoes, cocoa, peppers, sunflowers, pineapples, avocados, strawberries, vanilla, turkey and peanuts, besides gold and silver – also asserted that the old world brought benefits to the new – wheat, barley, onions, beans, lettuce, melons, sugar cane, parsley, cows, goats, chickens, pigs, cats, dogs, vines, olives, rice, bananas, apples, coffee, pears, lentils and garlic. To overlook this, he argued, would be dangerously Eurocentric; in 1492 bonfires burned on both sides of the Atlantic – the Inquisition burned heretics in Spain and the Aztecs burned human hearts. A simplistic apology for Conquest or for indigenous repressions would be equally misplaced.[3]

Uruguayan Eduardo Galeano considered that 'In 1492 America discovered capitalism' and his compatriot Mario Benedetti rejected the very term '*Descubrimiento*' in favour of '*llegada de Colón*' ('arrival of Columbus'), asserting that ordinary people would not celebrate an episode which led to the deaths of 70 million indigenous people; only governments and capitalists could do so. He also accused Spain of antagonizing Latin Americans while the very celebrations were taking place. As Spain prepared for the European Single Market, its Ley de Extranjería ('Foreigners Law') imposed new immigration restrictions on Latin Americans – proof that Spain's cultural and political future lay with Europe, not the Spanish-speaking world.[4]

Spanish intellectuals were less vocal, and most support for the commemoration came from politicians. Few of these anguished over the Black Legend, preferring to stress a common cultural heritage and contemporary co-operation between the Iberoamerican nations. Luis Yáñez, President of the Fifth Centenary Commission, even argued that thanks to the Conquest millions of indigenous Latin Americans preserved languages, cultures and lifestyles without apartheid.[5] However, José Luis Leal, formerly the Economics Minister, appeared to confirm Benedetti's cynicism, arguing that the Castilian language was the key to the Conquest: 'As Castille was a society of frontiers, of syntheses, Castilian was a language of frontiers, connections, a cosmopolitan language.' It was also the greatest aspect of the country's heritage, '*como valor económico*' ('economically speaking'), currently being used in 153 radio stations, 35 TV channels and 10 000 periodicals world-wide.[6] A poll of Spaniards in 1992 by the Research Council into Social Affairs (Consejo de Investigación de la Realidad Social or CIRES) showed that 61 per cent thought the Discovery was positive or very positive. However, when asked which area of the world they were more interested in, a mere 4 per cent responded 'Iberoamérica'; by contrast, 67 per cent mentioned the 'EEC' (CIRES, 1993, pp. 315, 335).

Discussion in Spain regarding the role of religion in the colonization of the Americas was rare. It took the visiting Bishop of São Paulo, Antonio

Celso Queiroz, to suggest that the church should apologize for the sins committed in the evangelization of America.[7]

One of the few Spanish writers to protest against the consequences of the Conquest was Juan Goytisolo. As the June 1992 Rio Earth Summit brought to public attention global environmental concerns, especially the overexploitation of Latin American resources, Goytisolo joined writers from 20 countries in the Morelia Declaration of the Grupo de los Cien (100 Group). They linked environmental damage with cultural loss, claiming that for 500 years the knowledge and the rights of indigenous American peoples were ignored, in the Americas and elsewhere. They deplored 'cultural contamination and the loss of traditions which have denaturalized lives'. Signatories included Octavio Paz, Carlos Monsiváis, Arthur Miller, Norman Mailer, Ernesto Sábato, Mario Benedetti, Margaret Atwood, and Seamus Heaney. Perhaps Alain Touraine was correct when he said that for Spain, Latin America was primarily an uncomfortable memory of '*la modernidad abortada*' ('aborted modernity'), and what Spain in 1992 was concerned with was indeed modernity.[8] The PSOE's May Day Manifesto did not mention the colonial past at all, focusing instead on Maastricht – '*una plataforma hacia el futuro*' (a springboard for the future).[9] While the colonial heritage was duly commemorated by the Spanish political establishment, therefore, the future for ordinary Spaniards lay in Europe.

Much more attention was paid in Spain to the country's considerable Arab heritage. The Middle-East Summit in Madrid in October 1991, in which tentative steps towards peace in the region were taken, encouraged a reappraisal of Spain's relations with the Arab world. In 1992, the Alhambra mounted 'Al Andalús', a major exhibition of Arabic art and culture, with 130 artefacts from 15 countries, reasserting the importance of Spain's Arabic cultural roots. King Juan Carlos reflected on this event and on the new openness of Spanish society when he inaugurated the Centro Cultural Islámico, which looms over Madrid's M 30. The king described the new edifice, Europe's largest mosque, as proof of modern Spain's tolerance and universality, open to all cultures, especially Arab culture which 'has a special place in our hearts'.[10]

One commentator pointed to the resurgence of the Moorish community in Spain. A map of current immigrant patterns superimposed on historic Moorish settlements prior to the expulsion of the Moriscos would reveal a remarkably similar geographical dispersion including Valencia, Catalonia and Murcia, with outcrops in Aragón, Andalusia, Extremadura, La Mancha and Madrid. While most of the 4 per cent of the population eventually expelled after 1492 were labourers and vassals of the latifundia nobility, nowadays most of the 0.2 per cent of the population which are Maghreb immigrants are farm labourers, domestic servants of the new middle classes, or workers in the service sector which needs 'easily-exploited labour to compensate for archaic competiveness'.[11] Spaniards' ease or discomfort with the re-emerging Moroccan community in 1992 was also investigated by CIRES.

The survey showed that Moroccans ranked 23rd in Spaniards' preferences towards other nationalities, one place ahead of 'Gypsies' and one place behind the English (CIRES 1993, p. 325). At some levels, Spaniards were still grappling with the question posed by the cultural collisions of 1492 – 'How to live with the other? How to understand that I am what I am only because another person sees me or completes me?' (Fuentes, 1992 p. 89). Spain's Moorish cultural heritage was widely appreciated, but doubts remained about current problems of ethnicity and integration.

Juan Carlos repeated the theme of contemporary tolerance when celebrating in Madrid's synagogue *'el encuentro con los judíos españoles'* ('encounter with the Jews of Spain'). Pointedly alluding to Franco's National-Catholicism, he described the 1492 expulsion of 100 000 Jews as the consequence of a state 'which saw religious uniformity as the basis of its unity'.[12] That Jewish community had been in Spain for 1500 years. Three thousand people from the Sephardic Diaspora assembled to commemorate their Spanish roots in an emotional ceremony in Toledo – Sefarad 92. Twenty from different countries carrying the surname Toledano were ceremonially presented with the keys of Toledo. Poignantly and coincidentally, the beleaguered 800-strong Sephardic community in Sarajevo celebrated their own Sefarad 92 with others opposed to intolerance and hatred, and reclaimed their Spanish roots: 'We feel we are fully Spanish. Spain is our second homeland and we consider King Juan Carlos I to be our own king'.[13]

Juan Carlos is credited too with the idea of Seville's Expo, suggesting it in 1976 as a way to celebrate the consolidation of democracy and restoration of Spain's place in the world. By common consent, Expo was a triumph and in many places established Spain's reputation as a modern, reasonably efficient and capable society. The bad auguries which preceded the opening – the sinking on launch of the replica of Columbus' ship in November 1991, the destruction by fire of the Pavilion of the Discovery (*Pabellón de los Descubrimientos*) and the sinking of two replica Viking longships *en route* to Seville – were unfounded. The protests of the *'Desenmascaremos el 92'* ('Expose the '92') organization provoked brief confrontations with the police, and some local residents in Seville attacked the unequal distribution of resources, but in general the Expo was well-received by its 41 million visitors. The 300 theatre, dance and music performances in the four principal venues averaged 69 per cent occupancy, despite poor advertising and ticket-sales arrangements. The major art exhibition 'Arte y Cultura en torno a 1492' presented 382 exhibits from Europe, Islam, the Far East and Precolombian America, tying culture to the theme of the Discovery, locating Spain's 1492 in a global context. 'Domestic' Spanish tradition was represented in Seville by no less than 65 bullfights (*corridas*) in the six-month season.

However, Expo was principally an affirmation that Spain now ranked among the world's developed countries. For Javier Solana, it was a 'fulcrum in the leap to modernization which Spain is taking in the field of scientific and technological development'; for the Canary Islands' President Jerónimo Saavedra, it represented 'the end of the old clichéd Spain of bullfighters and flamenco dancers'.[14] New construction projects trumpeted 'progress' – Seville's new airport, the new Santa Justa station for the AVE, the transformation of the Isla de Cartuja and the construction of seven new bridges across the Guadalquivir. Tellingly, opening the last stretch of the new *autovía* to Seville, Minister Borrell declared that not only was it now possible to drive from Expo to Barcelona in 10 hours; it was even possible to drive from Huelva to Copenhagen without passing a single traffic light – Andalusia was unmistakably integrated into Europe.[15] And to reinforce the point, in 1972, there were 849 kilometres of motorway in Spain and 576 kilometres of dual carriageway; in 1992, there were 1807 kilometres of motorway and 5887 kilometres of modern *autovías*. In 1992 alone, 52 bypasses were opened.

Significantly, in Expo, while Spain's pavilions reflected Arab styles, each of the *Autonomías* had their own pavilion, projecting the new regional diversity of Spain to the world. Andalusia's pavilion cost the most – six times that of Madrid's. The aftermath of Expo was intriguing; lasting benefits were hoped for – that 'reclamation and investment ... could achieve rapid and measurable change' (Evans 1994, p. 60). However, that the largest investment on the Cartuja site should be the Isla Mágica ('Magic Island') theme park rather than a hi-tech science park perhaps answers the question posed by Umberto Eco 25 years earlier in Montreal's Expo: 'But is an exposition today anything more than an adult Disneyland ... where concern for the Space Age is combined with nostalgia for a fairytale past?' (Eco, 1986, p. 293). A promotional triumph and an expensive advertisement for Spain, Expo confirmed the country's emerging modernity, but arguably was of doubtful value in confirming long-term benefits for Andalusia.

The Barcelona Olympic Games in July 1992 were also a commercial and technological triumph. The first modern Games to be free of ideological rivalry, with the Cold War over, they were the most harmonious and efficient in modern times. Spanish pride was confirmed by an unexpected 13 gold medals (the previous best was one!). The Games, however, also confounded sceptics who considered that Catalonia would hijack them to the detriment of Spain's national identity. The Generalitat did fund a media publicity campaign that cost 600 million pesetas and culminated in worldwide newspaper advertisements describing Barcelona as being 'in Catalonia, a country within Spain with its own culture, language and identity'; moreover, Pujol's relentless exploitation of the successful preparation for the Games achieved a major propaganda *coup*. While the Government funded 37 per cent of costs and the Generalitat 18 per cent, an opinion poll in April gave 25 per cent credit to the Generalitat and 28 per cent to the Government; by July the same poll gave the Generalitat 50 per cent and the Government 14 per cent. Pujol's strategy was proactive: he was quoted as saying in the Generalitat: 'the more the games are Catalanized, the more they will appear as something Catalan'.[16]

However, a clever theatrical compromise at the opening ceremony reconciled Catalan and Spanish sensibilities. Juan Carlos and Queen Sofía entered the renovated Montjuic stadium to the strains of the Catalan anthem *Els Segadors* – ensuring an ovation from both Catalans and Spaniards. While the extravagant pageant of the Fura dels Baus enacted an introverted metaphor of Catalonia's Mediterranean heritage (largely incomprehensible to global audiences), Catalan pride and identity were generously assuaged by Montserrat Caballé and Josep Carreras intoning *El Cant de la Senyera* – for singing which in the Palau de la Música Jordi Pujol had been arrested and imprisoned under Franco in the 1960s. PSOE Barcelona Mayor Pasqual Maragall paid homage to Lluís Companys, the Generalitat leader who declared Catalan independence in 1934, was President of the 1936 Barcelona anti-Nazi 'People's Olympics' and was executed under Franco. Throughout the Games, the coexistence of Catalan, Spanish and other *Autonomía* flags promoted the new Iberian consensus; in Maragall's words, 'We have proudly recovered a plural Hispanic identity.'[17]

The lasting legacy of the Games was the transformation of Barcelona and its infrastructure, especially its new road network, Villa Olímpica, restored beaches, renovated Montjuic, and modernized telecommunications systems. (Vazquez Montalbán, 1992; Montaner, 1997; Bohigas, 1991). It became 'again a city in which people longed to live and work'.[18] Three billion pesetas were spent on Barcelona; only 9 per cent of Olympic spending went on sports facilities. Sixty-six per cent of expenditure was by the public sector, but financial control of the Games was tight, and a profit of 340 million pesetas was reported. The European identity to which Spain (and Catalonia) aspired was readily identified in the organization of the Games, where, according to *El País* a 'Nordic dispassion', a 'Germanic punctuality' and a 'Swiss precision' were achieved, while retaining 'the overflowing and passionate enthusiasm of the Latin peoples'.[19] Catalan Terenci Moix offered less breathless and triumphalist descriptions of an event which he characterized as: 'A conspiracy between TV stations, a complete Masters in Business Arts, a crash course in advertising'.[20] The Games certainly did show world-class organization; they also confirmed full membership of the multinational corporate culture club; Games sponsors Coca Cola opined that the event might lift Spain's 150 bottles per capita annual consumption (7th world ranking) closer to the USA figure of 290.[21] The message of Mariscal's postmodern, anthropomorphic Games mascot Cobi – '*Amigos para siempre*' ('Forever friends') – scarcely challenged such thinking.

In October 1992, 700 Catalan organizations published the '*Bases para el Futuro Nacional de Cataluña*' ('Basic demands for the national future of Catalonia'), commemorating 1892 and claiming the right to have 'the institutions of a sovereign state' and most other rights except the actual term 'independence'.[22] Olympic success had far from satiated Catalanism.

Against the successful pyrotechnics of Seville and Barcelona, Madrid's year as European Culture Capital was widely held to be a damp squib. The dubious concept of European Capital of Culture had been conjured up by the European Council of Ministers and handed down as a poisoned chalice to Madrid. Although there were 14 art exhibitions, 189 dance performances, 531 concerts and 794 theatre performances during the year, surveys suggested that most Madrileños neither attended any event nor could identify them. Mayor Alvarez del Manzano set the tone in the opening events, with the Municipal Orchestra playing a selection of *pasodobles*, *zarzuelas* and *sainetes*. Madrid's *movida* of the 1980s, he had declared, was a 'great Socialist flop'. What was needed now was a new *movida* 'with Spanish music, *zarzuelas*, our own traditions'.[23] However, only 6 months later were the public at large involved, when a Calderón de la Barca *auto sacramental* (allegorical religious play), *El Gran Mercado del Mundo*, was performed in the city's Main Square (Plaza Mayor). Low investment in Madrid's '92 exacerbated political tensions between a conservative Partido Popular-led local Council, a PSOE-led Comunidad de Madrid and a Socialist Ministry of Culture, underlining serious confusion over whether the event was a celebration of local or international culture. However, the opening of the Thyssen Bornemisza museum opposite the Prado and the (much protested) installation of Picasso's *Guernika* in the Reina Sofia Museum was the real cultural triumph of Madrid that year – the creation of one of Europe's finest arrays of art galleries.

Ironically, within months of 'Spain's Year' ending, the electorate rejected Felipe González's PSOE. In the teeth of deepening economic recession and rising unemployment, he faced accusations of corruption on several fronts, and the humiliation of Mariano Rubio having to resign as Governor of the Bank of Spain – first sign of the declining power of the 'beautiful people' (Holman, 1996, p. 208). Budget cuts were ordered in September, including suspension of all cultural activities in foreign missions. The newly launched Instituto Cervantes's budget was lopped by 500 million pesetas. The Expo bill came under scrutiny: whilst a week after closure the organizers projected provisional profits of 7600 million pesetas, the reckoning in 1997 totalled losses of 130 000 million pesetas. By 2000 the state will have paid 228 000 million pesetas for Expo. When to this is added the huge cost of the AVE (equivalent to the entire RENFE budget for three years) and other infrastructural works, unsurprisingly in the *resaca* (aftermath) of 1993 the electorate, 'increasingly disenchanted by widespread greed and corruption', unhappily 'distracted by state-sponsored spectacles' (Petras, 1993, p. 101) deserted the PSOE. Far from Expo aiding the suffering Andalusian economy, by 1994 the jobless rate stood at 34 per cent – three times the EU average.

1992 was the year that Spain laid to rest some of the ghosts of colonial guilt, began to rebuild realistic and overdue bridges with the Spanish-speaking world, reaffirmed its long-undervalued Arab and Jewish cultural traditions, achieved a modern transport and telecommunications infrastructure, and above all graduated into Europe and the corporate world of the European Single Market, for which it had been preparing since the Stabilization Plan of 1959. Of course, as we have seen, Spain's definitive entry into modernity came at a price, which is still being paid by millions of Spaniards.

Notes

1. *El País,* 3 April 1992, p. 12.
2. *El País,* 17 July 1992, p. 31.
3. Aridjis, H. El Año 1492. *El País,* 6 May 1992, p. 16.
4. Galeano, E. Cinco Siglos de Prohibición. *El País,* 24 September 1992. Suplemento Temas, p. 4. Benedetti, M. En el '93 ¿Dónde Estaremos? *El País,* 27 February 1992, Extra, p. 26.
5. Yáñez, L. En el Año del Quinto Centenario. *El País,* 23 January 1992, p. 11.
6. Leal J. L. Lenguaje y Economía. *El País,* 23 April 1992, Suplemento Temas p. 8.
7. *El País,* 9 July 1992, p. 21.
8. Touraine, A. Imagen y Semejanza. *El País,* 21 February 1992, Extra p. 28.
9. PSOE Manifiesto del 10 de Mayo – Una oportunidad ganada. *El País,* 1 May 1992, Suplemento Madrid, p. 6.
10. *El País,* 22 September 1992, Suplemento Madrid, p. 1.
11. López García, B. El Retorno de los Moriscos. *El País,* 5 November 1992, Suplemento Temas, p. 8.
12. *El País,* 1 April 1992, p. 18.
13. *El País,* 15 September 1992, p. 28.
14. *El País,* 21 April 1992, p. 16.
15. *El País,* 11 April 1992, p. 17.
16. *El País,* 19 July 1992, p. 39.
17. España y Cataluña: en Estado de Gracia. *El País,* 3 August 1992, p. 25.
18. Rogers, R. Building Cities to Move the Spirit. The *Independent,* 13 March 1995.
19. *El País,* 5 August 1992, Suplemento El País Olímpico, p. 14.
20. Moix, T. La Antorcha de los Exitos. *El País,* 20 June 1992, p. 11.
21. *El País,* 2 February 1992, Suplemento Noticias, p. 6.
22. *El País,*1 October 1992, Suplemento Temas, p. 7.
23. *El País,* 2 January 1992, Suplemento Madrid, p. 2.

References

Anuario El País 1993, Madrid: Ediciones El País.
BOHIGAS, O., BUCHANAN, P. and LAMPUGNANI, V. 1991: *Barcelona, City and Architecture 1980–1992.* Barcelona: Gustavo Gili.
CENTRO DE INVESTIGACIONES SOBRE LA REALIDAD SOCIAL (CIRES) 1993: *La realidad social en España 1991–1992.* Barcelona: Ediciones B.
ECO, U. 1986: *Travels in hyperreality.* London: Picador.
El País January–December 1992. Madrid.
EVANS, B. 1994: A celebration of enterprise – expos and garden festivals. In Fladmark, J. M., *Cultural tourism.* London: Donhead Publishing, 50–64.
FUENTES, C. 1992: *The buried mirror.* London: André Deutsch.

HOLMAN, O. 1996: *Integrating Southern Europe – EC expansion and the transnationalization of Spain*. London: Routledge.

MONTANER, J. M.1997: *Barcelona, a city and its architecture*. Cologne: Taschen.

PETRAS, J. 1993: Spanish socialism: the politics of neoliberalism. In Kurth, J. and Petras, J., *Mediterranean paradoxes*. Oxford: Berg, 98-107.

WIARDA, H. 1996: *Iberia and Latin America*. Lanham MD: Rowman and Littlefield.

|6|

How Spanish is it? Spanish cinema and national identity

BARRY JORDAN

Introduction

As Marsha Kinder has argued (1993, p. 393), Spain has moved rapidly from the hermetic isolationism and monolithic control of a Castilian-speaking central state to a radically decentralized, semi-federal form of internal governance. While giving voice to the legitimate demands and aspirations of Spain's seventeen autonomous regions, this process has also given rise to a profound sense of unease regarding the definition of Spain and Spanish identity. As a recent editorial in *Cambio 16* put it:

> What do we call Spain? Is it a plurinational state? An autonomous state, comprising different nationalities and regions? A state without a nation? A nation of several states? It is becoming more and more difficult to know where we stand ... .
>
> (*Cambio 16*, 12 September 1999, p 3)[1]

Against such a background of political and cultural dislocation, our chances of talking about a Spanish cinema in the singular become very problematic. In this essay, I briefly consider some of the difficulties we face when dealing with Spanish cinema: (1) in terms of a national film industry and a national culture; (2) as a national cinema defined in terms of a European and foreign language cinema; (3) how certain post-Franco filmic stereotypes have come to stand for 'Spanishness'; (4) how our views of 'Spanishness' are being rearticulated for the 1990s.

National industry, national cinema, national identity

When dealing with the notion of a national cinema, the question of the relationship between a national cinema and a national film industry usually arises. Typically, arguments used to support the idea of a national cinema tend to stress the value of a national film industry to the indigenous economy in terms of jobs, investment, export earnings, etc., as well as the domestic and international projection of certain political and cultural values. But if we can talk of a national film industry this may not be the same thing as a national cinema. We can obviously have a national film industry employing many people and making lots of movies, but these may well not be 'national' movies, in the sense of offering representations of the lives, times and cultures of a country's population(s) and their everyday situations and concerns.[2] Moreover, while the economic and financial basis of film-making crucially shapes the sorts of films that can be made, this may be only one of a number of factors which determine the interplay between Spanish films and their constructions of 'Spanishness'. In other words, as John Hill points out, the economic arguments regarding the value of a national film industry do not necessarily imply the existence or functioning of a national cinema, which he claims, should be characterized by movies dealing with specifically national concerns and preoccupations (1992, pp. 10–12).

Such national concerns and the way they are constructed will clearly vary according to our definitions of Spanishness and the ways in which these manifest themselves through filmic representations of class, gender, sexualities, regional and ethnic identities, etc. Such representations will obviously reflect the choices made by film-makers but also, in the ways in which they are decoded, the reading habits and practices of film audiences. Of course, in a global media environment, the definition of what counts as a properly or recognizably 'national' concern becomes somewhat problematic. On the one hand, as Mark Allinson makes clear in this volume in his essay on contemporary Spanish youth cultures, media globalization has led to a significant refiguring of specifically 'Spanish' youth and subcultures. Thus, a young Spanish *aficionado/a* of Doc Marten boots, who also takes pleasure in raves, piercing, fanzines, Beavis & Butthead and Tarantino, is arguably difficult to distinguish from many other young people across much of the Western world. Of course, on the other hand, alongside such cultural homogenization, we have to acknowledge the variety of ways in which the same cultural artefacts can and do become appropriated by different groups in their own 'expressive cultures' (Gilroy, 1987) which, in their turn, suggests a plurality of possible appropriations at sub-national and subcultural levels. In other words, globally available cultural styles are subject to local inflection and re-signification, often with a certain stylistic combination achieving hegemony (for a while) within a specific cultural space.

Similarly, at sub-national level, definitions of the 'national' and national identity are bound to vary and change over time. For example, for all those citizens in Spain who hold Spanish passports and national ID cards, but who also hold on to their Basque, Catalan, Galician or other regional/geographical identities, and who assert their cultural differences from the central Spanish state, the ways in which they understand 'Spanishness' may differ, often radically, from official definitions. Such views may well be invested with counter-hegemonic, negative connotations, positioning 'Spanishness' in terms of its marginality, difference and its 'otherness'. If so, Spanish national identity emerges as irreversibly variegated, heterogenous and decentred (Kinder, 1993, p. 440). In this sense, though we may be able to talk of the Spanish state in political terms, we cannot sensibly talk of a unitary national culture or for that matter a uniform national cinema. Thus any notion of Spanish cinema needs to take this heterogeneity into account. It is obviously more appropriate to talk of national identities, cultures and cinemas in the plural. Of course, as we shall see, such sensitivity to plurality and difference has to be set alongside the fact that Spanish cinema may well be *perceived* by audiences according to a very narrow and ideologically loaded range of national stereotypes and images.

Spanish cinema as European cinema

When seen from the USA, Japan or the Middle East, Spanish cinema tends to be located and promoted as belonging to a wider category of European or 'foreign language' cinema. European cinema is conventionally defined as non-Hollywood, a cinema whose funding principles, working methods, cultural status and linguistic diversity supposedly make it distinctive. Yet, while linguistic difference is an undoubted strength in preserving cultural diversity, it remains an obstacle to creating a set of European film industries which can compete successfully with Hollywood (depending of course on our definition of 'competition'). Even where European film-makers seek to make films with wide international appeal, they find it difficult to overcome the marginalizing effects of marketing blurbs and audience expectations towards 'foreign language' films and the linguistic obstacles involved in promoting them (most notably the question of whether to subtitle or dub). Over the last few decades, co-production arrangements between different countries and companies have gone some way to mitigating the risk and costs of making films for Europe-wide consumption. Yet, as Kinder notes with reference to Trueba's 1989 co-production flop *El mono loco* (1993, pp. 502–3) too many film projects have turned into 'Euro puddings', becoming bland, rootless, committee-written narratives, dubbed or shot in English in order to overcome the language barrier and to appeal to an elusive wider audience. The concept of European cinema, thus raises major issues concerning financial, cultural and linguistic matters and also in relation to the increasing fragmentation of national film industries. In this sense, the Spanish film industry is a striking example of a national industry which has to deal politically and culturally with Spain's devolved, quasi-federal status and with claims for support from sub-national film cultures, such as those in Catalonia, the Basque Country, Galicia, Valencia and the Canary Islands. Given this subdivision of national identities, new minority voices have increasingly turned away from the central state and the dominant national culture and now look to Europe for financial support and cultural legitimation. As Wendy Everett argues, paradoxically, 'this apparent fragmentation may well constitute a strengthening of the notion of European film. Certainly it reinforces the conviction that European films matter' (1996, pp. 18–19).

If European or 'foreign language' cinema (including Spanish cinema) matters, it still tends to be too narrowly defined by the industry and by audiences as an auteurist-led, 'art cinema' – as opposed to the generically coded and industrially based products made in Hollywood. This expectation (reinforced by distributors and marketing departments) has tended to radically simplify a much more complex situation regarding the sheer variety and abundance of output generated by national cinemas, including popular as well as art house, independent as well as mainstream movies. Also despite pan-European public funding initiatives and co-production strategies, such as EURIMAGES and MEDIA, European cinema probably remains little more than a collection of works from different individual countries, films predominantly marketed as art movies usually with a strong aesthetic or high cultural bias (Vincendeau, 1996, pp. 444–5). In the past, this 'high culture/intellectualist' coding and perception of European cinema have given rise to a rather narrow view of national cinemas, unfairly reducing them to a few canonized texts, auteurs or movements, characterized by certain predominant representational strategies.

Paradoxically perhaps, most European films are also perceived as having a clear national identity, promising certain textual, thematic and stylistic features, as well as specific cultural values. For example, French art cinema conventionally promises sophistication, intellectualism, mature/adult issues, entertainment, romance, and 'high' rather than 'low' comedy. This may be the reason why Jean Marie Poiré's *Les visiteurs* (1993), a hugely successful popular comedy in France, was such a flop in Europe, since it signally failed to play to established audience expectations abroad, that is audiences conditioned to expect a high culture, arthouse product (Jaeckel, 1996, pp. 35–43). In similar fashion, Spanish cinema abroad tends to be perceived in terms of European art cinema, a 'foreign language' product, invariably subtitled, and sold on the basis of its 'auteurist' credentials, usually reflecting the marketing strength of the director's name. Spanish films also typically promise visual flamboyance, provocative and subversive narratives and torrid images of hot, often explicit sexual activity. However, beyond a certain charmed and very small circle, including Almodóvar, Bigas Luna, Aranda, perhaps Medem (for rather different reasons) and Saura, the work of dozens of other Spanish directors remains virtually invisible and other genres, such as popular comedies, are conspicuous by their absence. For example, this is arguably the case with Santiago Segura's *Torrente, el brazo tonto de la ley* (1998). Massively popular with national audiences in Spain and commercially outgrossing Almodóvar's record-breaking *Mujeres al borde de un ataque de nervios* (1988), *Torrente* has been picked up by Fox for distribution in Latin America and Europe but has encountered difficulties in finding a release in the UK and USA. This is partly due to the fact that the movie subversively reinvents the rich vein of 'bad taste' championed by Almodóvar's films of the 1980s. But as Sandra Hebron has argued, the main problem is that *Torrente* is an unashamedly macho-oriented, misogynist, racist comedy. It thus poses severe difficulties for some distributors, fearful that its overt political incorrectness and its cultural specificities will not play well to more sophisticated art house audiences.[3]

Such difficulties clearly reflect distinctions being made by distributors and exhibitors between what is assumed to travel and sell well abroad (i.e. art and heritage movies) and those films which do not travel well (i.e. popular genre movies, given that they allegedly contain too much indigenous cultural noise in the signal). If these do travel and manage to gain a release, perhaps by being shown at a film festival, they tend to get recoded by distributors for marketing purposes as belonging to the art house category. And here, as Vincendeau has argued, it tends to be the director who takes star billing rather than the national movie stars (1998, pp. 445–7). Indeed, unless they have achieved a degree of crossover and made it in Hollywood (like Gérard Depardieu, Jean Reno or Antonio Banderas; *see* Kinder, 1997, pp. 5–8), European film stars are few and far between and are normally unable to carry a film within a fiercely competitive and cluttered market, dominated by Hollywood. Most Spanish films, film-makers and national stars face major hurdles in achieving visibility and marketability in order to ensure some degree of economic success in the wider European context. Yet, while virtually unknown in the UK, Spanish stars such as Victoria Abril, Carmen Maura, Assumpta Serna, Rossy de Palma and Cecilia Roth are gaining increasing recognition and plaudits in European co-productions, in a process which sees a growing internationalization of Spanish movie making. What effects do such transnational processes have on our definitions of 'Spanishness'? In the 1980s, it was Spain's *movida* generation and its view of Spanishness which seemed to achieve a hegemonic position in defining the national, at home and abroad. It did so most emphatically through the subversive representations crafted by such popular auteurs as Almodóvar.

The Almodóvar effect

Emblematic figure of postmodern, post-Franco Spain, international ambassador for Spanish movie making, Almodóvar and his work have had a massive impact on filmic constructions of Spain's 'national' image for both Spanish and foreign audiences. Indeed, his work continues to enjoy an almost canonical, foundational status for post-Franco film-making, revered for its elevation of tastelessness, contemporaneity (perhaps until *Carne Tremula*, 1997), hedonism, fluid identities, female-centredness, generic mixing and its obsessive interest in sex. As Marsha Kinder has argued, almost single-handedly, in the 1980s and early 1990s, Almodóvar perfomed a sex change on Spain's national stereotype 'establishing a mobile sexuality as the new cultural stereotype for a hyperliberated Socialist Spain' (1997, p. 3). Conflating sexual liberation and modernity and transforming his generic filmic hybrids into an auterist trademark, Almodóvar hit upon a very successful formula commercially, though not always critically. From *Pepi Luci Bom y otras chicas del montón* (1980) through to *Kika* (1993), his eroticized and sympathethic focus on society's marginal figures (gays, lesbians, prostitutes, transsexuals, drug addicts, etc.) gradually established itself (with official support from the PSOE government) as a new and dominant articulation of Spanishness in the 1980s. His movies became increasingly successful abroad, gaining plaudits at international film festivals, generating very good business and opening the way for other Spanish film-makers to gain a foothold in foreign markets (e.g. Bigas Luna, Aranda and latterly Gómez Pereira). Foreign audience expectations of what a post-Franco Spanish film ought to offer were thus established in large part by Almodóvar's postmodern refiguring of the clichés of the traditional *españolada*. Moreover, Almodóvar and by implication Spanish film, became synonymous with sex and plenty of it, the steamier and more explicit the better.

Intererestingly, as Núria Triana Toribio usefully reminds us, from an historical perspective, the sexualization of Spanish cinema was taking place well before Almodóvar arrived on the scene.[4] Leaving aside the rather unique cases of Buñuel, Dalí and surrealism, Bigas Luna, for example, was already exploring the dark recesses of sexual transgression in such features as *Bilbao* (1978) and *Caniche* (1979) (Kinder, 1993, pp. 262–75). And well before that, in the late 1960s and early-to-mid-1970s, before the lifting of censorship, we find massively popular and commercially successful sub-genres, including the 'Iberian sexy comedy' and an indigenous 'cine de terror', both symptomatic of the 'sexualized' filmic responses to the repressions of the late Franco period (Jordan, 1995, pp. 128–31). Thus the critical construction of Almodóvar as the benchmark for 'Spanish' 'national' film output as well as the founding father of its 'sexualization' may be somewhat exaggerated.

Moreover, Almodóvar's legacy, in terms of the marginal filmic stereotypes he has used to construct 'Spanishness', may not have been altogether positive or beneficial, in the eyes of domestic or foreign audiences. Indeed, the equating of 'Spanishness' with sex and sexual perversion (however playful and camp) may have reinforced some rather unhelpful, negatively stereotypical, perceptions of modern Spain and Spaniards. As Toribio has proposed, over the years, Almodóvar has offered his audiences very strong, explicit, sexy images, often bordering on the pornographic, yet all the while safely contained within a highly stylized, auteurist, art-cinema wrapping. The ideological subtext of such filmic preoccupations with 'basic instincts' (at least up to the early 1990s) suggests a rather unflattering and 'unmodernized' view of Spaniards who, still supposedly traumatized by Francoist repressions, appear to have little on their minds except thoughts of libidinal satisfactions. In short, Almodóvar's filmic obsessions with sex and desublimation have probably bolstered those very negative stereotypes of Spaniards as 'randy latinos', thus reinforcing rather than exploding the embarrassingly folkloric images of sexual repressions found in the sexy Iberian comedies of the 1970s.

At the same time, and returning to a point made earlier, if we define the 'national' in terms of filmic choices and practices which highlight the real, everyday lives of ordinary people, then we might be rather hard-pressed to identify Almodóvar as a 'national' film-maker with 'national' preoccupations. Indeed, Almodóvar's emphasis on artifice, dislocation, generic mixing, role playing, filmic citation and so on suggests not so much realism or a concern with the everyday lives of ordinary people as an emphasis on marginality, stylization and fantasy. In this regard, Almodóvar's success – especially abroad and possibly the reason why foreign audiences are able to tap into his movies – has to do in part with his playful use of pastiche. Pastiche suggests hybridity not purity or authenticity. It smacks of fraud, putting in doubt the very idea of originality or essence. What Almodóvar gave us in the 1980s and early 1990s in stories of mainly female identity crises, obsession, unrequited love and the downsides of desire, etc., were arguably adventures in hybridity. Characters were involved in multiple forms of masquerade, using these as a vehicle for exploring other identities; spectators were thus encouraged to engage with these identity shifts and instances of cross-dressing, so much so that both spectator and character were in effect being 'licensed' to try on a variety of roles in the course of any one film. All of this was part and parcel of Almodóvar's mixing of styles and genres. His conflation of femininity and inauthenticity and his use of elements of travesty, transvestism and instability militate against any notion of fixed identities. Travesty, masquerade, pastiche, hybridity, generic mixing, the raiding of classic Hollywood melodrama, the recourse to textual homage and citation – there seems little that is particularly Spanish about such features or their combination. Indeed, given that Almodóvar's most successful film, *Mujeres al borde de un ataque de nervious* (1988), could be seen as basically an American high comedy shot in Spain, we might wonder whether there is anything particularly Spanish about Almodóvar's movies at all? For many critics and academics, Almodóvar's strident, lurid, sexually charged images represented to the world the boisterous, modernizing, brash, self-confident 1980s in Spain, showing Spaniards as ultramodern, flamboyant and sexually liberated, even if always on the verge of a nervous breakdown. How sociologically consistent this was with the lives of indigenous Spaniards and how true it was of Basques, Catalans, Galicians and of people of different social classes in Spain is anyone's guess. In the end, despite a strong vein of corrosive humour and irony, it could be argued that Almodóvar was (at least until recently) fundamentally a fantasist, offering largely escapist narratives to his admiring domestic and foreign audiences.[5] Thus, the dominant construction of Almodóvar as the quintessential post-Franco 'Spanish' and 'national' film-maker might require some revision.

Reinventing the 'national' for the 1990s

Despite a serious dip in the 1993–4 period, the 1990s in Spain have seen a remarkable upsurge in domestic film-making, a greater visibility internationally of Spanish films and a series of shifts in filmic articulations of the national. The main factor driving these developments has been the huge influx of new younger directors into the film business in the 1990s, comprising a range of people of between 25 and 45 years old. Beginning with Juanma Bajo Ulloa, Enrique Urbizu, Julio Medem and Alex de la Iglesia in the early 1990s and later including such figures as Daniel Calparsoro, Alejandro Amenábar, Ray Loriga and new wunderkind Santiago Segura, we also find many new female directors entering the field such as Marta Balletbó, Mónica Laguna, Icíar Bollaín, María Ripoll and Isabel Coixet. With a whole new raft of actors, writers, technicians and the like also coming on stream, this new generation of Spanish film-making talent is developing a set of images and representations which are appealing increasingly to younger film-going audiences. A new Spanish cinema of the 1990s has emerged, offering a vast array of different styles and genres, narratives and casting choices, with increasing numbers of directors turning to Hollywood for their inspiration. The new generation shows little sign of following any prescriptive political or cultural agenda. Indeed, the young directors of the 1990s appear not to be burdened by the weight of the past or the need to settle any political or ideological scores.

Perhaps now we are seeing the emergence of the conditions in which a 'national' cinema in Spain in the sense outlined earlier might be possible, in that many of the new films of the 1990s focus on problems affecting contemporary Spanish society. Many recent film narratives, for example, deal with the difficulties facing the younger generations, who feel increasingly alienated in relation to school, work, employment, family, the older generation and to a capitalist system which promises much and delivers very little. Films such as *La madre muerta, Alas de mariposa, Salto al vacío, Pasajes, Hola ¿Estás Sola?, Familia, Barrio, Historias del Kronen, Tengo una casa, Mi hermano del alma, Extasis* and *Solas* all reveal an interest in the everyday problems and concerns of a younger generation, of different class backgrounds, set adrift from mainstream society, looking to their marginal lifestyles and subcultures for emotional support and family structures. However, whilst a number of movies from the younger generations evince such 'national' concerns, they do so within an aesthetic framework and a set of styles heavily influenced by the transnational visual media (comics, ads, fanzines, video clips, design, etc.) and by a general assimilation of American genre cinema and its conventions, as seen for example in *El día de la bestia, Airbag, Boca a boca, Sólo se muere dos veces, Torrente* and *El milagro de P. Tinto*. As Alex de la Iglesia puts it:

> 'The *españolada* is history. Almodóvar poured a bottle of alcohol on the wound and cleaned it thoroughly. Now we have to convince people that a Spanish film can be funny, terrifying, exciting, intelligent, crazy, engaging, troubling, thrilling.[6]

> (Heredero, 1999, p. 57)

In this sense, since the 1980s, with more money available and bigger budgets, production values have risen considerably to a point where Spanish cinema has become fully internationalized, technically indistinguishable from its American competitors; it now forms part of a global, transnational film business. Moreover, Spain's younger directors, having mostly assimilated American film forms, are anxious to enter the commercial arena and make mainstream movies, telling stories in their own ways, emulating Almodóvar's auteurist status perhaps but moving beyond his obsession with libidinal desire (as he himself has done, to some extent, in *Todo sobre mi madre* (1999)). A number of them have already turned to America and especially Hollywood for their stories, styles, and working opportunities (for example, Isabel Coixet with *Cosas que nunca te dije/Things I never told you* (1996), shot in the USA and Alex de la Iglesia with *Perdita Durango* (1997), shot on the USA/Mexico border). The fact that Almodóvar himself has finally decided to mount his next project (*El chico del periódio/The paper boy*) in the USA and shoot it in English is perhaps symptomatic of the internationalization of Spanish film-making. Such a move may well alter and further complicate our perceptions of Almodóvar as the supposed benchmark of 'national' Spanish film-making and filmic definitions of 'Spanishness'.

What seems to be happening is that definitions of Spanishness and Spanish national stereotypes continue to be recycled, subverted and renewed, as in Segura's *Torrente*. At the same time, it is becoming increasingly difficult to distinguish what is Spanish from what is not; indeed, the search for signs of a putative, pre-existing, stable Spanish identity – as we have seen, in film as elsewhere – is rather elusive. Films, and especially contemporary Spanish films, raid and recycle filmic conventions, styles, narratives and forms from mainly American models and sources (as in Bajo Ulloa's *Airbag* (1997)). It may well be that now and in the future, Spanish national cinema will predominantly consist of a heterogenous amalgam of visual styles and formal strategies – appropriated from certain domestic traditions as well as being heavily indebted to other film cultures. Indeed, this is arguably the way film-making has always been, the result of a continuous process of assimilation and resignification of elements drawn from both home and transnational film cultures.

Acknowledgement

This is a rewritten version of a paper delivered at the Film Symposium, linked to Viva, Spanish Film Festival, held in Manchester, in March 1999, co-ordinated by Lorraine Ralston of Corner House Cinemas and sponsored by the Instituto Cervantes and Manchester City Council. I would like to thank the organizers for inviting me to speak and all the participants in the conference, especially Sandra Hebron and Núria Triana Toribio, whose papers provided ample food for thought for certain aspects of this essay.

Notes

1. '¿A qué llamamos España?: ¿Estado plurinacional, estado autonómico, de nacionalidades y regiones, estado sin nación, nación de varios estados ...? Cada vez resulta más difícil saber donde estamos ... .'
2. As argued in the editorial section of *Sight and Sound*, vol. 9, 3 (1999), 3.
3. Sandra Hebron. Paper delivered at Viva, Spanish Film Symposium. Manchester, 1999.
4. Núria Triana Toribio. Paper delivered at Viva, Spanish Film Symposium, Manchester, 1999.
5. Part of Almodóvar's reputation and indeed his success have been forged on the basis of the director's deliberate (if misleading) refusal to acknowledge Spanish history and the past, especially Francoism, in his movies. Ahistoricism has been one of the major features of his work which, in many respects, is arguably correct. Yet, at the margins, there are signs of historical embedding and concern (even as significant absences), if only we are prepared to look. More recently, both in *Carne Trémula* (1997) and *Todo sobre mi madre* (1999) (a powerful reprise of the director's interest in role playing and the theatrical), this cultivated disdain for the socio-historical appears to have been softened by a more overt embrace of the past, Francoist and post-Franco. Moreover, on receipt of the prize for best director at Cannes, in May 1999, while ironizing the lacrimose conventions of the Oscar ceremony, Almodóvar showed much political *savoir-faire* when genuinely acknowledging Spain's considerable political achievements since the Franco regime, stating: 'Excuse me if I don't cry. I would like to dedicate my prize to the democracy in Spain' (*Daily Telegraph*, 24 May 1999, p. 3).
6. 'La españolada es historia . .... Almodóvar vació un bote de alcohol sobre la herida y la limpió profudamente. Ahora hay que convencer a la gente de que una película española puede ser divertida, terrorífica, excitante, inteligente, frenética, encantadora, inquietante, apasionante... .'

References

EVERETT, W. (ED.) 1996: *European identity in cinema*. Exeter, Intellect Books.
GILROY, P. 1987: *There ain't no black in the Union Jack*. London: Routledge.
HEBRON, S. 1999: Spanish film in the UK and Europe. Unpublished paper delivered at Viva. Spanish Film Festival, Manchester.
HEREDERO, C. 1999: Cine Español. Nueva Generación. *Dirigido* (April), 50–67.
HILL, J. 1992: The issue of national cinema and British Film Production. In Petrie, D. (ed.), *New questions of British cinema*. London: BFI, 10–21.

KINDER, M. 1993: *Blood cinema. The reconstruction of national identity in Spain.* Berkeley, Calif.: University of California Press.

KINDER, M. (ED.) 1997: *Refiguring Spain. Cinema/media/representation.* Durham and London: Duke University Press.

JAECKEL, A. 1996: *Les Visiteurs:* a popular form of cinema for Europe? In Everett, W. (ed.), *European identity in cinema.* Exeter: Intellect Books, 35–43.

JORDAN, B. 1995: Genre cinema in Spain in the 1970s. *Revista Canadiense de Estudios Hispánicos,* XX, 1 (Autumn), 127–41.

TRIANA TORIBIO, N. 1999: Almodóvar and Spanish national cinema. Unpublished paper delivered at Viva, Spanish Film Festival, Manchester.

VINCENDEAU, G. 1998: Issues in European cinema. In Hill, J. and Church Gibson, P. (eds). *The Oxford guide to film studies.* Oxford: Oxford University Press, 440–8.

PART

II

NEGOTIATING THE PAST

Introduction

Spain's relationship with its own past is a complex and multifaceted one. The cultural, social and political changes which the country has experienced do not only affect the contemporary moment, but require the adoption of different modes of negotiating and representing the past.

A century ago, for example, Spanish cultural and intellectual life was dominated by a profound concern with the nation's cultural and political decline, particularly as an imperial power. Military disasters and the loss of the last Spanish colonies in 1898 provoked a generational reassessment of the past and the determination to reverse a dominant sense of malaise through a process of political regeneration and the rediscovery of the essential 'spirit' of Spain. In the 1930s, the forces of modernization posed fundamental challenges to the social, political and economic legacy of an outmoded feudal system. Reformist movements brought together an emerging revolutionary proletariat and a liberal–bourgeois intellectual class. The meeting point of these unlikely bedfellows resided in their shared sense of the importance of culture. Whilst liberal reformism promoted culture and education for the people, many writers and artists turned to popular cultural forms for their inspiration and to inject new vitality and meaning into contemporary cultural production. Francoism was both a violent and backward-looking response to these developments, appealing to its adherents by promising a nostalgic return to a particular notion of Spanish history and tradition. Under Franco, the state looked to Spain's imperial past to find a model for the present, constructing a monolithic version of the past to legitimize its own existence and authority. Indeed, history was rewritten to accommodate and reflect the regime's own national and racial mythologies and its centralizing and ultra-conservative agenda. The past itself was in many respects forcibly occupied by the victors of the Civil War who rewrote the history books and public records, and radically reconstructed the cultural life of the nation according to the moral, social and ideological tenets of a militant authoritarian nationalism. The regime's anachronistic cultural and political agendas were matched by a taste for monumental retrospection in its public buildings and spaces; innovation or experiment in the plastic, visual or performance arts was not encouraged.

After the death of the dictator in 1975, not surprisingly, there was a pressing cultural and political imperative to revisit and 'rescue' the recent past (and its perspectives on earlier histories) from Francoist manipulation and distortion. The retrieval and representation of the past became a central feature of the post-Franco modernization of Spain. The Ministry of Culture, newly created in 1977, and the new PSOE government, following its 1982 landslide victory, enthusiastically promoted cultural and artistic modernization through state-funded projects and by stimulating private investment and sponsorship. Acknowledging the new regional autonomies, the government also reaffirmed a (sometimes reluctant) official commitment to a policy of devolution of cultural and artistic heritage to the regions for their own local management and development. The relegitimation of Spain as a multicultural society was thus central to the post-Franco project of establishing Spain's identity as a modern, democratic European state.

In Spain's cultural life, the last two decades have been characterized by an apparently obsessive preoccupation with the past. Processes of retrospection seek tirelessly to represent the past in a variety of forms; indeed, the past is increasingly 'costumed', 'landscaped' and 'themed' into a culture of heritage. But what these processes articulate most clearly are continuing anxieties and dissatisfactions with the complexities of the present. Indeed, the past becomes the site on which the struggles of the present are re-expressed and remodelled. The essays in this section explore various aspects of these remodelling processes, focusing on their obsessions and denials, absences and nostalgias, as well as their motivations and meanings as forms of cultural understanding.

|7|

Heritage: devolution and the recovery of diversity

TONY MORGAN

'I'll bet,' said Sancho, 'that before long there won't be a wineshop or a tavern, an inn or a barber's shop where the history of our exploits won't be painted up.'

(Cervantes, *Don Quixote*)

Poor Sancho could not begin to imagine the royalties on T-shirt and statuette sales on the *Ruta de Don Quijote* heritage route four centuries later. But the search for the past in contemporary Spain and the struggle to understand its relics is about more than cheap souvenirs in La Mancha. Now that the turbulence of the transition has abated, and the dust raised by the economic miracle has settled, Spaniards evaluate what a generation of intense development has done to their heritage – buildings, traditions, language, environment, folkways. As Franco's centralism recedes and devolution advances, regions salvage identities which were obscured but not altogether lost, and individuals appraise Lowenthal's 'traumas of loss and change' (1998, p. 11).

Urban industrialism came late and unevenly to Spain; abundant monuments, even whole medieval complexes – many jewels like Santillana del Mar and Avila – survive today. The Civil War, though, left its mark; Belchite and the Alcázar at Toledo remained semi-destroyed by the victors as architectural *aides-mémoire* of the conflict. Falangist Giménez Caballero berated defeated Republican Madrid in 1939: 'Toledo means Spanish unity; El Escorial: Empire ... if you serve the Alcázar and El Escorial, you will rediscover your Destiny, Madrid!' (Juliá *et al.* 1994, p. 411). Even liberal Gerald Brenan bemoaned Republican despoliation of half Spain's churches during the conflict as 'an enormous artistic impoverishment for the country ... attacking the spirit of humanity' (1950, p. 177).

Franco's cultural policy resurrected the Catholic Kings and Philip II.

Memorials to José Antonio and fasces inscribed on cathedral walls nation-wide projected illusions of National–Catholic solidarity. Promoting Philip II's El Escorial as an emblem of unity led easily to forced construction of the Valley of the Fallen mausoleum nearby, where the *caudillo* basks in reflected glory from the monastery – Franco and Hapsburgs joined in death in the spiritual centre of their *patria*. Salamanca was proclaimed in 1939 a 'future imperial city ... an indestructible unity based on Catholic thought', with Franco commemorated alongside Columbus, the Catholic Kings and El Cid in stone carvings circling the Plaza Mayor (Gilmour, 1992, p. 117). The new Inquisition suppressed venues of local secular identity, whether trades union *casas del pueblo* or the Catalan Generalitat. The belt-tightening of the 1940s and 1950s prohibited reconstruction; instead, square-shouldered Civil Guard barracks stamped authority and bureaucratic uniformity across the land. The Spanish flag on the *ayuntamientos* saluted the *parroquias*, twin pillars of nationalism in cities and *pueblos*. At least the *Paradores* hotel chain – one success of the corporate state – preserved local architecture and cuisine for more affluent tourists.

However, the 'development years' of the 1960s also brought a more pervasive standardization – homogenous 'cosmopolitan' capitalist consumption. Coca Cola, Levi's, Pan Bimbo sliced bread, the SEAT 600, El Corte Inglés department store, the Beatles, and the like spread uniform tastes across Spain, overlaying local products and cuisine, music and regional styles (Hansen, 1977, p.158). The 'economic miracle' brought 'new, more effective and more pleasant forms of social control and social cohesion' (Marcuse, 1964, p. 14). Cities and regions increasingly resembled each other, the autochthonous displaced by the standardized and the modern. *Patria chica* meant less. The quaintly local became serendipity – flamenco *tablaos*, *tuna* musicians, *habaneras, botijas,* the *jota*. The *plazas de toros* filled with tourists as natives adopted the 'cosmopolitan' ethos of Real Madrid's San Bernabeu (under Franco's patronage) or Barca's Nou Camp (to defy him). Local fiestas became vehicles for inward tourism. The 1929 Poble Espanyol in Montjuich embodied people's kitsch – a pastiche of regional architecture, 81 buildings constructed in vernacular regional style, stitched together into a heritage theme collage where 'imperceptibly the real merges into the unreal', (Michener, 1968, p. 581) – as Andalusians, Murcians, Manchegans and Galicians were similarly deracinated and transplanted to Barcelona's industrial belt.

In the push for growth, it seemed atavistic to care overly about heritage. The 1964 Development Plan genuflected to the needs of 'the less developed geographical zones', but millions left them for a better life in Madrid, Barcelona, Bilbao, Valencia (García Nieto and Donezar, 1975, p. 482). In 1964, coincidentally, Marcuse's *One Dimensional Man* critiqued seductively centripetal industrial capitalism where 'the means of mass transportation and communications, the commodities of lodging, food and clothing, the irresistible outputs of the entertainment and information industry ...

bind the consumers more or less pleasantly to the producers, and through the latter, to the whole' (1964, p. 24). Culture Minister Fraga Iribarne would approve, scolding 'misconceived regionalism ... which could immobilize the lives and the social development of our regions'. He enthusiastically projected a network of 'Teleclubs' – community TVs to deliver state-approved 'culture' to remote *pueblos* 'and have the simple people observe the marvels the images bring, and talk about them, debate them'. Thus would the *pueblos* receive culture and civilization 'to bind their people fully into the modern world and society' (Fraga Iribarne, 1968, p. 332). In Giner's words, 'the real cultures of the non-Castilian peoples were belittled as mild, folkloric regional deviations from the norm' (1984, p. 86).

Ineffective planning controls, evasion and corruption destroyed much architectural heritage. 'Municipal vandalism' demolished parts of historic cities like Seville, for whose Mayor (and University Rector) José Hernández Díaz 'modernity must invade the city centre to prevent Seville becoming a museum' and Salamanca, where 1986 statistics recorded that 8000 of its 13 000 pre-1936 dwellings were destroyed in 1966–86 (Gilmour, 1992, p. 96). As Gilmour observed, 'Franco's was a regime which appealed to history for its justification yet expunged it where profits could be made' (1992, p. 30). As the cities mushroomed, developers and banks flouted Madrid's planning laws in the pursuit of expansion, and Barcelona's *laissez-faire* administration 'passively contemplated the most brutal changes in the historic centre, while creating ... monuments to bad taste and bare-faced contempt for the popular classes' (Vázquez Montalbán, 1992, p. 157). Imperial Catholic Toledo, in contrast, declared a national monument in 1940, was preserved.

No preservation societies defended heritage in Franco's Spain, and conservation was low on opposition agendas. However, the best efforts of an authoritarian regime and capitalist consumerism could not eliminate local identities entirely. In Spain's regions, as in the 'United' Kingdom or even tragic Yugoslavia, 'the felt and perceived collective past is still pre-eminently ethnic and national', and people try to rediscover that 'collective self' through 'philology, history and archaeology ... tracing one's roots in an "ethnic past", in order to ascertain the authentic identity beneath the alien accretions' (Smith, 1991 pp. 75, 159). Twenty years after Franco, 70 per cent of Spaniards, albeit inconsistently, still felt dual regional and national identity. In the Basque Country, 33 per cent felt 'only Basque'; 33 per cent in Navarre felt 'more Navarrese than Spanish'; 3 per cent in Cantabria felt 'more Cantabrian than Spanish' (Moreno, 1997, p. 134). Diversity, the 'common checklist of essentials: a common language, past, future, fate, folk culture, values, tastes, landscape' reasserted itself through regional and ethnic imperatives; 'even Madrileños now seek separate, noncentrist roots' (Lowenthal, 1998, p. 80).

Landscape, religion, music and *barrios viejos* (ancient quarters of towns) were refuges for identities. ETA volunteers renewed Basque language and traditions on mountain hiking expeditions. The only permitted Catalan organization, the Centre Excursionista de Catalunya (Catalan Hiking Club), conserved an attachment to place in mountaineering clubs which roamed Catalonia (García Ramón and Nogué-Fort, 1994, p. 202). Defiant, Montserrat gave services in Catalan. Madrid's Casco Viejo, San Sebastián's Parte Vieja, Valencia's Barrio Carmen, Barcelona's Barrio Gótico, Pamplona's Plaza del Castillo – inner-city *barrios viejos* which escaped the developers – became cultural refuges. Emigrant Centres such as *Centros Gallegos*, *Asturianos* or *Andaluces* conserved regional cuisine and traditions. *Asociaciones de Vecinos* (Neighbourhood Associations) started to defend local patrimony; in Barcelona they fought 86 urban disputes in 1969–75, 'their righteous gaze following any speculator who stalked the city' (Vázquez Montalbán, 1992, p. 185).

A sense of personal and collective identity survived, of bonds with the past being stretched but not broken. Displaced urban migrants visited their *pueblos* for weekends and *fiestas*, often returning to the family home for 'to cope amidst change, we also need considerable continuity with the past' (Lowenthal, 1998, p. 69). Franco's attempt to eliminate collective memory failed; instead, dug into 'trenches of identity for human warmth and safety', people reorganized their lives and found new ways of relating to this strange and unpredictable world.[1] Catalans reported the power of language and dance as traditions which 'bind you to the land and the people'. Under Francoism, they felt, traditions were their only authentic quality: 'traditions are what we have breathed, what has come from us; they are like our essence'. The *Sardana*, that gracefully mute dance of defiance, let them retain their collective identity: 'It was the only way they let us feel Catalan, because we had no other. ... The *Sardana* was the only thing in which we could see we were different to others' (Hernández, 1983, p. 163). For one Catalan woman, taking her wedding vows in Catalan in Montserrat reaffirmed her very self-perception; 'I wouldn't have felt married if the priest had done it in Spanish' (Michener, 1968, p. 593).

The 1978 Constitution, of course, restored the prime heritage symbol of centralism – the monarchy – but charged it with promoting diversity of cultures, traditions, institutions, and especially languages, 'cultural heritage ... demanding the highest respect and care' (Article 3.3). Article 48 defended the 'cultural ... heritage of the peoples of Spain' and, while Article 149 reserved a role for the state in the protection of national heritage, Article 148 devolved museums, libraries, conservatoires, and monuments. Regional flags and anthems were permitted (Belmonte, 1979).

The autonomy statutes, issued between 1979 and 1983, pledge various heritage priorities. Most defend identity, promoting historic, cultural and linguistic variety and local traditions. Aragón, Extremadura, Castilla la Mancha and Castilla y León – zones of great emigration in the development years – even aspire to promote the return of emigrants to their native region (and their heritage). Regional administrations established departments of culture. Some constructed new buildings for their seats of government;

others renovated historic buildings, rooting themselves in heritage. The Generalitat in Barcelona is emblematic, the Junta de Andalucía's renovation of Seville's Plaza de España recalls the 1929 Exposición Iberoamericana (Iberoamerican Trade Fair), while the restoration of Zaragoza's *mudéjar* La Aljafería for the Corts of Aragón (Parliament of Aragón) consolidates Aragón's muslim cultural roots. Madrid's conversion of Franco's Puerta del Sol Security Police headquarters exorcizes its demons, symbolically returning a building to the people who had feared it. New universities, metaphors of regional pride in restored cultural tradition, took names of local heroes – Catalan grammarian Pompeu Fabra in Barcelona, modernizing monarch and 'first mayor of Madrid', Carlos III, Valencian King Jaume Primer in Castellón. Juan Carlos himself pointedly shunned the majestic Palacio del Oriente as a family home, establishing the royal family instead in the low-profile Zarzuela palace.

Reinterpretations of history appropriated signs and symbols. Spray paint altered Castilian place names to Catalan, Basque or Galician originals, town halls renamed streets to remove Francoism's memory. Typically, the Caudillo's statue was dismantled in Valencia's renamed Plaza del Pays Valenciá (formerly Plaza del Caudillo). Avenidas del Generalísimo received fresh local or democratic titles – though not everywhere. In parts of Castilla y León the General's memory lingers in street names, alongside Onésimo Redondo and Generals Yagüe and Queipo de Llano, in still conservative nationalist communities. 'Contradictory renderings of our most recent history remain.'[2]

Local administrations promote heritage through conferences, publications, exhibitions, museums, *fiestas*, and urban renewal. Madrid's socialist Mayor Tierno Galván rehabilitated social life in popular *barrios*, culminating in the *movida* – 'ephemeral blend of pure tradition and postmodernism ... nostalgia for the city which had been lost' (Juliá, *et al.* 1994, p. 469). Madrid's revived Mardi Gras carnival even acquired a postmodern gloss with extravagant transsexual Bibi Andersen crowned as 1989's 'Muse' in the Plaza Mayor. The 1990s Partido Popular *ayuntamiento*, however, alienated popular feelings by curbing *movida* nightlife, and gentrifying the capital's streets with bulky 'heritage' street furniture.

Parallel with official urban renewal, in many cities old popular *barrios* came alive. Fortuitously, Franco's paternalistic tenant-friendly rental legislation left many run-down cheap city centre locations, easily converted into venues of post-transition hedonism. In Madrid's Malasaña and Plaza Santa Ana, Barcelona's Plaza Real and Viejo Born districts, Valencia's Barrio Carmen, Seville's Santa Cruz, Granada's Albaicín, radical conversions turned old locales into fashionable venues, reverberating with the styles and sounds of young democratic Spain. Coincidentally, rising concern for environmental quality encouraged *ayuntamientos* to recover at least parts of their city centres from the car – emblematically demolishing the Atocha 'Scalextric' flyover in Madrid, curbing traffic in historic Granada, Toledo and Cuenca and pedestrianizing historic areas, like the Pilar zone of Zaragoza, the Cathedral district of Santiago and the University zone of Salamanca. There was even a clean-up of buildings in such zones, albeit delayed and half-hearted. The PSOE's 1985 *Ley de Patrimonio Histórico* (Cultural Heritage Law) committed ministries investing more than 100 million pesetas on projects to allocate 1 per cent to heritage protection. The PSOE, however, bent on modernization, cared less for heritage identified with Franco: unsurprisingly, they seriously underfunded conservation of monumental church buildings.

Equally, *fiestas* revived to recover local identity. In rural Catalonia these bound the community together and distinguished them from outsiders. They served 'the building of a traditional-folkloric whole which sustains and dynamizes Catalan identity, promoting its radical and specifically local content' (Barrera González, 1985, p. 249). At the highest level, the *Diada* of 11 September (Catalonia's national day) brought 1 000 000 Catalans on to the streets of Barcelona in 1977 (Llobera, 1996, p. 199). On a lower level, a celebrant of the Berga *Patrona* festival (which celebrates the Virgin Mary) articulates how the fiesta unites people in an identity beyond time, place, or ideology: 'In the fiesta we rediscover the past and the living, and ourselves, dispersed during the rest of the year ... or separated by different ideologies' (Barrera González, 1985, p. 249).

Awareness of damage to the natural heritage grew as the impact of development was reassessed. Under-resourced Spanish environmental bodies at last received encouragement from national and regional governments. National Parks reversed some of the neglect; the establishment of Doñana, Spain's most important wetland nature reserve, as a world heritage site confirmed new priorities. As Spain returned to the world community, UNESCO and the EU made Spanish heritage protection an international concern. In 1984 UNESCO named ancient Córdoba, the Alhambra, Burgos Cathedral, El Escorial, Parque and Palacio Güell and the Casa Milá as World Heritage sites; by 1996 the list totalled 19 cultural sites, Doñana, and La Gomera's Garajonay National Park.[3] EU funds also bolster heritage restoration, restoring traditional Galician and Asturian farmhouses, or piloting efforts in Majorca to mitigate the excesses of mass tourism. The PSOE government banned highway advertisement hoardings which had disfigured the landscape (though sentimentally retaining the Osborne brandy bulls – a lingering attachment to disappearing *macho* Spain). Equally, they reclaimed beaches and coastline lost to mass tourism; the 1988 *Ley de Costas* (Coastal Protection Law) outlawed illegal buildings and exclusion zones.

Public and private initiatives also brought to Spain the heritage industry fast developing elsewhere: the Strawberry Train to Aranjuez, the Al Andalús 'Orient Express', the Basque Railway Museum, the Murcian Water Museum and sundry ventures to 'rediscover' tourist diversity – 'Journeys through the Asturian Pre-Romanesque', 'The Legacy of Al Andalus' (a tourist board promotion linking 240 *pueblos* in Andalusia which typify

Moorish heritage to 'revive the civilization of Al Andalús and understand our historic past'), 'Lorca's Granada'. The Ministry of Labour launched the internationally acclaimed *escuelas taller* (craft skills training workshops), which successfully train thousands of employable young artisans in skills needed to conserve buildings, fabrics, landscapes, art treasures. Some old traditions also took on a postmodern hue – the Rocío festival, Semana Santa Holy Week processions, the Camino de Santiago pilgrimage, all evolved from purely religious rituals into platforms for expressing personal identity and collective roots (Prat, 1991, p. 767). Even bullfighting – quintessentially 'pre-cosmopolitan' – after falling in 1971–81 from a peak of 682 *corridas* to 390, revived to 587 in 1992.[4]

Museums, of course – interpreters of heritage – can be polemical. The new Museo de Historia Catalana, itself a fine restoration in Barcelona's old port, presents Catalan history as a cameo of nationhood and victimization, with sections labelled 'The Birth of a Nation', 'On the Periphery of Empire' and 'Defeat and Recovery'. Staging an 1898 Centenary commemoration, it insinuated 'Spain's' (as opposed to Catalonia's) responsibility for the disaster. Archives, too, arouse passions. The Generalitat provoked uproar when demanding the return from Salamanca of 'their' Civil War archives; 50 000 *salamantinos* protested in the streets. Equally, most regions condemned Partido Popular Education Minister Aguirre in 1998 for proposing to revise school Humanities syllabi to give more weight to the 'centralist' dimension of Spain's history. A 1998 exhibition of Ibero culture opened schisms, as curator Professor Carmen Aranegui derided genetic, linguistic and archaeological evidence locating the origins of Basque and Ibero culture in Morocco; the Iberos, she insisted, were indigenous.

The recovery of minority languages is the most intimate and defiant reassertion of identity. Basque, Catalan, Valencian and Galician have expanded greatly under formal and informal pressures (Tejerina Montaña, 1996, p. 225; Henderson, 1996, p. 238). Their cultivation in a global cosmopolitan world is emotional, not rational, restoring continuity with the collective memory of communities – 'for hundreds of years ... the sign of identification of being Catalan' (Castells, 1997, p. 48). The preamble of the 1998 *Ley de Política Lingüística* (Catalan Language Policy Law) promotes Catalan as 'a fundamental element of the national personality of Catalonia ... in the modern world in which communication, information and cultural industries tend towards globalization' (Generalitat de Catalunya, 1998, Preámbulo 1).

Language was central to the 1997 Galician regional elections. Partido Popular's Fraga Iribarne, the old Francoist improver of the 'gente sencilla' (simple folk), triumphed as usual with 51.6 per cent of the votes. But the Bloque Nacional Galego (BNG) nationalist party for the first time since devolution came second with 25.5 per cent, a tenfold increase over 1979. The BNG campaigned to 'reunify the city and the countryside', advocated green policies, and promised cultural programmes to defend Galicia's artistic and historical heritage, to 'posta en valor, desfrute social, e garantía de transmisión as xeneracións futuras deste patrimonio que e selo de valor inmenso da personalidade nacional de Galiza e espello da historia como povo singular e diferenciado' (to revalue and spread widely, to bequeath to future generations this heritage which is the immensely valuable sign of Galicia's national personality and mirror of its history as a special and different people) (*Programa de Governo do BNG 1997* (IV).2.2, pp. 151–3). Above all, the BNG promised to promote the Galician language *galego*.

The striking aspect of the BNG success was the high proportion of young voters who supported them. In a relationship closer than in most of Spain, since city and countryside is closer in Galicia than elsewhere, the young whose parents had to abandon their linguistic and cultural values when they left the *pueblo* a generation earlier for the city, had, through contact maintained with their *galego*-speaking grandparents, reclaimed their heritage. This educated, urban democratic generation voted for the heritage which gives them meaning in a modern world (in which they may feel equally at home in Vigo, London or Madrid). The grandparents of these young people speak Galician, but for their parents, raised in the Franco era, it was part of the baggage that they had to abandon. Prestige, wearing ties, rising in the social scale, were incompatible with speaking Galician, which was relegated to the status of a code for poor people, country people, and fisher folk. 'Pero la llamada lengua materna sobrevivió, en efecto, como un hilo de leche.' (But the so-called mother tongue survived, as it were, like a stream of milk.[5])

Notes

1. Castells, M. Identidades. *El País*, 20 December 1997.
2. Solé Tura, J. 1997 '¿Qué Historia?' *El País*, 6 November 1997, p. 11.
3. UNESCO *World Heritage Sites in Spain* www.spaintour.com/heritage
4. *Anuario El País*, 1998, p. 251.
5. Rivas, M. 1997 La Galicia emergente. *El País Domingo*, 26 October 1997, p. 14.

References

BARRERA GONZÁLEZ, A. 1985: *La dialéctica de la identidad en Cataluña: un estudio de antropología social*. Madrid: Centro de Investigaciones Sociológicas.
BELMONTE, J. 1979: *La constitución. Texto y Contexto*. Madrid: Editorial Prensa Española.
BLOQUE NACIONAL GALEGO 1997: *Autonómicas '97 Programa de Governo*. Santiago: BNG.
BRENAN, G. 1950: *The face of Spain*. London: Turnstile Press.
CASTELLS, M. 1997: *The power of identity*. Oxford: Blackwell.
FRAGA IRIBARNE, M. 1968: *Horizonte Español* (3rd edn). Madrid: Héroes.
GARCÍA NIETO, M. A. and DONEZAR, J. M.1975: *Bases documentales de la España contemporánea, vol. 11, La España de Franco 1939–1973*. Madrid: Guadiana.

GARCÍA RAMÓN, M. D. and NOGUÉ-FORT, J. 1994: Nationalism and geography in Catalonia. In Hooson, D., *Geography and national identity*. Oxford: Blackwell, 197–211.

GENERALITAT DE CATALUNYA 1998: Ley 1/1998, de 7 de Enero, de Política Lingüística. Barcelona: Generalitat.

GILMOUR, D. 1992: *Cities of Spain*. London: John Murray.

GINER, S. 1984 Ethnic nationalism, centre and periphery in Spain. In Abel C. and Torrents, N., *Conditional democracy*. London: Croom Helm, 78–99.

HANSEN, E. 1977: *Rural Catalonia under the Franco Regime: the fate of regional culture since the Spanish Civil War*. Cambridge: Cambridge University Press.

HENDERSON, T. 1996: Language and identity in Galicia: the current orthographic debate. In Mar-Molinero, C. and Smith, A., *Nationalism and the nation in the Iberian Peninsula*. Oxford: Berg 237–51.

HERNÁNDEZ, F. 1983: *La identidad nacional en Cataluña*. Barcelona: Vicens Vives.

JULIÁ, S., RINGROSE, D., SEGURA, C. 1994: *Madrid. Historia de una capital*. Madrid: Alianza.

LLOBERA, J. 1996: The role of commemorations in nation-building. The case of Catalonia. In Mar-Molinero, C. and Smith, A., *Nation and nationalism in the Iberian Peninsula*. Oxford: Berg 191–206.

LOWENTHAL, D. 1985: *The past is a foreign country*. Cambridge: Cambridge University Press.

—— 1998: *The heritage crusade and the spoils of history*. Cambridge: Cambridge University Press.

MARCUSE, H. 1964: *One dimensional man*. London: Abacus (1972 edn).

MICHENER, J. 1968: *Michener's Iberia*. London: Corgi.

MORENO, L 1997: *La federalización de España*. Madrid: Siglo XXI.

PRAT, J. 1991: *Antropología de los pueblos de España*. Madrid: Taurus Universitaria.

SMITH, A. D. 1991: *National identity*. Harmondsworth: Penguin.

—— 1995: *Nations and nationalism in a global era*. Cambridge: Polity.

—— 1998: *Nationalism and modernism*. London: Routledge.

TEJERINA MONTAÑA, B. 1996: Language and Basque nationalism: collective identity, social conflict and institutionalisation. In Mar-Molinero, C. and Smith, A., *Nationalism and the nation in the Iberian Peninsula*. Oxford: Berg, 221–36.

VÁZQUEZ MONTALBÁN, M. 1992: *Barcelonas*. London: Verso.

8

Cultural memory, commerce and the arts: the Valencian Institute of Modern Art (IVAM)

TRINIDAD MANCHADO

Museums of contemporary art in Spain find themselves at different stages in an on-going process of change and redefinition of their roles and identities in Spanish society. Their endeavour to reconstruct new local and/or national cultural memories is a response to a rapidly changing society in which they find themselves subject to a high degree of political control. This chapter provides an insight into one museum, the Valencian Institute of Modern Art (IVAM), and its search for a distinctive artistic and cultural identity within its own political context. The chapter begins with an overview of the experiences and achievements of the major contemporary art museums in Spain over the last decade. It then focuses on the specific case of the IVAM, and concludes with a consideration of the developments that the IVAM has triggered in the region of Valencia.

Following Franco's death in 1975, an unprecedented number of public spaces dedicated to modern and contemporary art have opened in Spain, coinciding in the main with the Partido Socialista Obrero Español (PSOE)'s period in office (1982–96). Although this increase in the number of museums is a clear reflection of the international art market boom of that time, for Spain it takes on an extra dimension as part of a national drive to reinvent itself as a modern country. This new Spain has redefined its past by repackaging it for consumption through an expanding 'recuperation industry': museums, theatre, local history (Labanyi, 1995, p. 402). In this context, contemporary culture becomes a highly valued commodity and museums of contemporary art some of the best stages for the performance of this new dynamic Spanish identity. The PSOE based part of its cultural renovation on the long-awaited opening of prestige museological projects which were intended to create a new image of a modern society, firmly established as part of the international community to which Spain was eager to belong.

Central to this movement was the creation of the Museo Nacional Centro de Arte Reina Sofía in 1986 in Madrid with the purpose of becoming the main Spanish National Museum of twentieth-century art. The Reina Sofía suffered from excessive political intrusion, high expectations from the Spanish public and a troubled artistic project. The new National Museum was launched against a historical background of half a dozen failed attempts in this century to create a Spanish state museum of contemporary art (Bolaños, 1997, p. 217) with the pressing directive of building up a significant, permanent collection of contemporary art worthy of a national museum, as well as a successful programme of temporary exhibitions. The creation of the Reina Sofía was a state project with a clear political content, which suffered from short-term pressures eager to capitalize on impending successes. Evidence of this is shown by the rushed opening, the polemical renovation of the museum's historical building, and above all a succession of directors who, under intense public scrutiny, were faced with a desperate shortage of time for planning and development.

As an illustration, the Reina Sofía's first director, Tomás Llorens tried to build up a coherent collection for the museum by focusing on the great Spanish masters of the twentieth century while attempting to recover a different, at times forgotten, Spanish art history (one of his trademarks as founder of the IVAM's successful collection as we shall see below). Llorens was attacked on two fronts. On the one hand, the more conservative Spanish art world felt the collection focused too much on artists who had been in exile during Franco's dictatorship. On the other hand the new, younger Spanish art world associated with the recently created Spanish Art Fair ARCO (initiated in 1982), felt contemporary work deserved greater attention. As Tomás Llorens himself declared, 'There have been some complaints about the Reina Sofía's policy, especially from the market. The Reina Sofía's strategy went against the market, against ARCO'.[1] Tomás Llorens was ousted in 1990 after only two years, and the Reina Sofía's next director, María Corral, followed a similar process, plagued by numerous obstacles and criticisms while the museum was on the verge of collapse. As if to highlight this crisis, the almost overnight transfer of Picasso's *Guernica* from the Prado Museum to the Reina Sofía in 1992, against the artist's express wishes, proved to be a public relations disaster. Finally, when the Reina Sofía's collection was opened to the public in 1992, it met with overwhelming criticism from all flanks questioning its legitimacy (most notably from realist painter Antonio López who refused to exhibit his forthcoming retrospective there, claiming that the permanent collection did not offer an adequate representation of contemporary realist art).

Given these difficulties, the Reina Sofía's success story lies, not surprisingly, in its high calibre, temporary exhibitions (Eduardo Chillida and Richard Serra, Dada and constructivism, The Century of Picasso, Utopias of

Bauhaus, The Spanish Pavilion of the Second Republic, Saura, Tàpies, Viola, etc.) rather than in its permanent collection. The former mean instant public success, easily capitalized upon by politicians. The latter is geared to a long-term project, not necessarily visible to the public eye, with silent negotiations handled by art professionals and a need for continuity beyond the concept of current politicians. High politicization of museum work with very little room for medium- or long-term planning has been at the expense of Spain's historical project of building a coherent national collection of modern art.

Indeed, the need to fill this historical gap explains the acquisition of the two excellent imported Thyssen-Bornemisza and Guggenheim art collections in recent years. These two now-Spanish museums can be read as an instant contribution to the reconstruction of Spanish cultural identity by purchasing comprehensive, finished, ready-to-be-exhibited major art collections. The Thyssen-Bornemisza collection arrived in Madrid in 1992 after an expensive deal between the Spanish Government and the Thyssen family. By general agreement, Spain was ready to accept the financial sacrifice in order to claim its visibility on the international museological circuit and, as part of the 1992 extravaganza, to display Spain's new identity to the rest of the world.

The Guggenheim Museum in Bilbao, the most recent instance of politicians capitalizing on museological projects, gives an insight into why such an important art collection was established in the rather unknown and troubled region – at least from an American point of view – of the Basque Country, in 1997. The franchized deal – important works 'rented' from the Guggenheim in New York and exhibited as part of its core collection – was accepted by most of Spanish society. Nevertheless, the Guggenheim permanent collection is not entirely 'imported' as the museum administers a budget to build up its own specific collection emphasizing Basque and Spanish art. The Basque government went to great financial lengths in order to ensure that the Guggenheim collection came to Bilbao. Again, it is another attempt to reinvent a new identity for a region keen to enter postmodern society, in this case a society burdened with the troubles of a post-industrial city and the effects of terrorism. Basque politicians were equally aware that new wealth comes from new ready-to-consume cultural products. In this respect, the Guggenheim was planned as a crystallization point for the cultural and economic regeneration of the region. Attendance at the Guggenheim has surpassed all predictions in its first year (1 200 000 visitors instead of the 450 000 anticipated, of which a high proportion are foreign visitors), and the imposing titanium-silvery, ship-shaped museum is arguably fast becoming the most important cultural icon for contemporary Basque identity. An initially multinational, alien enterprise has thus been appropriated by the Basques. In this respect both the Guggenheim and the IVAM museums function in rather the same way as Richard Maxwell has commented in relation to regional broadcasters in Spain: as 'a challenge to the notion of the nation-state by hailing their public as global consumers, as participants in a transnational cultural exchange' (1997, p. 268).

Other regional museological projects sprang up around the same time as the IVAM such as the Museum of Contemporary Art of Barcelona (MACBA), the Andalusian Centre of Contemporary Art (CAAC), the Galician Centre of Contemporary Art, the Atlantic Centre of Modern Art in the Canary Islands and the Extremaduran and Ibero-American Museum of Contemporary Art (MEIAC) among others.[2] Based, albeit less successfully, on the IVAM model, these have by and large survived through the 1990s, but it is the IVAM which stands as the exemplary model for the end-of-the-twentieth-century museum. In contrast to the Reina Sofía's troubled history resulting from the high national expectations of such a symbolic, centralized project, the success of the IVAM, a modest, marginal project on the periphery of Spain, rests partly on its intelligent combination of exhibitions and acquisitions. However, ironically, its accomplishment is arguably also partially due to the initial constraints it faced, as well as its peripheral location, which shielded the museum from any early temptations of absorption and political cannibalization from Madrid.

As well as reflecting the tensions experienced by Spanish museums in their attempt to create a space for reflection, the IVAM creates a space for cultural memory in an ever changing and shrinking present. In addition to its art exhibitions combining national and international works, it has served as a stage for musical performances, fashion shows, book launches and poetry readings. As a venue for reflection on culture the museum has offered an active programme of conferences and courses, notably including its lively conferences on the role of museums in the present day and, as a centre for research into twentieth-century art, it has placed considerable importance on its publications. Always supportive of educational activities (its library is one of the best stocked of its kind in Spain) the IVAM's sense of permanence is not, however, exclusively associated with its collection but with the continual flow between local and international works.

The IVAM is one of the first examples of a general trend towards cultural decentralization first contemplated in the Spanish Constitution of 1976 (Article 148), and promoted by the Socialist government's plans to popularise culture with devolution of power to both local and regional governments particularly between 1983-86 when most *ayuntamientos* and *autonomías* were under PSOE control.

The idea of creating the IVAM emerged in 1983, and was consolidated in 1985 by the local government of Valencia's acquisition of a collection of work by Julio González – the under-represented Catalan artist of modern iron sculpture – and in 1987 by a further donation of paintings and drawings by Valencian artist Ignacio Pinazo. The IVAM's Charter was granted in 1987 and it finally opened to the public in February 1989. Unlike other similar projects, the founding team consisted of a younger generation of art professionals (including Tomás Llorens, Vicente Todolí and Carmen

Alborch, among others) who, with few political constraints, were able to build a rather personal, specific collection without external interference. From the outset it was clear that the museum's profile was to 'consider modern art from a historical point of view', and to show contemporary work which 'in the art world remains marginalized, forgotten or insufficiently valued'.³ Thus, the IVAM proceeded to establish a unique and unrivalled art collection by investigating the lesser known creative trends of well-known artists, or acquiring certain 'minor' art forms, such as drawings, graphic art, photography, photomontage, books, journals and book covers. Its resulting photography collection is considered to be the best in Spain, and its photomontage one of the best collections of its kind in the world.

The IVAM's original orientation also relates to a deep awareness of what art history has been in Spain: a succession of failed historical attempts to build up an art collection of national importance – as mentioned above in relation to the Reina Sofía, Thyssen-Bornemisza and Guggenheim collections – and the recognition that creating a comprehensive national art collection is no longer possible. In this context, the IVAM reconstructs a different cultural memory of Spanish art history: a history of what it could have been and never was. It focuses on diversity rather than congruity: 'We are interested in the side walks, however endless these may be.'⁴ Starting with local and national artists – initially Julio González's works which form the backbone of the collection – the IVAM has created several focal points around Spanish postwar artists such as Saura, Millars, Tàpies, Chillida, Renau, Eduardo Arroyo, Equipo Crónica and Equipo Realidad. From the local, it moves on to international references, always following lesser known paths such as the crisis of contructivist and Dadaist discourses relating to Julio González's work.

It is this fluid movement between the local and the global which is at the heart of the IVAM's success. The core collection of local and national work inscribes qualities corresponding to those of the international market-place and vice versa – the local becomes universal and the margins move to the centre. The IVAM collection thus reconstructs a new, marginalized cultural memory and gives a universal status to so-called 'peripheral' art. One might argue that this can be achieved only from the regional margins, away from the centripetal forces of Madrid and free from any canonical burden imposed by the centre. In many respects the unique assemblage of the collection reflects its financial constraints; in an inflated market-place a modest museum could only aim at the margins of the art world. However, the combination of wise investment, knowledge of the art market, and historical awareness of the reciprocity of art and culture has given the IVAM its distinct identity and enabled it to establish an international reputation through collaboration with major international museums such as the MOMA, Centre Pompidou and the Tate Gallery.

The IVAM is based in two main buildings, one being the newly constructed Centre Julio González characterized by a sober, clinical and unimposing architecture. The building clearly signals its role of sheltering works of art without overshadowing them. Behind this extraordinary simplicity and sense of space lies a complex and modern infrastructure of security and conservation systems. This centre exhibits the permanent Julio González collection as well as major temporary exhibitions. The Centre del Carme, located a few minutes away, is a group of historical buildings dating from thirteenth to the twentieth centuries with Gothic and early Renaissance features, and contrasts dramatically with the modern simplicity of the González Centre. The Carme Centre is dedicated to temporary exhibitions of contemporary local, national and international young artists, and, following the model of the *kunsthalle* galleries, has no permanent collection of its own.

Both buildings are located in the heart of Valencia's old quarter which offers a metaphor of the museum's historical vocation. Like any museum, the IVAM represents and reconstructs history, but this is a history of art reinterpreted from a postmodern perspective where present and past are recreated interdependently. In reflection of this reciprocal relationship, the more established work – such as that of Julio González or Paul Klee – is exhibited in the new González Centre venue, whilst younger, lesser known international artists – such as Allan McCollum or Tony Cragg – and young local artists of national significance – such as Miquel Navarro or Carmen Calvo – are located in the ancient buildings of the Carme Centre. This ironic articulation of synchronicity culminates in the very heart of the González building where, beneath the foundations of this contemporary construction, lie the original medieval walls of the city of Valencia, now an exhibit in their own right; this is another – rather more permanent – feature of the IVAM's collection.

The IVAM has assumed an emblematic value for Valencian identity, placing the city on the international art circuit and increasing its political significance. Under the direction of a succession of three directors fully in tune with Socialist Party cultural policy, the museum is one of the most prominent cultural successes of the PSOE government. Hardly surprisingly, following its victory in the Valencia regional elections, the new conservative Partido Popular administration was keen to leave its own mark on the IVAM and capitalize on its international reputation. The museum entered a period of uncertainty as it became the target of the PP's new cultural programme and a ferocious battle for its control began.

One might argue that the IVAM has never been completely free from political control since its establishment, although its emblematic status may have rescued it at least partially from total political asphyxiation. After a strong public campaign mounted by the local press demanding the IVAM's independence, a new director, Juan Manuel Bonet, was appointed in 1995. Known for his conservative views, Bonet was, none the less, respected in Spanish artistic circles. There were, nevertheless, individual concerns at his appointment, and some renowned Spanish artists – among them Tàpies,

Andreu Alfaro and Juan Muñoz – aired their views about the 'historical kidnapping' of the IVAM in the national press.[5]

The resignation in 1996 of Vicente Todolí, a key figure in the IVAM initiative and largely responsible for the collection since it opened, marked the beginning of a new and more tranquil phase in the museum's history. However, some fear that the greater emphasis on figurative and surrealist art under the new direction – a retreat into the safer territory of the canon – signals a more dormant, at worst a more provincial and conservative period for the IVAM. Whilst open to accusations of complacency, a more generous view would be that, in stepping back from the political turmoil, the IVAM's recent policy is making a significant contribution to the achievement of its original mission – a well-defined cultural discourse and identity. Despite its reorientation towards less controversial exhibits, recent acquisitions have continued to focus on 'lesser' or 'minor' art forms such as the book covers, posters and photographs mentioned earlier, giving visibility to otherwise forgotten art forms. The museum still functions as an art broker collaborating with major international museums and its exhibitions are regularly circulated abroad. Its promotion of local, otherwise marginalized, artists, at a national and international level, by showing and purchasing their work has not only increased their visibility, but also increased the IVAM's sphere of influence on trends within Spain's national art market. The museum's success has also acted as a stimulus for other art projects in Valencia, as is reflected in the proliferation of small, independent galleries since its opening.

One of the most significant manifestations of the impetus created by the IVAM is the establishment in 1996 of the Consorcio de Museos, an official body aiming to coordinate, promote and decentralize the numerous museums and artistic activities of the Valencian region. The fact that the Consorcio is led by the dynamic Consuelo Císcar, who had been a candidate for the directorship of the IVAM, and the ascendant profile of its flagship museum the S. Pío V, have led to speculation that this new macro art organization is set to overshadow the IVAM's independent role in promoting art in the region. It is certainly the case that the S. Pío V, originally dedicated solely to classical art, has made a major shift into showing contemporary, thought-provoking exhibitions, such as the June 1998 Pierre et Gilles, as good as any end-of-millennium museum uniting culture and spectacle. However, the Consorcio, not surprisingly, has embarked on a frantic programme of exhibitions ranging from the tranquil impressionist paintings of local artist Sorolla, through work by Renaissance artist Michelangelo, to provocative body art performances by Marina Abramovic, the kitsch art by gay couple Pierre et Gilles, and the work of Yoko Ono. The common denominator of these exhibitions is their popular appeal, attracting mass public attendance. The Consorcio has also produced an impressive display of publications by women, gay and other marginalized groups. As Consuelo Císcar declared, the Consorcio seeks to reflect 'the culture of miscegenation of our end-of-millennium'.[6] One might expect a vociferous reaction from conservatives confronted with such a radical programme of exhibitions promoted by their own party. On the contrary, however, it has received the blessing – albeit tacit – of the PP. A cynical explanation for this might be found in the enthusiastic public response to such spectacular *mise-en-scène* exhibitions and an unvoiced fear on the part of the right of accusations of being 'anti-contemporary'. These cultural and political reverberations stand as further evidence of the cultural influence emanating from the IVAM.

As Néstor García Canclini observes, heritage becomes political when it is theatricalized in museums (1989, p. 157). However, the IVAM has managed to negotiate the dangers of both cultural ritualization and political manipulation in order to provide a public space for the articulation of collective cultural memories and, indeed, identities and to establish itself as a mediator of cultural diversity and heterogeneity.

The latest museological multimedia project in Valencia – 'The City of Arts and Sciences' – where culture, art and science come together, captures more eloquently than anything else the IVAM's end-of-millennium spirit. Its impressive all-seeing, eye-shaped dome dominates the macro-futuristic complex. The sense of surveillance and control it emanates – a characteristic of the more traditional notion of the museum – is nevertheless subverted by its air of exploration and change, and its implicit invitation to engagement and play. Active engagement is the IVAM's trademark for the public.

Notes

1. Llorens, T. at IVAM Conference: La elaboración de un proyecto museográfico, IVAM, 9 September 1994.
2. For a discussion of the MEIAC and other recently created regional art museums in Spain *see* Holo, S. R. 1997, The art museum as a means of refiguring regional identity in democratic Spain. In Kinder, M. (ed.), *Refiguring Spain. Cinema/media/representation.* N.C.: Duke University Press, 301–26.
3. IVAM Proyecto Fundacional, 1984, unpublished.
4. Todolí, V. IVAM Conference. 6 September 1994.
5. *El País*, 25 October 1996, p. 40.
6. Consuelo Císcar in interview with the author, Valencia 3 June 1998.

References

BOLAÑOS, M. 1997: *Historia de los museos en España.* Asturias: Ediciones Trea.
GARCÍA CANCLINI, N. 1989: *Estrategias para salir y entrar de la modernidad.* México: Grijalbo.
KINDER, M. (ED.) 1997: *Refiguring Spain. Cinema/media/representation.* N.C.: Duke University Press.
LABANYI, J. 1995: Postmodernism and the Problem of Cultural Identity. In Graham, H. and Labanyi, J. (eds), *Spanish cultural studies, an introduction: the struggle for modernity.* Oxford: Oxford University Press, 396–406.

MAXWELL, R. 1997: Spatial eruptions, global grids: regionalist TV in Spain and dialectics of identity politics. In Kinder, M. (ed.), *Refiguring Spain. Cinema/media/representation.* N.C.: Duke University Press, 260–83.

|9|

Postmodernism and the contemporary Spanish avant-garde

ANTONIO SÁNCHEZ

A dominant feature of contemporary Spanish society is the fast growth in the design, production, marketing and consumption of cultural artefacts. Postmodernism's commodification of culture has weakened the avant-garde and exposed its dependency on the socio-economic structures it repudiates. While art has always been influenced by its 'mode of production' (whether based on a system of patronage or a consumer market) what has dramatically changed now is our awareness of it, which has helped demystify the idealized view of the modern artist as an individual struggling against society. Avant-garde artists have been stripped of their 'heroic aura' and forced to take a role as professionals, dependent on working contracts and the good will of local, regional and national cultural institutions. This has meant a shift in emphasis in the socio-cultural role and function of the avant-garde, and in the formulation of some of its central concerns. This study examines the concept of 'avant-garde' in contemporary Spanish culture, focusing on a range of examples of its operation in recent theatre and cinema. An introductory overview of the historical avant-garde which dominated the modernist culture of the 1920s and (to a lesser extent) the 1930s provides a background against which these contemporary inflections can be compared and contrasted.

The 'historical' avant-garde

The aesthetics of the avant-garde which dominated Europe during the first decades of this century were illustrated in Spain by the influence of movements such as futurism, ultraism, surrealism, Dadaism, Cubism, abstract art and the works of writers such as Lorca, Alberti, Max Aub, Aleixandre, Giménez Caballero, painters such as Picasso, Dalí, Gris, González, Miró and the film-maker Buñuel. The Spanish avant-garde can be best understood as a multiplicity of groups, united by their attempt to break with past cultural traditions and represent modern life through a constant emphasis on creativity. Their commitment to the idea of a new, modern society is often reflected in the exciting and relentless process of technical and aesthetic development which characterized their work. They radically overturned the basic values of romanticism which was rooted in a belief in spiritual and natural creativity and a nostalgic tendency to idealize the past, while rejecting the bourgeois aesthetics of realism. Avant-garde proposed the idea of art as a social engagement with the construction of a new, modern culture. This was often illustrated by an irreverent attitude towards social and aesthetic conventions, typical of surrealism and Dadaism, or by an embrace of either Communist or Fascist ideas of socio-political revolution.

We cannot talk, however, of the Spanish avant-garde as a homogenous trend, or even, in any straightforward sense, as a socially progressive and politically committed movement. Most Spanish avant-garde artists were members of the bourgeoisie, though this did not stop them empathizing with the condition and needs of the lower classes, as is illustrated by the socio-political commitment of most avant-garde artists before and during the Spanish Civil War. However, the crucial factor distinguishing them from previous movements is the engagement of their work, to different degrees, with the modern world.

Whilst European avant-garde artists revolted against dominant bourgeois norms, whether from the political left or right, they were also opposed to both popular culture and the incipient mass consumer society. Spanish avant-garde artists however seemed to have been more aware of the rift that modernization caused between popular culture and modernism, reinforcing the bourgeois distinction between low and high culture. They incorporated in their productions both traditional culture and elements of modern mass culture such as cinema and photography, thus anticipating the dismissal of high culture during the 1960s and subsequently in postmodernism. However, the difficult nature of the avant-garde rendered it inaccessible to both traditional rural audiences and the new urban masses.

After the military victory of the ultra-traditionalist forces commanded by Franco in 1939, Spanish society experienced a regressive process of 're-ruralisation' and any socially progressive ideas were quashed, as were attempts to speed up the processes of modernization. Avant-garde art was only permitted in so far as it remained confined to a social elite and did not constitute a real political threat to the regime's official culture.

Contemporary avant-garde

During the early 1970s Spanish avant-garde artists re-established contact with European and American avant-garde groups, particularly those working in experimental cinema and theatre. In Spain, after the political transition to democracy following the death of Franco (1975–82), aesthetics began to emerge from quasi-compulsory socio-political struggle against the Franco regime. A series of artists and cultural artefacts which, in a formal sense, belong to the avant-garde tradition came forth. However, while contemporary avant-garde or experimental art has retained an important role as an aesthetic strategy exploring and developing its cultural mediums, it has lost its status as a 'cultural alternative'. The claim to this role by the historical avant-garde must also be regarded with some caution since avant-garde has traditionally been an elitist and bourgeois aesthetic expression. In that particular sense, contemporary avant-garde or experimental art has not changed much.

An examination of examples taken from recent Spanish theatre and cinema will enable us to consider the role and characteristics of the contemporary avant-garde in contrast with its historical predecessors.

Avant-garde theatre in Spain

Throughout the 1980s Spanish theatre witnessed the integration into the official canon of some of its most experimental early playwrights such as Lorca, Valle-Inclán and Alberti. However, while this project of cultural recuperation was under way, a new wave of theatre was taking shape. 'Colectivos teatrales alternativos' (alternative theatre collectives) such as Bekereke, Ananda Dansa, Espacio Cero, Zotal Teatre, Teatro del Norte and La Tartana began to emerge, introducing new theatrical forms which moved away from traditional theatre (based in a literary text) and incorporated other aesthetic forms into a 'multimedia theatrical experience'. They enjoyed an extremely fruitful collaboration with the Centro Nacional de Nuevas Tendencias of Madrid, a state-funded institution aiming to promote research, production and staging of experimental theatre. The financing by national and regional government institutions of theatre companies such as Els Joglars, Els Comediants, La Cubana, Dagoll-Dagom and La Fura dels Baus (LFdB) in Catalonia or La Cuadra in Andalusia was also crucial to their development of an innovative theatrical language which was still based on the experimental theatre of the 1920s avant-garde artists. An example would be the current rejection by contemporary companies such as LFdB of conventional representational theatre and the aesthetics of realism, a feature already present in the work of early avant-garde artists such as Lorca and in the theatrical ideas of Antonin Artaud. In the case of LFdB, this new theatre only fully materialized in 1983 with *Accions*, premiered at the Festival de

Sitges in a derelict underpass beneath a railway level crossing. *Actions* (1983) signalled a shift from the traditional street theatre which they had been implementing since 1979 to performance without any apparent narrative structure. The work is based on a series of symbolic elements loosely associated with birth, death, destruction and purification which trigger sensations of fear, surprise, aggression and confusion in the audience. *Actions* was followed two years later by *Suz/o/Suz* (1985) and *Tier Mon* (1988), constituting a trilogy concerned with the search for a new theatrical language rather than any specific theme. This trilogy resembles Artaud's avant-garde Theatre of Cruelty and can be seen as pointing to the emergence of postmodernist theatre within the contemporary Spanish context.

It is surprisingly difficult to distinguish between avant-garde theatre and postmodernist theatrical experiments. Indeed, the initial impulse guiding LFdB's works echoes the historical avant-garde manifestos. However, unlike Artaud and other avant-garde artists and movements like Dadaism and surrealism, it does not perceive its theatre as a strategy for transforming society. Like Artaud, LFdB advocates a return to theatre as a subjective, sensorial experience but it does this by creating a collective ritual whose strength is rooted precisely in its refusal to be just a reference to an external reality. LFdB represents a new kind of theatre which has evolved further by incorporating pre-modern rituals of violence and catharsis into a hybrid postmodernist mass spectacle. In LFdB's productions, avant-garde or experimental theatre meets traditional ritualistic practices through state-of-the-art technology. This fusion creates a post-industrial urban imagery whose eclecticism underlines its postmodern nature.

LFdB's theatre is both a return to and a departure from the historical avant-garde theatrical productions which could provide an alternative to the dominant bourgeois realist theatre of their period. As Frenk *et al.* have indicated, 'The disturbances and shocks of the 1920s still resonate' (1995, p. 69) as throughout the 1980s Spanish theatre has rediscovered the progressive plays of Valle-Inclán and Unamuno and avant-garde authors like Lorca and Alberti, who in the 1920s and 1930s were already creating a theatre in which:

> The physical space of the stage began to be seen not merely as a familiar location in which dramatic business is carried out, but as a semiotic space, an expressive part of the overall symbolic structure. In some cases this meant schematic simplicity, in others, ambitious concepts far beyond the imaginative and technical resources of the theatrical establishment of the time.

> (1995, p. 66)

There are, however, some fundamental differences between the work of the historical avant-garde theatre and the more contemporary one. The avant-garde movements of the 1920s and 1930s tried to transform society by subverting the rational logic of bourgeois culture through their aesthetic projects, integrating elements of daily popular culture into their works to create something radically new. They also had an elitist and ambivalent position towards traditional popular culture and the developing mass culture. Their plays often illustrated the difficulties in mediating between the aesthetic and social elitism of their background and the traditional popular culture they were trying to reach. As Frenk *et al.* pointed out:

> [They] were united by a passionate belief in the cultural importance of theatre and an awareness of working within a problematic space between the ambition to address new, wider audiences and the reality of appealing to an intellectual minority.

> (1995, p. 65)

The attempt to integrate the audience into the theatrical experience, characteristic of postmodernist performances, illustrates the weakening of the 'high'/'low' cultural divide which previously hindered the dissemination of avant-garde aesthetics. The final critical success of historical avant-garde theatrical artefacts, almost 50 years after they were originally written, stands in contrast to the immediate success obtained by LFdB's theatre. Its participation in the official opening ceremony of Barcelona's 1992 Olympics emphasizes its popular appeal and growing acceptance of their postmodernist style of theatre which, until recently, was perceived as experimental and exclusive to intellectual elites.

The socio-political commitment attributed to many historical avant-garde artists is, however, absent from most companies and playwrights active in the current Spanish theatrical panorama. Despite the fact that most historical avant-garde artists came from privileged socio-economic backgrounds, they showed a concern with the precarious social and material conditions of Spanish society, the hopes and risks posed by modernization and the potential of art to change our social awareness. Critical engagement with socio-political issues in contemporary avant-garde theatre is limited to a few isolated examples such as Els Joglars and Alfonso Sastre.

Avant-garde cinema in Spain

As far as the cinema is concerned, the term 'avant-garde' has been used indiscriminately to describe a broad variety of cinematic forms from shorts to 8 mm films, from marginal to experimental work, and including independent and *auteur* cinema. As with theatre, it is difficult to use the term 'avant-garde' to refer to a single organized movement, but it is possible to talk of avant-garde cinema as a cultural practice outside the standard production and distribution structures of commercial cinema.

The historical references of Spanish avant-garde cinema are often traced back to the surrealist films of Buñuel and Val del Omar and, to a lesser extent, avant-garde artists such as Dalí, Gómez de la Serna and Lorca, whose experiments in this modern medium mirrored the interest of other European avant-garde groups and artists at the beginning of the century. During the 1950s it is Val del Omar, rather than Buñuel, who constitutes a referential point between the historical avant-garde and contemporary Spanish cinema. His concern with formal aspects and, following Eisenstein, the priority he gives to the close-up, reveal the influence of the historical avant-garde. However, his use of different formats and optical distortions are more typical of 1960s experimental cinema. Even more contemporary is his dismantling of the conventional boundaries between documentary and fiction. Val del Omar's work is best illustrated by his trilogy *Tríptico elemental de España* – comprising *Agua espejo granadino (La gran Siguiriya)* (1952–55), *Fuego en Castilla (Tactilvisión del páramo del espanto)* (1958–59) and *De Barro (A Carinho galaico)* (initiated in the 1960s but only fully completed in 1982) – which concluded a lifetime's research into the effects of light and movement on composition within the frame, whilst constructing a personal view of the Iberian peninsula's cultural roots outside the official versions of the past.

During the last years of Francoism the political tensions sharpened as did the reactions of radical artists within independent or non-commercial cinema. Changes in the socio-historical context following the collapse of the regime did not cause a transformation in the production or distribution of radical forms of cinema, although there was a brief revival of the documentary genre. Such films as *La vieja memoria* (1977) by Camino, *Canciones para después de una guerra* (1977) by Patino, and *El desencanto* (1976) by Chávarri fulfilled a cultural function of historical recuperation. Films such as *Animación en la sala de espera* (1981) by Carlos Rodríguez Sanz and Manuel Coronado, and *Cadalverles* (1982) by Angel García de Val, offered a radical discourse on madness and death and *Después de . . .* (1979–81) by Cecilia and Juan José Bartolomé was a remarkable personal testimony of the Spanish transition to democracy.

A new generation of film-makers emerging in the 1980s set about reformulating some of the narrative and visual concepts which typify independent cinema. In *Dos* (1980) by Alvaro del Amo, for example, the narrative structure is replaced by a cycle of actions and dialogues repeated with variations throughout the film. *Dos* lacks any historical background, or narrative beginning and end. Rather, it proposes a 'new narrative manual' where different possibilities, within a dualistic relationship, are being tested. The film has a circular quality; it opens with a global image of the interior of the house where all subsequent sequences take place and concludes with a reversal taking us back to the film's opening. It is a calculated cinematic structure within which the characters are forced to expose their ritualistic behaviour of union, dependency, domination, separation and desire. Throughout the film the word becomes the engine pulling the scene. The images are not relevant but their opaqueness and absence of obvious mean-ing create a strong sense of claustrophobia and anxiety. There is no sense of progression and time appears suspended. Nor are there any concrete refer-ences or anecdotes; there are only 'situations' – psychological patterns of individuals relating to each other – to which the actors lend their voices and their physical incorporation. Relationships are neither interpreted nor eval-uated, but presented with a detachment unqualified by gesture or acting. There is, therefore, no identification with the words and positions taken by the actors, merely recognition. The outcome is a cold, rational exercise which unsettles the spectator.

Iván Zulueta's films are dominated by a meta-cinematic theme. He uses collage and recycles sequences from other films shot by himself or others to create an ongoing commentary on the medium of cinema itself. His films stage the breakdown of cinema as a transparent representation of an exter-nal reality. In *Arrebato* (1979) cinema becomes the starting point for the main protagonist's internal journey of self-discovery which, eventually, leads him into an hallucinatory state. *Párpados* (1989) explores the cine-matic 'look', the active element which gives meaning to characters' relation-ships. The voyeuristic strategy central to the cinematographic experience becomes the real theme of the film; even the characters' relationships are secondary to a process of self-recognition and fascination with 'the look'. The film's narrative structure is based on two relationships: a couple (Carmen and Carlos) and a pair of twin sisters – two extreme instances of human proximity and identity, stressing the difference within the similar and vice versa. The film explores the way in which the inevitable frustration of human and cinematic desire for identification with the image leaves us 'hooked on the look'. *Párpados* represents a further step towards a cinema which takes the cinematic experience as its object of study and concern. The plot of these films is minimal, barely constituted by frames, fragments of the characters' memories or looks which, instead of narrating a story, sketch out a visual landscape where the nature of such representations can be explored.

Fluctuating between the personal and the experimental, José Luis Guerín's short and feature-length films in Super-8 are another example of this latest generation of avant-garde meta-cinema. His 1976 short *La agonía de Agustín* focused on the persecution and destruction of a beetle by a hand. The simplicity of the narrative subtly concealed a more sophisticated cine-matic discourse on the tension between surface and relief, between the two-dimensional quality of film and the three-dimensional reality represented. Although *Los motivos de Berta* (1983), Guerín's first feature, had a plot, it is a minimalist one; the film already displays an incipient interest in the meta-cinema discourse. It is, however, in his next film, *Innisfree* (1990), where cinema becomes the central subject. The film is a documentary set in the town of Innisfree, the birthplace of film director John Ford's parents, in County Galway, Ireland, and where he returned in 1952 to shoot one of his most successful films with John Wayne, *The Quiet Man*. *Innisfree* explores the past and its consequences but solely through the cinematic experience. Although it seems to follow the rules of the documentary genre, it does so only to subvert them by inserting fictional elements.

Tren de sombras (1996), Guerín's latest film, is another meta-cinematic exercise through which he explores the expressive materiality of cinema and its poetic nature. Rather than narrating a story, *Tren de sombras* articulates a melancolic fascination for the pure image, its photographic and material qualities.

Another important contemporary film director is Jesús Garay who, besides an impressive list of short films, documentaries and television documentaries, has already produced four features: *Nemo* (1977-78), *Manderley* (1980), *Pasión lejana* (1986), *La bañera* (1989). One of the latest additions to this young generation of avant-garde film-makers is Marc Recha, whose *El cielo sube* (1991) and *L'arbre de les cireres* (1998) further illustrate the 'narcissistic' obsession with the medium which characterizes contemporary avant-garde Spanish cinema. As Recha has himself revealed:

> In *El cielo sube* there is a desire, an attempt, to reconstruct cinema, to reinvent it. It was intended to be as if the film had been made by amateurs. It was a process demythicizing cinema ... a film about cinema, cinema in its purest form, in its primitive state and with its basic innocence.
>
> (1994, pp. 20–1)

With the exception of Buñuel's films, avant-garde cinema in Spain has never enjoyed the calibre and influence of German expressionism or the French new wave. However, there has been an important tradition of experimental cinema, and production of non-commercial cinema in Spain has increased since the 1960s, suggesting a stronger and more eclectic tradition than that from which Buñuel emerged in the 1930s. Arguably, the sheer variety of non-conventional forms of cinema has stretched the meaning of avant-garde cinema and the limits of commercial films.

Director Pedro Almodóvar began his cinematic activities in 1974 with a series of experimental films in Super-8, some of which resembled 1960s *performance art*. Almodóvar himself provided all the dialogues and songs during the films' projections. Some of these films are certainly amateurish, but this is offset by their contagious humour and spontaneity. It is also important to mention his short films: *Homenaje* (1975), *La caída de Sodoma* (1974) and *Trailer de ¿Quién teme a Virgina Woolf?* (1976), a critique of commercial cinema, *El sueño* (1978) and *Folle, folle, fólleme Tim* (1978). In 1980 he made what was to become his first commercially successful film *Pepi, Luci, Boom y otras chicas del montón*, initially shot in 16 mm and only later transferred to the 35 mm commercial format. With this film Almodóvar put an end to his experimental/marginal period and became the most successful modern film-maker in Spain.

Unfortunately, Almodóvar's smooth transformation from marginal, avant-garde film-maker to commercial cinema director is the exception rather than the norm. The practical constraints which have crippled the development of Spanish avant-garde cinema since its origins have hardly changed: a lack of infrastructure for the production, distribution and exhibition of these films. Avant-garde cinema has been exhibited in universities or cine-clubs in the past and, increasingly, at international film festivals such as Barcelona's International Festival of Independent Cinema, *L'alternativa*, and those in Gijón, Madrid and San Sebastián. However, this is 'too little, too late'. It is now relatively easy to see Spanish films in the experimental or avant-garde sections of these official film festivals, but almost impossible outside these limited and elitist events.

Following the election of the PSOE Socialist party in 1982 and the growing autonomy of the regions, art, including the avant-garde, was widely promoted through a variety of official institutions. Although painting and design benefited most, theatre and cinema also received different forms of national and regional support.

If the historical avant-garde of the 1920s ultimately renewed rather than destroyed bourgeois art, contemporary avant-garde in the 1980s gave an acceptable and progressive 'look' to the ultra-modern Spanish culture. The economic recession of the 1990s slowed down the promotion of culture pursued by the socialist government. In contrast to postmodernism's tendency to encourage heterogeneity, a tight process of selection was imposed which, according to Dent Coad, ensured that 'most investment was going to high-profile, elitist projects of a short-term nature. Little was being invested in middle- or lowbrow cultural activities or in long-term research and education' (1995, p. 375). This highlights the essential problem of avant-garde art or any other form of marginal culture. In contrast to traditional and consumerist cultural practices, avant-garde places its emphasis on the exploration of the medium (that is, the study of its materials and methods of production) rather than the promotion, distribution and consumption of its cultural output.

If the contemporary avant-garde artist has lost his or her role as a modern artist, so has the concept of avant-garde art, which can no longer constitute an alternative either to the official culture sponsored by the government institutions or to the postmodernist culture of mass consumer society.

One of the consequences of postmodernism's commodification of culture is the constant saturation of the cultural market and, alongside it, an increase in the ephemerality of its products. In this postmodernist context, the rejection of tradition which typified modernist and historical avant-garde art, has become meaningless. Spanish postmodernism is characterized by an eclectic incorporation and celebration of both old and modern cultural traditions. As the Spanish historical avant-garde maintained a more ambiguous relationship with popular culture than that of its European counterparts, it is possible to claim that, despite its elitism, it prepared the way for the postmodernist eclecticism of today. Contemporary avant-garde groups such as LFdB owe part of their success to the way in which elements of popular culture are integrated into their work. The avant-garde's previous pretensions of shocking and subverting bourgeois culture through works of art have now become rather more modest. Ironically, their earlier attempts to bring aesthetics into everyday life came to fruition in what, according to Fredric Jameson, is the 'cultural logic of late capitalism' where art becomes just another ephemeral commodity without social or spiritual relevance (Jameson, 1984).

Despite postmodernism's announcement of the 'death' of art in its transcendental meaning or as a way of transforming society, the relentless search for new forms of expression has continued. Avant-garde art has become an aesthetic practice obsessed with itself and the formal elements which constitute it. Although this may not apply to every single work of contemporary avant-garde, the focus on form and medium rather than on the socio-political emerges as the most frequent common denominator. In contrast with its historical antecedents, the contemporary avant-garde is no longer committed to socio-political concerns; it has become 'apolitical' in the strict sense of the word. Far from becoming an obsolete aesthetic tradition, however, avant-garde art still has a central role in the daily renewal and experimentation of culture in Spain. Rather than aiming to produce a total 'rupture' from the dominant social and cultural order (the objective of the historical avant-garde), this contemporary strategic avant-garde operates within it and seeks to expose some of the 'crises' and 'cracks' through which new possibilities might open up.

References

DENT COAD, E. C. 1995: Designer culture in the 1980s: the price of success. In Graham, H. and Labanyi, J. (eds), *Spanish cultural studies: an introduction.* Oxford: Oxford University Press, 376–80.

FRENK, S., PERRIAM, C. and THOMPSON, M. 1995: The literary avant-garde: a contradictory modernity. In Graham, H. and Labanyi, J. (eds), *Spanish cultural studies, an introduction.* Oxford: Oxford University Press, pp. 63–70.

JAMESON, F. 1984: Postmodernism, or the cultural logic of late capitalism. In *New Left Review* 146, 53–92.

RECHA, M. 1994: Reinventar la mirada: declaraciones de Marc Recha. *Banda Aparte* 1, November, 13–22.

|10|

Screening the past: history and nostalgia in contemporary Spanish cinema

RIKKI MORGAN-TAMOSUNAS

Introduction

Historical film in its broad range of manifestations – as documentary, historical reconstruction, period drama, heritage and nostalgia – has been prominent in Spanish cinema since its inception. However, the meanings it has embodied and the cultural significance with which it has been endowed have undergone many shifts as it has reflected and responded to changing social, political and cultural contexts, and its forms have been appropriated and re-appropriated to articulate different ideological positions and cultural meanings. Although the socio-political and production contexts for film-making have changed quite radically since the end of the dictatorship, the cinema of democratic Spain reveals a range of cultural preoccupations which form a continuum with the earlier period. The sheer range and proliferation of historical film in Spanish cinema of the 1980s displayed a seemingly obsessive concern with the past and this continues to have a strong presence in the 1990s. Recent examples produced in 1998 include Antonio Mercero's *La hora de los valientes* based in Civil War Madrid, Fernando Colomo's *Los años bárbaros* concerning anti-Franco students in the 1940s, in 1999 José Miguel Juárez's *Hijos de viento*, dealing with the life of Hernán Cortés, and other historical films with non-Spanish locations such as Bigas Luna's *La camarera del Titanic*, set mainly in 1912 France, and Gerardo Diego's *Frontera Sur*, set in late-nineteenth-century Argentina. The continuing popularity of historical genres is undeniable. Of the four Spanish films in the Madrid box-office top 10 in the week following the 1999 Goya awards, two were period pieces: José Luis Garci's adaptation of Galdós's *El abuelo* (1998) and Fernando Trueba's romantic comedy *La niña de tus ojos*

(1998) which has become one of the three highest grossing Spanish films to date.

Even when their main characteristic is one of rupture – a breaking with the past – many contemporary films and cinematic trends remain partially determined by the inescapable influence of the very past they seem to reject. Whilst, for example, the films of Pedro Almodóvar – that emblematic figure of New Spain – have always been self-consciously contemporary in style and subject matter, their dismantling of traditional concepts of gender roles and the advancement of alternative models for relationships, family structures, etc., clearly relate as much to the restrictive moral, social and sexual paradigms of the past, as to the radical possibilities of the present. Despite specific references to the dictatorship, his films have consistently offered a critical representation of the rigid patriarchal and paternalistic social structures and values that underpinned its arch-conservative ideology and its relation to a strict and dogmatic notion of Catholicism based on fear and guilt. Recurrent thematic references to such dogma and its manifestation in obsessive behaviour and psychological trauma (consider, for example, Angel's mother in *Matador*, 1986) clearly also have their roots in the psychological dramas of 1970s oppositional cinema (for example, Carlos Saura's *La prima Angélica*, 1973). Having never done so before, in his 1997 film *Carne trémula*, Almodóvar ventured into a period setting, opening the film with a critical vignette of the late Franco period. The sequence offers a characteristic combination of grating realism and studied stylization, steeped in the customary kitsch of Almodóvar's visual style – a glimpse of the past from a palpably contemporary perspective. Several of Spain's relatively new young film-makers are also making incursions into period drama. Isabel Coixet, whose first major success, *Cosas que nunca te dije* (1996), was not only contemporary, but based in the USA and made in English, has opted for historical drama in her recent *A los que aman* (1998), seeking the cultural roots of the present through studied period accuracy and emotional self-discovery. Also Fernando León de Aranoa, director of the acclaimed contemporary study in social realism, *Barrio* (1998), has recently declared his intention to make a film about the International Brigades and the Spanish Civil War.[1]

Despite this plethora of historical films, however, many critics have criticized their predominantly nostalgic mode and condemned their failure to examine the past in a critical or analytical way. Others have observed a neglect of contemporary issues resulting from both the glut of period cinema and a lack of engagement with the issues of the day in other genres with more contemporary settings (Alonso Barahona, 1992, p. 188). The following section will give a brief overview of certain trends in historical cinema since the end of the dictatorship and their cultural significance. It will also indicate some of the ways in which, notwithstanding the perceived limitations of some forms of the genre, its retrospective representations articulate important psychosocial perceptions of the past. The essay will then go on to discuss how, despite their narrative and thematic retrospection, these films inscribe perspectives and preoccupations which relate directly to contemporary cultural experience. Finally, it will consider the potential of the nostalgic affective mode for articulating a more radical or progressive discourse than the ideological conservatism with which it is usually associated.

History and identity: cultural projects of post-Francoism

Whilst it reflects the widespread obsession with the past in contemporary Western culture as a whole, Jo Labanyi demonstrates that the Spanish inflection of this phenomenon is particularly complex and relates to the specific social, cultural and political legacy of Francoism and Spain's accelerated modernization (in Graham and Labanyi, 1995, p. 398). Dominant institutional representations of past and recent history under Franco had been constructed according to the internal rules of the regime's social and political game and strictly enforced by the censor. It was hardly surprising, therefore, that one of the first cultural projects of the transition – in cinema and other forms of cultural production – was one of historical retrieval, with the purpose of rewriting recent Spanish history from the previously disenfranchised perspective of the losing side of the Civil War. Far from an exercise in nostalgia, a strong preference for stark documentary and testimonial realism was visible in early transitional films such as Jaime Camino's *La vieja memoria* (1977). Gradually this documentary style was displaced by the more populist mode of historical reconstruction in films such as Bardem's *Siete días de enero* (1978) or Pontecorvo's *Operación Ogro* (1980), and increasing licence in the dramatic enhancement of actual events – for example, *La fuga de Segovia* (1981) by Uribe, *Dragón Rapide* (1986) by Camino. The eighties were largely dominated by fictional dramas (often located in the early years of Francoism). In terms of the dominant political and cultural drive of the 1980s, the frequent focus on the deprivations and injustices of the past also offered a socio-political and cultural 'yardstick' against which the achievements of democratic Spain could be measured and contrasted. This can be understood, on the one hand, as a cultural expression of post-dictatorship euphoria, a reflection of the sense of optimism and air of real social and political change in the early years of PSOE government. However, it has also prompted less positive readings as a self-congratulatory articulation of the dominant discourse of middle-of-the-road liberalism and consensus politics at the time. Its emphasis on the contrast with the pre-democratic status quo also arguably diverted attention from current political performance and realities (Jordan and Morgan-Tamosunas, 1998, pp. 54–6; Monterde 1989, p. 56).[2]

In the 1980s Spain was also anxious to assert its image as a modern European state. In some senses this was a contradictory agenda in which the establishment of a contemporary national cultural identity sat uncomfortably alongside the desire for European identity and simultaneous commitment to the cultural diversity of the emergent regional autonomies. Film policy of the late 1970s and early 1980s reflected the European dimension by supporting European co-productions, the number of these more than doubling between 1976 and 1981 (Caparrós Lera, 1992, p. 411; Gubern *et al.*, 1995, p. 372). Subsequent criticism of the dilution of identity and formulaic homogeneity of 'Europudding' productions highlights the fact that, whilst this strategy may have helped to put Spain on the industrial map, it did little to promote notions of Spanish cultural identity itself.

The promotion of Spanish culture was enshrined in the Spanish Constitution of 1978 (Article 149.2) and PSOE film policy under both Miró and Semprún translated this into support for films which were 'representative of Spanish culture in any of its manifestations and forms of expression' (Gubern *et al.*, 1995, p. 407). Some of the new autonomous regions adopted a strong policy of financial support for their own film industries (for example, the Basque Country, Catalonia), and their main production trends tended unsurprisingly towards political and historical cinema. In particular they sought to retrieve cultural memory and identities which had been reduced to superficial manifestations of *costumbrismo* by the Franco regime's obsessive crusade against separatism (Jordan and Morgan-Tamosunas, pp. 160–3; 182–9). Josep María Forn's study of the martyred president of Catalonia during the Republic, *Companys, procès a Catalunya* (1978), was a notable example from the emergent Catalan cinema. At a national level, big-budget funding resulted in a flood of literary adaptations aimed at a middlebrow audience. The proliferation of financial agreements, first with Spanish Television (TVE) and later with the emerging regional and private channels, reflected popular demand and secured a healthy future for the Spanish heritage film well into the mid-1990s.[3] Despite some notable and controversial flops amongst the most expensive productions (e.g. Saura's *El Dorado*, 1987), there were a number of resounding domestic successes, such as Mario Camus's adaptations of Cela's *La colmena* (1982) and Delibes's *Los santos inocentes* (1984). More recently Pilar Miró's screen version of Lope de Vega's *El perro del hortelano* (1996) and Garci's Oscar-nominated *El abuelo* demonstrate the continuing popularity of the heritage film. Adaptations of work by contemporary authors with a historical theme have also been particularly successful (e.g. Imanol Uribe's 1991 *El rey pasmado*, based on a novel by Torrente Ballester), and have sometimes enjoyed a measure of international recognition (e.g. Pedro Olea's *El maestro de esgrima*, 1992, based on the Pérez Reverte novel). Recent examples include Mario Gas's adaptation of the Vázquez Montalbán novel *El pianista* (1998) and Antonio José Betancor's 1998 version of Rafael Arozamena's *Mararía*.

Engagement with the past?

Many critics have questioned the extent to which the plethora of retrospective films has really engaged with history, and issues of style, subject matter and absences from their narrative and thematic coverage have posed a series of questions which revive age-old debates about historical realism in the cinema. These issues are all the more loaded because of the complex and contradictory culture-specific meanings attaching to both the representation of history and the history of Spanish historical film itself. In its 'Crusade' against Communism, masonry and separatism, Francoism had appealed to retrospective models of Spain's imperial past, the Spain of the Catholic Kings, for inspiration and legitimation of its social, political and cultural values and structures. Institutionally approved film production – especially in the early years of the dictatorship – reflected this retrospection in its celebration of heroic deeds of the past, religious self-sacrifice and folklorism in historical and religious dramas, and *españoladas* (Higginbotham, 1988, pp. 18–24). The underlying discourse of these films consistently reinforced nostalgic notions of patriotism, family and continuity with a glorious past. The historical associations of Francoist period cinema with perceptions of manipulation, misrepresentation and the privileging of a highly prescribed socio-cultural and ideological discourse, have perhaps inevitably prompted critical wariness of the genre. The absence of contemporary films taking a clearly *analytical* approach to major historical events has tended to reinforce this view. José Enrique Monterde's much-quoted observation that Spanish historical cinema of the 1980s and early 1990s was a cinema of 'reconocimiento más bien que conocimiento' (recognition rather than discovery) epitomizes recurrent complaints about the lack of historical analysis (Monterde, 1993, p. 23).

One of the main criticisms has concerned the overwhelming preference for a personalized register, focusing largely on everyday domesticity or personal dramas. Despite its arguable limitations, however, the personalized representation of history can also fulfil an important cultural function, as a reflection and expression of history as subjective experience, particularly given its frequent focus on life at the social and political margins. It was to a certain extent inevitable that post-Franco attempts to retrieve the cultural memory of the Civil War's losers would focus on the private sphere since the perspective of the defeated Republican side and post-war opposition had been effectively excluded from the public domain of the dictatorship. A space was thus created within popular mainstream cinema for the articulation of previously disenfranchised voices and for the examination and deconstruction of some of the social, political and cultural bases of these marginalizations. The historical operation of a sexual economy resting on class- and gender-based inequalities, for example, is a theme clearly foregrounded in films such as *La colmena, Las cosas del querer* (1989) by Chávarri or *Libertarias* (1996) by Aranda. The appeal of these films inevitably rested partly on the familiarity of their references (through personal recollection, family anecdote, and collective popular memory), and emblematic films such as *Las bicicletas son para el verano* (1984) by Chávarri created a kind of nostalgically retrospective mythology of the everyday.

The mythologizing potential of film and the discursive function of personalization was also significant in the representation of historical figures from the public domain. Popular oppositional figures could be elevated from the margins to iconographic or even mystical status – as in Aranda's treatment of *El Lute* (1987 and 1988) or Gutiérrez Aragón's treatment of the *maquis* in *El corazón del bosque* (1978). At the same time public figures could be recuperated into the private world portrayed in the films to emphasize intimate aspects of their private lives and personae – whether overtly fictional, at best speculative or purportedly 'true'. The focus on private lives could be variously used to humanize and popularize such figures (e.g. García Lorca in Bardem's *Lorca, muerte de un poeta*, 1987), or diminish their stature (e.g. Franco in *Dragón Rapide*) (Jordan and Morgan-Tamosunas, 1998, pp. 23–8). Francisco Regueiro's later *Madregilda* (1993) plays mischievously with the contrasting iconographic status of both Franco and Gilda/Rita Hayworth. The Caudillo is reduced to a series of popular mythical caricatures and the popular subversive meanings attaching to Gilda are recognized in her newly elevated active oppositional status within the film.

Another central issue in the critique of heritage and period drama films relates to their emphasis on style and surface qualities. This, of course, is a difficult issue for the film industry. Vastly improved production values have been a major contributing factor to the retrieval of Spanish cinema from its previously disparaged image. Whilst dramatically reducing production, the controversial PSOE film policy of the 1980s focused on a range of 'quality improvements'. As *Moving Pictures* magazine put it, Spanish cinema has 'learned the art of looking good'.[4] However, Spanish critic Esteve Riambau identifies this look as one of the ingredients of a formulaic recipe which has led to the homogenization of Spanish cinema: a *cine polivalente* (multipurpose cinema) typically based on a combination of 'auteur direction, genre, literary adaptation, star casting and a characteristically stylish "look"' (Gubern *et al.*, 1995, p. 421).

This sophisticated quality can also create a visual disjuncture with certain thematic material, particularly in historical films where the narrative and thematic focus is directed at economic deprivation, political repression and social inequality. As early as in Pedro Olea's 1974 adaptation of the Galdós novel *Tormento*, Virginia Higginbotham remarked on the anaesthetizing effect of the film's colour: 'too luscious to visually convey hard times as anything but visual spectacle' (1987, p. 106), and John Hopewell later voices similar concerns about the sanitizing glossiness of *Los santos inocentes* (1986, pp. 226-8). Such polished visual surface qualities, together with other key formal aspects of period films, have a powerful capacity to inject images of the past with a 'cosy', nostalgic sense of well-being, even when they contain narrative or thematic material which would normally provoke quite contrary feelings. Generic hybridity can introduce further concerns with the location of particularly sensitive historical situations within the framework of genres generally regarded as 'lightweight'. Some of the most successful Spanish films (e.g. Berlanga's *La vaquilla*, 1984 and Trueba's Oscar-winning *Belle Époque*, 1992) merge periodicity with the major Spanish film genre of all time: comedy. The potential difficulties inherent in this mix are evidenced by the recent controversy surrounding *La niña de tus ojos*, a romantic musical comedy located in 1938 Berlin at the beginning of the holocaust.[5]

The centrality of the formal aspects of film to the establishment of the nostalgia mode in cinema is unsurprising if we consider nostalgia, as Raymond Williams argued in 1977, as 'a structure of feeling' (p. 172). The non-representational elements of film are able to appeal directly to the senses, privileging certain emotional responses in the spectator. These factors include particular techniques of camera work and lighting, such as the use of the 'romantic' soft focus and the predominance of mellow colours, the employment of camera angles recalling the conventions of retrospective genres – consider the sharp angles and dark shadows of classic *film noir* in Pilar Miró's period thrillers *Beltenebros* (1991) and *Tu nombre envenena mis sueños* (1996). They also, of course, include music – as is demonstrated by the powerful influence of retrospective melodies in contemporary films such as those of Pedro Almodóvar. It is significant that in many of the most successful historical films, the formal appeal of the musical elements has also been central to their narrative focus – e.g. *¡Ay, Carmela!* (Saura, 1990), *La niña de tus ojos*.

Apart from its anaesthetizing and escapist reputation, the nostalgia mode is often considered to inscribe an intrinsically conservative discourse because of its desire to establish continuity with the past, and as a result of its historical association with right-wing politics (Tannock, 1995, p. 455). In addition to Spain's specific cultural and cinematic legacy (mentioned earlier), a certain nostalgia for Francoism also circulated in popular parlance of the mid-1980s. This particularly related to the growing sense of urban insecurity in cities like Madrid and Barcelona which were witnessing rapid economic growth alongside increasing unemployment and a range of 'social problems' such as drug abuse, street violence, etc. The phrase 'cuando Franco' (in Franco's time) was frequently used to connote a utopian world of urban safety and moral certitude. This sentiment was reflected and perhaps fuelled in a series of Francoist nostalgic films which sought to discredit the Socialist regime by reference to its mounting political and economic scandals, and simultaneously dwelt on an artificially utopian recollection of the Franco years. This trend was perhaps epitomized in Rafael Gil's adaptation of Vizcaíno Casas's novel ... *Y al tercer día resucitó* (1981) in which

Franco was resurrected to pass judgement on the current state of affairs in Spain (Gubern *et al.*, 1995, p. 389–90).

However, the consignment of nostalgia to the ideological rubbish heap may be tantamount to throwing out the baby with the bath water. Stuart Tannock points out that nostalgia has characterized both right *and* left politics in the past and that the desire for stability can be decoupled from the notion of regression: 'Nostalgia approaches the past as a stable source of value and meaning; but this desire for a stable source cannot be conflated with the desire for a stable, traditional and hierarchised society' (1995, p. 455). Indeed elements of nostalgia in the cinema can have a particularly important function in the positioning of the spectator to empathize with sometimes radically different propositions advanced by narrative and characterizations. Such potentially subversive elements are present in *Belle Époque*, for example, which introduces a range of radical departures from the moral codes and social structures normally associated with its early 1930s location. Traditional attitudes are ridiculed in the exaggerated behaviour and acting styles of the upper-class mother and son played by veteran comic actors Chus Lampreave and Gabino Diego. At the same time Fernando Fernán Gómez's unusually bohemian family displays a range of sexually transgressive behaviour – particularly in the female characters' assertion of their sexuality, and in the gender fluidity introduced by the cross-dressing and sexual encounter between Violeta (Ariadna Gil) and Fernando (Jorge Sanz). The film apparently endorses this transgression through a nostalgic discourse which casts them as utopian.

In a contemporary narrative context, Almodóvar's films of the 1980s provide prime examples of this appropriation of nostalgia in support of a progressive discourse. In *La ley del deseo* (1987), for example, the nostalgic romance of the Los Panchos soundtrack is a key element in positioning the spectator to empathize with the protagonists of a final homosexual love sequence still unusual in mainstream mid-eighties cinema. Similarly the traditional *cruz de mayo* (spring altar) provides a narrative focus and ironical backdrop both for the positive representation of a far-from-conventional family unit (comprising an adolescent child with a transsexual surrogate mother and a homosexual uncle in the paternal role), and for the film's closing images in which Pablo nurses his dead lover in front of the burning altar – a striking tableau which powerfully subverts the traditional associations of the Pietà. Similar instances occur in *Entre tinieblas* (1983) and *Tacones lejanos* (1992) where nostalgic melodies support representations of lesbian desire and transvestism respectively.

Engagement with the present?

Despite its location in the past, the popular appeal of the nostalgia film signals it as an important cultural barometer of the present. Case and Shaw note that the conditions for nostalgia crucially hinge on some sense of the present being 'deficient' (1989, pp. 2-4). Many argue that in contemporary Western societies, the process of modernization and the successive introduction of industrialization, consumer society, globalization of the economy and the growth of the mass media have produced a sense of confusion and alienation in both society and the individual. Cultural and political postmodernity is experienced as a series of disorientating effects producing a sense of loss of individual identity, roots and community. As the boundaries between public and private spheres, and between image/representation and reality are eroded, the notion of reality itself is destabilized. Nostalgic cultural manifestations respond to this sense of disorientation by appealing to some notion, albeit fictitious, of 'a past that was unified and comprehensible, unlike the incoherent, divided present' (David Lowenthal in Case and Shaw, 1989, p. 29). Richard Dyer's work on entertainment provides a useful conceptual framework for mapping the utopian qualities of nostalgia onto identifiable absences and confusions in contemporary society. Dyer relates specific 'inadequacies in society' – 'scarcity', 'exhaustion', 'dreariness', 'manipulation', 'fragmentation' – to corresponding pleasures and solutions associated with non-representational aspects of popular entertainment forms: 'abundance', 'energy', 'intensity', 'transparency', 'community' (1981, pp. 183-4).

If contemporary Spanish period films indulge current fixations with (retro) style, they also simultaneously betray the gulf between lack and 'abundance' which is central to the desire on which contemporary capitalist consumerism is predicated. However, despite the thematic focus in a number of period films on social inequality, the connection between this and the underlying implications of the stylistic indulgence of the film itself are rarely signalled. Exceptions might include films such as *Las cosas del querer* (Chávarri, 1989) where the allure of material abundance is specifically problematized.

The role of formal aspects in creating the structure of feeling which (in combination with its historical setting) defines the nostalgia film clearly relates to Dyer's notion of 'intensity' as a direct, 'authentic' experience of unrestrained emotion which he contrasts with the 'monotony, predictability, instrumentality of the daily round' (1989, p. 184). In the era of the 'death of the subject' and the simulacrum, the 'intense' and 'transparent' experience of 'excitement, drama, affectivity of living' (Dyer, 1989, p. 184) is one of the self-evident appeals of the nostalgia film to contemporary audiences. Even when it is cast within a hyperbolic mode signalling its own artificiality and condition as a cinematic construct – e.g. the exuberant reunion of the itinerant opera-singing mother with her ecstatic children and husband in *Belle Époque* – the pleasurable intensity of the experience is not diminished.

Fredric Jameson has argued that the retrospective trend in contemporary Western culture in general indicates that we are 'incapable of achieving aesthetic representations of our own current experience' (1983, p. 117). However, these articulations of the experience of contemporary cultural reality within the formal discourse of nostalgia point to a less pessimistic reading. Indeed the inscription of an identifiable sense of 'lack' also points to a potentially more constructive role for nostalgia associated with Dyer's notions of 'energy' as a sense of empowerment and potential effective agency, and 'community' in terms of shared interests and 'collective activity' (1989, pp. 180–1). The nostalgia film has the potential to promote the very engagement and agency it is generally regarded as stifling, as a number of films located in the historical context of the Civil War can demonstrate. The translation of social reformist and anti-Fascist Republican agendas into an emotional, humanistic discourse permits a potentially energizing experience of community and agency related to a political or ideological cause, and locates them within a readily accessible mode of address. In *¡Ay, Carmela!*, for instance, Carmela's indignation at the inhuman treatment of the Polish prisoners of war, the humiliation of the Republic, and her own degradation are the humanist and emotional corollaries of political commitment and integrity.

Vicente Aranda's *Libertarias* provides a particularly powerful example of the energizing possibilities of nostalgia. The film's utopian discourse is flagged in its opening text frames which refer to the events of 18–21 July 1936. The contextualizing statements culminate by telling us that on 21 July 'The Spanish Civil War has begun, the last idealist war, the last dream of a people propelled towards the impossible, towards utopia.' Moving from simulated black and white 'archive' images to full-colour action, the opening sequence of the film represents the celebratory mood following the initially successful resistance to the Nationalist uprising, and the revolutionary euphoria which this critical moment had unleashed. Unusually for its type, the film is protagonized by an ensemble group of women brought together by militants of the anarchist-influenced Mujeres Libres (Free Women) and comprising ideologues, former prostitutes and a nun. Here Dyer's notions of abundance, energy, intensity, transparency and community are clearly at work, producing a nostalgic discourse which speaks of the revolutionary potential of the moment. More specifically it captures the sense of energy, optimism and empowerment generated by the female solidarity of a group of women taking charge of their own destiny for the first time.

Through the operation of a complex set of identification processes and the juxtaposition of different points of view, the film brings about a gradual shift in perspective from potential cynicism to emotional engagement with the ideological positions of various central characters. The film moves, for example, from Concha's (Laura Maña's) apparently genuine but formulaic recitation of revolutionary clichés, to Pilar's (Ana Belén's) assertion of women's right to active participation in the struggle. Pilar delivers her speech in angry response to party exhortations for women to abandon their arms and return to their tradionally supportive role. Her explanation of what this self-determination means for women is articulated with a winningly embarrassed candour and simplicity, powerfully enhanced by the use of close-up and reaction shots. The sequence is underwritten by an extra-diegetic soundtrack accompanying her words with the ever-increasing tension of a combative drum beat. Later in the film María's (Ariadna Gil's) religious devotion is aligned with the egalitarian reformism of the revolutionary discourse. In contrast to many films about the Civil War, *Libertarias* (like Ken Loach's highly acclaimed Spanish–British–German co-production *Tierra y Libertad/Land and Freedom*, 1995) also addresses some of the ruptures and factional splits which contributed to the eventual defeat of the Republic. It shows, for example, the friction between anarchist resistance to hierarchical structures and pressures to adopt more formal military structures. It also offers a critical representation of attitudes to gender which ran counter to the otherwise egalitarian rhetoric of the left. *Libertarias* thus avoids some of the shortcomings of other films taken to task for their uncritical account of Republican resistance. At the end of the film most of the women are brutally killed by Moorish troops allied to the invading Nationalist side. This dramatically tragic resolution provides a stark point of contrast with the prevailing discourse of revolutionary euphoria, and ensures the consignment of the latter to the preserves of nostalgia.

Although such films are associated with the specific historical context of the Spanish Civil War, they may have more general resonances and relevance for audiences of the nineties. When the pleasurable qualities of nostalgia are associated with ideological commitment and action, they have the capacity to promote the desire and will to achieve a level of engagement and empowerment which many would define as absences in contemporary cultural experience.

Notes

1. *Fotogramas*, March 1999, p. 158.
2. Certainly the latter-day antics of the PSOE regime suggest that what might have seemed negative cynicism at the time, accurately predicted the dangers of complacency and licence this attitude implied.
3. The gradual reduction in investment by public television thereafter, and the restrictive terms of their deals introduced what, by mid-1998, had become a major threat of destabilization into the unprecedented healthy and promising state of Spanish cinema (Abad y Ponga, 1998: ¿El cine español va bien? In *Fotogramas*, May 1998, pp. 81–90).
4. Holland, Jonathan, 1998: Dreams come true. In *Moving pictures at the London screenings* Day 3, 28 October 1998.
5. This film ironically coincided with the mixed critical reception of Roberto Benigni's Oscar-winning film *La vita è bella*, 1997.

References

ALONSO BARAHONA, F. 1992: El cine en la cultura española contemporánea. In *Breve diagnóstico de la cultural española*. Madrid: Ediciones Rialp, S.A., 174–90.

BAUDRILLARD, J. 1983: The ecstasy of communication. In Foster, H. (ed.), *Postmodern Culture*. London: Pluto Press, 126–34.

CAPARRÓS LERA, J.M. 1992: *El cine español de la democracia*. Barcelona: Editorial Anthropos.

CASE, M. and SHAW, C. (EDS) 1989: *The imagined past – history and nostalgia*. Manchester: Manchester University Press.

DYER, R. 1981: Entertainment and Utopia. In Altman, R. (ed.) *Genre: the musical*. London: Routledge and Kegan Paul, 159–74.

GRAHAM, H. and LABANYI, J. 1995: *Spanish cultural studies: an introduction*. Oxford: Oxford University Press.

GUBERN, R., MONTERDE, J. E., PÉREZ PERUCHA, J., RIAMBAU, E. and TORREIRO, C. 1995: *Historia del cine español*. Madrid: Cátedra.

HIGGINBOTHAM, V. 1988: *Spanish film under Franco*. Austin Texas: University of Texas Press.

HOPEWELL, J. 1986: *Out of the past. Spanish cinema after Franco*. London: British Film Institute.

JAMESON, F. 1983: Postmodernism and consumer society. In Foster, H. (ed.) 1983: *Postmodern culture*. London: Pluto Press, 111–25.

JORDAN, B. and MORGAN-TAMOSUNAS, R. 1998: *Contemporary Spanish cinema*. Manchester: Manchester University Press.

MONTERDE, J. E. 1989: El cine histórico durante la transición política. In *Escritos sobre el cine español 1973–1987*. Valencia: Filmoteca de la Generalitat Valenciana, 45–63.

MONTERDE, J. E. 1993: *Veinte años de cine español (1973–1992). Un cine bajo la paradoja*. Barcelona: Ediciones Paidós.

TANNOCK, S. 1995: Nostalgia Critique. In *Cultural Studies* 3, October, 453–64.

WILLIAMS, R. 1977 *Marxism and literature*. Oxford: Oxford University Press.

|11|

Sects and secularity: another cinema, another Spain

RYAN PROUT

Today I'm unofficial, but tomorrow I might be official! And vice versa, of course, or even something worse.

(Bulgakov, 1997, p. 79)

The cults, as well as the sects ... owe their rise, in part at least, to the shortcomings of the churches.

(Van Baalen, 1956, p. 364)

Américo Castro, the iconoclastic chronicler of Spain's genesis as a nation, has suggested that 'In essence, at least, Hispanic history is the history of a belief system and of a religious sensibility' (quoted in Payne 1984, unnumbered). If Castro's assertion is valid, we should not be surprised to find that Spanish film-makers interested in uncovering and portraying the contrary motion between change and stasis in their society have returned to the subject of religion and religious sects, both during the Francoist regime and during the period of democratic transition and consolidation. A juxtaposition of Luis Buñuel's *La Voie lactée*, made in 1969, and José Luis Borau's *Niño Nadie*, released in 1998, illustrates this point. While Buñuel's film was made in the penumbra of a regime which had sent the director into exile, and Borau's was made following tremendous religious and political upheavals in Spain, both films nevertheless delve into the marginal world of sects and secret societies as a means of discovering the norm against which these anomalous belief systems have arisen. Similarly, the two films which are the primary reference point of this essay, José María Zabalza's *La de Troya en el Palmar* (1984) and Javier Palmero's *Manuel y Clemente* (1986a) both attempt to produce social satire through an engagement with the history and activities of a deviant religious congregation.

The similarities between the two pairs of films mentioned here are only of a general kind, however. Whereas Buñuel's film reflects the director's personal fascination with the obduracy of historical heretical figures, such as Priscillian, the fourth-century Gnostic bishop of Ávila (Buñuel, 1994, pp. 244–5), and Borau's film culminates in the exposure of an imaginary group of naked autosoterists, both films from the 1980s are concerned with what was then, and is still, an actually existing schismatic Catholic sect, the Carmelitas de la Santa Faz, often referred to simply as El Palmar de Troya after the name of the Andalusian village nearest to where the sect took hold.[1]

The breakaway order was founded in 1974 on the back of a series of apparitions and mystical communications initiated in 1968 when four truant schoolgirls claimed to have seen a vision of the Virgin Mary. By the late 1970s, the order could boast of having its own Pope, Gregorio XVII, as well as its own Holy See located some 40 kilometres outside Seville. Adherents of this ultramontane sect believe that the Roman Catholic Church has fallen into the hands of Communists and freemasons who have conspired to keep the official occupant of the throne of St Peter under heavy sedation (Cardinal Father Isidore María, 1980). They reject the moderate reforms of the Second Vatican Council (1962–65) and persist in performing religious ceremonies in Latin and in keeping a strict separation between clergy and laity in the celebration of the Eucharist. Whilst the sect emerged in the dying days of the regime, it developed and grew coetaneously with the process of democratic reform. Following celestial nomination (the first since St Peter's), in 1978 its leader was crowned as Pope Gregorio XVII only weeks before the promulgation of the Spanish Constitution. An exemplary manifestation of the atavistic and nostalgic tendencies of a *nacionalcatolicismo* oblivious to shifts in the surrounding socio-political landscape, the sect provided ideal material for a satirical treatment of the paradoxes produced by the co-existence within the same society of some elements 'which would not look out of place in a Golden Age picaresque tale' (Palmero, 1986b, p. xx) and others belonging to the rapid process of modernization and secularization which Spain had been undergoing since Franco's tardy demise.

Such satirical possibilities are exploited by Zabalza, for example, when he frames alongside each other bikini-clad tourists and followers of Gregorio XVII, their eyes turned heavenward in expectation of a miraculous event which will cure them of their illnesses and free them from poverty.[2] By contrasting Almodóvarian punks with religious fanatics in mediaeval outfits, *La de Troya en el Palmar* emphasizes the gulf between those sections of Spanish society with their eyes set on the future and other groups looking for reassurance in the past. With plenty of sexual antics and elements of bedroom farce, the film looks like a straightforward sex comedy. However, this definition would be inadequate since, in the midst of its comedy, Zabalza's film also picks up on contemporary concerns about the changes in the relationship between church and state. The mainstream Catholic priest depicted in the film is obsessed with destroying his church so that he can sell the plot of land it occupies, a reference to the economic quandary in which the church found itself following the suspension of government subsidies in 1983. Interlaced with this sub-plot are impressive scenes of the command-ing presence of the Palmarian sect's imposing basilica over the Andalusian landscape. Released in 1986, close on the heels of *La de Troya en el Palmar*, Palmero's film also blends documentary and dramatic scenes. However, as its title suggests, it focuses more closely on the established biographical facts known about Clemente Domínguez (later Pope Gregorio XVII) and Manuel Alonso (later Gregorio XVII's Secretary of State). As it follows the develop-ing relationship between its two protagonists from 1968 to 1978, *Manuel y Clemente* also crosses the border between Francoism and democratic transi-tion. The director always had it in mind to create a dramatic confrontation between 'contemporary Spanish history [and] social phenomena of the utmost significance' (Palmero, 1986c, p. 3).

Rather than reinforcing the notions of consensus, compromise, and rec-onciliation, which were arguably the preferred watchwords of the transi-tional process, Zabalza's and Palmero's films were indicative of the schisms within the nascent post-Francoist society. Despite the clear potential of the unrivalled Palmarian 'collective fossil' (Alonso-Fernández, 1993, p. 220) for comedic and documentary treatments, both films which portrayed the Palmarian sect were regarded as anomalous and have been largely over-looked in historical overviews of Spanish cinema. This can be explained by generic and political constraints, two distinct yet closely allied forces which determined the look and content of the transitional era's most successful cinema. As José Enrique Monterde argues, the generic range of post-Francoist cinema in the period from 1976 to 1992 was largely restricted to comedies and thrillers. Furthermore, within the successful comedic sub-gen-res he identifies, there was no place for satire (1993, pp. 130–4). This was a limitation which some critics had already recognised when *Manuel y Clemente* was released in Spain. For example, Nuria Vidal (1986) observed that:

> Palmero's film is an anomaly. Esperpento [the theatre of the grotesque], satire, and the *sainete* are all genres which possess a vener-able tradition in Spanish culture. ... Sadly, these genres have been all but forgotten by a contemporary Spanish cinema more concerned with the development of new wave comedy and auteurist works. *Manuel y Clemente* is an exception to this rule in that the director makes a point of trying to revitalise the neglected genre of black comedy.

The policing of genre suggested by Monterde and Vidal reflects and artic-ulates a political reticence with regard to topics which seemed to suggest the seepage into democratic Spain of recognizably Francoist features. As is clear from reviews in the Spanish press as well as from Palmero's unsuccessful efforts to have the value of his film recognized by the state, an essay in satire like *Manuel y Clemente* was regarded as suspicious and untimely by the bodies responsible for subsidizing and promoting Spanish film.[3] While the concept of transition implies a gradual shift between past and present, the films remembered from the eighties are more likely to be those which posited a clean break with the past (of the sort embodied in the hedonistic counter culture of the Madrid *movida*). The blank denial of the past would simply not have been possible in a satirical, archaeological film focused on the living fossil of the Palmarian sect. Explaining the difficulties he encountered in securing the government subsidy for *Manuel y Clemente*, Palmero says 'They tried to persuade us that since the subject would inevitably bring back memories of the Francoist era, it was better to avoid the theme of religion altogether'.[4]

Although *Manuel y Clemente* received bad reviews at home, it was better received (if not better understood) at festivals in Berlin and San Francisco where the putative homosexual relationship between Gregorio XVII and his Secretary of State was read as the film's main interest. The differing interpretations of the film in Spain and in the United States indicates that estimates of its quality had as much to do with distinct levels of sensitivity to specifically Spanish cultural markers as they did with any kind of absolute measurement of technical accomplishment. The same documentary disregard for the invented impermeable frontier between Francoism and democracy which made *Manuel y Clemente* unacceptable to a Spanish audience brought approval outside Spain from gay viewers, a fact which did not escape the attention of the film's director:

> It's not an old-fashioned cinema, with images of fascists, that I'm trying to create. Take the question of homosexuality in the film, for instance. Far from going about it in a heavy handed way, we treated the theme symbolically, letting the images speak for themselves. When *Manuel y Clemente* was shown at the San Francisco Film Festival, this considerate approach to the topic was something which was appreciated. By contrast, I've had my knuckles rapped [in Spain] by other people precisely for *not* going out of my way to lampoon the film's protagonists, but that didn't seem to me to be the right thing to do.[5]

One of the scenes Palmero leaves to speak for itself is the film's closing sequence where an aerial view of the Palmarian basilica provides the backdrop for a roster of individuals canonized by the sect (including Francisco Franco, Patron Saint of Spain, and Saint José Antonio Primo de Rivera, Martyr) and others who have been excommunicated by it, such as viewers of the musical *Jesus Christ Superstar*, Spanish priests engaged with workers' rights, and Cardinal Tarancón, primate of Spain from 1969 to 1981 (Palmero, 1986b, pp. 130–1).

The dislike of *Manuel y Clemente* among Spanish film critics was general, but the exact source of their discontent was more varied and ambiguous. *ABC*'s reviewer believed the film to be sacrilegious and offensive to even the most casual of Catholics, whilst *Diario 16*'s opined that the film's satirical intent failed on account of an inadequate production budget.[6] This consensual yet contradictory critical response finds a parallel in the uncertain place accorded religion in the Spanish constitution of 1978. The position adopted by the constitution is far removed from that of the regime, which had instituted the 'broadest assortment of religious regulations seen in any twentieth-century Western state' (Payne, 1984, p. 185). Nevertheless, it stops short of removing the Roman Catholic Church from the constitutional equation of national identity. Paragraph three of Article 16 states that:

> There shall be no State religion. The public authorities shall take the religious beliefs of Spanish society into account and shall in consequence *maintain appropriate co-operation with the Catholic Church* and the other confessions.
>
> (emphasis added)

If it is allowed that terms such as 'the state' and 'public authorities' are essentially synonymous, it can be seen that the two clauses of this paragraph flatly contradict each other. As well as reflecting the adversarial forces which must have been at work in the elaboration of the constitution, this semantic vacillation also underscores the problematic position of the religious issue in contemporary Spain. Twenty years after its promulgation, the constitution has been defended as valid in every particular, a fact which suggests, furthermore, that the ambiguities it enshrines also continue to be an important part of Spanish culture and society today.[7] If the disquiet produced by *Manuel y Clemente* was due in part to its trumpeting of these ambiguities, it seems fair to suggest that the film will remain relevant in a present moment where a degree of obfuscation about the place of the church in Spanish identity is carefully maintained.

Although sects have been pursued since the constitution was ratified, by bodies such as the government-backed Committee for the Study of Religious Sects (Rodríguez, 1997, pp. 19–35), the new laws on freedom of worship were sufficiently liberal to allow all manner of alternative religions, cults, and sects to take root in Spain in the late 1970s and early 1980s. A significant literature has grown up around these non-Catholic confessions, often focused on the dangers and challenges they represent for the vulnerable sectors of Spanish society (Rodríguez, 1997; Pinto, 1998; Vidal Manzanares, 1995 and 1998). Within Spain, experts on sects have tended to read them as by-products of a deregulated secular consumer society (Rodríguez, 1997, p. 399). Stacked up on the shelves of the Belief System Superstore, Rodríguez identifies a vast array of groups including the scientologists, Jehovah's Witnesses, the Moonies, Soka Gakkai, practitioners of Heavy Yoga, Tierra Nueva, Nueva Acrópolis, and Edelweiss. Rodríguez estimates that between them the sects may have as many as 500 000 followers in Spain. In 1989, the Jehovah's Witnesses alone claimed to have a Spanish membership numbering 71 471. These figures underscore the relevance of an attention to sects within cultural studies of democratic Spain. The writer of the prologue to Rodríguez's study compares the author's enterprise to the uncovering in the United States of the Watergate affair. Rodríguez himself goes on to assert that a significant number of politicians and university lecturers in democratic Spain have come under the sway of the Moonies and the scientologists. The perceived threat from these groups is sufficient that members of the official commission set up to study them have at various times been assigned police protection (Rodríguez, 1997, 19–35).

Whilst studies such as Rodríguez's make for compelling reading, like the critical responses within Spain to *Manuel y Clemente*, they show an unwillingness to conjoin an investigation of the social consequences of religious diversity with a socio-political historical perspective. In studies of the sects in Spain, Franco is scarcely mentioned and the continuities between *nacionalcatolicismo* and the continuing power exercised in Spain by the Roman Catholic Church are collapsed into oblique references to a classic or traditional religion. Many of the features which Rodríguez pinpoints in order to distinguish potentially harmful organizations, which he calls *sectas delictivas* (criminal sects), from innocuous non-Catholic religions, are also characteristics which might have been used to describe aspects of the Francoist regime. If sects exploit personality control, persecution of deviance, the imposition of uniform opinion and the fetishisation of arms to control their adepts, so did Franco to establish his regime. But these sorts of parallels would lead one to the conclusion that Francoism itself was a large-scale criminal sect, and thus Rodríguez avoids making them by simply ignoring the past. It is unsurprising, then, that the Palmarian sect, in existence well in advance of Franco's death, should receive only the most cursory mention in *El poder de las sectas*.

In order to understand why a sect as reactionary as the Palmarian one prospered at the intersection between dictatorship and democracy, it is important to take stock of the fact that in the latter half of the regime, Franco's crusading brand of *nacionalcatolicismo* had itself become divorced from influential currents within the mainstream of the Roman Catholic Church in Spain. Although it has become customary to presume that there existed a perfect union between church and state from the beginning to the end of the regime, as José Manuel Cuenca Toribio notes (1989, pp. 146–8), the relationship between the two had become somewhat strained and dislocated during the reigns of John XXIII (1958–63) and Paul VI (1963–78). Indeed, Paul VI was labelled 'The Communist Pope' by certain elements among Franco's keenest supporters (Payne, 1984, p. 194). Paul VI's reformist programme (the continuation and consolidation of the Second Vatican Council inaugurated by his predecessor) and his unfriendly encyclicals produced a virulent strain of right-wing anticlericalism towards the end of the regime. Critical statements from the 'Communist' Pope had given the left-wing hierarchy and younger priests (increasingly significant as Franco's supporters were depleted by death) the authority to take up the rights of the poor and to express solidarity with the Catholic workers' groups, which, despite the regime's efforts to contain them, had assumed a political role. Ironically, it was Franco's own decision to exempt the clergy from laws pertaining to detainment and censorship which gave the priests and bishops the opportunity to turn against their former ally. Much to the chagrin of the regime, under John XXIII, the Vatican ceased referring to the events of 1936–39 as a 'crusade' and for the first time used instead the term, 'war' (Cooper, 1975, p. 28). In his biography of the dictator, Paul Preston describes Franco's complete bewilderment in the face of the left-wing realignment adopted by the same church which he felt owed its salvation to him (1995, pp. 736–37).[8]

The Second Vatican Council had stressed the need for aperture within the church. This aperture was something that Franco was unable to countenance within the machinery of government and so he simply ignored the reforms within the same church to which he had tethered his state. Stanley Payne suggests that the regime 'sustained its traditional national Catholic identity to its dying day, continuing on frequent public occasions to reaffirm its own peculiar theology, as if the position of the Roman Catholic Church in general had not changed' (1984, p. 207). Like the founders and followers of the Palmarian sect, then, Franco took refuge in a nostalgic and fossilized form of a creed which had always been a partner of convenience, in any case. In the General's Pronunciamiento of 1936, religion had not even been mentioned among the future dictator's plan for national salvation (Cooper, 1975, p. 6). In the second half of the regime, certain sectors within the same institution which had served as a fig leaf for Franco's brutalities and atrocities reinvented themselves so that by the 1970s 'The Church had become the regime's number one domestic political problem' (Payne, 1984, p. 206). The special prison in Zamora for offenders inspired by Vatican II (the *carcel concordatoria*) bulged with dissident priests who had identified themselves with nationalist identities in the Basque Country and Catalonia and with the plight of the underclass in the south of Spain (where Gregorio XVII's alternative Holy See would later emerge). By the time Carrero Blanco (Franco's most likely successor) was murdered by ETA in 1973, angry protesters were calling for Cardinal Tarancón, then the leader of the church in Spain, to be executed by firing squad (Payne, 1984, p. 205). Those who had formerly been the chief political advocates of the church hierarchy had become its most bitter opponents.

If the Palmar de Troya sect is a fossil, then, it is an imitation of the already fossilized *nacionalcatolicismo* which was the official belief system for the entire duration of the regime. Therefore, representations of the sect, in *La de Troya en el Palmar* and *Manuel y Clemente*, for instance, constitute an unsettling mirror parody of the theology of dictatorship which lasted into the 1960s and 1970s. Since it traces events across the imaginary borderline between dictatorship and democratic transition, *Manuel y Clemente* is especially troubling. It situates within the time span of the regime the origination of a reactionary theology, which could only have come about in response to the threat posed by a more populist, more liberal church. The film's documentary chronology also underscores the discontinuity between the pace of religious and political evolution, an uncomfortable proposition, perhaps, for a new wave of government (the PSOE elected in 1982) which 'assumed the identity of leader of a muted ... anticlericalism' (Payne, 1984, p. 214). As has already been noted, however, the film's unpopularity was bipartisan. If it was unpopular with the left for hinting at the role of the church in accelerating political evolution, it was unpopular with the right on account of its satirical portrait of the mercenary partnership between the church and the right-wing government. The subtitle originally envisaged for the film (dropped in the actual production) was 'I'll Get the Money, You Look After the Visions' (Palmero, 1986b, unnumbered). Even without the subtitle, the film's dialogue emphasizes that it was the effective interplay between Manuel's financial talents and Clemente's gifts for mystical drama which lent success to the sect (and to the regime which it unintentionally parodies). The artful combination of money and mysticism also harks back to the fortuitous coming together in 1953 of the legitimization from ecclesiastical and political quarters which was to give the regime a new lease of life. In August of 1953 a Concordat was signed between the Spanish state and the Vatican. One month later an agreement on economic and military aid was reached with the United States. The Palmarian Vatican, and the two films based on its evolution, play out in fast-forward the course of church–state relations through the dying days of the regime and into the more recent past. The sect's existence serves as a reminder of 'A past which remains very close to us chronologically even if it has already become very distant in the public imagination' (Cuenca Toribio, 1989, p. 166). Such a reminder was never likely to be popular in a country where it was and still is rare to discuss the past, either in public or on the big screen.

By considering the historical, social and cultural context which gave rise to the Palmarian sect in Spain, we have seen that as part of their bequest to their democratic successors, Franco and his regime left behind at least two currents of religious practice: the one a nostalgic fossilized political instrument, the other, at least initially, a more progressive focus of social antagonism.[9] Like Franco's macabre mausoleum at the Valley of the Fallen, the Palmar de Troya Vatican can justifsiably be regarded as a living monument to Francoism since it enshrines the petrified form of Catholicism which the dictator had institutionalized during his regime. This was the achievement of orthopraxy through the enforcement of orthodoxy, remembered by one writer as 'the monolithic religious structure ... which measured and quantified everything' (Tusquets, 1985, p. 7). Since Franco's Catholicism was in essence an authoritarian tool used for ideological control, it bears comparison with the creed of scientific atheism which thrived under Stalin in the former USSR. Just as the Soviets enforced rational atheism with the determination of religious zealots, so the Francoists instituted an official Catholicism with the calculating expedience of mercenary Bolsheviks.

Arguably, in both cases, the net result of the carefully planned conflation of ideology and religion may have been the same: an ethical vacuum feeding on the inadmissible schizophrenic division between professed and actual beliefs.

The Russian novelist, Mikhail Bulgakov, a survivor of the Stalinist terror, foresaw that political perversion of religion would leave Russians vulnerable to any quack or charlatan who offered them a scheme to bridge the gap between policed atheism and a more intimate agnosticism. In *The Master and Margarita* (1997), the black magician Woland and his demonic retinue find easy prey among the already brainwashed denizens of Moscow. The novel's central character, John the Homeless (Ivan Bezdomny), is lost in an ethical and relativistic nomansland where it is impossible to figure out any distinction between good and evil. Written somewhat later than Bulgakov's novel, Juan Goytisolo's *Juan sin Tierra* (1975) features a similarly dispossessed Spanish protagonist. Where Ivan Bezdomny loses his ethical co-ordination on account of Stalinism, Juan the Landless loses his in the face of Francoist *nacionalcatolicismo*. Perhaps the Russian novel is more pertinent to this discussion, however, since it underlines the eventual vulnerability to a black market belief system which dictatorship theology produces in its victims. The recent flourishing in Russia of sects and cults is readily connected with the 70 years of enforced Soviet atheism, yet students of sects in Spain seem reluctant to make a connection between the same phenomenon and the country's subjection to four decades of phoney religion (*see*, for example, Rodríguez, 1997, p. 51).

In their temperament, *La de Troya en el Palmar*, *Manuel y Clemente*, and *Niño Nadie* are reminiscent of *The Master and Margarita*, a novel which has often been described as cinematic. Like Bulgakov's novel, these films approach sects, charlatans and religious quackery not only as effects of an immediate social malaise but also as historical symptoms which have their roots in past oppression. Borau's anonymous child is left without an identity when his father abandons parental responsibilities in order to become the disciple of a fake professor who is himself duped out of his savings by a secret Madrid sect dedicated to the worship of pagan deities. The contemporary setting of Borau's film suggests that the child's anonymity is the result of a postmodern society breaking down into a morass of featureless relativism. However, the anonymous baby's parents were raised in the past and the sect which is at the core of their drama is, like the Palmarian one, as much an historical symptom as the product of a deregulated spiritual market-place. Niño Nadie, then, is not only a child of the present but also the son of Juan sin Tierra and a grandson of Gregorio XVII, a papal reincarnation of the General's *nacionalcatolicismo*.

Acknowledgements

My thanks are due for the generous help I was given at the Biblioteca Nacional, the Filmoteca, and the Ministerio de Educación y Cultura in

Madrid as well as to my colleagues in the sub-faculty of Spanish at Oxford University and to the editors for bibliographical references.

Notes

1. The origins and growth of the sect are detailed by Goméz Burón and Martín Alonso (1976), and by Barrios and Garrido Conde (1976). A more recent study by Francisco Alonso-Fernández (1993) recounts the same details more concisely and also studies El Palmar de Troya's record-breaking stigmatizations.
2. Of the 17 films directed by Zabalza, all but two were made during the regime. Alongside thrillers and *Paella* Westerns, Zabalza also made *El milagro del cante* (1966) and *Divorcio a la andaluza* (1968) which dealt respectively with the controversial subjects of the exploitation of Spanish culture by tourism and divorce. These early films, a musical and a comedy, anticipate the technique also used in *La de Troya en el Palmar* of incorporating awkward subjects and social satire in an apparently formulaic genre.
3. Trenas, M. A. 1986: Estreno con carácter nacional del filme *Manuel y Clemente*. *La Vanguardia*, 29 May; Palmero, J. 1986c: Letter to the Spanish Minister of Culture, 9 April.
4. Quoted in Flores, F. 1986: La cinematográfica historia del 'papa' Clemente. *La Vanguardia*, 31 May.
5. Quoted in Bayón, M. 1986: Manuel y Clemente: Dos pícaros treparon de Sevilla al cielo. *Cambio 16*, 9 June, p. 139.
6. *See* Crespo, P. 1986: Review of *Manuel y Clemente*. *ABC*, 28 May; Marinero, F. 1986: *Manuel y Clemente*, la película del Palmar. *Diario 16*, 1 June.
7. Anonymous, 1998: Los 'padres' de la Constitución defienden su plena vigencia. *El Pais Digital*, 27 November.
8. In the eyes of anthropologists like Stanley Brandes (1976), the role of the church had changed so dramatically in the latter half of the regime that it was even possible to analyse it as a catalyst in the process of secularization.
9. Notwithstanding his role in the crusade against so-called Communism, many observers are agreed that under the papacy of John Paul II (1978–) the Roman Catholic Church has returned to the more conservative stance of Pius XI (1922–39) and Pius XII (1939–58). John Paul II has spoken out against democratization within the church, insisting that 'The truth is a gift from God [and] is not revealed through democratic votes and opinion polls' (quoted in Willey, D. 1998: Despatch on Vatican in *Newsdesk*. London: *BBC World Service*. 21 November). Theologian Hans Küng suggests that John Paul II 'Always takes an extremist stand. ... He has a certain paradigm from which he considers everything. Basically, I believe it is the paradigm of the medieval church, with a great papacy and with all that makes Rome great. [He] is a rather contradictory person who asks for religious freedom in the world but who represses it within the Catholic church, who speaks out for justice, but who does not give justice in the Catholic church in many ways' (quoted in Ewart, E. 1998: *Absolute truth: smile of history*. London: *BBC Television*, 4 October). In so far as the hierarchy of the Spanish church have followed John Paul II's lead, such attitudes will clearly have had repercussions for the evolution of post-Francoist Catholicism in Spain. The Pope's most recent anti-democratic comments figured in his address to Austrian bishops (Pope John Paul II, 1998: Discorso del Santo Padre Giovanni Paolo II agli Ecc.mi Presuli della conferenza episcopale dell'Austria in visita 'Ad limina Apostolorum'. *Vatican Daily Bulletin*, 20 November).

References

ALONSO-FERNANDEZ, F. 1993: *Estigmas, levitaciones y éxtasis: de Sor Magdalena a El Palmar de Troya*. Madrid: Temas de Hoy.
BARRIOS, M., and GARRIDO-CONDE, M. T. 1976: *El apasionante misterio del Palmar de Troya*. Barcelona: Planeta.
BORAU, J. L. 1998 (film): *Niño Nadie*.
BRANDES, S. 1976: The Priest as Agent of Secularization in Rural Spain. In Aceves, J. B., Hansen, E. C., and Levitas, G. (eds), *Economic transformation and steady state values: essays in the ethnography of Spain*. Flushing, NY: Queens College Press, 22–9.
BULGAKOV, M. 1997: *The Master and Margarita*. London: Picador.
BUÑUEL, L. 1969 (film): *La Voie lactée*.
BUÑUEL, L. 1994: *My last breath*. London: Vintage.
Constitución española. 1979. Madrid: Oficina de Información Diplomática, Ministerio de Asuntos Exteriores.
CARDINAL FATHER ISIDORE MARIA [alias ALONSO, M.] 1980: Pope Gregory XVII: short biographical sketch. Palmar de Troya Web Site: Geocities.com.
COOPER, N. B. 1975: *Catholicism and the Franco Regime*. Beverly Hills, Calif.: Sage Publications.
CUENCA TORIBIO, J. M. 1989: *Relaciones iglesia-estado en la España contemporánea*. Madrid: Alhambra.
GOMEZ BURON, J. and MARTIN ALONSO, A. 1976: *El enigma de El Palmar de Troya*. Barcelona: Personas.
GOYTISOLO, J. 1975: *Juan sin Tierra*. Barcelona: Seix Barral.
MONTERDE, J. E. 1993: *Veinte años del cine español 1973–1992: Un cine bajo la paradoja*. Barcelona: Paidos.
PALMERO, J. 1986a (film): *Manuel y Clemente*.
—— 1986b: *Manuel y Clemente: Yo el dinero y tú el vidente* [unpublished script].
—— 1986c: Letter to the Spanish Minister of Culture, 9 April.
PAYNE, S. 1984: *Spanish Catholicism: an historical overview*. Madison, Wis.: University of Wisconsin Press.
PINTO, R. 1998: *Las sectas al descubierto*. Madrid: CCS.
PRESTON, P. 1995: *Franco: a biography*. London: Fontana.
RODRIGUEZ, P. 1997: *El poder de las sectas*. Barcelona: Grupo Zeta.
TUSQUETS, E. 1985: *Love is a solitary game*. London: John Calder.
VAN BAALEN, J. K. 1956: *The chaos of cults: a study in present day isms*. London: Pickering and Inglis.
VIDAL, N. 1986: Review of Manuel y Clemente. *La Vanguardia*, 5 June.
VIDAL MANZANARES, C. 1995: *El desafío de las sectas*. Madrid: San Pablo.
—— 1998: *Nuevo diccionario de sectas y ocultismo*. Pamplona: Verbo Divino.
ZABALZA, J. M. 1984 (film): *La de Troya en el Palmar*.

|12|

Spectacle, trauma and violence in contemporary Spain

CRISTINA MOREIRAS MENOR

The historical period that witnessed the installation of democracy in Spain has been the subject of much debate in recent years. One of the fundamental questions that has been asked regarding the transition from dictatorship to representative democracy is whether this process implies a continuity with the prior Franco regime, or whether it is founded on a complete break with the political, social and cultural conventions of the past. Twenty years after the death of Franco this question remains relevant to the work of cultural analysts and literary critics to the extent that contemporary cultural production continues to examine the bases of democratic freedom upon which Spanish contemporaneity was established. The present study will investigate certain ideas that have surfaced in Spanish cultural production over the last 20 years and which, in my view, take on new cultural (and psychosocial) meanings as they address the ways in which the contemporary subject reflects on the present and on history. My interest is in exploring certain concepts underlying the cultural construction of history in literature and film, particularly the ways in which Spanish history is narrated following the death of Franco. How is the recent history of the Civil War and of the Franco dictatorship presented in the cultural production of today? How does the memory of a traumatic historical period and its abrupt end figure in cultural representation? Why do important areas of 1980s cultural production ignore this past, while others address the recovery of such memory? In response to these initial questions, I propose to explore three concepts that I consider fundamental to Spain's cultural trajectory: spectacle, trauma and violence. Although all three concepts point to the continuing open cultural wound of the post-Franco years, they also mark important differences between the cultural representation of the first decade of democracy and that produced after 1992. A fundamental difference distinguishes the 1980s from the 1990s: the eighties are marked by a collective desire to integrate Spain and its people into Europe. The nineties, by contrast, are characterized by the absence of such collective designs. Absence, negativity, and the lack of a utopian outlook define post-Olympic Spain. If cultural production of the eighties constituted, in the words of Eloy Fernández Porta, 'a happy marriage with the government project' (1996, p. 35), that of the nineties is marked by a total absence of state, governmental, or global European-style projects other than that of monetary integration.

In order to examine how the contemporary subject experiences the present, this essay will consider a range of subject positions or narrative perspectives that are privileged in recent cultural production. Writers and film-makers as diverse as Juan Goytisolo, Bernardo Atxaga, Ray Loriga, José Angel Mañas, Juan Madrid, Alejandro Amenábar, Pedro Almodóvar, Lidia Falcón, Bigas Luna, and Carlos Saura broach reality and the violence of the everyday from three key perspectives: as distant spectators from without, as traumatized witnesses from within, and as abject subjects at the centre of the crudest and most terrifying folds of that violence. The sections below examine the articulation and cultural significance of each of these subject positions in turn. As we shall see, all three positions – or modes of confronting the real – are clearly grounded in affliction, and inscribe the logics of a wounded culture, a culture in shock.

Spectacle

In the early years of post-dictatorship in Spain an overriding demand to spend and consume emerges, not only as a result of the important economic upturn (itself based on image), but also due to a profound shift in the relationship between subject and object. In its desire for full integration into Europe, Spain itself becomes an object of consumption: a tourist destination. Now completely integrated into the market-place, the Spanish subject adopts a new self-image and, as a consequence, the relationship between the individual and his or her own image takes on the kind of privileged status identified by Fredric Jameson as characteristic of postmodern culture in general. I am referring to the three main features which, according to Jameson, condition the relationship established between the contemporary (or postmodern) subject and his/her experience: a privileging of the culture of image and of simulacrum, the lack of historicity, and the waning of affect (Jameson, 1991, chapter 1). Image and appearance are now of paramount importance for a citizenry whose collective aim is to sell itself to Europe. Thus, Spain unreservedly embraces the culture of spectacle, while focusing on a dehistoricized present. In an ideological move to eliminate a past that situated Spain in a position of inferiority with respect to the rest of the world, new models of identification – or signs of identity – are adopted for the newly established democracy.

Dehistoricization, simulacrum, and profound immersion in the superficiality of appearance – key features of what has come to be known as the society of the spectacle (Debord, 1983) – allow the Spanish subject of the early post-dictatorship to articulate new signs of identity. Total identification with the world of consumption and spectacle disassociates Spain from its recent past of repression, silence and homogeneity. This 'new Spain born from the tomb of Franquismo that aspires to identify with the symbols of international mass culture' (Subirats, 1995, p. 12), is fully integrated into the society of spectacle. What we confront now is a gaze which locates the subject at the border between subject and object. Caught up in a culture of image and appearance, the individual begins a process of self-fetishization, representing himself or herself as alienated from the spectacle being contemplated and is, at the same time, positioned as his or her own object of desire. The individual becomes a subject of contemplation – a spectator assuming a position of total passivity in the face of reality. Such a stance finds parallels in the following statement by Ray Loriga: 'If an enemy army invaded the country it would have to reach my can of beer before I worry about it' (1994, p. 94). Reality, now conceived exclusively as representation and spectacle, no longer has an impact; indifference becomes the characteristic position of these years.

In contrast to the final decades of Spanish dictatorial history, and through full insertion into the logics of the society of spectacle, processes of identification are now constructed according to the rubric of an ostensibly non-ideological and fundamentally dehistoricized depoliticization. The Spain of repression and censorship becomes the Spain of excess, in defiance of the Francoist maxim – 'We have not come to pamper ourselves nor to enjoy this peace that many of the bourgeoisie love' – quoted in Carmen Martín Gaite's *Usos amorosos de la posguerra española* (1987, p. 23). The well-documented *movida* (the youth culture movement active in the 1980s, particularly in Madrid, Barcelona, Bilbao, and Vigo) was the epiphany of the new culture of spectacle, opening up new and important spaces for the construction and representation of identities.

Trauma

If the cultural production of the early years of Spanish democracy is dominated, on the one hand, by the culture of spectacle (as in the work of Ana Rossetti, Eduardo Mendicutti, Pedro Almodóvar, Ouka Lele and Lidia Falcón, among many others) and, on the other, by the expression of identity politics (as demonstrated by the work of Rosa Montero, Esther Tusquets, Soledad Puértolas and Lourdes Ortiz, to name but a few), there also exists another area of cultural production that posits the present not simply as a privileged moment for representation, but more specifically as part of a process of historical becoming. These texts view the present as one moment in a continuous process of historical transformation, and offer an interpretation of the present through the recovery of historical memory. What is at stake here is the notion of Spain as a national entity – as in Atxaga's *Obabakoa* (1989), *El hombre solo* (1994), *Esos cielos* (1996) – or the subject as a social entity constructed on the basis of historical essence as in Vázquez Montalbán's *El pianista* (1986). Moreover, they are examples of a cultural production structured around the idea of trauma as it is understood by Cathy Caruth (following Freud) (1996, p. 5). In this sense trauma is conceived not as a symptom of the unconscious, but rather as a symptom of history; the traumatized subject either carries the weight of an intolerable history or is trapped both in the past and in the present, becoming the symptom of a history that the subject cannot possess in its totality. Motivated by the desire to perceive an origin or originary cause, this subject desperately seeks to possess history by narrating it, unaware, however, that the unveiling of a 'traumatic origin' through the narration of history is ultimately impossible. In the words of Baudrillard, 'we shall never experience the primal scene, but at every moment we experience its prolongation and its expiation' (1996, p. 2). In this sense these historical narratives reveal not only that the origin is traumatic (an accepted fact), but that trauma is also present in the very act of narration that confronts the impossibility of unveiling origin. These texts demonstrate that whilst trauma is always displaced, dislocated and symbolized at the margins of the narrative edifice, it will always also remain essentially inscribed within it.

Authors such as Bernardo Atxaga, Antonio Muñoz Molina, Lourdes Ortíz, Manuel Vázquez Montalbán, Juan Benet, Juan Goytisolo, Juan Marsé, Jorge Semprúm, Luis Llamazares, and Alejandro Gándara approach Spanish reality from this historiographic (and therefore traumatic) position. Their works appear to reflect on reality from the place of trauma; they do not address reality as an attempt to 'cure it' and therefore to disposses themselves of it, but rather present trauma as the cause of an apparently unrelated contemporary situation. Such authors think Spanish democratic society in the light of its historical continuity with Franquismo and, in particular, with the Civil War. Their narratives – *El pianista* (Vázquez Montalbán, 1986), *Beatus Ille* (Muñoz Molina, 1986), *Coto Vedado* (Juan Goytisolo, 1985), and *Cristales* (Gándara, 1997), to name only a few – uncover and give narrative structure to a desire to consider the past as a direct yet absent cause of the contemporary social and cultural configuration. Not unlike Benjamin's Angel of History, they maintain that the past must direct its flight toward the future, while dragging along the debris that the storm of progress piles at its feet (Benjamin, 1985, p. 257). The traumatic event is therefore ever present; it is the catastrophe of the moment. Through their idealistic search for the origin of the affliction, these texts show that history and contemporaneity are structured by trauma and its absent moment of origin. Montalbán expresses this idea masterfully in *El pianista* through a narrative reflection in which the Civil War, the key moment in the protagonist's life, remains unnarrated. Whilst the text conveys the desire to narrate the history of Alberto the pianist, his history is quickly forgotten amid a complex narrative displacement of characters and situations. The narrative begins in the present when Alberto enters the lives of three couples facing the 'horror' of democracy (disease, absence of meaning, lack of political drive, and the absence of a state power against which to direct affect) and ends with what the discursive chain has constructed as the origin of this catastrophe: the Civil War, the unspeakable primary scene of the protagonist's historical process of becoming.

Violence

Parallel to this preoccupation with history for the historical subject (identity), and for the historical construction of Spanish subjectivities (nations), another type of literary and filmic production emerges alongside the works of the culture of spectacle. The young writers of the 1990s – sons and daughters of the 'fucking Marxists and hippies' whom José Angel Mañas blames for the current situation (1994, p. 67) – produce texts that not only reject any trace of history but also fail to articulate a desire that might serve as a driving force of their narratives. Paradoxically these texts seem to lack the desire to narrate for they neither tell stories nor relate life histories. Instead, they describe urban cartographies, depict acts and events, and record – much like a video camera – the happenings of the present moment. The gaze of the abject subject of this moment is grounded in the terror produced by the subject's realization that the sense of dislocation comes from within the self (the uncanny). Despite this estrangement, however, the excess of information characterizing multimedia culture has fostered in the contemporary subject a sense of certaintly that she or he will possess the truth. The gaze focuses on a present characterized by its own isolation and on the 'foreignness' of historical experience. It is a horrified gaze that hides its own dread through a fascination with violence and a perpetual acting-out designed to conceal the absence of meaning and eliminate any possibility of demonstrating affect. Affect is now represented as an apathy that becomes intolerable due to its inability to express itself. Hence indifference and the representation of this (vicariously experienced) affliction predominate. The subject represented in the cultural production of the post-Olympic 1990s is dispossessed of will-power and, following the Nietzschean analogy, dispossessed of originary affect. Moreover, the subject is lost amid the violence generated by the erosion of the state which coincided in Spain with the dawn of the society of spectacle and of the market-place.

In order to understand this influential literary production which is, after all, the literature that contemporary youth consumes, it is important to remember that Spain is now fully integrated into Europe and located within a transnational postmodernity. In these post-Olympic years triumphant celebration in the wake of 1992 has given way to economic, social and polit-ical realities marked by instability, corruption and violence. While this group of texts does reveal a preoccupation with history (in terms of both the erasure and the recovery of historical memory) it also offers a reflection of reality at its most immediate and most severe. These narrations are driven by concerns that are no longer national (despite sometimes containing tra-ditional Spanish elements, as in Bigas Luna's films and Loriga's novels), nor are they integral to identity formation (sexual, racial, or other kinds). Rather, they focus on the new reality of the 1990s in which 'nationalist loy-alties (or those of any other kind) grow weak to the benefit of other forms of social union' (Juaristi, 1994, p. 47).

Unlike previous modes of narrative production, the common theme of these texts is the difficulty (or the impossibility) of narrating the desire that gives rise to them in the first place. Novels and films such as *Historias del Kronen* (Mañas, 1994), *Mensaka* (Mañas, 1995), *Días contados* (Madrid, 1993), *El día de la bestia* (Alex de la Iglesia, 1995), *Tesis* (Amenábar, 1996) *Plenilunio* (Muñoz Molina, 1997), and *El estrangulador* (Vázquez Montalbán, 1994) inscribe a narrative gaze directed at the horrific under-side of reality, presenting subjects completely lacking in any object of desire. These are primarily urban writers and film-makers bearing witness to the erosion of the state, the end of public life, and even of the Other (in the Lacanian sense), through the representation of a threatening, borderless space which becomes the site for the dispersion both of the group and of the individual. The city of the 1990s becomes a container unable to contain, a building without walls (Jameson, 1994, pp. 156–9) – unable to provide shel-ter, yet at the same time closed in by an overwhelming feeling of restriction – where the abject subject, dispossessed of identity, wanders without trace. In this Spanish city, which at the same time could be located in any part of the world, acts of extreme and senseless violence occur: murders of friends, suicidal behaviour, matricide, gang beatings, serial killings and filmed tor-ture. Characterized by their fast pace, the exclusion of memory as a struc-turing principle, and a disinterest in articulating ideas or identities, these texts emulate the logic of the video-clip in that they portray simple action devoid of affective or intellectual meaning. In contrast to the celebratory happiness and glamour of the 1980s, the affects that dominate here are boredom and discontent. Spectacle and its appearance have been displaced by reality in its excess, by a virtual reality which remains omnipresent in its desperate inaccessibility, and the alienated spectator-subject of the 1980s becomes what Jean Baudrillard has identified elsewhere as the all-knowing actor-subject of representation (Baudrillard, 1996, p. 27). Spanish culture is now characterized by this space of horror and death – an extreme excess of reality – that situates the subject simultaneously inside and out, producing, as Baudrillard would say, a collapse of the signifying process: 'Our culture of meaning is collapsing beneath the excess of meaning, the culture of reality collapsing beneath the excess of reality, the information culture collapsing beneath the excess of information – the sign and reality sharing a single shroud' (1996, p. 17).

The absence of an explicit motivating desire or object in these texts prevents the subject from 'speaking' or from even producing meaning. In my view, this collapse in signification stems from the fact that these texts are engaged in a process of thinking through that 'obscure object of desire' which belongs to the realm of the unspeakable and of the indeterminable. As this object is not comprehended, it cannot be made to mean, nor can it be ordered in history; the narrative is thus rendered unthinkable. It becomes a performance which fills the void produced by the impossibility of discursive signification. Through a hopeless, yet inevitable acting-out, uncomprehended meaning is contained and projected at the very moment it is produced. Consider, for example, the following text from Loriga's *Días extraños*:

> I liked to stay home and watch TV. ... One night Apocalypse Now was on. I had already seen it two or three times in the theater, but I had never brought the war home before. ... I had a half gram and a fridge full of beer. I went down the river in search of Kurtz. Halfway through the movie, I stopped drinking beer and switched to whisky. When Willard got to that damned island, I was as high as a kite. I did my last line and took a long swig out of the bottle. I felt nauseous and then a pain my head. As if they'd shot me in the head. I grabbed a knife from the kitchen. I advanced silently through the jungle with Willard. I was all excited. Like I was happy for the first time. I cut myself on my arms and hands. Not very deep cuts. The blood started to flow. I took off my shirt and rubbed the blood all over my face and chest. I was in my element. I knew it was a war that wouldn't be able to take me. I was tough. Bled like a pig. I was tough and alone. I didn't have to prove anything to anyone. I just wanted to stay there in the middle of the jungle, cut off, piling up silent victories. When I woke up there was blood all over the place. I cleaned up the worst of it, showered, and went to work. The blood on my face was dry like a scab.

> (1994, pp. 81–2)

Loriga's narration of the experience of a solitary subject in his Apocalypse Now home reflects Baudrillard's contention that art (and I would add, culture in general) 'is simply the paradoxical confusion between art and reality, and the aesthetic intoxication that results from them' (1996, p. 29). In this exceptional illustration of acting-out, Loriga contrasts the immediacy of violence in modernity – in this case, the Vietnam War – with its second-hand experience in the 1990s, mediated by video and acted out through a parodied performance of individual heroism and daring. The text reflects on the experience of reality and the (no longer apocalyptic) end of history that inhabits the body of a generation. Contemporary reality is no longer examined through desire, but through the production of acts in which the subject hides fantasies that he cannot sustain. In contrast to the symptom discussed earlier in which desire presents itself as displaced, acting-out permits the subject to dispel such fantasies, not by displacing them, but by transferring them to reality as in the extreme example of the snuff movie, or as demonstrated in such films as *Tesis* (Amenábar, 1996) or *Acción mutante* (Alex de la Iglesia, 1995). However, this transferral does not make the fantasy real. Baudrillard writes:

> Acting-out only expresses the impossibility of the fantasy to remain fantasy by projecting itself in a fictional, chance world for which there is no other motive than this violent opening up to ourselves. Fashioning ourselves in a perfect virtual world so that we can opt for one outside reality. Or even yet, in the case of history, getting rid of incoherence and contradictions in a unique and unpredictable act.

> (1996, p. 35)

Loriga's experience, not unlike the experience of terror presented in snuff movies, is completely outside the real world, while at the same time totally immersed in the most pressing reality.

Due to the absence of an object, or of a driving desire, the subject of the nineties is represented in terms of annihilation rather than construction. Violence, sex, disease, addiction, terror and, above all, boredom, are the affects and drives that dominate this cultural experience. To a certain extent, the subject of the nineties represents the antithesis of the eighties subject. While the eighties subject became willingly immersed in postmodernity, the nineties subject allows us to see postmodernity's most terrifying side.

Spain has had little opportunity to assimilate the abrupt arrival of modernity, and with it, the society of spectacle dominated by modern communications media and the forces of the market-place. Ushered overnight into the postmodern era, Spain emerges as a traumatized and defenceless society – what Mark Seltzer would call a 'wound culture' (1997, p. 4). The society of spectacle and of communications technology exposes the weakened borders of the public sphere. As Amenábar's film *Tesis* illustrates, absolute privacy becomes increasingly threatened, causing the private realm to disappear. The invasion of the private sphere is also illustrated by contemporary culture's fascination with violence, pain, the tortured body, and a history in shock: 'The wound is where private and public cross: the transit-point between the individual and collective, between the body of the individual and the collective body of men' (Seltzer, 1997, p. 25). While this violence is expressed in many ways and reflects a multitude of events, it inevitably points to a continuing open cultural wound.

References

BAUDRILLARD, J. 1996: *The perfect crime*. London: Verso.

BENJAMIN, W. 1985: Theses on the philosophy of history. In Arendt, H. (ed.) *Illuminations*. New York: Schocken Books, 253–64.

CARUTH, C. 1996: *Unclaimed experiences: trauma, narrative, and history*. Baltimore: The John Hopkins University Press.

DEBORD, G. 1983: *Society of the spectacle*. Detroit: Black and Red.

FERNÁNDEZ PORTA, E. 1996: Poéticas del prozac: tres líneas en la novela española de los noventa. *Quimera* 145: 35–9.

JAMESON, F. 1991: *Postmodernism or the cultural logic of late capitalism*. Durham, N.C.: Duke University Press.

—— 1994: *The seeds of time*. New York: Columbia University Press.

JUARISTI, J. 1994: Identidad en la intemperie. In Aranzadi, J., Juarasti, J. and Unzueta, P. (eds) *Autodeterminación. Raza, nación y violencia en el país vasco*. Madrid: El País/Aguilar, 45–61.

LORIGA, R. 1994. *Días extraños*. Madrid: El Europeo & La Tripilación.

MAÑAS, J. A. 1994: *Historias del Kronen*. Madrid: Destino, 1994.

MARTÍN GAITE, C. 1987: *Usos amorosos de la posguerra española*. Barcelona: Anagrama.

SELTZER, M. 1997: Wound culture: trauma in the pathological public sphere. *October* 80, 3–26.

SUBIRATS, E. 1995: *España, miradas fin de siglo*. Madrid: Akal.

P A R T

III

MEDIA: REGULATION, MARKETS, PUBLICS

Introduction

Media issues come in all shapes and sizes, including the following: the constitutional control of the media, media freedoms and the extent of government interference at policy and programme level; whether the media distort/reflect/repackage/mediate reality; whether they enrich or impoverish the consumer's sense of life or are manipulative and ultimately self-serving; deregulation and the prevalence of the free market; the impact of globalization on the ability of nation-states to determine cultural policy. Issues around media in Spain, as elsewhere in a global media environment, are dominated by questions of regulation, ownership, control, choice and diversity. These have become increasingly problematic over the years because of profound social changes: (1) the spread of new diversified media technologies, yet often with highly concentrated forms of ownership; (2) the increase in globalized media access (for example, through the use of the Internet for business and leisure purposes); (3) a greater diversity of values, beliefs, tastes and cultural traditions among national populations, especially in multi-ethnic, multicultural societies. Though responses to these changes have taken various forms (such as civil and legal redress, privacy laws, official watchdogs, non-governmental organizations and self-regulation), they arise by and large in a neo-liberal climate which favours the market and deregulation. Spain is no stranger to these kinds of problems and changes; indeed, the rapid shift from a highly interventionist media landscape under Franco to the current broadly deregulated situation reveals paradoxically that highly politicized and partisan traditions of official government interference refuse to disappear.

Under Francoism, the media (press, news agencies, radio, television, cinema, publishing, as well as public entertainments etc.) were all subject to censorship and political control, including the many privately run operations (especially in radio) which none the less happily cohabited with the state-run media. Before 1975, instances of oppositional pressure for democratic change began to surface in the press (e.g. in publications such as *Cuadernos para el Diálogo, Triunfo, Madrid, Informaciones, Cambio 16*). During the transition period, alongside established papers such as *ABC, La Vanguardia* and *Ya*, we see the emergence of papers such as *El País, Diario 16, El Periódico* and *Interviú* seeking spaces to act as mouthpieces for the newly emerging democratic polity. But only with the accession to power of the PSOE in 1982 do we find the basic structural and financial changes which allow the emergence of a media industry as such along 'neo-liberal', market-oriented, European lines. (And even then, as in the case of Spain's film industry, significant economic and infrastructural change would only really begin to make a serious impact in the 1990s.)

During the 1980s, we witness the gradual dismantling of the old statist/Francoist media operations, the selling off of state-run newspaper chains, the concession of radio licences, the rise of regional television and press groups and the reluctant approval in 1988 by the PSOE government of three new private television channels (Antena 3, Tele 5 and Canal Plus). Indeed, the PSOE was very reluctant to open up the television market, fearful that it would lose control of the political agenda, which a state-run television service virtually guaranteed to the political party in power. All these moves towards media pluralization and 'marketization' tended to encourage major levels of concentration within specific media, plus significant levels of foreign investment in television stations. We also see the emergence in the 1990s of two important Spanish multimedia groups, PRISA and ZETA and the crucial influence of the big banks as major investors in press, television and satellite/cable groups. Of course, one should not underestimate the importance of foreign capital in Spain's media industries: the influence of the American majors in film distribution and multiplex development as well as transnational capital in film financing; the presence of Murdoch interests in Antena 3 and those of Berlusconi, Kirch and foreign banks in Tele 5; French ownership of Canal Plus; German groups such as Springer and Bertelsmann in book publishing; the advertising field dominated by international agencies, etc. Spain's media industries have thus been rapidly thrust into modernity and though a healthy pluralism appears to exist, problems of concentration, globalization, foreign ownership, weak official regulation and government interference (especially in television news and current affairs agenda setting) may not bode well for the future in terms of public accountability, public access, programming diversity and the maintenance of quality and standards.

This section tackles many of the regulatory aspects of the new media environment in Spain. Essays here seek to highlight some of the unresolved tensions and issues, the significant flashpoints which characterize a rapidly evolving media environment. Clearly, notions of regulation and control have to do with processes of power encompassing both governmental policies and laws, editorial interventions (say, in television news management and agenda setting) as well as other processes of cultural reproduction which shape how media discourses operate. In other words, regulation and control are dynamic processes, crucially affected by dominant economic and political forces, yet power is also to some extent dispersed and contestable. In Spain, however (as revealed by the example of digitial television over the last three to four years), the margins for contestation and serious public debate about regulatory issues seem rather limited.

The essays in this section seek to provide insights not only into matters of cultural policy but also cultural politics. The latter depend on processes of struggle between individuals and social groups over meanings and interpretations ascribed to texts and discourses concerning values and tastes as well as forms of identity and subjectivity. In Spain, in a context of market deregulation, entry into the new media arena has its price, with Spanish media consumers increasingly dividing into two distinct classes, those who can afford the new services and those that cannot. Ability to pay thus largely determines the ability to participate in the struggle over meanings and the debates alluded to above over regulation and control. While these processes jockey to impose some form or structure of meanings and values in the field, such discourses are not entirely nor eternally fixed; nor do they offer the last word, but are open to different forms of appropriation. As we shall see, and despite the relatively low levels of awareness, articulacy and leverage of Spaniards as consumers/audiences of media services, the rearticulation of meanings and the contestation of official versions of events can play a key role in the functioning of cultural and media politics in contemporary Spain.

|13|

Public accountability and private interests: regulation and the flexible media regime in Spain

PHILIP DEACON

The purpose of this essay is to examine the changing situation of the press, radio and television in Spain as they responded to government measures to make the media more accountable, setting the process in the context of the country's political, economic and social evolution in the last third of the twentieth century.

The legacy of Francoism

On his death in November 1975, General Franco bequeathed to posterity a media system subservient to government diktat: two television channels directly under state control, an array of radio stations, mainly state-run but some in the hands of the church, and a little-read press, emasculated by censorship and government directives, and controlled by sympathetic interest groups, monarchists (*ABC* and *La Vanguardia*), the Roman Catholic Church (*Ya*), and the state's own political organization, the *Movimiento* (*Arriba*). Given the complementary mechanism of censorship, disciplinary measures to ensure conformity were hardly necessary in the early years of Franco's rule. Prior approval of all printed materials, imposed in 1938 during the Civil War, gave way under foreign pressure in 1966 to a much-trumpeted, though minimal, freedom, but publications still had to be deposited with the authorities before appearing on the street, allowing for subsequent confiscation and possible punishment; and the state held the trump card in reserving the right to deny companies permission to operate.

The serious monthly journal *Cuadernos para el Diálogo* acted after 1963 as a safety valve for democrats, though constantly suffering from censorship, and in the final decade of Francoism the weekly magazines *Triunfo* and *Destino* operated on the edge of the permissible, subject to censorship, fines and suspensions (up to four months) which entailed uncertain operating conditions, diminished revenues and a loss of face with the buying public. Self-censorship and government directives, particularly at moments of political crisis, kept circulation figures low, while radio and especially television, funded via advertising and government subsidy, provided apparently unpaid-for sources of news and entertainment. Televisión Española (TVE), the state monopoly in television, was a mouthpiece of government, providing opportunities for apparatchiks (a subsequent Prime Minister, Adolfo Suárez, was Director-General, 1969–73), while political conformity favoured career prospects in an organization not subject to normal commercial principles and whose purpose was to keep the population compliant, largely ignorant of internal affairs and entertained by a diet of sport and popular imports.

Commercial vitality, accompanied by market-oriented efficiency, led to the launching of new-style press ventures in the 1970s. The weekly magazine *Cambio 16* started up in 1971, working within the prevailing restrictions on coverage (economy and society, though not politics) but reflecting international values in terms of design and presentation. The company which would launch *El País* in 1976 (PRISA) was set up four years earlier but denied permission to publish by a suspicious, ailing regime.

The media during the political transition: 1976–1982

Once political horizons opened up on Franco's death in November 1975, and more especially on Adolfo Suárez's accession as Prime Minister in July 1976, state regulation yielded ground to market forces driven by the population's desire to be informed. The governmental relaxation of restrictions allowed daily newspapers in Catalan (*Avui*, 1976) and Basque (*Deia*, 1977), as well as new titles in Castilian, notably *Diario 16* (1977) and *El Periódico* (1978). Consumer enthusiasm led to the establishing of a variety of news-oriented publications, weekly rather than daily, all driven by a desire to explain the new political situation.

State-run television and radio served new masters, seemingly intent on manipulating the media in their political favour, while ostensibly focused on achieving democratization. The new, non-regime press reflected majority opinion, providing a political lead and drawing the state-owned media in its train. The lifting of restrictions on areas subject to moral, in particular church-inspired, censorship, led to the appearance of *Interviú* (1976), a magazine of glossy pin-ups and sensationalist, investigative reporting, and foundation stone of the future Zeta group. A society liberated from overt repression boosted *Interviú*'s circulation as well as fuelling the launch of other similar publications, many imitating, or versions of, tried and tested models from abroad.

As in other areas, the Constitution of 1978 established ground rules for the new media. Article 20 guaranteed freedom of expression and expressly prohibited censorship, while its third clause foreshadowed a law to regulate the organization and parliamentary control of broadcasting, indicating a wish to reflect pluralism of various kinds, including regionalism. The affirmation in article 38 that Spain was an 'economía de mercado' (free market economy), was balanced by the second clause of article 128 which allowed government to 'reservar al sector público recursos o servicios esenciales' (reserve for the public sector essential resources or services), without specifying further.

As far as state-run radio and television were concerned, the major regulatory instrument followed a year later (January 1980) when the *Estatuto de la radio y la televisión* (Radio and Television Statute) became law. Radio and television were declared essential public services and mechanisms were set up to supervise them. A parliamentary committee (*Comisión Parlamentaria*) would exercise general oversight (article 26), while a 12-member Administrative Board (*Consejo de Administración*) would directly control Radiotelevisión Española (RTVE) in conjunction with the director-general, advising on appointments, finance, advertising, and day-to-day administration. Members of the board would be selected in proportion to parliamentary representation and hence appear to reflect the will of the electorate. The director-general would be appointed for four years, the same duration as parliament, though might be replaced earlier if a general election was brought forward, reflecting the underlying assumption that the post was political in a party-related sense. Nevertheless, the first post-Statute appointee was agreed between government (UCD, Unión de Centro Democrático) and the main opposition party (PSOE, Partido Socialista Obrero Español), in accordance with the consensus policies favoured at the time.

Having benefited from a pro-democratic, even impatiently progressive press, Adolfo Suárez's government hesitantly proclaimed its market principles in deciding to sell off the state-owned newspaper titles. Regionally based papers, dependent on local advertising revenue, found initial buyers in regional business interests, but most ended up as part of nation-wide groups which increasingly proliferated (Correo, Prensa Ibérica, Zeta). A few titles closed through lack of commercial interest, whereas others, notably the football-centred *Marca*, could be relaunched by new owners in the hope of finding or creating a new readership capable of sustaining them commercially. The disposal process was slow (1977–84).

The PSOE in power: 1982–1996

Whereas the UCD governments (1977–82) successfully managed the transition to democracy, major economic change only began in the 1980s after the socialists came to power and Spain's commitment to European integration focused attention on the country's relations with its neighbours. PSOE policy combined cautious, social democratic principles allied to monetarist economics, fuelled by a desire to innovate and release creative energies. Old established daily newspapers (*ABC, La Vanguardia*) felt the effects of competition and proceeded to restructure. Many weeklies, born in the enthusiasm of political euphoria accompanying the shift from dictatorship to democracy, disappeared as the population faced the harsher economic climate of the 1980s, with politics less all-absorbing now that a modern constitutional system was in place. Market-driven creative talents, focused on developing existing trends or inventing new ones, launched magazines catering for special interests such as consumerism, hobbies, self-betterment, sport. Given the economic significance of Spain's incorporation into Europe, experienced players from outside (Bertelsmann, Hachette) bought into or launched Spanish equivalents of formulae successful elsewhere.

Whereas the print media adapted to European models and attitudes, the broadcast media evolved slowly, restrained by a cautious government. The Radio and TV Statute had envisaged state-owned television channels operating within the territory of each autonomous community, and two communities anxious to promote their languages via broadcasting, the Basque Country and Catalonia, moved to set up television services even before legislation was in place. The *Ley reguladora del tercer canal de televisión* (Law Regulating the Third Television Channel) of 1983 made clear the subservience of the third channels to the two nationally based channels serving the whole of Spain. RTVE would have priority in areas deemed to be of national interest, allowing the third channel to cover an event in the co-official language of the autonomous community when RTVE provided coverage in Castilian. In the case of programming in Basque, Catalan or Galician the existence of such a service responded to a political imperative deriving from the region itself. In communities without a distinctive language to protect and foster, the justification for another channel seemed less compelling. Yet, given that revenue would derive from advertising, the resources required for programming seemed unproblematical, especially since no rivals to RTVE existed at the time.

Areas with distinctive cultures followed the lead of the Basque Country and Catalonia: Galicia (1985), Andalusia (1989), Valencia (1989), Madrid (1989); others have toyed with the idea and most thought better of it. In practice, the consistently loss-making third channels have required substantial public subsidy (up to 75 per cent), which has been financed from the budgets of autonomous community governments. And just as RTVE, run from Madrid and subject to government appointees, toed a political line on news and current affairs, so the third channels reflect the pressures of power groups at autonomous community level. One feature, foreshadowed in the 1983 law, came into existence as more regions set up services. The umbrella Federation of Autonomous Radio and Television Organizations (FORTA), established in 1989, was designed to promote co-operation between regional channels, facilitating the joint purchasing of programmes, especially films, and promoting savings through shared activities.

From the outset of democratization, radio enjoyed similar fortunes to the press, requiring substantially less resources than television and finding suitable niche areas to exploit. Public and private radio stations multiplied and became more focused in the mid-1980s with the improved signal quality of FM. Stations existed at national, autonomous community and municipal levels, with linked services from large groups able to switch between national and local coverage. The major protagonists have been the state-run Radio Nacional de España (RNE), PRISA (Ser, Antena 3 Radio, Sinfo Radio), the Catholic Church's COPE (Cadena de Ondas Populares Españolas), and Onda Cero, with the make-up of groups frequently changing as new licences are granted or mergers occur. Regulation is light and from the early 1980s operated at autonomous community level. Targeted programming focuses on youth (*40 principales*), classical music (Sinfo Radio), and talk shows (*magazines*) based on nationally famous celebrities. General programming (RNE, COPE) offers a broad range to listeners, with community radio and so-called free radios (*libres*) allowing a high degree of pluralism. The next major change will take place when digitalization becomes the norm, a process initiated in 1997 when a number of radio channels became available on Canal Satélite Digital. Some stations might prefer to continue on FM, but the option may not remain open under the pressure of the new technologies.

Competition and the increased play of market forces seemed sufficient for the print media, with no detailed regulatory framework. The general tendency has been towards concentration of titles in media groups (PRISA, Zeta, Recoletos, Correo) which publish dailies, financial news, weeklies and books, in some cases extending to radio and television. Consolidation has not, however, excluded failure. Jesús de Polanco's PRISA group launched the weekly *El Globo* (1987–88), which accumulated unacceptably heavy losses in its brief, six-month existence; the Grupo Anaya ventured into the competitive field of dailies with *El Sol* (1990–92), which lasted 21 months; and the publishers of *ABC,* in conjunction with the German Springer company, experimented with the sensationalist daily *Claro*, which nevertheless proved unappetizing to Spanish readers, lasting less than four months in 1991. The overall pattern during the 1980s and '90s was constant manœuvring for position, often with foreign companies taking shares in mainly Spanish ventures. Among notable incursions was the entry by the British Pearson group (*The Economist,* the *Financial Times*) in 1993 into the Grupo Recoletos (*Marca, Expansión, Actualidad Económica*), of which it became majority shareholder in 1996, before further diversification into Antena 3 television in 1997, and a major stake a year later in *El Mundo,* the second most popular daily (after *El País*).

The legalization of commercial television

The PSOE government, first elected in 1982, proved reluctant to unleash the full effects of commercial criteria in television, yet events beyond Spain's frontiers exerted pressure. Satellite television broadcasting, capable of circumventing national legislation by beaming programmes from outside a country's borders, stimulated Spanish press-based companies to plan for multimedia operations involving commercial television. Antena 3, a potential television operator, was set up by the Barcelona-based *La Vanguardia* group in 1978, a decade before the government enacted plans to regulate a commercial system. Multimedia groups in France, Germany, Italy and the UK provided models for Spain, but fear of cultural imperialism in the government party delayed action. Foreign-based groups, already established in the print media, saw the Spanish market as ripe for televisual exploitation, with the prospect even more enticing once Spain entered the European Community in 1986.

When the eventual plan for commercial television was unveiled in April 1987, caution was evident, though the government pledged itself to quality programming by limiting the number of licences to three companies, who would be required to offer a service for the whole country. Safeguards were included in the original *Proyecto de ley* (bill) in order to prevent exploitation: limits on cross-media ownership, restrictions on the percentage of non-home produced programmes and a public supervisory body. The government proclaimed its desire to preserve and reflect Spain's political, social and cultural diversity and, what appeared uppermost in the minds of the PSOE legislators, to prevent commercial domination by large groups.

In the course of the year-long debate before the *Proyecto* became the *Ley de televisión privada* (Commercial Television Law) in May 1988, a number of significant modifications took place. As far as licence operators were concerned, no one person or company could own more than 25 per cent of the shares, and no more than 25 per cent of a company could be in foreign hands. However, the original restrictions on cross-media ownership were dropped. The government would award licences for a 10-year operating period, based on programme plans as well as financial competence. It was argued that restricting licences to only three companies, as opposed to allowing the free play of market forces advocated by the opposition Grupo Popular, would guarantee the flow of advertising revenue and hence benefit programme quality. The Law set minimum quotas on programming: 15 per cent must be in-house; 40 per cent should originate from countries of the European Community; 40 per cent of films must be European, of which half should originally be Spanish. However, a central feature of the original bill, the supervisory body, was dropped and instead the operating companies would be answerable to government.

The lengthy discussion of the bill brought mergers between up to a dozen groups who at some point expressed an interest in competing for the franchises, with the result that only five companies eventually entered the contest: Antena 3, led by *La Vanguardia* and Antena 3 Radio, but also including Spanish newspaper interests and foreign investment companies; Canal Plus, based around PRISA, Canal Plus France, and four leading Spanish banks; Gestevisión-Tele 5, centred on the Spanish publishing group Anaya, Silvio Berlusconi's Italian media company Fininvest, and the ONCE (the Spanish, semi-official organization for the blind); Univisión-Canal 1, principally Antonio Asensio's Grupo Zeta, Rupert Murdoch's News International, Servifilm, and the remaining 40 per cent comprising other miscellaneous investors; and Canal C, composed of some 25 Catalan businessmen. The first three groups obtained the licences and went on air in 1990; Canal Plus had to request a three-month extension, having decided that part of its service would be encrypted, requiring a decoder in order to obtain access to its premium broadcasts (principally films and football matches).

Although the adjudication of licences brought accusations of political bias and even court action, the system allowed modification as a result of market forces. Nothing had been laid down to prevent partners in companies operating the concessions selling out to rivals. The key restriction was the 25 per cent limit on individual participation and the similar 25 per cent ceiling on foreign ownership. Hence a losing bidder or even a previously unknown company could buy up to 25 per cent in an existing licence holder. Having lost out two years earlier, Asensio's Zeta Group, in conjunction with Rupert Murdoch, bought into Antena 3, though 18 months later Murdoch sold his holding to the Banco Central Hispano. By early 1994 Antonio Asensio, via Zeta and other companies controlled by him, had what appeared to be an illegally large share in Antena 3. However, in 1997, he sold Zeta's 25 per cent stake to Telefónica, who henceforth controlled the company with support from Spanish banks. Tele 5 rapidly lost the Anaya Group who sold out in 1990 to KIO (Kuwait Investment Office) led by Javier de la Rosa, whose shareholding was later purchased by Leo Kirch's German media company; similarly, the ONCE sold its shares to Radiotélévision Luxembourg (RTL). Tele 5 thus appeared to breach the 25 per cent limit on foreign ownership in the original law, provoking judicial investigations in 1997. Of the three original companies granted licences, only Canal Plus, led by Jesús de Polanco's PRISA group, has maintained an almost identical set of shareholders throughout its existence.

If media companies, both Spanish and European, have bought into and out of television since 1989, the other significant presence has been that of major Spanish banks (Bilbao-Vizcaya, Central Hispano and Santander), both directly and through their financing of participating companies. Precise, up-to-date details of shareholdings are elusive since operating companies are not publicly listed. Government, in the person of the *Secretario de Estado de Comunicación* (Secretary of State for the Media), has been loath to intervene, in accordance with a prevailing spirit of deregulation, interpreted by some as a market free-for-all. More vociferous guardians of legality have been rival media interests who use their mouthpieces in the press to bring to public attention their competitors' apparent disregard for the law.

Before the advent of commercial television, media specialists attempted to gauge whether advertising would provide sufficient revenue to make the new channels viable. Sophisticated measuring techniques soon provided audience figures for individual programmes – readily accessible in the *Anuario El País* (*El País* Yearbook) – and advertising tariffs respond to the number of viewers delivered by the new channels. After making the expected initial losses consequent on setting up, all three companies were generating profits by 1995, especially healthy in the case of Canal Plus, whose subscription service provided a source of secure revenue. The existence of three new televisual rivals brought a deterioration in the market share and consequent financial position of RTVE, which registered increasing losses from 1990. Viewing figures for January 1998 reveal that whereas Antena 3 takes about 23 per cent of viewers at peak evening viewing times, a figure more than matched by TVE1 at 27 per cent, Tele 5 captures some 20 per cent, ahead of the autonomous community channels on 17 per cent, while TVE's La 2 picks up some 6–8 per cent compared with Canal Plus at 3–4 per cent, the latter reflecting its subscription basis. However, the same survey revealed that the third channels in Catalonia and Madrid (TV3 and Tele Madrid) were the stations preferred by viewers (22-23 per cent) in those communities.

The changing media scene under a PP government

The commercial channels increasingly complain of the unfair competition which TVE and the third channels offer, benefiting from official subsidy while competing for advertising. By the late 1990s, many voices expressed the need for a new method of funding the public channels, possibly via an annual licence fee, as is frequent in comparable European countries. Yet government cannot be unaware of the unpopularity which the introduction of such a method would provoke.

Just as the legalization of terrestrial commercial television had been accelerated by outside technological advances, so another technical revolution, digitalization, combined with satellite delivery of signals, set the pace from 1996. Although digital encoding provides better technical quality, what broadcasters envisaged was the possibility of interactivity (the television sale of products), and the ability to link payment to viewing habits and thus charge selectively for premium programming. Many operators saw the ultimate goal as *pago por visión* (pay-per-view), whereby programme providers could charge for single programmes, in particular new films and football matches. Canal Plus had already paved the way by codifying peak viewing programmes, though charged on a monthly basis. The purchase of rights to broadcast top football matches was seen as the key to capturing audiences for satellite digital television and Audiovisual Sport was set up in 1997 to commercialize the possibilities.

The controversy in Spain over digital satellite television revealed a lack of clear policy decisions from government, resulting in a clash with the European Union, and even allegations that the ruling Partido Popular wished to influence the outcome in its own political favour. Canal Satélite Digital, led by the PRISA-based Sogecable, originally controlled through Audiovisual Sport (owned by Sogecable, Antena 3 and TV3) the rights to broadcast football matches. Canal Satélite Digital was launched on 30 January 1997 on the basis of access to Spanish football and a multi-channel offer of television and high-quality audio programmes. No sooner had the new service started than the government introduced, by the normally emergency method of a *Decreto-Ley* (Decree Law), a series of restrictions relating to signal decoders, registration and financial safeguards (1 February 1997). Sogecable protested, alleging that the government was attempting to obstruct Canal Satélite Digital's advantage over the, as yet, unconstituted rival service to be offered by a group sympathetic to the governing party. The rival Vía Digital, led by Juan Villalonga, government appointee in the recently privatized Telefónica, brought together RTVE, the Mexican Televisa (headed in Spain by Luis María Ansón, former editor of *ABC*), the international Direct TV, the autonomous television companies of Galicia and Valencia, and the Recoletos group. However, Vía Digital was unable to launch until September 1997.

Within a month of its first hurried legislation for digital satellite television, the government announced the *Decreto-Ley reguladora de emisiones y retransmisiones de competiciones y acontecimientos deportivos* (Decree-Law Regulating the Broadcasting and Transmitting of Sporting Competitions and Events) – soon popularized as the *Ley del fútbol* (football law) – in order to prevent restrictive monopolies in the televising of sporting events of national interest. The measure was seen as an attempt to undo commercial agreements, to allow Vía Digital a share of football coverage, and even as an attack on the PRISA group and its chief, Jesús de Polanco. Parliamentary debate followed, with the PSOE opposing the legislation and questioning its constitutionality. A spirit of compromise was forthcoming from Sogecable, which proceeded to offer freer access to competitors to broadcast matches than initially seemed likely, and until negotiations broke down (October 1998) football coverage was shared. The rival digital services were to use different satellites, requiring different (or adjustable) dish aerials and different decoding hardware, whereas commercial considerations made it imperative to have one system using compatible hardware and shared software in order to reduce operating costs. Spain entered 1999 with both systems in operation and the number of subscribers looking relatively healthy (Canal Satélite Digital: 512 000; Vía Digital: 289 000. *See El País*, 26.2.99).

The 1990s witnessed the return to a more politicized media system. If the

PRISA group and its linked multimedia interests appeared to benefit from the period in power of the PSOE (1982–96), the arrival in government of the Partido Popular in 1996 was accompanied by a more doctrinaire attitude towards RTVE and the alleged favouring of sympathetic interests in the fields of independent radio and television. The PP government is expected to oversee the renewal of commercial television licences in 1999, and in November 1998 announced its intention to raise the 25 per cent limit on individual holdings in operating companies to 49 per cent, heralding a period of renewed media turmoil.

Whereas regulation of the media in many western democracies operates at arm's length from the executive, Spain's governments since 1978 have adopted a less formal approach, defending the adequacy of parliamentary supervision, while reserving detailed administration of regulatory processes for a ministry sub-department. Informed commentators on the media nevertheless complain of the lack of clear guidelines and call for regulatory bodies independent of the executive, empowered to establish non-partisan procedures in a sphere where government seems unable to resist partiality. In the absence of publicly accountable institutions, market forces and commercial considerations are allowed to operate with minimal interference. Given the shortcomings in official regulation, the main responsibility for scrutiny is assumed by rival media interests, who are hardly disinterested observers.

Further Reading

BARRERA, C. 1995: *Sin mordaza. Veinte años de prensa en democracia*. Madrid: Temas de hoy.

BUSTAMANTE, E. 1989: TV and public service in Spain: a difficult encounter, *Media, Culture and Society* 11, 67–87.

Comunicación social 1989 [–1996]/Tendencias (Informes anuales de Fundesco). 1989–96. Madrid: Fundesco.

DEACON, P. 1999: The media in contemporary culture. In Gies, D. T. (ed.) *The Cambridge companion to modern Spanish culture*. Cambridge: Cambridge University Press, 309–17.

—— 1995: *The press as mirror of the new Spain*. Bristol: Dept. of Hispanic, Portuguese and Latin American Studies, University of Bristol.

Informe anual de la comunicación 1997–1998. Estado y tendencias de los media en España. 1998. Barcelona: Zeta.

MAXWELL, R. 1995: *The spectacle of democracy. Spanish television, nationalism, and political transition*. Minneapolis, Minn.: University of Minnesota Press.

REIG, R. 1998: *Medios de comunicación y poder en España. Prensa, radio, televisión y mundo editorial*. Barcelona: Paidós.

SÁNCHEZ TABERNERO, A. *et al.* 1993: *Media concentration in Europe. Commercial enterprise and the public interest*. Düsseldorf: European Institute for the Media.

VILLAGRASA, J. M. 1992: Spain: the emergence of commercial television. In Silj, A. (ed.), *The new television in Europe*. London: John Libbey, 337–426.

|14|

Politics and television news in Spain

IÑAKI ZABALETA

Introduction

Spain, with its 38.2 million people, has three main state-wide television channels: one public, TVE1, and two private, Antena 3 TV and Tele 5. These three are now the core terrestrial broadcasters, with a 69.7% average audience share, offering general programming for all tastes, families and classes. With regard to the other two state-wide channels, the public TVE2 or La 2, with its much smaller audience share, is complementary to TVE1, with its programming emphasizing culture and sport. Canal Plus, with its encrypted analogue signal and its small subscription audience, offers mostly thematic programming, predominantly movies and sport. There are also eight regional television stations and about 20 local providers. This essay aims to explore the nature and functioning of television news across the main public and private channels in Spain over the last two decades and to gauge the extent to which news agendas are influenced by mainly political but also other factors.

News audiences, viewing figures and programme content

Over the 1993–97 period, TVE1 lost a seven-point audience share during the main evening news bulletin – broadcast in prime time – in favour of the private channels. Yet, taking into account the fact that during the period the private operators were attemping to grow their audiences and consolidate their operations, such a degree of slippage is not inordinately high. And even with such losses, TVE1 remains the reference point for Spain's news pro-grammers, with a 32.6 per cent average audience share. Ratings for Antena 3 TV went up during its first three years of operation but after that they began to fall continuously, losing significant share until 1998. Nevertheless, it lies second, with a 21.9 per cent average audience. Tele 5, by contrast, is the channel with the lowest share of the news audience (16.2 per cent average), although it has been trying hard to increase its proportion year by year. All of which indicates that, in relation to audience share for news programming, the private channels have not seriously eroded the main public channel's ratings. By 1998, audience viewing figures for news had stabilized for the three main channels, as seen in Table 14.1.

Table 14.1 Audience share of newscasts between 1993–97 (%)

	1993	1994	1995	1996	1997	1998	1993–98 mean
TVE1	37.2	33.6	32.9	31.6	30.9	29.7	32.6
Antena 3	17.8	22.9	25.4	23.6	22.1	19.8	21.9
Telecinco	14.3	15.1	16.9	16.6	17.1	17.3	16.2
Mean	*23.1*	*23.9*	*25.1*	*23.9*	*23.4*	*22.2*	*23.6*

Source: SOFRES and the author's elaboration of their figures
Note: The audience share relating to 1998 covers the period from January to the end of September.

With regard to programme content, the analysis of Spain's television news bulletins requires us to move beyond a conventional view and avoid the dispersion of content categories. In this regard, the most frequently visited single category is sport (19.1 per cent), an area that has acquired much greater relevance during the 1990s, when in the wake of competition from the new private stations, news bulletins have been revamped as more lively and entertaining 'shows', with significant sporting coverage. Politics (16.5 per cent), the classic category of current affairs and the public sphere, has dropped to second place whilst those of the economy (10.5 per cent) and the weather (8.4 per cent) have maintained a reasonably solid and consistent presence. These four categories are basic staples in any news bulletin, but even more than these single categories, the important source of comparison has to be made between two main 'compound categories', that is, between 'good' and 'bad' news: on the one hand, crime, accidents and terrorism (which corresponds to negative, conflictual and violence-related news at 14.4 per cent) and, on the other, pro-social categories (comprising more positive reports on social and consumer issues, health, environment, culture and science, at 27.9 per cent).

When made, this comparison highlights the fact that, in quantitative terms, the compound category of pro-social news stands at more than double that of conflict-oriented news. This finding is perhaps surprising and is normally one which remains hidden. With regard to our comparison of the three dominant public and private broadcasters, the main conclusion is that in relation to the categories of sport, politics and accidents and crime, relative percentages of programme composition are fairly similar, within a 2 per cent tolerance.

Despite the evident similarities across channels in information and content in regular daily news programming, we should not forget that in electoral campaigns, the coverage by public television has been much more diverse, balanced and fair than that of the private channels, largely because it is closely monitored and controlled by an independent Central or Regional Electoral Board (Zabaleta, 1997).

Politics and the news

The influence of politics in the news is a perennial issue taking very different guises according to the *political viewpoint* of the interpreter and the *level of abstraction* according to which the event in question is positioned and understood. In any case, it is widely accepted that the influence of the political party in power is very much present in the way the news is constructed and broadcast in public European radio and television systems (Blumler, 1992; López-Escobar, 1992; Siune and Truetzscheler, 1992); such influence is not so clear, however, in relation to private channels. This frequent allegation, even in many democratic countries, has found fertile soil in Spain, a country that until 1978 did not have a democratic Constitution and had been ruled by a dictatorial regime. With regard to the notion of political viewpoint, the factor that determines the influence of politics in the news output of public television is arguably not so much ideology as power; that is, whether or not the interpreter or his or her ideological peers are in government or opposition.

As regards the level of abstraction, any analysis has to be framed in terms of two basic and distinct concepts: on the one hand, *politics*, that is, the practical, day-to-day, political activities within the political system – understood in terms of a low level of abstraction – and on the other, *policy*, comprising issues, events and news that affect the political system as a whole (national security, military issues, the functioning of the democratic system, etc.), understood as matters involving a higher level of abstraction.

The news treatment of an issue will thus differ according to whether the media consider it – or are 'encouraged' to consider it – as pertaining to the domain of politics or to that of policy. In the first case, the media will treat the issue following their conventional journalistic standards and their ideological standpoint. In the second, and certainly in the Spanish case, almost all the media behave in a roughly similar manner, choosing to insulate and prioritize the policy issue in question – national security or military matters, for example – over journalistic ethics or the obligation to investigate and inform fairly. And sometimes, an event that clearly belongs to the domain of politics is converted into a policy matter in the media and its journalistic treatment is developed accordingly. In Spain, in this regard, state-wide public and private channels almost coincide in their news treatments by reinforcing a high level of abstraction. Whilst their news is thus broadly homogeneous, normalized and even personalized in many cases, both public and private channels tend to treat issues which belong to the domain of 'politics' as if they were state-level, policy issues, particularly in conflicts of national identity, as seen in events and issues relevant to the Basque Country and Catalonia.

Socialists in power: the strategy of the cat

The PSOE governed Spain for 14 years, between 1982 and 1996, during which time it made great and positive efforts to modernize the country. Yet in relation to two key, linked areas, those of terrorism and information policy, the government acted in a more dubious and questionable fashion. Indeed, it implemented two parallel strategies in public radio and television news reporting, the first of which can be inferred from a statement made by Felipe González, and widely publicized in the media. During his first official trip to China in 1985, González is reported to have said: 'Black cat or white cat, what matters is whether it catches the mouse', an aphorism he allegedly picked up from Chinese leader Deng Xiao Ping, whom González publicly admired.

This highly pragmatic line of reasoning – enthusiastically endorsed not only in Spain but in most Western countries during the 1980s and 1990s and called upon to legitimate the use of almost any means (political or other) as long as it achieved the desired ends – became the cornerstone of the Socialist government's anti-terrorist and information strategy in the domain of policy.

With regard to terrorism, the result was state-supported counter-terrorism (basically torture, kidnappings, bombings and assassinations) against radical Basque nationalists and members of ETA. By the end of the decade, this strategy was largely abandoned – save for instances of torture. Regarding the information strategy, the Socialist government exerted a far-reaching and arguably fierce control of RTVE, which monopolized the air waves until the arrival of private television in 1990.

To understand the 1980s in Spain, it is also necessary to briefly describe the struggle between the Socialist government and the banker Mario Conde, owner of the major Spanish bank Banesto. Conde became the role model for both young and old Spanish people, a symbol of eighties-style success; awarded a doctorate *Honoris Causa* by the University Complutense of Madrid, he was also a close friend of King Juan Carlos; he thus offers another notorious example of the 'strategy of the cat' in matters of finance and behind-the-scenes politics. Moreover, Conde was also the president of the bank that, by means of loans, owned the majority of the shares in Antena 3 TV.

During the first half of the 1990s, Conde showed interest in becoming the political leader of Spain's conservatives. In order to prevent such an eventuality, Felipe González helped manœuvre Spain's Central Bank into investigating Banesto on charges of false accounting and bankruptcy. As a result, Conde was tried and sent to prison, yet he did not go quietly. He used his powerful economic muscle and, as consistently argued in the media, counterattacked with information leaks and reports about illegal activities by members of the Socialist government – corruption, phone tapping and state-terrorism – allegations which seriously affected the electoral prospects of the Socialists. Also, national daily newspapers such as *El Mundo, ABC* and *Diario 16* uncovered the same activities through their own investigative reporting. In protest, Felipe González accused several newspaper directors of organizing a 'crime union' (*sindicato del crimen*) with the aim of overthrowing him.

The Conservative party took advantage of the situation to exert pressure on the Socialist government and create an impression of a major political scandal in Spain. The political turmoil gradually filtered into the consciousness of ordinary Spaniards. At that moment, too late perhaps, Felipe González made another enigmatic statement that signified another shift in the Socialist strategy towards news and information: 'If one opens the window, flies enter with the air'. This second statement was made in China too, on his second trip during February 1993, and once again Felipe González borrowed it from the Chinese leaders he admired so much.

During that conflictive period, public radio and television were a battleground of primary importance. Numerous journalists, scholars and politicians agree that Felipe González's government implemented in RTVE a strategy of silence, secrecy and distortion of information, in relation to governmental corruption and state terrorism activities. Details of certain specific cases may help to illustrate this assertion.

On 21 February 1993, the newspaper *El Mundo* revealed that a congresswoman of the conservative Popular Alliance (PP) was about to claim that Spain's most important weekly television news magazine, 'Informe Semanal' ('Weekly Report', broadcast by TVE1) had made two purchases of heroin and given it to an addict in order to illustrate a report on drugs. Two days later, a spokesperson from TVE acknowledged this fact, but a day later the director of the news department, María Antonia Iglesias, contradicted that version saying the drugs were bought by two people who had nothing to do with the programme. A few days later, TVE denied any contradiction between both versions, but by 10 March, *El Mundo* published a new report proving that TVE had admitted before the Public Accounts Committee its irresponsibility in using public money for drugs purchases. Finally, on 1 April 1994, the same newspaper confirmed this version and that of the conservative MP by publishing a first-person account by an eyewitness.

It is undeniable that this case was politically exploited to the full by the conservatives in order to undermine the government's credibility. Even so, it has to be admitted that the case clearly showed a lack of ethical standards on the part of the journalists involved and the management of TVE. One could argue that the case followed and illustrated perfectly the strategy of the cat, that is to get the story by whatever means and whatever the costs, even to journalistic integrity.

A second illustrative case occurred on 11 July 1995, triggered by the Administrative Council of RTVE, which unanimously condemned the journalistic treatment of a report – broadcast on 25 June by the same 'Informe Semanal' magazine show of TVE1 – on the long-term phone tapping of members of political parties, including King Juan Carlos, by Spain's secret service, CESID. With the facts of the case originally uncovered by *El Mundo*, the television report was condemned across the political spectrum for being confused, economical with the facts and heavily biased towards the government, in that it tried to exonerate the Socialist Minister of Defence, Narcís Serra, from any wrongdoing.

A third case occurred on 18 January 1995, when the evening news bulletin of TVE1 opened with a special interview (from inside prison) with the former Head of State Security, the Socialist Julián Sancristóbal, accused of state-terrorism activities. During the interview, Sr Sancristóbal denounced a conspiracy against Felipe González, allegedly organized by Judge Baltasar Garzón (the scourge of General Augusto Pinochet). From a journalistic viewpoint, the content of the interview was not a matter of controversy, but the style, timing and presentation of the interview were seen as matters of concern. There was little or no introduction and contextualization of the item, just an exaggerated and rather sensationalistic, pro-government spin given to the case. One could mention other similar cases which would reinforce the impression that Felipe González's 'strategy of the cat' was being tacitly implemented in public television news. The private channels were not nearly as conspicuous. They had enough to do in order to cope with their own economic difficulties.

Conservatives in power, conservative news style

The conservative Popular Alliance (PP) won the General Elections of 3 March 1996 with an extremely narrow margin, and brought to an end the era of Socialist government. The new prime minister, José María Aznar, kept his electoral promise and appointed a media professional to the position of RTVE's director-general. She was Mónica Ridruejo, 33 years old, trained in the USA and hailed as one of a new breed of high-powered media administrators, yet she lasted less than a year. The appointment of the second director-general in 1997 entailed a break with Aznar's electoral promise, since the new incumbent, Fernando López-Amor, was a conservative member of parliament. His reign was also short-lived, lasting little more than a year; he was eventually forced to resign in rather bizarre circumstances. Finally, at the end of 1998, Pío Cabanillas Alonso, a non-politician, son of the 'liberal' Minister of Information and Tourism during the last Francoist cabinet (1974), became the third and current director-general of RTVE.

During the first three years of conservative government, two aspects of television news policy have become salient: on the one hand, the sheer abundance and excess of televisual attention devoted to Spanish-style socialite news and on the other, the marked increase in coverage of the Spanish military.

News concerning weddings and similar social events involving members of aristocracy and other ranks – including bullfighters, sportspeople, etc. – are fast becoming considered newsworthy by television news journalists and editors. So widespread is this phenomenon that parliamentary questions have been tabled and RTVE executives have been called upon to justify and defend such coverage. Soft, uncontroversial and trashy, such items of 'news' arguably accord with the tone and values of conservative Spain. The reporting of these events takes two main forms: on the one hand, daily newscasts offer quite detailed items about them and on the other, there have been whole programmes offering special live coverage, which may last several hours.

The lead in this type of news policy is perhaps surprisingly being taken by public television, and is enviously followed by the private channels. An excellent illustration of this symbiosis of media and high society can be found in the wedding of Eugenia Martínez de Irujo, daughter of the Duchess of Alba, to the bullfighter Francisco Rivera on 23 October 1998 in Seville. As the event was getting closer and the media were 'trailing' it with increasing intensity, a massive wave of 'social interest' – which could hardly be described as 'public interest' – was being generated in society at large. Top television executives and journalists engaged in heated debate as to whether Spain's main public channel, TVE1, should broadcast the event exclusively or share it with the private channels. This conflict of interest became a matter of national concern, a state affair, and the supervisory parliamentary commission for RTVE debated the issue and divided along political lines: the left, in opposition, were against it; the right, in favour. Finally, the family of the Duchess of Alba stated that they wanted TVE1 alone to broadcast the wedding. Though loud and fierce, the protests of the private stations proved ultimately futile.

TVE1 deployed 35 cameras, 15 trucks, and 10 mobile production units. The live coverage of the wedding did not restrict itself to the ceremony itself but relayed well over five hours of insubstantial pictures, poor information content and much nonsensical chit-chat by the announcers about umbrellas and dresses. The average viewing audience was 57 per cent and at certain moments it reached an 80 per cent share. The director-general of RTVE is said to have regarded the occasion as one of the most important social events of the year. Indeed, government press officers, echoing the director-general of RTVE, claimed that public interest in the wedding derived from two objective facts: the huge interest shown by the private channels in wishing to broadcast it and its enormous audience appeal.

Other nuptial events that have dominated the national news during the last few years have been the weddings of the two daughters of the King of Spain: the Infanta Elena to Jaime de Marichalar in 1996, in Seville; and the Infanta Cristina to the Basque handball star Iñaki Urdangarín in Barcelona. A futher series of weddings involving bullfighters – Enrique Ponce and Manuel Benítez, among others – and soccer players have filled newscasts and magazine shows too. This news trend is present in almost equal measure in both public and private television.

The second aspect of news policy which is symptomatic of the Popular party in power is the increasing and favourable attention given by public television to the Spanish military. On Saturday evenings, at 7:30 p.m., close to prime time, we find (1999) a news magazine programme named 'Código Alfa' ('Code Alpha') on the cultural channel, TVE2. It offers uncritical, advertising-style reports about the Spanish military, giving us only the most favourable view of the Armed Forces. The fact that the Spanish military is becoming professional and abandoning compulsory national service may well be the explanation for the presence of this show, yet this should not be used as a justification for its low-quality journalism.

The battle of the newscasters

'News bulletins are the identity cards of the television channels' said Gabriel Campo, executive of the TVE news division. This seems to be true if we consider the changes that have taken place between 1996 and 1999 in Spanish newscasts.

On 14 September 1998, the first day of the fall–winter schedule, the race to attract audiences for news programmes began. Since the ratings leadership of TVE1 remained undisputed, the struggle for the second position focused on the two private channels.

Prior to that day, the private stations had fought a hard battle in order to hire new anchorpersons. And through an unprecedented series of events, none of the TVE newscasters who were fronting the three main newscasts – afternoon, evening and night – in 1996 remained in their posts in 1998. This shake-up also affected directors of the news divisions.

Antena 3 TV, controlled by Spain's mighty telecommunication corporation *Telefónica Española*, developed the most aggressive strategy, hiring famous anchorpersons as new media stars. It lured away from TVE the evening newscaster and head of the news division Ernesto Sáenz de Buruaga. Since this anchorperson was appointed by President José María Aznar to manage and present the news on TVE and enjoyed his total confidence, this move was interpreted as a clear manœuvre by the conservatives to strengthen their position for the forthcoming General Elections, likely to be called in 2000. The news policy adopted by Sáenz de Buruaga could be inferred from the closing statement of his daily bulletin: 'That's how things looked today, just like we told you'. This assertion, in my opinion, suggests a somewhat rigid and determinist conception of reality, one which exclusively constructs reality in the singular and, morever, presupposes only one way of conveying that reality, which happens to be the version delivered by Sáenz de Buruaga. Another Antena 3 TV initiative that made the headlines was the hiring of one of the most valuable and versatile news programme presenters of TVE, Matías Prats, who left public television after 23 years service and now presents the afternoon newscast in the new station.

Tele5 differed in its strategy and did not hire already famous national newscasters but turned to less well-known regional television anchors and radio announcers. This policy seemed to work since during the winter of 1998, their newscasts achieved a better audience share than those of Antena 3 TV. But the confrontation was far from over and by the beginning of 1999, Antena 3 TV had recovered some ground in its ratings.

Self-censorship or government intervention

The case of the Madrid Forum for Peace is an important example of information self-censorship in modern times as well as government intervention in the way the mass media organize their information policies and news production. As noted earlier, it is an illustration of the transformation of a normal *political* activity into a *policy* issue. The Madrid Forum for Peace is made up of prominent Spaniards, recognized democrats, whose activities have been limited to expressing their opinions, in search of a framework for a fair and just peace process in the Basque–Spanish conflict.

On 20 January 1998, there was an important and very newsworthy meeting in the Ateneo of Madrid. It was named 'Event for a Dialogued Peace in the Basque Country' and more than 600 people attended, including a high-ranking member of the former Socialist cabinet, plus twelve deputies of the Spanish Congress, several high-ranking judges, and many Spanish intellectuals, writers, lawyers, and so on. Five speakers outlined various ways forward for the search for peace in the Basque Country. Just before the event, the organizers and speakers invited the media to a press conference, yet none of the national television channels reported the event in their news bulletins, nor did any of the national newspapers. There occurred what can only be described as an information blackout. Two months later, as a follow-up to that first public presentation, 147 prominent and influential Spanish people (again including judges, lawyers, writers, journalists and university professors) agreed, signed and presented to Spanish society a document named the *Madrid Manifesto*. A press conference was held in Madrid on 26 March 1998, yet even though the presence of the media was abundant, no national TV – public or private – offered any information about it. The next day, the national newspapers did not publish anything either. Again, it was an almost complete information blackout. On the other hand, the coverage of that same press conference and the Madrid Manifesto in the Basque media was prioritized and given front page prominence. It seemed as if the media based in Madrid and the Basque media inhabited two totally different worlds.

The third significant event occurred at the end of September 1998, a few days after the cease-fire declared by the terrorist group ETA. The signatories to the Manifesto sent a press communiqué to the media regarding the cease-fire and the need for a process of dialogue to reach a peace. For the third time, no national Spanish television channel bothered to report the event.

The fourth nationally newsworthy event took place on 20 October 1998 when the signatories to the Manifesto announced in a second communiqué that they were about to form the Madrid Forum for Peace. Only now did TVE1 decide to report the announcement. Why the change of policy? The cease-fire declared by ETA obviously had a major bearing on this shift. In which case, one has to question the degree of media independence regarding the newsworthiness of events related to the Basque–Spanish conflict, when seen as a policy issue. Interestingly, the private channels did not report the formation of the Madrid Forum for Peace, an indication perhaps of how they tend to lag behind public television. Finally, the fifth major event organized by the Madrid Forum for Peace took place in Madrid on 2 December 1998, when members hosted the presentation of the 'Lizarra Accord' (an agreement, signed in the town of Lizarra (Navarre) between all Basque nationalist parties and groups who supported the rights of Basques to self-determination). For the first time, this event was covered by all television stations, public and private.

According to leading figures from the Forum, the national media operated a double standard, refusing to cover the Basque peace process until ETA declared its cease-fire in September 1998. By doing so, they deliberately silenced events and initiatives which had previously argued for a negotiated solution to the conflict; they also tended to criminalize all political activities by peace campaigners relating to the Basque country. Forum members maintain that the conservative Home Office Minister, Jaime Mayor Oreja, held meetings with national media news programmers in order to exert undue pressure on them to maintain strict control over coverage. In practice, this often meant total news blackouts, even of genuinely democratic political initiatives, especially where the latter did not coincide with government policy. Such heavy-handed official intervention in news management, in practical terms, was to all intents and purposes censorship, official or unofficial. This seems to represent a widespread, worrying and continuing tendency of government interference in the Spanish news media to convert *political* issues into *policy* matters, especially with regard to questions of regional autonomy.

References

BENNETT, W. L. 1983: *News: The politics of illusion*. London: Longman.

BLUMLER, J. G. 1992: *Television and the public interest: vulnerable values in West European broadcasting*. London: Sage.

CONSUMER 1998: Telediarios: muy alejados del ciudadano. *Consumer*, 4–7.

DE LA CALLE, P. 1998: 'Sillas calientes' en los informativos. *El Mundo*, 30 September 1998, 77.

GALLO ROSALES, I. 1998: 'Las masas querían ver la boda', según López-Amor. *El País*, 30 October 1998, 77.

LOPEZ-ESCOBAR, E. 1992: Spanish media law: changes in the landscape. *European Journal of Communication* 7, 241–59.

SIUNE, K. and TRUETZSCHELER, W. (EDS) 1992: *Dynamics of media politics*. Euromedia Research Group. London: Sage.

SOFRES, AUDIENCIA DE MEDIOS 1997: *Anuario de audiencias de televisión*, 1997. Madrid: Sofres Audiencia de Medios.

ZABALETA, I. 1997: Private commercial television versus political diversity: the case of Spain's 1993 general elections. In Kinder M. (ed.) *Refiguring Spain. Cinema/media/representation*. Durham: Duke University Press, 284–301.

|15|

New media technologies in Spain: a healthy pluralism?

RICHARD MAXWELL

This essay charts the rise of cable and digital satellite TV in Spain. The first part describes how two companies emerged from a moribund cable industry to compete for digital satellite TV. The ruling Popular Party (PP) backed one company controlled by the Spanish transnational telecommunications giant, Telefónica. The other company was owned by a subsidiary of PRISA, the Spanish media transnational and ally of the main opposition party, the Spanish Socialist Workers Party (PSOE). The conflict between these forces became known as *la guerra digital*: a digital war for new media in Spain. The second part focuses on the structural consequences of the digital war: globalization of ownership and control, augmentation of Hollywood film and TV imports, and commercialization of domestic production. The essay concludes with an assessment of the health of Spanish media pluralism as measured by the availability of new, commercial media technologies.

La guerra digital

Until recently, Spanish cable television (CATV) was a haphazard and local business, mostly low-quality, community video strung together within apartment complexes. Cable businesses popped up around the country with the permission of local authorities, who took advantage of a Constitutional Court judgement that said that the absence of a cable law did not prohibit the building of cable systems. The life of cablers in legal limbo was prolonged by a dispute among the regional governments, municipalities, and the central government over who should have the right to grant cable licences. By 1994, central, regional and local authorities agreed to rules that provided only a modicum of regulation too weak to stop cablers from multiplying.

In December 1995, the PSOE pressed a Cable Telecommunications Law through parliament to regulate CATV nationally. The law set coverage zones at a minimum of 50 000 inhabitants, effectively excluding many cablers which the PP – the projected winner of the coming national elections – had licensed in towns it controlled. The law also limited to two the number of operating licences the regulatory authority would grant in each market, but guaranteed that one of those licences would go automatically to Telefónica nine months after the other licence had been issued (the waiting period was meant to give other cablers a head start on the mighty Telefónica).

Two large cable companies formed during the shake-out and consolidation of the cable industry. Cableuropa was a consortium established by a cable operator, Multitel, in partnership with two national banks, Banco Santander and Banco Central Hispano (BCH). For Banco Santander and BCH, the investment extended their media holdings and positioned them against rival banks, Argentaria, Banco Bilbao Vizcaya and La Caixa, which were major shareholders of Telefónica. Cableuropa sought additional investors to finance CATV in major cities and eventually sold a controlling interest to a US company, SpainCom (owned by General Electric, Callahan Associates and the Bank of America).

The second company was Cablevisión, which Telefónica set up with Canal Plus, a pay TV operator controlled by Sogecable. Sogecable's business of programme production and packaging is vertically integrated with a film production company (Sogetel), TV and film distribution outfits (Sogepac and Warner Sogefilms), and venues for both theatrical film exhibition (Warner Lusomundo Cines de España) and pay TV (Canal Plus). Sogecable is owned by Canal Plus France, PRISA, and major Spanish banks. PRISA owns the largest circulation newspaper in Spain, *El País*, and the top commercial radio station, Ser. Telefónica operates the most extensive telephony network in Spain with control over about 98 per cent of the market.

Cablevisión did not last a year. The European Commission (EC) had opposed the alliance, and the PP disliked any business involving the PSOE-friendly PRISA. The EC suspected that Cablevisión constituted an illegal monopoly, and the 1995 Cable Law compounded that impression by promising Telefónica a licence in every cable market. In June 1996, following their electoral victory, the PP revised the Cable Law to force Telefónica to wait two years before beginning cable operations. PP's law also returned licensing power to local and regional authorities, lowered the minimum market size to make it easier for smaller towns to get cable, and lifted the cap on foreign ownership of cable firms. In July, a Spanish court ruled that Telefónica was illegally using its phone network for Cablevisión and ordered Telefónica to stop all cable services. The partnership officially dissolved in November 1996.

As the cable partnership unravelled that summer, Sogecable and Telefónica began separately to jockey for position to become the first to offer digital satellite TV in Spain. It was a logical move for Sogecable, whose

Canal Plus already furnished numerous channels of pay satellite TV in the analogue format using France's Astra satellite. Telefónica's controlling interest in the Spanish Hispasat satellite would give them low-cost entry to the TV market while they waited out the two-year restriction to start their cable services. Telefónica was first to announce their new service, saying it would start on Christmas Eve 1997, but Sogecable beat them by 12 months. By January 1997, Sogecable's new satellite TV service, Canal Satélite Digital (CSD), was busy signing up subscribers.

Whereas CSD was familiar business to Sogecable's owners, Telefónica needed partners with expertise in media buying and programming. The PP helped Telefónica form a new consortium, Distribuidora de Televisión Digital (DTD), to promote a service named Plataforma Digital Española. Major investors included Telefónica (35 per cent), the Mexican TV transnational, Televisa (17 per cent), and the Spanish public broadcaster, Radio Televisión Española (RTVE) (17 per cent). Local press and radio stations friendly with the PP bought shares, and the rest went to the Madrid-based publisher, Grupo Recoletos, a subsidiary of the Pearson group, a British media conglomerate and publisher of *The Financial Times*. Initially, the Spanish private TV firm, Antena 3, was going to invest in 17 percent of DTD, but then changed camps to take a 15 per cent share of Sogecable's CSD, a deal which also set up Sogecable and Antena 3 in a joint venture giving them exclusive rights to televise top football (soccer) matches in Spain.

The first skirmish occurred in January 1997. Worried that CSD would capture all of the potential audience before Telefónica entered the market, the PP introduced a law to block the distribution of CSD's digital decoder. Sogecable appealed and continued to sign up subscribers. Then the PP appointed a special prosecutor to investigate personal business records of Jesús de Polanco and Antonio Asensio, respectively PRISA's and Antena 3's chairmen, in apparent retaliation for Asensio's defection with the prized football rights to Polanco's camp.

Throughout 1997, DTD repeatedly postponed the launch of its service, which it renamed Vía Digital. To obstruct CSD and help Vía Digital, the PP issued two new laws: one obligated all satellite services to use Telefónica's preferred digital decoder, and another aimed to weaken Sogecable's and Antena 3's control over televised football rights. At this point, the EC intervened and began proceedings against the Spanish government for attempting to use executive power to shut down CSD's existing satellite service. The EC eventually forced the PP to modify its anti-competitive laws.

Toward the end of July, at the height of conspiratorial schemes that included a wire tap on Jesús de Polanco's office telephone, Telefónica won a major victory that changed the fortunes of the war. Telefónica's director, Juan Villalonga, convinced Antonio Asensio to sell all of his controlling interest in Antena 3 to Telefónica. In addition to Antena 3's private TV business, the deal gave Telefónica 15 per cent of CSD and, perhaps the biggest bonus, the joint licence for televised football rights. Villalonga remarked that the buy-out of Antena 3 was a small investment for a company the size of Telefónica. As he put it, the deal cost '... peanuts. A mere day or two of our company's cash flow'.[1] Vía Digital finally began broadcasting in September 1997.

By January 1998, CSD had grown to 250 000 subscribers with an equal number on their waiting list. In contrast, Vía Digital had not surpassed 85 000, but claimed 120 000 were wait listed. CSD had sealed broadcasting rights for major Hollywood film and television programmes. Unable to secure a deal with a major Hollywood supplier, Vía Digital opted to compete on price, extending a free promotional offer well beyond a prudent period for any company other than one with Telefónica's capital reserves (total revenues for 1997 exceeded $15 billion).

Then, in July 1998, the two sides agreed to merge. The merger would have combined CSD's programming know-how with Vía Digital's technological and financial muscle. It would have also resolved the dispute over the rights to televise football matches. However, the merger agreement, scheduled for completion in September 1998, implied a complex inter-corporate arrangement, involving Mexican, British, Japanese, French, American and Spanish investors as well as rival national banks. The problem of ownership and control was matched by the question of how to standardize accounting and technical systems. On the accounting side was the problem of distinct subscriber management practices. On the technical side, the problems were incompatible decoders and different satellites with reception dishes set at divergent angles. Before the merger could proceed, not only would these issues have to be resolved but the deal would have to be approved by the EC, which had recently prohibited a similar merger in Germany. Nevertheless, the truly vexing question was how these companies could possibly get along after the aggressive war that they, and their political patrons, waged against one another.

The answer was, for the time being, that they could not. In September, Telefónica called off the merger after CSD published advertisements reclaiming their exclusive rights to football matches. Apart from the football row, disagreement over each other's company's value was probably the most important and basic barrier to restructuring the ownership of the merged companies.

The war dividend

The short and fuzzy truce notwithstanding, the war over digital satellite TV accelerated three economic trends that started in the 1980s: globalization of Spanish media industry ownership, growth in film and TV imports, and increased commercialization of domestic production.

Globalization

In 1998, Vía Digital's ownership was distributed among Telefónica (35 per cent), RTVE (17), Televisa (17), DirecTV, a subsidiary of Hughes electronics, a General Motors' company (6.9 per cent), Itochu (5 per cent), Pearson (5 per cent), TV3, Catalan TV (5 per cent), Telemadrid (4 per cent), Canal 9, Valencian TV (2 per cent), TVG, Galician TV (2 per cent), with the remainder held by the regional and business press. The US-based DirecTV entered this partnership through its Latin American subsidiary, Galaxy Latin America, and pledged to raise its ownership of Vía Digital to 25 per cent. The Japanese trading firm, Itochu, has holdings in the Japanese digital satellite service, PerfecTV, and owns a few million shares of Time Warner's preferred stock.

On the eve of its launch of Vía Digital, Telefónica paid the Pearson group $154 million plus a 5 per cent stake of Antena 3 in exchange for 20 per cent of Pearson's Madrid-based publisher, Recoletos. The deal gave Pearson a piece of Sogecable's CSD in addition to its 5 per cent of Telefónica's Vía Digital. CSD meanwhile continued to be controlled by Sogecable, with the small remaining percentage split between Telefónica and Pearson. Sogecable owners are PRISA (25 per cent), Canal Plus France (25 per cent), with powerful minority interests held by major banks, including Banco Bilbao Vizcaya, which also owns a significant stake in Telefónica.

The telecommunication privatizations of 1997 and 1998 led to the rapid globalization of CATV ownership, in particular of Telefónica's two main rivals, Retevisión and Cableuropa. Retevisión owned the entire land-based television network infrastructure when the PP came to power. In accordance with European Union directives, the PP sold 60 per cent of Retevisión in 1997 and approved a provision that licensed Retevisión as the second national telephone network, breaking Telefónica's 70-year monopoly. A controlling 21.7 per cent of Retevisión was sold to a Telecom Italia subsidiary (STET), and another 21.7 per cent to Endesa, the leading Spanish power company, then also privatized. Unión Fenosa, the third largest power company bought 8.6 per cent. The remainder went to regional banks and Euskaltel, which the Basque government formed in 1992 to build a regional digital network. Over the same period, Telefónica was completely privatized and allied itself with new global partners, MCI WorldCom and Portugal Telecom.

SpainCom (General Electric, Callahan Associates, and the Bank of America) holds a majority stake of 32 per cent in Cableuropa. The rest of the company is held by Spanish banks and media firms. France Telecom formed an alliance with Cableuropa to set up local CATV subsidiaries, bringing with it Global One partners, Deutsche Telekom and Sprint. France Telecom has also agreed to join Cableuropa in its bid to become Spain's third national telephone company.

Retevisión set up CATV subsidiaries in cities throughout Spain to compete with Cableuropa for the second cable licence (one goes to Telefónica automatically). In March 1998, a Retevisión subsidiary, CyC Telecomunicaciones Madrid, won the licence for Madrid, a city prized for comprising 30 per cent of Spain's cable market.

Imports

Vía Digital and CSD needed programmes for hundreds of their planned channels and so began a spending spree in 1997 to buy rights to show films and other entertainment goods in Spain. They wanted exclusive contracts for long-term broadcast rights in order to deny programming to their rival and thus raise the market value of their brand name. In such competition, all roads lead to Hollywood, home of the dominant exporters of filmed entertainment, where the total value of digital war deals came to an estimated $3 billion ('Spain tries to get along').

Sogecable signed exclusive deals with all of the major Hollywood studios except MGM. They sealed a $250 million, 10-year deal with Paramount, and one with Time Warner for Turner cable channels that included an exclusive contract to develop the Spanish version of CNN. They acquired rights to Disney channels, Universal's action movie channels, and to televise 20th Century Fox's recently released films in Spain, including exclusive pay TV rights to the blockbuster, *Titanic*. CSD gained further advantage through Sogecable's Warner Sogefilms, a distribution partnership with a Time Warner subsidiary that fosters trade and marketing of Hollywood and domestic films. Finally, CSD benefits as part of Canal Plus France's empire which provides programme packages to a dozen countries in Europe and parts of Africa.

Although Vía Digital acquired exclusive rights to MGM films and its libraries, it has a weak record of Hollywood deal making. Vía Digital focused instead on working with such national distributors as Media Park, which put together programming for nine channels and provided Vía Digital non-exclusive rights to Fox's film library. Vía Digital also cut deals with Playboy TV, BBC World, BBC Prime and Eurosport.

The global independent film distributors were also tapped by programme-hungry broadcasters and satellite operators, making Spain the third-largest importer of independent cinema in the world after Germany and Japan in 1997 (Hopewell, 1998a, p. 36).

Domestic production and commercialization

Apart from movies, satellite TV programming consisted mostly of sports and documentaries, staples of domestic production. Of course, football dominates, but celebrity bullfighting has become new stock in trade. Vía

Digital outbid Sogecable for exclusive rights to three classic bullfights during the festival seasons in Seville, Madrid and Pamplona. For the San Isidro festival of Madrid, for example, Vía Digital paid more than $3 million for rights to televise the main fights, paying star bullfighters upwards of $60 000 to use their images to promote the pay per view events (Webster, 1998, p. 39). Vía Digital has also invested over $6 million in the Spanish film industry, with smaller sums going to national distributors, co-productions with Latin American producers and the production of TV movies. A small investment by international standards, it still represents Vía Digital's commitment to domestic production. Apart from this, Telefónica also has a controlling interest in Lola Films, a powerful producer of Spanish cinema.

Conclusion

This essay has shown how the development of new media in Spain accelerated globalization, with French, American, Japanese, British, Spanish and Italian corporations giving direction to new digital satellite and cable services. The multiplication of satellite and cable channels has in turn created unprecedented demand for imported films and TV shows from Hollywood. And finally, increased investment in commercial film and TV production, primarily sports and documentaries, has benefited domestic producers but it has also imposed market criteria to determine what gets produced, broadcast, and who can see it.

While this latest and most unrestrained phase of media privatization shares many features with the period leading up to the legalization of private television in Spain (Maxwell, 1995), the most striking similarity has been the way in which commercial media corporations have profited from the political intrigues surrounding the emergence of new media. As John Hopewell (1998b, p. 38) noted in *Variety*, the digital war was 'perhaps the most powerful marketing campaign ever launched in favor of digital pay TV.' Indeed, in less than 18 months, the new satellite services reached twice as many homes as cable. Hopewell added that while the 'back-stabbing, blackmail, conspiracies, phone-tapping, midnight takeovers, and Byzantine lawsuits' may have confused people, the 'confusion made front-page news, week in, week out, convincing Spanish citizens that whatever digital TV was, it was not to be without.' What Hopewell does not mention is that the front-page news ultimately failed Spanish citizens, leaving them without a way to consider and debate the necessity, function, or appropriateness of such technologies in a democracy.

It is important to understand that digital media are not just rivals to analogue media but are going to be phased in under a legal mandate to *replace* all analogue media systems. Consider the magnitude of this replacement in Spain as of 1998: there were nearly 12 million households in Spain, all of which had at least one colour TV set; 90 per cent had a phone. Over 61 per cent had a VCR, under 4 per cent had a cable subscription, while over 7 per cent subscribed to satellite services hooked up either to a collective dish (satellite master antenna television, SMATV) or direct-to-home dish (DTH). Of these households, 2.5 per cent were equipped for Internet access, a figure sure to grow with fierce marketing of cable and satellite services.

The consumer's price tag for a digital make over has been estimated at $11.5 million for television hardware alone (Martínez Soler, 1998, p. 111). In this context, any consideration of new media must take into account the potential profits motivating operators who plan to integrate media services through digital distribution into Spanish homes. Services as diverse as phone, television, radio, Internet and interactive media can potentially be marketed by a single provider who has criss-crossed investments in digital cable networks, digital satellite and over-the-air digital broadcasting. This explains why Telefónica expanded to offer CATV and satellite TV services; why a TV network, Retevisión, became a phone company, a CATV service, and, eventually, a digital terrestrial TV service; and why Cablevisión grew from CATV to make a bid to become a national phone company. The fundamental goal was to get their brand names into the digital market-place. That was, in short, the reason for the digital war: all the fuss was no more than a relatively cheap way for the likes of Telefónica and PRISA to secure brand-name recognition in the new digital environment in a short period of time.

To conclude, the new media promise a healthy pluralism for Spanish citizens who can afford to pay a premium for better quality images, more programming choices, and the variety of multimedia and interactive services that digital satellites and fibre optic cable will carry. By the same token, the large majority of Spaniards will probably see a decline in the quality and timeliness of domestic productions broadcast free of charge. This decline could occur if top national programme makers and distributors find more lucrative work in the subscription and pay-per-view market. Affluent consumers will get high-quality services and home equipment, poorer viewers will be increasingly cut off from such innovations. More distressing will be the lock out of viewers from popular televised sports, as digital operators manoeuvre for control over broadcasting rights, especially to football.

Unless the EC or the Spanish Parliament offer a viable political solution to halt this division of Spanish culture into two classes, the majority of Spanish citizens will be forced to view the new media through store windows, their noses pressed against the glass as they marvel at the latest special effects in the spectacle of Spanish democracy.

Note

1. 'Apenas unos días de cash flow de nuestra compañía' (quoted in Martínez Soler, 1998, p. 256).

References

HOPEWELL, J. 1998a: Distribs enter a vibrant market. *Variety*, April 20–6, 36.
—— 1998b: Country readies for digital fireworks. *Variety*, April 20–6, 38.
MARTÍNEZ SOLER, J. A. 1998: *Jaque a Polanco: la guerra digital: un enfrentamiento en las trincheras de la política, el dinero, y la prensa.* Madrid: Ediciones Temas de Hoy.
MAXWELL, R. 1995: *The spectacle of democracy: Spanish television, nationalism, and political transition.* Minneapolis, Minn.: University of Minnesota Press.
Spain tries to get along as Hollywood watches sceptically. *European Media Business and Finance* 8 (15), 27 July 1998, 1.
WEBSTER, J. 1998: Matadors cash in on a bull market. *The Sunday Telegraph*, 24 May, 39.

16

The Spanish film industry in the 1980s and 1990s

BARRY JORDAN

Introduction

Industrially underdeveloped, structurally fragmented, aesthetically impoverished and politically hamstrung, between 1939 and 1975 the Francoist film industry – if such a term is appropriate – was an isolated, poverty-stricken, state-controlled backwater on the margins of Europe (Besas, 1985, pp. 17–30 and 1997, p. 246; Hopewell, 1986, pp. 63–71; Gubern *et al.*, 1995, pp. 181–294; Monterde, 1993, pp. 29–65; Evans, 1995, pp. 215–22). The death of Franco in 1975 promised longed-for freedoms and new opportunities. However, the period of political reform which followed (1977–82) coincided with the deepest economic recession since the Stabilization Plan of 1959 and was intensified by the political uncertainty over the succession to the dictator and whether the transition to democracy would hold. It was against this troubled background that the Spanish film industry, no stranger itself to almost permanent crisis conditions, faced the multiple challenges of political, industrial, technical and cultural modernization and reform. In this essay, I attempt to trace some of the decisive moments in the story of the modernization of Spain's film industry, with particular reference to political, institutional and legislative changes over the last two decades.

Flukes and short-termism: the reform period 1977–1982

Like the process of democratic reform in the country as a whole, the arrival of political and institutional reform in the Spanish film business came in stages, but not in a planned, coherent fashion. In fact, it is difficult to relate the rapid pace of political change in Spain in the late 1970s and early 1980s to changes in the film industry which, when they did happen, were usually lagging behind other trends, discontinuous with real political changes and largely piecemeal (Monterde, 1993, pp. 19–21).

The reform process mainly took the form of the legislative dismantling of the old Francoist administrative apparatus which was incompatible with a new plural and democratic Spain. This process was characterized by a number of developments: the supression of the official Francoist newsreel NODO; the dismantling of the vertical syndicate structure in the film industry; the official ending of state censorship in November 1977, replaced by a new Board of Film Classification; the retention of the existing film protection system, with domestically produced films receiving as of right subsidies of 15 per cent of box-office receipts, with a further 25 per cent available for bigger-budget projects; the retention of dubbing licences for foreign (i.e. American) films and the elimination of distribution quotas (thus disadvantaging at a stroke the obligation on distributors to market and distribute Spanish films – a measure rescinded and revised in 1978) (Monterde, 1993, pp. 67–81; Hopewell, 1986, pp. 176–9; Gubern *et al.*, 1995, pp. 346–52). Unfortunately, during the reform period, it is difficult to discern any serious commitment to change, let alone any coherent, overarching policy towards the film industry. Indeed, it was difficult for the ex-Francoist administrations of the period to develop a consistent strategy or a general law when between 1977 and 1982 there were no less than six ministers responsible for the General Cinema Board (*Dirección General de Cine*): Rogelio Díaz, Félix Benito de Lugo, José García Moreno, Luis Escobar, Carlos Gortari and Matías Vallés Rodríguez. In brief, by the early 1980s, Spanish film-making had changed very little. The 'industry' remained decapitalized and vastly under-resourced, film production was totally fragmented, with dozens of fly-by-night production companies making one film and then disappearing. As Imanol Uribe has argued, films got made largely by 'pure fluke' ('por pura chiripa') (cited in Payán, 1993, p. 23). Paradoxically, however, film production boomed, with mainly low-budget, pot-boiler genre films being made (comedies, horror, spaghetti westerns, soft pornography, etc.). This was possible only because of the system of state subsidies inherited from Francoism, which significantly diminished the degree of financial risk involved in domestic film-making (while seriously hindering the achievement of viable financial returns) and helped support a fairly large though transient commercial sector as well as a much smaller art-house enclave.

Nationalizing Spanish cinema: PSOE film policy 1982–1988

In October 1982, the PSOE won a landslide electoral victory against a divided and discredited governing party, signalling the effective consolidation of democracy and the beginning of fundamental change, or so most Spaniards hoped (Preston, 1986: 189–227). In the film arena, political and institutional change came via PSOE film policy (though not by a general law), its vision heavily influenced by French Socialist film legislation and by a cohort of liberal-left art-house directors and producers identified with PSOE thinking, including José Luis Borau, Manuel Gutiérrez Aragon, Vicente Aranda, Mario Camus, Victor Erice, Pilar Miró, Carlos Saura, Elías Querejeta and Andrés Vicente Gómez. Their time had come. Government policy reaffirmed the PSOE's pre-electoral commitment to the concept of a subsidized national cinema, defining the cinema not simply as a commercial product but as a 'cultural good' ('bien cultural'), which formed part of the people's cultural heritage ('el patrimonio del pueblo') and served as an instrument of emancipation ('instrumento de liberación') (Hopewell, 1989, p. 400; Gubern *et al.*, 1995, pp. 400–1). Such principles indicated a decisive shift towards a view of cinema as an artistic and cultural artefact, a serious 'quality' product and as a crucial element in the state-sponsored, PSOE-inspired re-education of the Spanish nation.

In October 1982, Pilar Miró Romero was appointed Director-General of Cinema *(Directora General de Cinematografía)* taking up her post in December of that year. (Later, she was appointed Director-General of the Institute for Cinema and Audio Visual Arts – *Instituto de Cinematografía y de las Artes Audiovisuales,* or ICAA, set up in 1985 – which replaced the old Francoist General Cinema Board *(Dirección General de Cine).* Miró's appointment was significant for several reasons. She was the first woman ever to hold such a post, a sign perhaps of the PSOE's desire to promote women politicians in a traditionally male-dominated public sphere. She was a practising member of the profession, one of the very few female graduates of the regime's Film School *(Escuela Oficial de Cine)* and someone who had developed a long and successful career in both film and television (Triana Toribio, 1998, pp. 234–7). Miró was also a Socialist activist, relatively senior in the party and a personal friend of the new prime minister. She had also been a victim of deep-rooted professional mysogyny, not only in media circles in Spain but also in connection with her debut film *La petición* (1976) and with the lengthy ban imposed by the (military) courts on her controversial critique of the Civil Guard, *El crimen de Cuenca* (1979). Nevertheless, given her background and experience, Miró seemed eminently qualified to deal with the awesome problems facing the Spanish film industry.

When Miró took up her post, American cinema totally dominated the Spanish national market (Hopewell, 1989, pp. 396–7). Also, up to the early 1980s, indigenous Spanish film production was broadly of three types: (1) S-rated films (that is, low-budget, poor-quality pot-boilers, mainly soft pornography, sex comedies, horror films, gore, etc., whose *raison d'être* was to be traded by distributors in order to qualify for dubbing licences); (2) co-productions with foreign companies (again sex films, westerns, horror movies – many of which were fraudulent and again made cheaply in order to secure dubbing licences); (3) a small number of artistically more ambitious, art-house films, made by liberal-left auteurs, largely for international festivals and for raising Spain's cultural profile abroad. To make any headway on reforming such a polarized production landscape, Miró had to operate on several fronts. She had to find ways of reducing the degree of American dominance in distribution and exhibition (by varying distribution and screen quotas to ensure better and more numerous release dates for the local product, as well as more aggressive and effective marketing). She needed to tighten controls on the bogus nature of many low-cost co-production proposals and budgets as well as rationalize (i.e. radically diminish subsidies for) the whole 'S' category of films. Above all, in line with her political mandate, she had to reorient funding arrangements in order to improve the general quality of indigenous movies, involving greater use of collaborative production and screening agreements with the state television provider, RTVE. As a corollary, she would also have to improve the marketing and visibility of Spanish films abroad, by way of supporting domestic film events and exhibitions as well as international film festivals (Gómez Bermúdez de Castro, 1989, p. 8).

In strategic terms, the so-called Miró Law of December 1983 (in fact a set of Reales Decretos or Royal Decrees) focused on the need to raise dramatically the 'quality' of Spanish films as well as encourage new directors, children's cinema and experimental work. At the heart of the new legislation was a measure, based on the French *avance sur recette* system, which took the form of subsidies of up to 50 per cent of total film production costs paid in advance to producers/directors from the Film Protection Fund. Later, such advance subsidies would be supplemented by other financial benefits, including extra credits paid to film producers who had not received advance subsidies. (Though always precarious, film-making in Spain thus remained, at least financially, relatively risk-free, with the state picking up an ever larger proportion of production costs, but only for 'approved' projects.) Apart from direct injections of public subsidy, funding would be financed from the monies recouped for dubbing licences paid by distributors, as well as from the rolling return of subsidies and loans from films already funded from the public purse and (theoretically) earning returns at the box office. (Gómez Bermúdez de Castro, 1989, pp. 119–25). Yet, as Besas puts it rather disparagingly, by lavishing a great deal of public money on her ageing, left-wing, auteurist 'centurions' (1997, p. 247), all of whom were keen to develop an intellectually respectable, anti-Francoist and internationally competitive film 'culture', Miró's policy would effectively mean fewer, if bigger-budget productions, virtually none of which would ever cover their costs.

Not unexpectedly, the Miró Law had a devastating effect on Spanish film production totals. In 1982, whilst 142 features were made (including dozens of low-budget genre films) and attracted basic state subsidies, by 1989 this number had plummeted to 48, with many commercial film-makers (of mainly sex and horror movies) having been discouraged from applying

(Gubern *et al.*, 1995, p. 402). On a more positive note, however, the new legislation radically transformed the general technical level of film production, the quality of sets and costumes, the overall 'look' of Spanish films, as well as improving the level of salaries and the duration of shooting schedules (Hopewell, 1989, p. 401). All of which implied, as a corollary, significant cost inflation. Also, as Monterde observes, directly encouraged by the new legislation, there developed something of an obsession among those Spanish film-makers favoured by Miró to propose ever bigger and more ambitious film projects, with correspondingly higher budgets, in imitation of international production standards (1993, pp. 107–9). Over time, this resulted in what Riambau has called a 'cine polivalente', an increasingly standardized, 'quality', official film product, based in large part on literary adaptations such as *La colmena* (1982) and *Los santos inocentes* (1984). The latter, both by Mario Camus, were successful movies in their own right but they gave rise to a much less successful (commercially and critically) art-house bandwagon (Gubern *et al.*, 1995, p. 421) which signally failed to attract Spanish audiences. And while Miró did much to raise the profile of Spanish film internationally through a myriad of international festivals, prizes, promotional film weeks, and so on, despite one or two notable exceptions, Spanish films struggled to gain visibility and compete seriously in any of the major international markets (Monterde, 1993, p. 107–9).

At bottom, rather than satisfy the tastes and interests of mainstream audiences and the market, too many officially subsidized film projects were designed to fulfil an a priori PSOE-led, 'cultural' remit. They were conceived in accordance with what film producers thought would satisfy official cultural agendas and please the various committee members responsible for disbursing the advance subsidies. Specific criteria for awarding subsidies were nebulous and at times arbitrary, thus leading to industry-wide dissatisfaction with the adjudication system. So, apart from the danger of uniformity of film product, as noted above, there was far too much room in the system for influence peddling, favouritism (*amiguismo*) and corruption (Hopewell, 1989, p. 404; Gubern *et al.*, 1995, p. 403). A further criticism levelled at the Miró legislation was the fact that it became, in effect, a form of political manipulation, if not control (Gómez Bermúdez de Castro, 1989, p. 127). Moreover, virtually the only cinema being made by the late 1980s in Spain was that financed by the state. In 1985, for example, 53 out of 77 films were made in Spain without subsidy; in 1987, this figure had dropped to only 19 out of 69. The state had rapidly taken on the role of dominant, indeed hegemonic, film producer; and in effect, as Berlanga argued, the PSOE had 'nationalized' the film industry (Payán, 1993, p. 35). This, plus alarming levels of cost inflation, tended to dissuade private/commercial film interests from (re)-entering the market; it also brought with it excessive bureaucracy and charges of official incompetence, as well as manipulation of committee decisions on film projects and corruption, to which the Miró administration was not immune (Gómez Bermúdez de Castro, 1989, pp. 129–35). In the wake of a number of high-profile cases, (involving accusations of favouritism and leading to a parliamentary enquiry) Miró resigned at the end of 1985 (Payán, 1993, p. 33; Gómez Bermúdez de Castro, 1989, pp. 131–3). She also left her post at an awkward moment, just before Spain's accession to the EEC in January 1986 (upon which new norms, concerning screen/exhibition quotas and dubbing licences for 'non-EEC' (American) films, would come into force) and without having managed to properly restructure the fields of distribution and exhibition, which were increasingly controlled by the big US distributors and their agents. Miró was succeeded as head of ICAA in January 1986 by Fernando Méndez Leite, film and television director and film critic, who broadly continued existing policies regarding selective advance subsidies. He was also anxious to defend the basic principles of state film support in the face of criticism from EEC ministers over excessive protectionism being lavished on the Spanish film producers (as noted above, Spanish film subsidies could total up to and sometimes exceed 50 per cent of production costs, whilst the EEC average among member states was 25–30 per cent) (Payán, 1993, p. 37).

Spain's entry into the EEC had unfortunate consequences for the domestic film industry, given that EEC (EU) films – despite their extremely poor box-office potential – now qualified for inclusion into the screening quota hitherto reserved for Spanish films alone and on the same terms. This meant a worrying dilution in the already low number of Spanish films being distributed and exhibited at home. During Méndez Leite's term of office, it was also clear that the ICAA Protection Fund was simply inadequate to cope with the demands being placed upon it (as seen in the case of superproductions like Saura's *El Dorado* (1988) or Ridley Scott's *1492* (1992), a Spanish co-production subsidized to the tune of 2 million dollars by the Spanish government (Besas, 1997, p. 250). More alarmingly, but not unexpectedly, state-subsidized films were making little or no return at the box office and thus failing to replenish the Protection Fund (Monterde, 1993, pp. 105–6), raising the spectre of its imminent bankruptcy.

The reform of the reform: 1988–1994

In July 1988, Javier Solana was replaced by Jorge Semprún as Spain's new Minister of Culture. Given Semprún's background as an anti-Nazi war hero and renegade Communist, plus his literary credentials and his links with the cinema (as scriptwriter, for example, on Costa Gavras' *Z*, (1969), on Renais' *Stavisky*, (1974) and as director of a documentary on the Civil War, *Les deux mémoires* (1973)), his appointment was greeted with enormous anticipation among Spain's film professionals. Unfortunately, this was soon dashed when the new minister, following the PSOE's 'neo-liberal' economic policies, its new European commitments and a determination to roll back the adverse financial effects of the Miró Law, adopted a particularly hardline policy on film funding, especially in regard to selective advance subsidies, inflated budget applications and box-office fraud. Indeed, Semprún argued that the Miró legislation had led to a 'dependency' culture among film-makers, which discouraged private funding initiatives. So disillusioned was he with Semprún's stance that Méndez Leite (already the target of legal action by film professionals in 1987) resigned from his post at ICAA on 9 December 1988.

Méndez Leite was replaced by Miguel Marías (son of the renowned Spanish philosopher Julián Marías), translator, film critic and academic, director of the *Filmoteca Española* (Spanish Film Archive, 1986–88), but someone who had little practical experience of the film industry as such. Marías was charged with implementing the measures emanating from the so-called Semprún Decree (Decreto Semprún), whose funding objectives had given rise to such a massive storm of protest from the film industry. In principle, while acknowledging the need for the state to support the cinema, the Decree simply enshrined in law the government's decision to make the film industry more self-sufficient, while encouraging the entry of independent entrepreneurs and various forms of private capital. Semprún now linked pre-production subsidies to funds raised by producers, while exploring alternative forms of financing and means of raising credits, such as 'soft loans' from banks, certain types of tax breaks and more extensive co-production arrangements (production advances, domestic and foreign screening rights) with RTVE (Gómez Bermúdez de Castro, 1989, pp. 128–30; Besas, 1997, p. 251).

In January 1990, Marías stepped down and was replaced at the ICAA, not by an academic or film professional, but (as if harking back to the old Francoist days) by a career civil servant, a Euro technocrat named Enrique Balmaseda, specialist in European media legislation. It was the latter's task to prepare the groundwork for a new film law (involving production initiatives and improvements to technical infrastructure and professional training) and to complete the financial reforms of the Semprún Decree. In this regard, the PSOE government was relying mainly on those co-production arrangements and advances (which were helping to subsidize 20–30 film features per year) between the film industry and RTVE to get it off the financial hook. Unfortunately, following the launch of private television in Spain in 1990, RTVE began to experience severe pressure in its advertising income. This resulted in the public corporation reneguing on a film co-operation agreement signed in June 1990 and the withdrawal of its promised 2000 million peseta investment in film financing and purchase of film rights for the small screen. This forced the ICAA in December 1990 into emergency negotiations with the Banco de Crédito Industrial concerning loans to the film industry, heralding a period of acute and almost terminal financial crisis. Given the need to provide some form of collateral or guarantees of repayment, bank loans/credits were not particularly attractive to film producers (Besas, 1997, p. 254). With production levels an all-time low, a general strike on 12 December 1991 by film and theatre actors demonstrated widespread professional dismay and anger at government policy. As a result, Balmaseda resigned from the ICAA, being replaced in January 1992 by PSOE stalwart Juan Miguel Lamet. The latter presided over an agreement between ICAA and the Banco Exterior de España which would provide a source of low-cost credit for film production, backed by an 800 million peseta guarantee fund. But still, criticism of government policy continued unabated. Moreover, in 1992, out of 52 film releases, only three (including Trueba's *Belle Epoque*), grossed more than their production costs, with 14 failing to achieve a release at all, including four state-subsidized movies (Besas, 1997, p. 255).

In March 1993, with its electoral support seriously in decline, the PSOE still managed to win a fourth term in government. Before its return to office, at the San Sebastian Film Festival in September 1992, a collection of 19 Spanish film producers, led by ex-UCD minister Albert Oliart and film producer José María Otero, had come together to form a powerful new pressure group, PROCINE, intent on lobbying government for radical changes in state film funding. At the heart of their proposals was a call for a shift in the nature of financial support for the industry away from the arbitrary and discredited system of selective advance credits towards a system of automatic subsidies for all film projects based on box-office receipts, financed by taxes on ticket prices, advertising, television rights, video sales, etc. The basic subsidy of 15 per cent of box-office returns given to all state-supported movies would remain in place; however, advance credits would be limited to supporting more risky projects and new directors.

The PROCINE proposals coincided with further elaboration of the government's *Plan Integral de Cine* (begun in 1990, as noted above) emanating from the Ministry of Culture, which would form the basis of a new Film Law to be passed in 1994. The government plan anticipated a Film Protection Fund totalling some 4000 million pesetas yearly, to be made available in the form of soft, low-cost credits. It also foresaw the need to increase the national market share of Spanish film to a highly ambitious 25 per cent, as in France, but over a period of years. In the preceding months in parliament, Partido Popular politicians and lobbyists had championed an alternative film bill and argued vehemently for the wholesale removal of film funding from state budgets, the suppression of advance credits and dubbing licences, a change of screen quota rules (arguing that 50 per cent of European Community films should be treated as Spanish) and for a major shift towards automatic (not selective) subsidies based on box-office receipts. As a result, after numerous rectifications to the text of the PSOE bill and massive filibustering pressure from Partido Popular (as well as the resignation of Lamet in January 1994, who was replaced at the ICAA, for a second term, by Enrique Balmaseda in March 1994), the new Film Law came into effect in June 1994. Initially, this new Socialist law supported the *status quo*, continuing the disbursement of advance subsidies as well as imposing a screen quota of one day of Spanish/Community film for two days of film from so-called third countries (*terceros países*), in essence the USA. (In other words, American subdistributors in Spain would be required to buy and screen a greater proportion than before of 'Spanish/Euro' films in order to secure dubbing licences for American films.)

However, under immense pressure from the US-dominated film distribution and exhibition sectors to amend the legislation in favour of more deregulation, at the San Sebastian Film Festival in September 1994, the new Socialist Minister of Culture, Carmen Alborch, signalled a major shift in government policy. She announced publicly that the June Film Law of 1994 was to be amended, with effect from October. Changes included the scrapping of the system of advance production subsidies (the very heart of the Miró legislation) and the adoption of automatic subsidies, now geared to box-office takings, with a sliding scale of subsidies taking effect at various stages, according to the type of film involved and its revenue profile. So, a film taking 30 million pesetas would receive an automatic subsidy of one-third of the cost of producing the film, to which would be added 15 per cent of total costs automatically, up to a limit of 100 million. (In the case of films by new directors, the threshold would be 20 million and for films shot in languages other than Castilian, the target would be 10 million pesetas of revenue, before the subsidy kicked in.) Despite an outcry from Castilian producers and directors, ICAA director Balmaseda was persuaded that regional film industries, such as the Catalan sector, would probably collapse if Catalan films were obliged to take 30 million pesetas in sales before securing a subsidy.

Thus, under the Socialist mandate, beginning with the so-called Semprún Decree of 1988 and now with Alborch's apparent U-turn in policy, we see a complete reversal of the main principles which had inspired the Miró Law in the early and mid-1980s. Government support was no longer rigidly predicated on advance subsidies for high-quality, art-house movies with negligible audiences but increasingly on the commercial viability of the product in the market-place. Even so, the principles of a state-subsidized film industry would remain intact, an approach which would characterize Socialist policy up to the following election of 1996.

Meanwhile, production of Spanish films reached its nadir in 1994, with a mere 44 full length features being made, including in that number 8 co-productions; only 39 features reached the screen.[1] Also, of a total of 1259 films shown in Spain in that year, only 187 were Spanish. At the same time, at 6.8 million, audience figures for Spanish movies were at their lowest levels for nearly a decade. Official figures revealed a slippage of 1.5 million spectators in 1994, resulting in a loss of 550 million pesetas of revenue compared to 1993 and a relatively low market share of 7 per cent.[2] In part, this situation reflected the fierce competition the domestic film business was facing from television and video, as well as US dominance. It also suggested a vote of no confidence by Spanish film audiences in the type of Spanish films available. By and large, despite a few exceptions (Almodóvar's *Tacones Lejanos* (1991), Alex de la Iglesia's *Acción Mutante* (1992), and Enrique Urbizu's *Todo por la pasta* (1991)), Spaniards continued to ignore Spanish films.

Paradoxically, 1994 saw a number of positive developments. The same year saw the Oscar award and significant international acclaim for Trueba's *Belle Epoque* (1992) and the release of a small number of successful Spanish films including Bajo Ulloa's second feature *La madre muerta* and Manuel Gómez Pereira's top-grossing comedy *Todos los hombres sois iguales*. Also, we see the creation of Sogetel/Sogepaq, that is, the film production and distribution/sales arms of the Spanish media conglomerate PRISA, (owner of *El País*) following a merger with IberoAmericana, Polygram and Canal Plus. This new international combine announced plans to invest 6000 million pesetas in local film production, supporting 16–20 film features during 1995 and 1996. In a similar but more cautious vein, RTVE announced an 8000 million peseta injection of investment into film production and transmission rights over a four-year period, dependent on the availability of funds. There was also a new building for the Filmoteca and the revival of Franco's old Official Film School (*Escuela Oficial de Cine*) to be headed by Méndez Leite and run by the Comunidad de Madrid. Above all, Balmaseda announced a record ICAA Film Protection Fund for 1995 of 16 900 million pesetas. In turn, he demanded a much better market share for Spanish film upwards of 13–15 per cent in order to justify the increased subsidy. After a disastrous 1994, 1995 would be the year in which the Spanish film industry would have to turn the corner, which it did.

Reversal of fortune: 1995–2000

Since 1995, the Spanish film industry has experienced major changes giving rise to a series of transformations which, almost for the first time, may well be leading to the emergence of a viable national film 'industry'. After the March elections in 1996, with the narrow victory of Aznar's Partido Popular, conservative government film policy was set firmly on the path of deregulation and commercial viability. José María Otero, head of ICAA, announced a series of measures including the following: the suppression of advance subsidies and dubbing licences; the phasing out of screen quotas; the retention of automatic subsidies according to box-office revenue; support for new directors and scriptwriters; and help for special or higher risk projects. Such measures clearly indicated the beginning of the end for a subsidized Spanish film industry, with government acquiescing to pressures from multinational distributors and exhibitors as well as indigenous entrepreneurs in their quest for greater market freedoms.

During the mid to late 1990s, film production totals in Spain have been around 70–80 features per year, at an average declared cost of approximately 250 million pesetas, though in 1998, 16 films had budgets well in excess of 400 million.[3] Market share holds reasonably steady at 13–14 per cent per year, with Spanish films attracting roughly 13 million spectators in 1998, indicating strong public and commercial success in a number of cases, including Trueba's *La niña de tus ojos* (1998), Garci's *El Abuelo* (1998), Fesser's *El milagro de P. Tinto* (1998), Gómez Pereira's *Entre las piernas* (1998) and especially Santiago Segura's *Torrente, el brazo tonto de la ley* (1998). As noted above, with the consumption of media services in Spain on an upward curve and Spanish film now representing a more attractive commercial proposition, major infrastructural changes are under way in the film sector. We find significant levels of merger activity in distribution and exhibition, with new companies emerging such as Media (linking Manga Film and Sherlock Distributors) and Nirvana (incorporating Sogedasa, Amanda & Wanda Films). We also find the expansion of companies such as Catalan Distributor/Exhibitor Cinesa into the Basque Country as well as established players such as Lusomundo, Dehesa and Lauren building new multi- and megaplexes, an area now attracting Tele 5 and its partner TriPictures in a new distribution venture calling itself 'Premier Megaplex'. Such activity has resulted in 200 new cinema screens being opened in Spain in 1998. And whilst film production in Spain remains fundamentally fragmented, there are numerous signs of new production company formation, particularly in Catalonia, with Prisma, Castelao and Barcelona Audiovisual, as well as Filmax/Sogedasa, a grouping which intends to specialize in the production of 'cine de terror' (horror movies).

A key element in all of the above changes is the crucial role played by the television companies in the co-financing of film production and the provision of opportunities for exhibition, through contracts for domestic and foreign transmission and repeats on the small screen. In this connection, as a subscription film channel, Canal Plus is a key investor in production as well as a crucial distribution outlet, regularly filling its schedules by purchasing lots from commercial film distributors as well as cross-buying bundles of Spanish films from TVE and other television companies. Just as important, however, are recent developments in digital television. After the breakdown in October 1998 of the proposed merger between Telefónica's *Vía Digital* and PRISA's *Canal Satelite Digital* (originally negotiated in July 1998), the two giant conglomerates appear to be following separate development strategies, one with its own highly advantageous football coverage (CSD), the other without (VD). This 'poker game', as it has been called, was preventing the companies from giving clear signals as to their investment intentions in film production and transmission, though VD had stated that it intended to invest 6000 million pesetas in film activities up to the year 2000. However, in May 1999, the situation was clarified. The Spanish parliament approved EU directives on the harmonization of television and media financing (the so-called 'television without frontiers' directives). These new rules will now oblige all Spanish television companies to invest 5 per cent of their annual revenues in domestic film production and transmission. This represents a major new source of finance for Spanish film production and exhibition (upwards of 13 000 million pesetas for 1999–2000, if the legislation is implemented and properly enforced). It also provides a basis for longer-term financial stability, allowing Spanish producers to make more competitive, bigger-budget movies, with greater resources for casting, shooting schedules, marketing and promotion.

Most importantly, perhaps, since the mid-1990s, there has been a veritable renaissance of attractive and commercially viable domestic film production in Spain. This has arisen in part through changes in film financing and the greater role being played in film budgets by foreign, transnational capital, which demands projects that promise a commercial return. It is also the result of the huge injection of new blood into the industry, with new young(ish) directors, actors, writers, technical crew, etc. (aged between 25 and 45), some with training, many others without, but who desperately want to make mainstream, commercial movies. For example, since 1990, nearly 160 new directors, 30 of them women, have made a movie in Spain, giving rise to 15 films per year from debut directors (not all of which achieve a release, however) (Heredero, 1999, pp. 51–2). Such a colossal generational renewal has had a major impact not only on production totals, but on the emergence of a broadly commercial Spanish cinema involving a new set of narrative, generic, thematic, stylistic and casting choices, which are proving highly attractive to Spanish audiences, especially the younger genererations. Add to this process of renewal the fact that national and international film festivals have proved invaluable in raising the profile and in some cases the commercial success of Spanish movies. Like Garci's *El Abuelo* (1998), Saura's *Tango* (1998) was nominated for an Oscar in 1999. While neither won Best Foreign Film, the Oscar effect significantly improved Saura's box office take in the USA (though not in Spain). Almodóvar's recent success at Cannes in 1999 as prizewinner for Best Director has helped to reaffirm his stature as an international auteur and boost an already healthy domestic and foreign box office for his *Todo sobre mi madre* (1999). Also, Trueba's *La niña de tus ojos (*1998), already fêted at Berlin, found its returns increased by 30 per cent in Spain after winning a Goya for best picture in January 1999 (the very prize José Luis Garci tried to secure for his *El Abuelo* through an alleged 'compra de votos' (purchase of votes) of Spanish Academy members, a scam somewhat reluctantly denied by Academy President Aitana Sánchez Gijón; such a manœuvre, if true, clearly indicates the crucial effect of the Spanish Goyas on the domestic box office).[4]

In the context of this burgeoning new commercialism, perhaps the most striking film phenomenon of the last two years has been the remarkable success of Santiago Segura's debut feature *Torrente, el brazo tonto de la ley* (1998). Shown at Cannes in 1998, *Torrente* has become the Spanish film sensation of the decade, seen by over 3 million Spaniards and outgrossing Almodóvar's record-breaking *Mujeres al borde de un ataque de nervios* (1988). *Torrente* is a subversive generic hybrid, combining elements of

Spain's sexy Iberian comedy of the 1970s (seen in the casting of seventies veteran Tony Leblanc), drawing on aspects of the *esperpento* tradition of black humour as well as features of John Woo's violent Hong Kong action thrillers. These styles are cleverly interwoven to produce an ironic, satirical chronicle of urban Spain, a savage skit on those embarrassing Iberian sterotypes which Almodóvar so successfully and profitably reinvented in the 1980s. The difference is, however, that where Almodóvar substituted traditional national stereotypes (macho matadors, gypsies, Fascist cops, etc.) with outrageous though positively imaged marginal sexualities (gays, lesbians, transsexuals, drug addicts), *Torrente* lambasts the very 'eroticised marginalia' which Almodovar helped to 'normalize' and make visible. Indeed, through the activities of its macho, racist, misogynist cop hero determined to bust a drugs gang, Segura's film is a subversive provocation to the image of a sexually liberated, politically correct Spain which gained hegemony in the Socialist Spain of the 1980s and 1990s, particularly through Almodóvar's camp comedies (Hernández Ruiz, 1998, pp. 38–9). In similar 'backlash' mould and also enjoying breathtaking commercial success, we find (ex-Almodóvar protegé) Alex de la Iglesia and his fourth major feature *Muertos de Risa* (1999), which exploits the vehicle of the ageing comic duo to deliver a biting, ironic critique of Spain's economic and cultural modernization. Such movies are proof not only of a dramatic shift in constructions of Spanishness for the late 1990s but also of the ability of new Spanish film-makers to connect with and attract mass (mainly young) film audiences with well-made, commercial, yet thought-provoking movies. Perhaps at last, such signs indicate the emergence of a credible and viable industrial and commercial base for film-making in Spain.

Notes

1. *Fotogramas*, February 1995, 36.
2. *Fotogramas,* February 1995, 35
3. *Fotogramas*, March 1999, 160.
4. *Fotogramas*, February 1999, 142.

References

BESAS, P. 1985: *Behind the Spanish lens. Spanish cinema under Fascism and democracy*. Colorado: Arden Press.
BESAS, P. 1997: The financial structure of Spanish cinema. In Kinder, M. (ed.) *Refiguring Spain. Cinema/media/representation*. Durham and London: Duke University Press, 241–59.
EVANS, P. 1995: Cifesa: cinema and authoritarian aesthetics. In Graham, H. and Labanyi, J. (eds), *Spanish cultural studies: an introduction*. Oxford: Oxford University Press, 215–22.
GOMEZ BERMUDEZ DE CASTRO, R. 1989: *La producción cinematográfica española. De la transición a la democracia (1976–86)*. Bilbao: Mensajero.

GUBERN, R., MONTERDE, J. E., PÉREZ PERUCHA, J., RIAMBAU, E. and TOR-
REIRO, C. 1995: *Historia del Cine Español*. Madrid: Cátedra.
HEREDERO, C. F. 1999: Cine español. Nueva Generación. *Dirigido* (April),
50–67.
HERNANDEZ RUIZ, J. 1998: La peliculilla del amiguete. *Dirigido* (March), 38–9.
HOPEWELL, J. 1986: *Out of the past: Spanish cinema after Franco*. London: British
Film Institute.
HOPEWELL, J. 1989: *El cine español después de Franco*. Madrid: El Arquero.
MONTERDE, J.E. 1993: *Veinte años de cine español (1973–1992). Un cine bajo la
paradoja*. Barcelona: Ediciones Paidós.
PAYÁN, M. J. 1993: *El cine español de los 90*. Madrid: Ediciones J.C.
PRESTON, P. 1986: *The triumph of democracy in Spain*. London: Routledge.
TRIANA TORIBIO, N. 1998: In memoriam. Pilar Miró (1940–1997). *Film History*
10, 231–40.

|17|

Marketing with local culture in Spain: selling the transnational way

RICHARD MAXWELL

This essay endeavours to explain how global marketing research works in Spain. The essay follows a marketing network from the ground up, starting with the structured encounter between the marketing interviewer and respondent, in order to show how a transnational firm creates identities for products it wishes to sell in Spain. It describes the process whereby the widely divergent responses of interviewees and focus-group subjects are narrowed to fit into a marketing framework that reflects the transnational corporation's interpretation of the value of goods and services. The essay analyses the significance of the corporate effort to scan and assess popular tastes for big international commercial clients in Spain and how this integrates the local culture into the global market.

Is Spain different?

As every global marketer knows, Spain is different. But for the global marketer, so is every other country in the world. The sale is the goal, and the sale is always local. Hence, global marketers have learned to localize transnational products. They initiate this process by conducting surveys and convening focus groups that will help them track the desires, tastes, opinions and habits in places where potential customers live, shop and die.

From start to finish, the job of global marketing research is one of familiarization. At first, the interviewer appears as a stranger; in fact, according to rules of survey research, they must be unknown to the people being interviewed. Then the interviewers take steps to insinuate themselves into people's lives, using a range of techniques that convey empathy: a winning smile, a gift or payment, expressed knowledge of neighbourhood, town, or city life. In the next stage, the actual interview and questionnaire function like a machine that intermixes the everyday language of interview subjects with the commercial discourse of the marketing survey, creating in the end the appearance of a congenial exchange where before there had been difference. And finally, the product returns to the consumer, packaged, promoted and advertised in that uncanny and knowing form that, if it works, hits close to home. In this context, Spain's differences make it identical to other advanced capitalist economies where a marketer must ply his or her trade (Maxwell, 1996a).

Consider the marketing research firm ALEF, a Spanish subsidiary of the transnational research company, Millward Brown International (MBI). MBI is headquartered in London and forms part of a conglomerate controlled by the Kantar Group Ltd., which is part of the world's second largest advertising and marketing mega-conglomerate, the UK-based WPP. As a part of WPP, ALEF connects to a network of operations providing research, advertising, public relations and other communications services to hundreds of Fortune 500 companies. The WPP empire includes, for example, the powerful public relations firm Hill & Knowlton and the massive advertising agencies of J. Walter Thompson and Ogilvy & Mather Worldwide. Taken together, WPP's subsidiaries combine to form a vast economy from which each of its operations may benefit. Indeed, this economy is of such a large scale that the internal exchanges of business referrals among WPP companies alone account for about a quarter of WPP's total business. ALEF is just one informational node within this worldwide network, a potential source of local market knowledge for any of WPP's subsidiaries' global clients. Some of the past clients linked to ALEF through the marketing research web of the Kantar Group include American Express, Guinness, IBM, Kraft Jacobs Suchard, Levi Strauss, PepsiCo, S.C. Johnson, Unilever, United Distillers, Abbey National, British Airways, British Telecom, De Beers, Ford, Phillip Morris, Time Inc., Argos, AT&T, Beiersdorf, the British Government, Danone, Royal Mail, Shell and Tenneco.

ALEF carries out a range of marketing functions in Spain, including polling, consumer research, and tracking studies of brands and brand recognition among consumers. Like most WPP subsidiaries, ALEF is hired to furnish corporate clients with 'global brand stewardship', a strategy aimed at understanding what happens to brands as they cross borders and how best to help those wayward brands make the journey. By putting local knowledge to work within its global research and analysis network, ALEF can help its transnational clients sell to Spanish markets.

Consumer surveillance from the ground up

Of course, none of this global machinery can function without the labour of the technicians, survey designers, and the interviewers who work on the front line of consumer surveillance. This is where ALEF comes in.

ALEF has deployed teams of interviewers in six marketing research zones across Spain, positioning them in strategic locations that have been identified by a peculiar mapping system created by the rival A. C. Nielsen marketing research company. This strange cartography depicts a world in which traditional political regions have been reconfigured into geo-commercial spaces called Nielsen zones. These zones have the familiar sounding names of Andalucía, Centro, Levante, Norte, Galaico-Astur-Leonesa, and Catalano-Aragonesa. Though carved from the realist geopolitics of the Spanish territorial state, the boundaries on this marketing map serve the singular purpose of distinguishing populations for surveys and other consumer studies. Nevertheless, the standard political map and the Nielsen map share one feature: they are both hierarchically organized with Madrid on top, seconded by Barcelona, followed by the Mediterranean coast and the other zones.

Manuel Ameijeiras, ALEF's Director of Production and Field Research, described the organization of ALEF's realm:

> We have our headquarters and two field research centers in Madrid. We have one research center in Seville and another in Granada in order to handle Western and Eastern portions of Andalucía. Badajoz is included in the Western Andalusian zone. Ciudad Real is included in Eastern Andalusian zone (our choice, not Nielsen's). There's one for the Levante zone in Valencia, another in Bilbao, one in Galicia, and one in Barcelona. We also have one in Lisbon, though that isn't a part of the Nielsen zones. This decentralization is important. What we do is change a bit of the boundaries of the Nielsen zones for our own purposes so that Asturias is in the same zone as Bilbao.

> (Interview, 26 January 1995)

Each of the six research zones also has between two and four teams, totalling twenty teams of varying sizes. Apart from the research centres, four additional team leaders provide direction to teams dispersed in Oviedo, Valladolid, Salamanca and Badajoz. Mallorca also has one team and team leader.

Short of installing surveillance devices in every Spanish home, a transnational client of a marketing firm must rely on the hard work of the interviewer who performs such tasks as telemarketing or the face-to-face interview described here. Interviewers are sent into the streets to question people using a random route method or quota system. The quota system looks for a particular kind of person to interview whereas the random route compels the interviewer to follow a pattern of door-to-door encounters that are supposed to end up furnishing a sample that represents a scale model of Spanish opinion, tastes and preferences. The quota applies to studies in which a known type of consumer is identified and then asked a series of questions that build on the profile of the existing type. For example, owners of a particular brand of luxury automobile might be specified targets of research for a product that only they are likely to buy, such as expensive alarm systems, additional insurance, or diverse luxury goods and services. Other typical interview subjects for a quota method might be recent arrivals at international airports, pet owners, or unemployed youth. Although diminishing in importance, the random route method by contrast provides the most surprises for the interviewer, largely because they do not know who they are looking for as they would with a quota-based survey that obligates them to find a predetermined number of interview subjects with proscribed characteristics.

In the random route, the interview takes place in locales that are proportional in size and demographic variety to a given population under study. In order to ensure that each site has the same probability of representing a designated portion of the entire population, ALEF statistically matches cities, towns and villages of varying size to other similar cities, towns and villages. In theory, an interviewer may go to any one of a number of interchangeable habitats or place categories. Under this statistical criterion, Cadiz is the same as Badajoz, Bilbao is Seville, La Coruña is Córdoba. In short, if research calls for a representative sample from such a habitat, then these diverse places will be treated as if they were identical.

From a strictly statistical angle, then, the mapping system reconfigures divergent spaces and experiences using the market criteria which are compatible with their transnational client's interpretation of life's values. Such an interpretation favors the sameness of consumption over the complexity of cultural differences, though there is some accounting for the putative diversity of consumer lifestyles. Thus for marketers like Ameijeiras the question of regional or national identity 'doesn't really affect consumer products'.

> Take banks for example. Differences of identity don't really figure into a bank's services, its products – savings, credit, etc. Of course, if a man wants to make an investment in Cataluña, he has to go to La Caixa. But that doesn't mean he's getting a different product; it's simply the change of brand in banks one works with. The same thing occurs with general consumer goods.

Ameijeiras's statistical imagination cannot, however, automatically contain all the diversity of regional and local cultures in Spain. It takes a little more discursive work to make people fit inside such marketing knowledge. 'Cataluña is industrialized', Ameijeiras offered, 'and is located near the border with France. Well, this might influence the level of travel, for example, which demonstrates a clear cultural difference with Galicia, where it's more rural, not as mobile.' For Ameijeiras, some people might desire certain services that others reject because of cultural influences that vary among Spain's regions, but knowing this does not change how that product or service will be marketed. As he eloquently put it: 'Cheese is cheese.' The reasons people like cheese 'don't vary between regions,' he said. 'Of course,' he added, 'if you're in Galicia, it's Galician cheese you'll want; in Cataluña, Catalan cheese.' Still, he concluded, while 'more of the local cheese is consumed, the reasons why are not different.' Hence, cheese is cheese.

If the marketing researcher interprets difference in this narrow commercial manner, then not only can cheeses be rendered identical by an empirically demonstrable universal taste for cheese, but Bilbao can magically become Seville, Palma can stand in for Málaga, and so on as long as the designated populations represent similar proportions of the total population under study.

After picking a locale that meets the basic statistical protocol, ALEF's zone managers will choose a district within the locale and pick a place at random to begin the interview. For example, a zone manager might choose an arbitrary number, say three, and then pick up a listing of businesses. It does not matter if this list shows the locations of pharmacies, churches, or stores. The manager simply looks to see what business appears in the third place on the list. The manager will then label that address as the point of departure on the log sheet distributed to the interviewer. A supervisor will ensure that the route is viable and also that the interviewer assigned to the route is not known there, since, as a rule, familiar faces skew results.

At the start, the interviewer looks toward the point of departure and turns left and walks. A number, which is also chosen at random, is given to the interviewer to indicate what door they should knock on first. At ALEF, for example, 2.6 may appear at the top of their instruction sheet, meaning that they will stop at the first address with either a two – 52, 22, 32, etc. – or a six. They have to stop at each of the random numbers as they come upon them. If no one is home or there is anything inappropriate about the person who is home (not a household authority, for example), then the interviewer must pick an alternative. After the interview, they leave the building and turn left again until they find another two or six. They might do two turns to the left and then two to the right, or one left and one right. They do this until they get their ten or eight interviews. They are also instructed to note exactly what happens in the street while they walk. A four-hour walk could take someone a good distance across a city the size of Madrid. However, in the life of an interviewer four hours probably means eight interviews within a mere ten Madrileña blocks, including numerous hikes up and down stairs of apartment buildings.

When the interviewer comes to the door, they do not know who is going to answer nor what conditions they will find. Interviewers at ALEF have confronted many different circumstances, some terrifying and some humourous, but most have been mundane and even boring. Female interviewers are especially alert to possible dangers with unpredictable or aggressive interview subjects. The men are concerned as well about violent domestic scenes that they might happen upon. For the most part, however, the work is tedious and routine, physically demanding, and psychologically draining, especially when the interviewer repeatedly faces the anxious moment that precedes each new encounter (Maxwell, 1996b). However, the job of the interviewer requires that they be relaxed in order to put the interview subject in the right frame of mind for the interview. 'If people are at ease', said one interviewer at ALEF, Gabriel Fernández, 'it's easier to convince them.' 'Exactly!' said Valle Rodríguez, another ALEF interviewer. 'It's easier to convince them to do the interview when you and they are both having a good day, when you're both at ease. And if they are not, well, you just move on to the next one' (Interviews, 16 March 1995).

Once the interviews are collected, they are screened by the supervisors for any errors or unusual results. 'There are times when the interviewer does something not really right, not really within the guidelines,' said Ameijeiras. For instance, an interviewer might fake the responses from people living in a building they were instructed to survey. 'In neighborhoods of rich people,' Ameijeiras explained, 'you'll find that doormen won't let interviewers enter. If the interviewer put down that they interviewed someone in that building, then the supervisor can easily check with the doorman.' The supervisor is obligated to ensure that at least 15 per cent of the interviews done under their charge have been done correctly. They have to do this by re-walking the route done by the interviewer. The supervisor then informs the delegate in charge whether or not the interviews are valid. They only check a few places and if there is no problem they go on to check another route. 'There is some latitude in this,' said Ameijeiras, 'since not all unplanned outcomes can be avoided. But if there is one incorrect one, we check again, and if there is another, this annuls the interview, ruins the information, and we throw out the route.' If 20 to 25 per cent of the work is badly done, ALEF will throw it out and do it over completely.

Ameijeiras added that 'even when the interviewer does everything perfectly, there are still faults in the random method. One is non-response.' Non-response is probably the most common problem facing marketers, as people become increasingly worried about their privacy and how their personal information will be used. There are other problems with the random route method that can skew the results. 'One skewing problem is associated with lower class neighborhoods,' said Ameijeiras,

> where people might be unemployed and hence at home more often than someone who is working. Another bias is associated with female respondents who are at home during the day when the interviewer comes or calls. In this case, when you tabulate the findings you discover you have more women than men – which is not representative since Spain, like most countries is composed of an equal amount of men and women. Another problem has to do with the fact that in Spain there is not a long tradition of surveying, so until recently we've not had sufficient knowledge of all the variables involved in quantitative research. Since the integration with Europe, there has been a marked improvement in methods.

After the survey has been vetted and the information has been processed, the client will receive the summary report from ALEF or MBI. In some cases, ALEF's marketing research goes into a multicountry study of consumption of goods or services which a transnational corporation wants to market globally. In Spain, such global goods could be anything from household cleaning products to imported whisky.

The integration of local identity into global goods

As this process demonstrates, marketing researchers hold a strategic position between the lives of ordinary people and the aims of global merchants. Their labour creates a social presence for an otherwise undifferentiated brand as they endeavour to detect brand awareness in the minds of interview subjects. Their work helps to integrate local culture into transnational salesmanship by retelling the stories that constitute collective identity as if people were merely fellow travellers in the life of a commodity. For this reason, marketers are incapable of gathering information that could tell a story resembling people's complex identity narratives. Recall the homogenizing inscription of Nielsen zones upon diverse experiences in Spanish cultural geography, and consider how the survey questionnaire's protocol grounds down divergent stories of taste and preferences into anonymous bits of detail. Once memorialized in digital fragments of consumption habits and desires, marketers recombine their findings into a data image of a virtual Spanish consumer whose myriad traits refract and distort the identities of hundreds of interview subjects. In a world defined by market knowledge, this composite figure is the authoritative representation of those Spaniards to whom a specific product or sales pitch can be targeted.

Nevertheless, the interviewers' place in the distribution chain of goods and services allows them to see, however briefly, the complexity and diversity of Spanish life as well as the extent to which their research succeeds in helping to shepherd global brands into local experiences of Spanish culture and vice versa. As the following exchange demonstrates, while they understand and sometimes get a kick out of their role in the commercial marketplace, the interviewers at ALEF do not always agree about their impact as the stewards of branded goods and services (Interviews, 16 March 1995).

TO: Okay, so I'd have to say that there is very little influence of what we do in the final product.

VR: What?

ER: I disagree. I think we do influence.

TO: Man, are we that important? [laughter]

ER: I think so ...

VR: There are studies that we participated in that have come out very well and had influence. I'll see an ad on the telly and think to myself that I had a hand in that.

TO: Come on. You only interviewed people on what they thought about what was already there. In the end it's the ad agency that decides, and you know it.

ER: Yeah, but if you work on one ad and then they change it or bring out another after the research is done, then you think you might have had something to do with it.

Conclusion: process over product

Marketers will never know with certainty whether or not Spaniards recognize themselves in the products sold with the aid of this transnational network of marketing research. The problem of knowing is chronic, and the cycle of research is interminable. This condition elevates the importance of the role that faith has in marketing research – the faith that marketers and their clients bestow in the techniques of consumer surveillance and the categories of consumers they concoct. This faith is the pre-eminent symbolic currency exchanged among advertisers, marketing researchers, and their corporate clients. Its symbolic power not only holds together a vast network of commercial relationships but legitimates multi-billion-dollar corporate investments in surveillance technology and expertise designed for the extraction, collection, storage and processing of personal information.

From this perspective, the most significant feature of marketing research in Spain is the institutional arrangement it has installed and maintained within Spanish society. Starting with the interviewer and the labour organized around the interview, marketing research transforms Spanish life into an informational commodity. People are mapped into geo-commercial zones and then picked out of the population for random questioning of their desires and hatreds for commodities. Their life stories are transformed into an appendage of the commodity's life in order to make sense within the marketing imagination and the corporate client's interpretation of people's value. This is marketing research's vision of Spanish culture, a place like any other where data images of consuming subjects live out their days in Nielsen zones.

References

MAXWELL, R. 1996a: Out of kindness and into difference: the value of global market research. *Media, Culture and Society* 18 (1), 105–26.
—— 1996b: Ethics and identity in global market research. *Cultural Studies* 10 (2), 218–36.

PART
IV

OTHER VOICES

Introduction

Since the end of the dictatorship a whole range of previously invisible, marginalized or disenfranchized voices and identities have become visible. This is also true of various political and ideological positions and perspectives which were excluded from public life and cultural production by legislation and censorship under Franco. It is also the case for many lifestyles and patterns of behaviour which diverged from the conservative social and moral norms enforced by the regime.

The newly permissive, post-Franco context has favoured the representation and articulation of attitudes and behaviours which, in some cases, have broken quite radically with tradition and their impact has sometimes attracted considerable media attention. This has led some cultural commentators, particularly in the 1980s, to regard Spain as the epitome of postmodern social, moral and cultural eclecticism and hedonism, and an oasis of tolerance and liberation, particularly in sexual matters. Such emphatic and celebratory views may suggest a rather more widespread and radical social revolution than is actually the case in democratic Spain. Nevertheless, the changes which the country has undergone in terms of its social structures and cultural values are highly significant. The driving force behind these changes has been Spain's accelerated modernization and the economic and legislative structures and patterns of employment which have accompanied it. In particular, these have had a major impact on traditional gendered roles for both men and women.

Prior to the Republican period (1931–36), Spain was a profoundly conservative country. The Republic brought significant legal advances for female emancipation including votes for women, eligibility to stand for parliament, basic civil and employment rights, and other previously absent legal and administrative entitlements, as well as the introduction of civil marriages and flexible divorce laws. Despite such progressive legislation, however, its implementation was never seriously supported or enforced. The Civil War created new and active opportunities for women, especially on the Republican side, but the moral, social and political structures of the Franco regime reversed the political advances made under the Republic and aggressively reinstated the most traditional values of patriarchy and conservatism.

Since the end of the dictatorhip, advances in equal opportunities legislation and practical changes such as the availability of contraception have radically changed the composition of the workforce, enabling large numbers of women to become economically independent or financially significant in the family structure. Such changes have thus had an inevitable impact on established notions of male and female roles and gender relations. Alternative lifestyles – such as widespread solo living, the legitimacy of openly homosexual relationships, etc. – have become possible as result of legislative changes and a significant reduction in the influence of the Catholic Church.

The visibility of these changes in the cultural products, practices and lifestyles of post-dictatorship Spain is self-evident. However, some of the more subtle meanings inscribed within the ways in which different identities are represented or different subject positions are articulated are less obvious. The essays in this section explore a series of issues relating to representation and subjectivity. They variously trace the development of models of behaviour and changing values as these are portrayed in the media and various forms of cultural production. They also scrutinize the underlying assumptions of contemporary representations – for example, those of alternative sexual orientations and disability – in order to assess the extent to which these indicate positive and progressive developments.

|18|

Gendered images: constructions of masculinity and femininity in television advertising

ELVIRA ANTÓN

Notions of gendered identities and their representation in Spain have undergone some radical changes since the strict paradigms, particularly in the early years, of Francoism. Previously marginalized identities have ceased to be officially persecuted or denied and new models have become visible, sometimes co-existing alongside the persistence of more traditional articulations.

Femininity and masculinity are, of course, never fixed identities, but a constantly renegotiated set of alliances and identifications. They both help to determine, and are in turn influenced by, what we consider normative patterns of morality and behaviour or typical and acceptable ways of behaving within the social setting. The range of identities circulating in a particular society at any one time is neither of essence nor of anatomy, but rather the product of culture(s). In their representation of gender identity and difference cultural products and practices not only reflect, but help to constitute these identities. The sustained circulation and reproduction of those representations may result in the establishment of apparently 'fixed' identities and with them the conventional codes that make it possible for the viewer/reader to understand particular subject positions, whilst also offering a point of reference. An examination of these representations can therefore provide a key to the models of gender identity privileged and promoted at any one moment, and offer points of comparison for measuring shifts in those models over a period of time.

This essay will look at a number of representations of masculinity and femininity in Spanish television advertising, and the way in which these have helped define and shape gendered identities. In order to give some sense of how those representational codes and images have evolved alongside the social, political and economic development in Spain, the first section below offers a brief consideration of the Franco period. Images from cinema and other cultural products from the early years of the dictatorship (before the widespread availability of television) provide a point of departure for a consideration of television advertising of the later period of Francoism, and a more detailed examination of the 1980s and 1990s.

Gendered identity in the Franco period

Institutionally preferred notions of masculinity and femininity during the Franco regime were clearly determined by the patriarchal structures on which its social, political and economic organization depended, and the patterns of behaviour and morality established by the Catholic Church. In its dual role of both constructing and reflecting models of gendered identity and behaviour, cultural production during the dictatorship played its full part in reflecting, promoting and reproducing these models.

Ironically, it is often in their most extreme articulations that these models most visibly betray their underlying contradictions. Idealizations of womanhood in the heroic figures of Santa Teresa de Jesús, Isabel la Católica or Agustina de Aragón, found everywhere from printed biographies to cinema in the early 1940s, are just one example. These representations fulfilled a dual function as models of both femininity and masculinity, posing evident contradictions for women, not least because of the intrinsic incompatibility of the idea of the 'warrior leader' with the conventional role of mother/housewife (Martín Gaite [1987] 1994, pp. 150–1; Graham 1995, p. 184). Representations of masculinity could pose similar contradictions when men were figured as traditionalist, soft and charming – the protagonist in *El, ella y sus millones* by Orduña (1944), for example (Evans, 1995, p. 222), or as 'half monk and half soldier' (Martín Gaite, 1994, p. 23), as in the case of historical icons like Don Pelayo or Philip II.

In the 1950s and 1960s, through the proselytism of the Sección Femenina de Falange (the women's section of the Falangist party), the regime offered a representation of the ideal Spanish woman in which she should 'appear soft, sweet, kind natured' (Martín Gaite, 1994, p. 40). It was a passive and submissive image inspired by the Virgin Mary. As Miguel Delibes' arch example of Catholic womanhood, María declares in *Cinco horas con Mario* 'purity is a woman's most prized possession' (Delibes [1966] 1977, p. 187). Women's role in life was largely limited to that of wife and mother, keeping her well away from the work-place (Graham, 1995, p. 186). Alternatives to marriage were the convent or the 'misfortune' of remaining an 'old maid', fit only to 'vestir santos' (to 'dress saints'), as the saying goes. In this manichean society, as María again informs us, there were 'two kinds of women, decent women and fallen women' (Delibes [1966] 1977, p. 188). Unless they could be recuperated into the family structure, thus restoring the social order, there was a price to pay for those breaking the rules and disrupting the socio-familial order: death, ostracism, and relegation to the category of Other. In *Balarrasa* (Nieves Conde, 1950), for example, one miscreant sister runs away with a gangster and dies in a car crash realising the spiritual emptiness of her life only too late, whilst the other sister is 'saved' by the intervention of her priest-brother. Similarly in *La muerte de un ciclista* (Bardem, 1955), María José (Lucía Bosé) is 'punished' by death in a car accident, having killed her lover in order to win back her wealthy husband.

The social status of the 'ideal man' rested mainly on his professional position, and his role as head of the household. Men who acted against the social order could also be punished, as in *La muerte de un ciclista* again, where, as a result of self-doubt and lack of confidence in the system, the professional failure of male protagonist Juan (Alberto Closas) resulted in his humiliation, ostracization and, ultimately, death.

The construction of masculinity required men to be physically strong, successful, determined, articulate and self-confident (Martín Gaite, 1994, p. 173). Another key element in privileged concepts of masculinity focused on the virility and sexual prowess central to the idea of the 'macho ibérico' (Iberian male). One of the most widely circulated images of masculinity in Spanish advertising, introduced in the first half of the sixties, promoted *Soberano* brandy with the slogan: '*Soberano. Es cosa de hombres*' ('*Soberano.* It's men's business'). The brand name itself (meaning 'sovereign') inscribed the notion of authority, and marked out an exclusive and clearly delineated male sphere of activity. The advertisement also crucially linked masculinity to the visual image of the bull – a key cultural signifier connoting bravery, strength, aggression, virility and purity of race, a range of qualities associated with the (male) 'true-blooded Spaniard'. The idea of the 'stud' appealed to the 'unquestionable' notion of the virility of the Spanish man, as it did in the sixties promotion of other products such as *Gillette* razor blades: '*Para hombres con toda la barba*' ('For full-bearded men').

The potentially disruptive, animal associations of masculinity, were contained within the civilizing conformity of the staid 'civil servant' look – dark suit, white shirt and tie – which became the 'look *par excellence*' for the Spanish man of the 1960s Spain of the technocrats. This preferred look began to change during the 1970s, although, despite the more informal and relaxed clothing, masculinity continues to be measured in terms of romantic and sexual success with women. The executive was born in the seventies – a dynamic, educated man, successful in both social and professional spheres. Indeed, by the end of the seventies and into the early eighties, men tended to be presented as younger, more energetic, 'on the up', in line with the aspirations of change and regeneration which were the watchwords of the incoming Socialist Party. Although his look begins to change in the mid-seventies, the male figure remains a 'caliph' at home, as in the *Turrón El Panal* confectionery advert (1974) in which a male voice-over narrates images of a centuries-old legend of the seduction of a caliph. The images then change to show a contemporary patriarch waiting to be pleased by a woman tempting him with *turrones* (nougat-style sweets) as the voiceover exhorts female viewers to 'conquer your caliph with *turrones El Panal*'. The *Byass 96* liqueur advertisement (1974) similarly casts the male breadwinner as a warrior. Associative cross-cutting between images of a medieval knight in armour after a battle and of a busy contemporary executive on the telephone in his office are accompanied by a female voice-over, which confirms the analogy: 'He is my warrior. Every day he has to fight a hard battle. For him: all my gratefulness, my love and *Byass 96* . . . the brandy of the new warriors'. The male figure continues in the position of authority, usually middle-aged and married, strong, confident, and with a distant attitude towards his family. He is relaxed in his abode, where the lounge is his domain, separate from the domestic sphere of his wife. Emerging notions of equality remain at the level of protective paternalism, as in the *Kelvinator* washing machine advert of 1975 which exhorts male viewers to 'Be a man and help your wife to do the washing with *Kelvinator*!' The word 'help', of course, implies 'by buying her' this domestic appliance, thus crucially linking social modernity with technical modernity, and placing consumer activity at the centre of both. Women continue to be modelled as good mothers and housewives, passive and subordinate to the husband and *his* desires, as the female voice-over in the *Barón Dandy* men's cologne advert of 1975 demonstrates: 'Tú eliges y por eso estoy contigo. *Barón Dandy*, porque tú decides' (*You* choose, that's why I'm with you. *Barón Dandy*, because *you* make the decisions). Female agency is still largely focused on the development of subtle manipulative skills which, though presented as an area of – albeit very limited – female power, are clearly directed at maintaining the status quo. The *Kelvinator* advert again illustrates this in its advice to female viewers: 'Be a woman, get your husband to buy you a *Kelvinator*.'

Women in advertising in the 1980s and 1990s

In 1975, the International Year of Women, the first timid attempts were made at speaking publicly of equality, yet publicity seemed to move faster than society – in that same year the *Banco de Bilbao* proclaimed itself the first 'Woman's Bank'. Overlaying images of a woman entering the bank in its television advertisement, a male voice-over comments that 'this determined walk is the symbol of the woman of our time, of a woman with responsibilities, who works and lives in today's world. To her the *Banco de Bilbao* sends a message of friendship. The *Banco de Bilbao* believes in women's rights.'

With the greater participation of women in the work place, a new image of the executive woman, always on the move and in control, is offered as an ideal. No longer is she only the happily married woman, she is now represented as an independent woman, respected and valued for her work. Her look becomes more assertive and determined, displaying attributes which had until then been exclusively associated with masculinity.

Despite this new professional identity, the contemporary executive woman also often protagonizes advertisements for cosmetics or other beauty products, implying a relationship between female autonomy and professional success and the maintenance of youth and beauty – still important characteristics associated with female identity, and the conditions *sine qua non* for the successful seduction of men (Peña-Marín and Frabeti, 1990). Carmen Maura, in a mid-eighties advertisement for *Monki* coffee, for example, plays both roles to perfection. In her appearance (as well as because of the actress's own public image) she embodies the idea of the successful woman who is also a prudent housewife (saving money by buying this brand of coffee) and a suggestive seductress with her alluring comment about economizing with every cup she drinks: 'tacita a tacita' (one cup after another).

The increased centrality of female subjectivity which Jordan and Morgan-Tamosunas have noted in Spanish cinema of the eighties and nineties (1998, pp. 133–8) is also visible in advertising, especially in the foregrounding of relationships between women and female complicity. One particularly interesting recent example is the series of television adverts for *Evax* sanitary towels (1998) directed by Isabel Coixet. Both actresses in the various versions of the advertisement had previously appeared in female-bonding movies – Silke in *Hola, ¿estás sola?* (Icíar Bollaín, 1995) and Rossy de Palma in *Mujeres al borde de un ataque de nervios* (Almodóvar, 1988). For Spanish spectators, therefore, they were already referents of female subjectivity and particularly associated with the idea of 'cosas de mujeres' (women's business). In the *Evax* advertisements they enjoy an intensely active day in the company of a female friend. The tenor of the images and the sisterly relationships imply that that other 'women's business' – menstruation – can also be equally natural and uninhibited ... if you do it with *Evax*.

Despite visible changes in representations of femininity, certain negative stereotypes continue to persist. A recent *Movistar* mobile telephone advertisement (1998), for example, perpetuates the cliché of women as at best chatterboxes, and at worst gossips. Whilst adopting an apparent complicity with potential female customers, it invites them to 'gabble to your heart's content' ('¡Ahora ya puedes hablar más de la cuenta!').

The woman as housewife, now presented as both young and satisfied with life, continues to advertise food and products related to the needs of family and children, as in the *Dan-up Danone* advertisement of 1998, in which a mother offers her expectant children a drink, 'to them it is a soft drink, to me it is nourishment'. However, when the advertised product needs the authority of an expert, this is invariably supplied by a male figure or voice-over. Men have ceased to be portrayed as the patriarch dominating the family structure, yet more subtle articulations of a continuing deference to male authority are common. To the surprise of his wife, for example, and despite evident unfamiliarity with the domestic domain and its incumbent chores, the man of the house might discover a new and better cleaning product – in the late-1990s *Don Limpio* advertisement a husband offers to do the cleaning while his wife takes a bath, and we become accomplices to his cleverness in discovering a product whose effects duly surprise and dazzle his wife when she emerges from the bathroom.

Representations of men in advertising in the 1980s and 1990s

The advertisements of the 1980s showed men that had changed not only their looks, but also their attitudes. The achievements of the feminist movement, the progressive incorporation of women into the labour market, and their more active role in society seemed to have precipitated a crisis in masculine values and a search for new models. The advertising industry has reflected and indeed promoted those models and the masculine image has distanced itself from the *machismo* characteristic of the previous decades (Rey, 1994, pp. 187–207).

In television advertising the stronger presence continues to be male, promoting an ever more diversified range of products. Alongside more traditionally 'masculine' consumer goods (alcohol, tobacco, automobiles, banking services, technology), men now also promote more conventionally 'feminine' articles such as clothing, beauty products and cosmetics, household appliances and food-stuffs.

The traditional father-figure combining strength and self-confidence with an air of distance and inaccessibility is now replaced with an equally self-confident, but manifestly more affectionate and caring figure. This 'New Father', in addition to a new physical look, has also established a tender and affectionate relationship with his wife and children, often appearing with a smaller child to permit a display of his new-found capacity for tenderness. In a 1990s television advertisement for *Sobaos Martínez* sponge cakes, for example, a young father is shown out cycling in the country with his young son. While the father repairs a puncture, the little boy eats a sponge cake – 'tan tiernos que son irresistibles' ('so irresistibly tender'), remarks the female voice-over, referring to both product and father and son. As Juan Rey observes (1994, pp. 107–22), today's modern father is seeking a new model that neither implies violence, nor disallows sensitivity.

Similar shifts are illustrated in a late-1990s *Bimbo* sliced bread advertisement where two men in their late fifties speak knowingly to one another at the office about recipes, a subject once pertaining exclusively to the female realm. One tells the other of a new recipe he has discovered, an easy one of course, making it clear that, as men, they have by no means taken over in the kitchen, but seem more likely to be living alone – divorced, perhaps – and therefore requiring no-fuss, easily fixed recipes. The advertisement not only reflects what has become a more frequent experience of solo living, previously inconceivable in a society whose ultimate aim had always been to promote the family unit. It also importantly lends validity, a seal of approval, to independent living even when it is the implied result of divorce or separation.

The long-standing proverb – 'El hombre y el oso, cuanto más feo más hermoso' (suggesting that both men and bears are most attractive at their ugliest) – is now visibly dated; brutality and ugliness are no longer 'men's business'. Indeed the modern man is required to be young and good-looking (features previously more typically associated with feminine identities). Preferred physical models of masculinity have also taken on a series of traditionally 'feminine' attributes: features and gestures that have been softened, a body that is not only virile, but beautiful. 'Cada vez son menos los que no se cuidan' ('Fewer and fewer men are failing to care for themselves') declares the male voice-over in the television advertisement for *Natrem* sweetener, in which we see three overweight men going through the motions of a 1960s dance routine. For this project a whole range of cosmetic products and health foods are required. However, as is demonstrated by a late-nineties *Nivea* aftershave advertisement claiming that the product is 'the best thing that can happen to a man', notions of male success are still essentially associated with physical prowess and sexual conquest. The good-looking young man in the advertisement receives a sports award followed by a deep kiss from a young woman clearly desired by the surrounding group of men.

Women in advertising have traditionally been represented as young and beautiful, needing model bodies if they were to triumph with the opposite sex. In today's advertising this also applies to the representation of men. What the male image has lost in sexual aggression (the bull) it has gained in eroticism – indeed, transformed into the new 'beautiful man', the male body is now displayed totally or partially nude in a number of advertisements (Juan Rey, 1994, p. 125). In the late-nineties advertisement for *Boss* men's cologne, for example, an attractive young man with a bare torso looks directly to camera in flirtatious defiance. The male figure has willingly become the object of the gaze, subverting once and for all any remaining notion that it is men who look and women who are looked at.

Alongside these new and radically different inflections of contemporary male identity, more conventional associations clearly continue to persist and are readily reproduced for the purposes of product promotion. Another late-nineties advertisement for *Movistar* mobile phones specifically targets a male market, appealing to conventional notions of courage and the male role of adventurer 'para los que corren riesgos' ('for those who take risks'). Another contemporary *Movistar* advertisement is located at a horse race, where the idea of masculinity attaching to the product is constructed through images of strength, power, decision and speed – as well as a 'characteristic' male competitiveness.

In general, in television publicity in the 1980s, and even more so in the 1990s, we find both masculine and feminine representations of a more positive and complex nature, showing both continuities and discontinuities with the traditional model. Women are no longer represented as passive, dependent beings, nor is heterosexual love represented as women's only emotional need. Although men are still rarely seen at the heart of the family domain in the house itself, and, when they are shown taking care of the house or the children it is more frequently in a recreational, fun situation, the male figure is now represented as just another member of an apparently more democratic family structure; he is no longer modelled as the patriarch occupying a dominant position in the hierarchy. Men have been integrated, and while still strong, they are also tender, not only protective, but now caring.

Notions of gender have become more fluid, as the 1998 version of the *Osborne* brandy advertisement significantly shows. It is a postmodern pastiche, a collage which not least demonstrates how contemporary images can be emptied of their meanings and ceaselessly re-directed and re-invented: a beautiful woman brands a man with a kiss, leaving on his skin the mark of a burning bull; Ester Cañadas, one of Spain's top international models, reverts to one of the most traditional female roles as object of desire, performing a seductive dance; Javier Bardem emerges from crashing waves, bare-torsoed, stealing the role of Venus, then changes role to preside over a barren landscape, the triumphant conqueror of nature. This latter set of images in particular plays ironically on the meanings attaching to the actor's screen image as the ultimate contemporary *macho ibérico*, through persistent visual references to the bull, the image which has been so closely linked to the historical promotional representation of *Osborne* brandy. This collage of images offers representations of masculinity and femininity that have become interchangeable – male and female icons are both objects of the spectator's consuming gaze, and both display elements of characteristics traditionally coded as 'masculine' *and* 'feminine'. *Osborne* is no longer exclusively 'men's business'.

References

DELIBES, M . [1996] 1977: *Cinco horas con Mario*. London: Harrap.
EVANS, P. 1995: Cinema, memory and the unconscious. In Graham, H. and Labanyi, J. (eds). *Spanish cultural studies. An introduction*. Oxford: Oxford University Press, 304–10.
GRAHAM, H. 1995: Gender and the state: women in the 1940s. In Graham, H. and Labanyi, J. (eds) *Spanish cultural studies. An introduction*. Oxford: Oxford University Press, 182–95.
JORDAN, B. and MORGAN-TAMOSUNAS, R. 1998: *Contemporary Spanish Cinema*. Manchester: Manchester University Press.

MARTÍN GAITE, C. 1994: *Usos amorosos de la posguerra española*. Barcelona: Anagrama.
PEÑA-MARÍN, C. and FABRETI, C. 1990: *La mujer en la publicidad*. Madrid: Ministerio de Asuntos Sociales: Instituto de la Mujer.
REY, J. 1994: *El hombre fingido: La representación de la masculinidad en el discurso publicitario*. Madrid: Fundamentos.

|19|

Representation of alternative sexualities in contemporary Spanish writing and film

JACKY COLLINS and CHRIS PERRIAM

It would be a misrepresentation both of fact and, probably, of the intentions of men who desire men and women who desire women in the Spanish state to say that there was a categorizable gay, homosexual, lesbian, bisexual, or queer 'culture'. However, an increasing number of films and imaginative writings – many of them mainstream – are witness to a liberating and lively set of contestations for meaning around questions of identity and terminology. Because studies on Spanish culture, society or sexuality have had little to say on lesbians or lesbianism in Spain, with the exception of a number of recently published works,[1] the first part of this essay is devoted to perceptions of the emergence of lesbian cultures from the margins into mainstream society, as borne out in contemporary literature and film. Three novels published in Spain in the 1990s – *Con la miel en los labios* by Esther Tusquets (1997), *Si tú supieras* by Antonio Gómez Rufo (1997), and *Beatriz y los cuerpos celestes* by Lucía Extebarría (1998) – and three films – Fernando Trueba's *Belle Epoque* (1992), Pedro Almodóvar's *Kika* (1993), and Marta Balletbò-Coll's *Costa Brava (Family Album)* (1995) – have been selected to ascertain the extent to which they offer representations of a visible, autonomous character who has accepted and is comfortable with her own sexuality and who has also been socially accepted.

As Jay and Glasgow point out, there is always a danger of universalizing the fluid, multifaceted identity of a 'lesbian' (1990, pp. 1–9). There exist numerous theories and positions on the lesbian identity, and a broad spectrum of definitions between the essentialist and the constructionist schools of thought. Moreover, it must be borne in mind that 'prevailing concepts of sexuality vary according to the time, the culture and the most prominent moralities' (Gibbs, 1994, p. 2). However, for the purposes of this brief account our definition of 'lesbian' is broad: a female subject whose object of desire is another woman, whether or not such desire achieves physical fulfilment in a same-sex genital relationship.

Con la miel en los labios is not the first novel in which Esther Tusquets deals with the subject of lesbian relationships. *El mismo mar de todos los veranos*, 1978 (discussed by Smith, 1992, pp. 91–128), inaugurated a trilogy in which bisexuality and lesbianism are central preoccupations. In *Con la miel en los labios* the relationship between Andrea and Inés is first referred to in terms of friendship, echoing the romantic friendships and 'Bostonian marriages' of the nineteenth century discussed by Faderman (1981). As their 'friendship' develops there is an obvious sexual attraction between them that subsequently leads to physicality, but also gives rise to a revealing discrepancy in the way each explains to themselves their sexual feelings; for Inés it is 'amistad' (friendship), but for Andrea it is 'amor' (love).

As in the trilogy, Tusquets repeats the triangular dynamic where a woman (Inés) has to choose between the love of a woman (Andrea) or that of a man (Ricard). When Ricard intervenes to warn Inés of the 'unhealthy' relationship that exists between Andrea and herself, Inés questions how a supposedly liberal, emancipated person could have such negative views of same-sex female relationships. However, she herself has declared earlier that it would be impossible for her to accept Andrea's suggestion that they live together and this response, like Ricard's, mirrors that of a society that at worst believes that such relationships are 'unnatural' and impossible and at best ignores them. Finally, Inés accepts Ricard's proposal of marriage and thus chooses a socially approved lifestyle, even though it means sacrificing what may have been the love of her life. In the end, Tusquets presents a lesbian subject who not only loses the object of her love and cause of her happiness, but she (Andrea) also loses her dignity and self-respect in a final outburst of uncontrollable emotions that characterize the Lesbian as one who operates outside the acceptable behaviour of a civilized, ordered society.

In *Si tú supieras*, Gómez Rufo deals with the problematic theme of the fluidity of sexuality. Here Andrea has struggled with her attraction towards other women. Taught from an early age that such emotions and desires are sinful and dirty, she suffers through fearfully internalizing her feelings until she falls in love with Carmen. She tries temporarily to form relationships with men and perceives an affair with Carmen's husband as a haven from the emotional turmoil she has known in the struggle to accept her sexuality, supposing that he will lead her to 'the promised land' of 'normality'. Similarly, in consonance with what heterosexual, patriarchal society considers as the 'natural' order – that women's sexuality should be expressed only in relation to men – her previous girlfriend Marta had ended their relationship for 'a tall, handsome yuppie from a well-heeled family'. In Andrea's parents' reaction to her sexuality it is possible to observe what has been and still is the experience of many Spanish lesbians. Her father rejects her, and her mother, although she supports her, insists on taking her to see two psychologists. In dealing with alternative sexuality there appear to be two common options: perpetuate its invisibility by denying its existence or treat it as an illness. To be treated 'naturally' and 'normally', Andrea decides to hide her lesbianism at work and the comments made by her colleagues represent popular contemporary Spanish attitudes towards lesbians and lesbianism: it is unusual for a young woman (Andrea) not to have a boyfriend; her female colleagues are disgusted by the thought of two woman having sex together; her male colleagues are initially titillated by the idea of observing this sexual act, but conclude that sex with a prostitute is preferable since a lesbian cannot be considered to be a woman (a notion frequently raised in lesbian feminist theory).

With *Beatriz y los cuerpos celestes,* Extebarría offers an even more troubled image of female sexuality in a novel that focuses on the search for identity. One should bear in mind that this is not a 'lesbian' novel, nor does it focus specifically on lesbian relationships. Rather it presents lesbianism as located within a range of sexualities that women should be free to choose from, a notion supported in the novel by quotations from Jeanette Winterson and Cristina Peri Rossi. In this first-person narrative such a range of sexualities finds embodiment in Beatriz (Bea), on her journey of self-discovery. Although she refuses to identify as any specific sexuality, through the various stages of her life it is possible to trace aspects of a lesbian development, her close friendship with the wayward Mónica being like a schoolgirl crush with its provisional sexual experimentation, and her feeling of isolation and of being 'other' clearly expressed as she remembers her convent education and the conformist behaviour of her classmates. Explicit self-examination is undertaken around the debate of 'nature or nurture' that surrounds the development of identity and sexuality.

The relationship that she does enter into with Caitlin (Cat), raises a number of issues and also reinforces prevalent stereotypes regarding lesbianism as degenerate behaviour and the gay and lesbian community as a ghetto of vice and perversion. Bea and Cat both come from dysfunctional families where they had had very close relationships with their mothers. In the same vein, it is possible that both have been sexually abused by older men. Reactionary social convention would imply that such experiences might well lead them to choose a lesbian lifestyle. Indeed, Cat and Bea's involvement in drug dealing and Cat's early work as a striptease artist and the sense that they are lost souls searching for somewhere to belong, appear to conform to such a view. However, the author treats the development of Bea's relationship with Cat without any reference to it being unnatural or immoral, and offers non-sensationalist, explicit descriptions of their lovemaking, thus affording same-sex female desire the expression that it is so often denied. The significance of this novel should not be underestimated, given the success it has had with the general public and the acclaim it has received in literary circles.

Male homosexual desire has found explicit representation in Spanish cinema since the end of the 1970s through directors such as Almodóvar,

Aranda, Bigas Luna and Eloy de la Iglesia (Evans, 1995, p. 327). Moreover, Almodóvar in particular has created a number of lesbian characters (in *Pepi, Luci, Bom y otras chicas del montón* (1980) and *Entre tinieblas* (1983)). Nevertheless, although the lesbian has attained visibility, the taboo of explicit sexual lesbian desire still remains to be challenged in contemporary mainstream Spanish cinema. In *Kika,* the lesbian, Juana (Rossy de Palma), is a maid, a subordinate. Moreover, she is perversely submissive: when her brother, an escaped criminal and porno star arrives at the flat, she suggests that in order for his intrusion to appear as if it were a robbery he should tie her up, gag her, punch her and later rape her. Her apparent consent and complicity in this brutal treatment figuratively expose the experience (in the main) of the contemporary Spanish Lesbian. Her sexuality has remained invisible, since lesbians have allowed themselves to be silenced and oppressed and have permitted their rights to be violated, often by those closest to them – their families.

At a more obvious level, a conventional caricature of the Lesbian is present in the business of Nicholas (Peter Coyote) accidentally sending a draft of his latest novel, *A Lesbian Killer,* to Andrea Caracortada (Victoria Abril). The book is based on real events, he says, but admits that not all the crimes were committed by the same person and not all necessarily by lesbians, or by women. He alleges to have made the central character lesbian to give the novel more 'bite'. The 'dangerous' lesbian is allowed to exist, since she serves a commercial purpose by attracting more readers, either in response to the current 'lesbian chic' or out of 'morbo' (morbid fascination). As Andrea and Nicholas battle with one another to the death, he reveals that he is the serial killer in the novel, to which she responds 'That ridiculous lesbian is you!' Her words echo the archaic nineteenth-century psychological theory, that lesbians were really men trapped in women's bodies. When Nicholas finally urges Kika to change the title of the book and replace the character's name with his own we see a replacing of the lesbian by the male. By the end of this film the lesbian, both living and fictional, who had appeared in mainstream society with a certain degree of acceptance, has been disappeared once more, either dismissed (Juana) or replaced by a man (Nicholas).

In *Belle Époque,* the action does not take place in contemporary Spain, but rather in pre-Civil War 1930s. Nevertheless, as Jordan and Morgan-Tamosunas (1998, pp. 58–9) have suggested, the values and attitudes that emerge from this film are more reminiscent of those found in present-day society, more specifically, the opinions concerning sexual behaviour. With regard to the character Violeta (Ariadna Gil), she transcends the lesbian sexualities prevalent in the 1970s and 1980s, to represent an even more contemporary lesbian sexuality that is located in the queer/post-lesbian theory of the 1990s. *Belle Époque* touches on such issues as cross-dressing, the troubling of gender and the fluidity of sexuality. As Violeta arrives with her sisters from Madrid, she is wearing what could be considered as 'feminine' clothing (skirt, blouse, etc.), but the style is more severe than those worn by her sisters. Once inside the house the difference becomes more accentuated: Violeta is wearing overalls and a beret (traditional 'male' attire). Moreover, her activity suggests a fusion or blurring of gender. Not only does she perform the 'female' task of cleaning, but she also takes responsibility for the 'male' task of repairing the vacuum cleaner. Furthermore, she works within a traditionally 'male' profession, as a veterinary surgeon. As a consequence she is able to live without the economic support of a man, unlike her sisters. The blurring or transgression of gender-defined boundaries is repeated to a greater degree through the carnival scenes as Violeta dons Fernando's (Jorge Sanz's) uniform and paints on a moustache. In doing so, she appropriates the 'maleness' that will allow her to fulfil her desire to love a woman – Fernando, dressed in a maid's costume. This multiple subversion of identity allows a performance of Violeta's lesbian sexuality within a constructed heterosexuality and also renders these identities ambiguous and uncertain. As Violeta has sex with Fernando, a queer disruption to lesbian sexuality occurs that challenges the simplistic theory that a lesbian who engages in heterosexual sex becomes a heterosexual. As post-lesbian theory has suggested, such an act in fact allows lesbians to challenge male supremacy by engaging with the phallic power base. In some ways, then, this otherwise extremely conformist film contains some of the most advanced representations of lesbianism in Spanish cinema.

The internationally acclaimed low-budget *Costa Brava (Family Album)*, as Smith suggests, goes some way in breaking new ground in Spanish cinema by placing a lesbian, Ana, and her bisexual lover, Montserrat, as the central characters (1997, p. 43). It could be argued however, that in order to limit the social transgression that this image presents, the director stops short of radically challenging accepted conventions as the couple appear to ape a heterosexual partnership, cohabiting, emphasizing the importance of monogamy and conforming to notions of what is male/female-specific behaviour. In addition, in spite of the 'happy ever after' feel of *Costa Brava*, the tourist setting could imply a transience in their relationship or that lesbianism is not an identity but rather a sexual location to be visited.

Through the 'housewife' who features in Ana's monologue the lesbian identity is also presented in a non-threatening way. This character has a good job, she is a model neighbour and she is understanding. But she is still a possible 'danger' to the housewife's children. This structure of a performance within a performance facilitates the raising of further issues: women who enjoy sex with women but would not renounce their heterosexuality; and the bond of female identity. Montserrat also poses a number of questions that centre around lesbianism: when is the moment of realization of one's lesbianism? What are the implications for identity of having sexual relations with another woman? And could lesbian relationships ever be socially acceptable? Her struggle to own a lesbian identity reflects the power of naming and the fear of social rejection.

It would appear that there are certain differences between the textual and filmic representations of lesbian identities considered in this essay. In the former, they appear to reinforce the traditional negative view that lesbians are 'mad, bad and dangerous to know'. They represent a distorted, inferior sexuality that cannot be allowed to exist within a patriarchal society. To a degree the Lesbian has become invisible and achieved a measure of autonomy, but she is far from self- and social acceptance. By contrast, in the latter there is evidence of a reversal of the demonization of lesbianism, a departure from an identity whose demise and destruction is inevitable. It now remains for this alternative sexuality to receive explicit treatment, the lack of which reinforces the absence of desire between women.

Sex between men, on the other hand, has been a persistent and growing presence in film and literature. In the mid- to late 1990s in Spain, alongside a sudden rebirth of indigenous queer cinema, a new phenomenon on the literary scene emerged – a small market for more or less popular fiction by and for lesbians and gay men, boosted by the establishment of a lesbian/gay publishing imprint, Egales, backed by bookshops in Barcelona and Madrid. However, with the possible exception of Carlos Sanrune's rentboy's tale *El Gladiador de Chueca* (1992) and the unevenly written though arresting *Sígueme* by Cristóbal Ramírez (1998), stories about male homosexuality have stayed safely gay in their interest in love, lifestyle and their assumptions about sex and identity. They have not on the whole followed in the radical footsteps of works by better known writers who had already in the 1980s marked out the way towards more complex, less polarized, more queer writing. Juan Goytisolo's *Makbara* (1980) and the autobiographical volumes *Coto vedado* (1985) and *En los reinos de taifa* (1986) had given radical and often illuminatingly contradictory perspectives on the formation of homosexual desire and its politics (Epps, 1996; Smith, 1992) at a level of complexity which is reflected in the structuring of the text (making Goytisolo perhaps more discussed by intellectuals internationally than widely read by queer Spaniards). Lluis Fernández and Alberto Cardín had, like Goytisolo, explored the diversity of homosexual desire within a matrix of political and social dissent, revealing queerness and perversity in the straightest of institutions, but (unlike Goytisolo) exploiting exuberantly the radical potential in transsexuality and cross-dressing, and often employing a comic modality to underscore their political points. Eduardo Mendicutti's hilarious and sharp perspective on the *tejerazo* in *Una mala noche la tiene cualquiera* (1982), using a less difficult style, also had exploited this strategy. Terenci Moix, now a best-selling name frequently using camp overstatement and obvious outrageousness to subvert entertainingly the mores of comfortable urban Spain (for example *Mujercísimas*, 1995), had made radical linkages of homosexuality and national identity in writings of the 1980s and *Mundo macho* (1986) is a transgressive homoerotic text which worries at the knot binding sex, power, decadence and violence. His ongoing autobiographical cycle – part 3, *Extraño en el paraíso* (*Stranger in*

Paradise), appeared in 1998 – is a personalized queer genealogy of some seriousness. Luis Antonio de Villena in poetry, biography and narrative fiction has since the early 1980s been constructing a complex and richly embellished set of images of sex between men which is variously realist in its revelations and idealist in its high-cultural eclecticism (Perriam, 1995). It owes much to an established gay tradition, but in refusing any connection with the identity-politics or the role models of *lo gai,* verges on being queer in its aesthetic. Many of Villena's protagonist narrators are fired in their quest for impossible love and beauty and in their flight from the mundane by a sense of exalted marginalization. But the isolated middle-aged protagonist of Álvaro Pombo's novel *Los delitos insignificantes* (1986), in his sexual obsession with a younger and not-gay man, is presented as both the victim (in his damaging loneliness) and beneficiary (in the enforced acuteness of his perceptions of his difference) of the rejection by Spanish society of the single person and the impossibility for a generation born in the 1940s fully to come out as gay.

In film, Jaime Chávarri's *Un dios desconocido* (1977) had also powerfully explored loneliness and marginalization, in the person of a middle-aged stage magician whose profession is a tacit metaphor for his being under the spell of García Lorca's 'Oda a Walt Whitman' (a poem which is in part a complicated meditation on labels and meanings for same-sex love among men) and for his conjuring with conflicting emotions to do with his own (and Spain's) past and with a future he is trying to forge with his communist, bisexual boyfriend. More militantly queer were Eloy de la Iglesia's box office successes *Los placeres ocultos* and *El diputado* (1976 and 1978), in as much as they explicitly disturbed the structures of marriage and the state by emphasizing homosexual desire but eschewing coupledom or a commercially inflected lifestyle.

In the second half of the 1990s in cinema a sub-genre placed between gay and queer has emerged. Alfonso Albacete, Miguel Bardem and David Menkes's *Más que amor frenesí* (1996) looks back to early Almodóvar in its provocative and self-consciously postmodern representations of sexuality, desire, and alternative social configurations (though not in its relatively glossy production values and emphatically mid-nineties look) and is as notably daring in its sex scenes as it is laid back in its assumptions. Félix Sabroso and Dunia Ayuso's *Perdona, bonita, pero Lucas me quería a mí* (also 1996) uses a murder – that of the handsome straight boy Lucas who comes to rent a room in a flat of very gay gay men – as an excuse for Almodovarian gags on police ineptitude, wild coincidence, frenetic excess, and gay iconography while reclaiming and reinforcing gay stereotypes. Yolanda García Serrano and Juan Luis Iborra's *Amor de hombre* (1997), in contrast, takes a more decorous and cosy line in its desire to show (middle-class white) homosexual lifestyles in Madrid as 'normal'. A group of professional gay men live their thirty-something lives, protected by Esperanza, the beautiful but single straight best friend ('normal men aren't normal. Believe me, I know from bitter experience' is her rueful view) of Ramón (Andrea Occhipinti bringing in an element of glamorous Eurogayness) who inconclusively debates within himself the relative benefits of monogamy and promiscuity. In recent writing too a number of such normalizing versions of homosexuality have been emerging, as has already been suggested. Much less comfortable and less fixed in its ideas is Armando Rabazo's *Las paredes del acuario* (1996) which exploits the cult and culture of youth in two contrary ways. The first-person narrator, twenty-something, pretty *malagueño* Paco, escapes the provincial by associating with older, richer men (and women) whose worlds are those of painting, antiques, lavish parties, travel and drugs; the narrative is conventionally linear and based on adventure, with Paco and his emotionally close but physically absent buddy Héctor being motivated by a line from the poet Luis Cernuda: 'Go ever onwards, never looking back'. This is similar to Villena's literary world. However, less conventionally gay-tradition oriented is the novel's representation of male sexual identities. While a diversity of same-sex desire is represented in different characters attracted to Paco, from openly upper-middle class gay, through bisexual male Cuban prostitute, to chaste, French and platonically infatuated widower, he himself in his narration shifts between positions and hides from singular identification. He protects himself from unwanted advances by maintaining his straightness, pretends to women (for various motives, including that of proving his sexual fidelity) that he is *marica,* and pretends to himself that he is not. In fact, though, his whole adventure is structured around his search for the equally beautiful Héctor of whom other characters have but fragmentary news, visual memories, or photographs. Its emphasis on the fragmentary and provisional in sexual identity and its tacit questioning of its narrator's continued state of closeted denial gives the novel a special queer edge.

Cultural representations of gay and bisexual subjectivities appear to have attained a degree of acceptance in contemporary Spain, as witnessed to by the mini boom in queer cinema and the emerging market for gay male popular fiction. It is to be hoped that the belated emergence of lesbian sexualities in print and on screen will prompt fuller explorations and construct a more visible audience; were the Lesbian to be once more relegated to the status of passing phase or lifestyle gesture it would be a serious obstacle to the possibilities of positive 'queer' cultural expression in Spain.

Note

1. See Brooksbank Jones, A. 1998: *Women in contemporary Spain.* Manchester: Manchester University Press; Jordan, and Morgan-Tamosunas, 1998; Smith, 1992.

References

EPPS, B. 1996: *Significant violence: oppression and resistance in the narratives of Juan Goytisolo: 1970-1990.* Oxford: Oxford University Press.

EVANS, P. 1995: Back to the future: cinema and democracy. In Graham, H. and Labanyi, J. (eds), *Spanish cultural studies. An introduction.* Oxford: Oxford University Press.

FADERMAN, L. 1981: *Surpassing the love of men: romantic friendships and love between women from the Renaissance to the present.* London: The Women's Press.

GIBBS, L. (ED.) 1994: *Daring to dissent: lesbian culture from margin to mainstream.* London: Cassell.

JAY, K. AND GLASGOW, J. (EDS) 1992: *Lesbian texts and contexts: radical revisions.* London: Onlywomen Press.

JORDAN, B. and MORGAN-TAMOSUNAS, R. 1998: *Contemporary Spanish cinema.* Manchester: Manchester University Press.

PERRIAM, C. 1995: *Desire and dissent. An introduction to Luis Antonio de Villena.* Oxford and Provincetown: Berg.

SMITH, P. J. 1992: *Laws of desire: questions of homosexuality in Spanish writing and film. 1960–1990.* Oxford: Clarendon Press.

—— 1997: Review of *Costa Brava (family album)*, *Sight and Sound*, 7(3), 43–4.

|20|

Changing subjects: gendered identities in ETA and radical Basque nationalism

CARRIE HAMILTON

> In the modern world everyone can, should and will 'have' a nationality, as he or she 'has' a gender.
>
> (Anderson, 1983, p. 14)

> ... not only does everyone have a nationality and gender in the same imagined way, but these imaginings constitute us as modern subjects.
>
> (Sommer, 1990, p. 120)

In recent years scholars across cultural and disciplinary boundaries have paid increasing attention to the constructions of social subjectivity and collective identities. In Spain, a multinationed nation where nationalism – both central and peripheral – has been a powerful driving force in history, academic interest in identity politics has focused largely on the national, and more specifically on the tensions between 'Spanish' and 'regional' identities. In privileging the national as a category of identity, however, scholars of Spain and its 'autonomies' or 'historical nations' have tended to marginalize other forms of identity. Although most have acknowledged class as a crucial factor in the construction of national identities, to date few have taken seriously the question of gender and its relationship to both national and class identities.

Nowhere is this absence of gender analysis more glaring than in the case of ETA and radical nationalism, which have been the subject of countless studies over the past 25 years. Yet gender identity has been at the root of Basque national identities and nationalisms in their various incarnations throughout the century. This essay outlines how concerns about gender identities and relations shaped the growth of ETA during the late Francoist and transition periods, and how nationalist women – whose stories have largely been written out of the history of radical nationalism – renegotiated the boundaries of gender and national identity in a quest to forge new female subjectivities.

The gender conflict at the root of radical nationalism is inextricably linked to a more general identity crisis stemming from fundamental tensions within ETA between essentialist nationalism, on the one hand, and the new social/cultural landscape of Francoist Spain in the 1950s and 1960s, on the other. ETA emerged in 1959 out of a generational conflict between a group of young middle-class nationalist men (members of the clandestine cultural group Ekin) and the older leadership of the traditionalist Basque Nationalist Party (PNV), a conflict which revolved on a political level around the question of how to achieve and define a future Basque state. Beyond this strategic dispute, however, the founding of ETA was impelled by a dual urge among young Basque men to *break* with their father's generation, and simultaneously to *continue* their father's political struggle. One early male militant, for instance, has suggested that for his generation entry into ETA was

> a way of reacting against the generation before, against the soldiers' generation. On the one hand, in the family circle we were handed down a heroic legend of the war, and of course, were told about all kinds of horrors of Francoism. But, at the same time, whether out of fear of repression or of losing whatever – lots or little – had been gained, they didn't move a finger against the dictatorship. We went to continue their war.

> (cited in *Jauristi* 1994, pp. 191–2)

This desire for both continuity and change within the patriarchal nationalist tradition suggests a crisis in patterns of political inheritance, and indeed of masculinity more generally, in the late 1950s and 1960s, a period of rapidly changing economic and social relations in the Basque Country and throughout Spain. In fact, ETA's literature during its first decade reflects a profound preoccupation with virility, as epitomized in this excerpt from an early editorial in ETA's clandestine newsletter *Zutik*:

> The Resistance is many-sided: peaceful women dedicated to cultural and humanitarian work; violent men who await only a little more strength and an order; honest priests, who fearlessly raise the voice of the Truth.

> (*Zutik* 10, 1961)

Notwithstanding its breakaway from the PNV, therefore, ETA held on long and strong to narrow notions of nation and national identity very similar to those laid out by PNV founder Sabino Arana at the turn of the century. In this tradition, men were the citizens and activists of the movement, while women were the guardians of national tradition. Like women in the PNV women's section during the 1930s (Ugalde, 1993[1]), women in early ETA were largely positioned in 'support' roles akin and parallel to their domestic position. This practical sexual division of labour simultaneously reflected and was reflected in the organization's theory. Throughout ETA's first decade women appear only sporadically and on the margins of debates over culture, class and armed struggle.

Yet an abiding concern with gender relations is at the heart of all these debates. In the early writings of ETA there is little attention to women *per se*, and more to a universal Woman or Mother, who appears primarily as a symbol of Basque cultural and national difference. A 1961 issue of *Zutik* contains a reference to Basque mothers which, in both its essentialist vision of women and its juxtaposition of Basque and Spanish values, recalls the words of Arana himself:

> Against such a general concept of woman as a pleasant promise, against the 'Don Juan' mentality, against the concept of the 'Lady' – a beautiful and idealized, but depersonalized thing – the Basque opposes his transcendental conception of Woman as Mother and Lady of the House: that is, as a fundamental human element and of primary importance in social organization.

> (*Zutik* 15, 1961)

Here the Basque citizen is clearly gendered as male, while 'Woman' functions as a marker of Basque identity. Women, then, are not individual or collective subjects in the nationalist struggle, but rather the emblems of all that struggle stands for.

Like other nationalisms across geographical and historical borders, radical Basque nationalism has always reserved a privileged space for the Mother as the repository of cultural values, and as the symbol of national 'uniqueness'. As comparative studies of gender and nationalism convincingly demonstrate, the maternal myth is one of the basic myths at the root of all nationalist movements (Yuval-Davis and Anthias, 1989). I define 'myth' here not as something 'false', i.e. the opposite of historical 'truth', but rather as a collective story giving insight into what a community holds most sacred. Myths function by definition on the symbolic plane. Therefore, while myths tell us a great deal about what a community believes about itself and the world, if read literally as revealing the daily lived practice of members of that community, they grossly simplify people's experiences.

This has been a mistake in many studies of radical Basque nationalism, which have tended to interpret women's roles (when they have interpreted them at all) in a very limited context as replicas of the *mythic* role of the Mother, thereby reducing all 'real' women to mothers of male ETA militants or prisoners. Furthermore, while there has been much lip service paid to the *symbolic* importance of these mothers, their major material contribution to the survival of ETA and the radical nationalist community has gone largely unrecorded.

The confusion of 'real' women with the symbolic Woman further obscures the historical meaning of the maternal myth within Basque society. The association of Basque women with an imaginary family unit free from the gender and class conflicts of the modern world functioned as an ideological stabilizing force in the face of the tremendous transformation of Basque society. During the 1950s and 1960s, the family and women's position within it, like the Catholic Church, came to symbolize for nationalists, and for Basques in general, the bastions of a disappearing culture and language in the midst of a world overwhelmed by the impact of modernization – industrialization, urbanization, migration. Changes in women's positions was but one consequence of these developments.

With the impact of economic expansion during the 1960s, and the consequent partial liberalization of Francoist work legislation, more and more women throughout Spain began to leave home to work for wages. Combined with the influence of 'outside' ideas which the Franco regime could no longer keep at bay, the boundaries between women's 'private' and 'public' roles became increasingly fluid. This boundary displacement was indicative of the broader changes of the decade, in which the archaic and ultra-nationalist social and cultural vision of Francoism was increasingly undermined by the regime's own push to modernize the Spanish economy. Francoists strove to achieve full integration into the Western market without being corrupted by the 'foreign' influences of pluralist Western societies – a project which of course proved impossible. The rise of a consumer culture, the influx of foreigners brought by the state-sponsored boom in the Spanish tourist industry, rising incomes, and increased opportunities for middle-class youth to travel and study abroad, all inevitably brought with them the liberalizing influences of Western European culture. In the long run the thwarted project of economic modernization free from social and cultural change would lead to the disintegration and demise of the regime itself.

Although it would be years, even decades, before the full impact of many of these changes was felt in the lives of 'ordinary' women, in the short term their influence was felt on a variety of fronts, including within ETA and the radical nationalist community. While many of ETA's male founders and early militants reacted to shifts in gender roles by harking back to 'traditional' family relations, and in particular to the figure of the Mother, young female nationalists looked to both the old and the new in order to forge identities for themselves in a society which had confined them discursively, and to a large extent physically, to the home.

In spite of the enormous body of work on ETA, women's participation in and around the organization has been almost entirely ignored. In my own historical study on the gender politics of radical nationalism (Hamilton, 1999), therefore, I have endeavoured to 're-gender' ETA through an oral history project involving former female militants.[2] In reading their life stories we see that women's actions and identities sometimes mimicked those of the roles set out for them in wider society, while at other times they contradicted and challenged these expectations. Moreover, because of their very uniqueness in blending personal and political perspectives, the oral sources offer an alternative not only to the 'official' radical nationalist narrative, but also to the startlingly simplistic portrayals of radical nationalist activists found in many studies of ETA.

Negotiating patriotic motherhood

If it is true that the importance of women's work in guaranteeing the survival of the community has not been given its due place in the recorded history of radical nationalism, it is equally true that many women derived a clear sense of personal and political identity from these roles. As Shireen Hassim has noted in her study of women in Zulu nationalism, 'the conservative discourse ... has not merely been imposed by men from above, it is a discourse produced out of a resonance of ideas of motherhood and family that are held by women themselves and which fit into their daily reality' (Hassim, 1993, p. 12). This identity, then, was clearly a *choice*, one which brought both sacrifices and rewards, as the following excerpt from an interview with a Basque woman whose children were born in the 1970s, indicates:

> I transmitted to the children the ideas we both had. And that their father went to demonstrations and meetings, because *I* stayed and looked after them. I mean, I stayed and protected, in one way, the nucleus of the family. And I guaranteed its survival, and its continuity. If we had both gone ... for sure we wouldn't have had children and so, with us the family project would've ended. In some way we've given continuity, in our children. And that, well, that's the project ... of those kinds of things, otherwise the nation would end. (b. 1947)[3]

The theme of 'complementary roles' is common in the oral sources. While this model does not directly contest the gendered division of labour which locks women into 'support' capacities, nationalist women who have chosen to take on these roles none the less challenge the maternal myth by stressing the *practical* as opposed to *symbolic* value of their labour:

> ... and who is looking after the children? And, because in the end, I have *always* said that the toughest years for the organization, which were in Iparralde, the ones they had to live in hiding and that, and the ones who led were the men, but the ones who really put out for the survival of this and that, were the women. And that work has never been recognized. Not, not even the analyses of that period recognize

that very important role of the women of, of, in some way, of the militants. (b. 1948)

One crucial element in the re-gendering of the history of ETA, then, is a full, material account of women's 'support' roles within the organization, and in particular their choices in making motherhood a political act. However, we must also go beyond these support roles to the other activities of women in the radical nationalist movement. For the maternal myth has served not only to simplify motherhood as practice; it has also had the effect of marginalizing, and to a large extent making invisible, those women who chose to enter ETA not as reproducers of male militants, but as militants themselves.

Female activism as an act of rebellion

The opening up of greater opportunities for women in Basque and Spanish society during the 1960s and 1970s was reflected in the increased participation of women in ETA.[4] Although the organization's early leadership and rank and file had been almost exclusively male, and notwithstanding the gendered division of labour laid out in its literature, by the end of ETA's first decade women were involved as militants in a variety of capacities. For many of these women, becoming politically active required a rejection not only of the oppressive gender politics of the Francoist state, but also of the more local constraints of family, church, and community. Not surprisingly, then, in the life stories of former female militants a common metaphor for the construction of a new female identity is that of rebellion.

The oral historian Luisa Passerini has suggested that women's stories of rebelliousness form part of a female oral tradition:

> the rebel stereotype, recurrent in many women's autobiographies, does not primarily aim to describe facts and actual behaviour, but serves a markedly allegorical purpose, which changes continually through contact with different life experiences. It is a means of expressing problems of identity in the context of a social order oppressive of women, but also of transmitting awareness of oppression and a sense of otherness, and hence of directing oneself to current and future change.

(Passerini, 1987, p. 27)

In oral narratives, then, the stereotype of the rebellious woman represents an identity based not so much on individual character as on the performance ('acting') of certain roles which subvert traditional gender norms.

Even for those women raised in families with a fierce sense of ethnic identity, the stark contradictions between nationalist nostalgia for a pure Basque past, and the opening up of new social, economic and cultural worlds, gave rise to an identity crisis. This crisis is clear in the account of the following informant, who was raised in the French Basque Country and was one of the first young women to join ETA in the mid-1960s:

> The fact is I vacillated in being Basque, in identifying myself as Basque, because for me being Basque was *euskaldun fededun* [Basque-speaking person of faith]. ... Here the Basque thing was supported or aided by priests and people on the right. The 'whites' were Basques, Catholic, and the 'reds' were French and secular. ... And the thing about *fededun* I would have, even though I'd participated in [French] Catholic Action activities and all that, well I was a bit of a rebel and *fededun* among other things I couldn't put up with were all the social constraints. ... And, and that's why, I wanted so much to be French and modern. (b. 1941)

The urge to be modern was in many ways even greater on the other side of the border, where a staunch regional Catholic tradition was reinforced by a dictatorship founded on the ideal of 'National Catholicism'. Although commentaries on ETA commonly focus on the role of 'red' Basque priests in opposing the Franco regime and fostering radical nationalism, for female activists the church represented a mixed blessing. On the one hand, it did offer new spaces for political activism in the form of coeducational mountain climbing and cultural groups organized by Catholic Action. On the other hand, however, the church, like the family, tended to reinforce the sexually repressive policies of the regime. Consequently, for many young women the construction of a new political identity meant a move away from a religious upbringing, as one woman active in ETA in the mid-1970s recalls:

> The whole thing about religion, I rebelled a lot and so I took up, it was my first public protest, to stop going to mass, talking, well, believing. Let's say I got out all the fury I felt. There was no way I could talk to the priest, no matter how nice he was, no matter how leftist; but I, I thought God was allowing so much injustice, God didn't exist, and all that in my family was like a big bomb. (b. 1956)

Likewise, another woman who became a militant in the 1970s describes her struggle against injustice in terms of rebellion:

> And little by little, well, you start to get involved, in, in more things, and, and well everything which could seem like an injustice, well I rejected it and well we could say that I was a rebellious woman. That's all. (b. 1961)

Being a 'rebellious woman,' then, signified a renegotiation of both gender and *national* identities, among other things because Basque nationalist tradition, like Francoism, had defined women chiefly in terms of their domestic and maternal roles. For female ETA militants activism almost invariably meant postponing or relinquishing motherhood altogether. Becoming political subjects, then, meant challenging popular definitions of Basque womanhood, as one former female ETA prisoner notes:

> ... when we insisted that we were prisoners, or when we put the feminine in all the, the documents or, when we demanded that different treatment, what we were trying to do was to be recognized as political agents. Against what? Against the traditional model of the Basque woman as mother. Sure. Because we weren't mothers, and on top of it we weren't at all sure about the question of maternity. ... The majority of us weren't out to be mothers. Why? Well because first of all we were political beings, and it was in direct contradiction with the traditional figure of the mother, looking after of the children and all that. (b. 1957)

Women militants, therefore, experienced a tension between celebrating a tradition of women's support roles in the nationalist movement, and struggling against the restrictions these placed on their own political activities and identities. The remaining part of this study will examine one final attempt by women nationalists to resolve the contradictions in radical nationalism, through the construction of a nationalist feminist movement.

New nationalist feminist subjects

> Both nationalist and feminist movements are engaged in the politics of identity, but the interests of the latter are usually submerged to those of the former.

> (Condren, 1995, p. 175)

The height of Spanish and Basque feminist mobilization corresponded with the transition in Spain from dictatorship to liberal democracy. During this period – from the mid-1970s to the early 1980s – there were several feminist initiatives within the radical nationalist movement. In defining themselves as nationalists and as feminists, women involved in these new organizations contested the gender hierarchies not only of their own movement, but also of wider Basque and Spanish society.

The symbol of the new nationalist feminist identity was the term Mujeres Trabajadoras Vascas (Basque Working Women), – a feminist reworking of Pueblo Trabajador Vasco (Basque Working People), an ETA catch-phrase from the late 1960s. One former activist outlines the importance of women bringing together different elements of their political identities:

> You're an activist all at once. Not an activist five times over. I mean, and when you're active, you have to be active as, as a woman, like

everything at once. I mean, you can't duplicate yourself. I mean, now I'm going to, and I'm, a feminist. And now I'm going I don't know where, and I'm a nationalist. (b. 1958)

By designating themselves MTVs, nationalist feminists set out to define a new female subjectivity which combined gender, ethnic and class identities, in a way which resonates with much recent feminist theory of subjectivity (Braidotti, 1994, p. 4). However, they were much less successful in having their demands incorporated into the radical nationalist movement. Ultimately, the struggles of nationalist feminists to have their feminist demands recognized as legitimate within their movement is the story of an attempt to create modern female identities within a largely traditionalist nationalist framework. Whether they acknowledged it explicitly or not, by demanding recognition as active political subjects nationalist feminists, like women in ETA, were directly challenging the essentialist gender politics of the radical nationalist project.

To the extent that their aims were consistently frustrated by the male nationalist mainstream, then, nationalist feminism had a limited influence on the movement as a whole. Notwithstanding these limitations, and indeed the persistent privileging on the Basque political scene (among non-nationalists and nationalists alike) of national above gender identity, the study of radical nationalism is incomplete without an investigation into the ways in which nationalist women – as feminists, as ETA militants, as mothers, and in many other capacities – became active subjects in the struggles to redefine the Basque nation. In highlighting the complex connections between national and gender identities, and in demonstrating that these identities are neither 'natural' nor fixed, the life stories of female nationalists uncover the 'gender trouble' at the heart of ETA and radical nationalism, and indeed in the broader histories of Basque and Spanish nation-building.

Notes

1. See also Ugalde, 1992, pp. 695–700.
2. During 1995–6 I carried out some 25 interviews with former female activists from the 1960s and 1970s.
3. All translations from original interviews in Spanish are the author's own. Because the interviews are direct translations of spoken words, they do not always conform to the conventions of written language. Interview excerpts will be identified in the text by interviewee's date of birth, as here.
4. According to arrest and prison statistics gathered for my Ph.D. thesis, during the 1970s women constituted about 10 per cent of ETA militants. The majority of these women were accused of collaboration, as opposed to direct military action or leadership roles.

References

ANDERSON, B. 1983: *Imagined communities: reflections on the origins and spread of nationalism.* London: Verso.

ARANZADI, J., JUARISTI, J. and UNZUETA, P. 1994: *Auto de terminación.* Madrid: El País/Aguilar.

BRAIDOTTI, R. 1994: *Nomadic subjects: embodiment and sexual difference in contemporary feminist theory.* New York: Columbia University Press.

CONDREN, M. 1995: Sacrifice and political legitimation: the production of a gendered social order. In *Journal of Women's History* 6, 4 and 7, 1 (Winter/Spring 1995), 160–89.

HAMILTON, C. 1999: *The gender politics of ETA and radical Basque nationalism, 1959–1982.* Ph.D. Thesis, University of London.

HASSIM, S. 1993: Family, motherhood and Zulu nationalism: the politics of the Inkatha women's brigade. In *Feminist Review* 43 (Spring 1993), 1–25.

JUARISTI, J. 1994: Un cadáver en el jardín. In Aranzadi, J., Juaristi, J. and Unzueta, P. *Auto de Terminación* . Madrid: El País/Aguilar, 191–2.

PASSERINI, L. 1987: *Fascism in popular memory.* Cambridge: Cambridge University Press.

SOMMER, D. 1990: Love and country in Latin America: an allegorical speculation. *Cultural Critique,* Fall 1990, 109–28.

UGALDE, M. 1992: The discourse of gender and the Basque nationalist movement in the first third of the 20th century. *History of European Ideas* 15, 4–6, 695–700.

UGALDE, M. 1993: *Mujeres y nacionalismo vasco: Emakume Abertzale Batza 1906–1936.* Bilbao: Universidad del País Vasco.

YUVAL-DAVIS, N. and ANTHIAS, F. (EDS) 1989: *Women–nation–state.* London: Methuen.

21

Re-registering Spanish feminisms

MARGARET ANDREWS and ANNY BROOKSBANK JONES

In her recent study of women and social change in democratic Spain, influential feminist philosopher Victoria Camps notes that feminism 'has lost its way and is boring' (Camps, 1998, p. 13). Legal equality has been largely achieved, she notes, but 'a change of register' is needed if remaining egalitarian feminist demands – such as parity of pay and promotion opportunities, and a more equitable distribution of domestic tasks – are to have resonance for women born after the feminist boom of the 1960s and 1970s (p. 13). In this section we look at two examples of cultural practices which suggest fresh registers for feminist discourse: first, a film, *Hola, ¿estás sola?*, by Madrid-born Icíar Bollaín; and second, work by Catalan women Internet users. These new registers are not necessarily the product of explicit feminist reflection. Some of the women discussed do not consider themselves feminists at all, while, of those who do, many are happy to accept feminist discourse, wholly or partly, as it stands. Intentionally or otherwise, however, their interventions are helping to open up fresh perspectives for Spanish feminism in the new millennium.

The majority of the Internet material accessed focuses on extending, rather than transforming, women's communicative possibilities. In the case of feminist sites, emphasis is placed on enabling women to create and exploit new spaces in which long-standing feminist objectives can be more effectively debated and pursued. The significance of this process is underlined by Catalunya's Technology Institute: Internet use and other technological practices, it observes, involve pleasures of which men will remain the chief beneficiaries unless women become more technologically autonomous (Institut Català de Tecnologia, 1997). And this autonomy is crucial, since major technological change is inextricable from 'social and lifestyle changes' in which women as well as men must play their part (p. 51). There is thus an urgent need for women to establish 'new prototypes ... a new culture, a new way of doing things and of creating teams and networks' (pp. 67–9). This need resonates in the discursive changes advocated by Camps. Its emphasis on a renewal of women's organizational and communicational culture also features in the work of the Barcelona-based women journalists' group, Dones Periodistes. This influential group is convinced of the Internet's potential as a new public sphere more easily and equitably available to women than the traditional one. It has worked to unlock this potential for women in journalism and elsewhere, and is currently participating in a European project to establish a flow of Internet communication on subjects appealing to women, in a form that is both 'pleasurable and inclusive' (Dones Periodistes, 1997, p. 1).

Like Dones Periodistes, Ciberdones see the Internet as providing a more efficient, up-to-the-minute, and pleasurable way of accessing other women. But despite the much-vaunted global potential of the Internet, the European activism of some of its members, and references to 'Internet citizenship', Ciberdones' homepage focuses on the creation of an emphatically local, family-type, space. Internet users are invited to become mutually supportive 'virtual friends' in 'a little land named CyberCatalunya' which welcomes women 'of all ages and from all over Catalunya ... married, single, widowed and separated', and which acknowledges the support of technologically inclined men (Ciberdones, 1998a, p. 1). The network's strong regional base means that virtual friendships can even be 'realized' over occasional social dinners. This combination of virtual and non-virtual encounters raises interesting questions about how such 'Möbius-practices' condition the circulation of ideas which, in their Internet form, remain theoretically open to intervention and revision.

The Ciberdones site referred to deploys some familiar feminist strategies – most notably the appeal to solidarity between women as women – but, unlike that of Dones Periodistes, it avoids using the term – because of the group's desire to be inclusive, perhaps, or because regional associationism is given priority over any explicitly feminist aims. Ciberdones is a heterogeneous network, however, and certain other sites present an explicitly feminist face, though not necessarily a univocal one. For example, *La plana de les Ciberdones* juxtaposes multilingual policy-talk on cyber equality with the image of Lara Croft and references to cyborgs and 'la net-revolution' (Ciberdones, 1998b: 1). The Castilian-language webzine site of Riot-grrrls offers a similarly rich and ambivalently feminist mix. Its homepage uses girl-power rhetoric to underscore more explicitly than does Dones Periodistes what is represented as the Internet's 'great potential for connecting and organizing the atomized ... feminist movement' (Riot-grrrls, 1998a, p. 1). Elsewhere, however, Riot-grrrls seem less comfortable with the 'f' word: to describe the webzine's aims, for example, they observe half-defiantly, half-apologetically that 'feminist seems a good enough word' (Riot-grrrls, 1998b: 4). Underlying this ambivalence is a desire to recruit young women to feminism by confronting, and thus partially neutralizing, some of the reasons why they might feel alienated from it. Although the Riot-grrrls homepage sets out to unite individual women, their range of reference – from Cabbage Patch to Tomb Raider – is emphatically international rather than regional. The Ciberdones sites referred to offer a primarily social connectivity which builds on familiar Spanish models of egalitarian feminist associationism. By contrast, Riot-grrrls' recourse to an international consumer imaginary also licenses its appeal to the Internet's more intimate, expressive possibilities. Users are exhorted in the language of New Age self-help manuals to respond spontaneously to the items posted: 'express your feelings; use your emotional vulnerability as a positive force'. The feminist changes to which it appeals are primarily personal: the revolution it repeatedly affirms 'is inside you' (Riot-grrrls, 1998a, p. 2).

The ambivalence highlighted in the work of Ciberdones and Riot-grrrls is a crucially important factor in the development of new feminist registers. Its causes have been explored in the work of young Catalan women's group, Col.lectiu de Dones joves Desobediencia. There are two commonly held objections to feminism, the Collective notes. First, they ask, why should any young woman seeking a positive self-identification align herself with feminism? Feminists are, after all, a minority with certain negative characteristics – characteristics that derive in part from aspects of the women's movement, and in part from the movement's roots in social conflict (Col.lectiu, 1994). Forms of conflict have been increasingly marginalized in the current pluralistic social climate, leaving less scope for the ideological commitment associated with much of Spain's early egalitarian feminism. This basis in conflict has been a factor in the stigmatization of activists in certain sections of the media and the public sphere which have worked to undermine feminist innovations by discrediting their sources.[1] Interacting with this stigmatization of feminism is the widely held view that it is now superannuated, that it has nothing more to offer young women who have grown up with the notion that they enjoy unprecedented equality with men in law. This notion has been reinforced by the fact that legal equality has meant the institutionalization of some key feminist insights as 'common sense' in mainstream political and broader social discourses. Although these fragments usually figure without reference to the ideology or broader objectives that gave them their force, they are widely seen as supporting the view that 'feminism' has filtered though all aspects of Spanish life.

The significance of these processes, at a time when (equality feminists stress) real-life equality has yet to be attained, emerges with a telling ambivalence in Icíar Bollaín's *Hola, ¿estás sola?* (Hallo, are you alone?). The film concerns two young women for whom feminism is simply not an issue: they make no reference to it. Yet their attitudes and possibilities are everywhere marked by it. They enjoy key freedoms associated with feminist-led social advances: the availability of contraception which enables a more relaxed and unpathological relationship with their bodies; the confidence and autonomy to initiate (sexual and other) relations with men on equitable terms; an enviable sense of freedom and mobility hardly troubled in the film by a shortage of money. But it is suggested that their lives bear a negative as well as a positive debt to feminism. Twenty years earlier their mothers had been members of the first generation of women to question Francoist models of maternal self-sacrifice and to begin to revalue personal happiness and self-fulfilment. Both are presented as having left their families and their daughters in a search for personal autonomy that has marked both 'unmothered' girls in different ways and made mothers a site of crisis throughout most of the film. Yet the film as a whole is a pleasurably naturalistic representation of young women making choices about their own lives and, in the process, finding happiness and lasting friendship. These tensions, we suggest, make *Hola, ¿estás sola?* a post-feminist film in three different and apparently contradictory senses. First, it is 'post' feminist in the sense that it takes for granted certain advances for women in which feminist activists played a key role, and suggests (by ignoring them) that feminist projects for the future are of no relevance for young women today. Second, it is post-feminist in a more critical sense, in its condemnation of what figure as some of feminism's negative side-effects. Third, and more positively, it suggests a fresh approach to the impasses of equality feminism which many younger women will find attractive: the possibility of forms of autonomy that include negotiated friendships between women, motherhood and loving, symmetrically powered relations with men, all presented in an upbeat setting that neutralizes some of the old complexes and recriminations.

So, *Hola, ¿estás sola?* is not a 'feminist' film in any simple sense. In cutting themselves free from their mothers the two girls also detach themselves from the mothers of feminism. Rather as the generation before them had to detach itself from the maternal self-abnegation of the 1940s and 1950s, the girls have to 'matar a mamá' ('kill off mum'). In each case, the assertion of independence implied in 'el relevo de las generaciones' ('generational change') brings gains and losses. As noted, these include the decline of often contradictory forms of extra-institutional feminism in favour of more normative institutional discourse (Brooksbank Jones, 1997). But this normative dimension makes it difficult for women to recognize or express dissatisfaction with social features presented to them in a positive light: if they are told that they have the same possibilities open to them as men, for example, difficulties in realizing these possibilities might be experienced as the result of women's own, personal shortcomings. This in turn might lead them to choose alternative courses which they then represent to themselves as the result of individual choice (Col.lectiu, 1995). The emotional investment of *Hola, ¿estás sola?*'s protagonists in idealized notions of motherhood and romantic love could be viewed in this light. From this perspective, it seems that young women and men who forget their history, wilfully or otherwise, are condemned endlessly to repeat it. And such a loss of historic memory – among a generation that keeps its edits largely as style – would seem particularly poignant to those feminists who laboured to find, or construct, predecessors. Yet as Catalan feminist group Espai Dones Joves notes, history never simply repeats itself. At a time when many young women find the positivist discourse of progress less compelling than discourses of individual autonomy, Espai Dones Joves claim 'the chance to make mistakes and repeat processes similar to others that may already have arisen within the movement' (Espai Dones Joves, 1996, p. 76). They are aware that the contexts in which they experiment with old and newer ideas are always changing, conferring new significance on discourses and tactics alike.

This helps to explain the new significance invested in feminist discourses and tactics by their deployment on the Internet. In the examples cited, this significance often seems to owe more to the medium's technical and formal novelty than to users' conceptual or other innovations. These new technical possibilities have their own conceptual implications, however. Some appear to usher in dramatic possibilities for feminism; others seem to shake key feminist assumptions to their foundations. For example, posting material on the Internet is a radical public act to the extent that it inaugurates the possibility of interaction between the cybermaterial and the unknown audience. When a feminist critic publishes a non-virtual account of a text, for example, or a pen-friend replies to a letter, their interventions exist alongside the text or the letter that motivated them. But on the Internet each intervention can, in theory, revise, supplement or displace what succeeded it. To this extent, the Internet foregounds relations, processes of 'transformation and change ... emerging and becoming' at the expense of fixed and enduring authority (Lebrero Stals, 1996, p. 110). Above all, it questions the truth status conventionally attributed to text, image and ideas (Echeverría, 1996, p. 114–5). Information flows across the Internet through 'rhizomatic' or root-like processes rather than primarily linear, sequential, or accretive ones. And this tends to foreground the possibilities and processes of communciation itself rather than questions of conceptual 'depth'. The Internet's undermining of notions of enduring authority, history, progress and truth represents a challenge to traditional feminism's methods and objectives. It challenges feminism first as a primarily modernist project, a historically grounded emancipatory discourse oriented towards enduring social change. But it also questions the traditional organization of the public sphere – its grounding in truth, consensus, the separation of the public and private domains – in which institutional feminists have made their most notable advances. Attempts to rethink feminism from within these new parameters open up possibilities for some of the most innovative and thought-provoking work by women net-users.

Sherry Turkle, Donna Haraway and others have suggested that technology can open up spaces for new, postmodern subjectivities for women (and men) that are no longer subject to the old phallocratic dualisms. Internet users, it is argued, can (in principle) evade the pressures of identity and history, free their imagination, exploit the possibilities of technological pleasure and subversion to become who they want to be. The rhetoric of pleasure and subversion is deployed at the website of Dones Intrepides which, like Riot-grrrls, targets younger users. In its attempts to encourage playful and imaginative uses of the network, however, the Dones Intrepides site illustrates how far the scope for imagining what one wants to be in the future is limited by what one is, or imagines oneself to be, in the present (Espai de Dones/ Dones Intrepides, 1998).[2] As noted, the development of Spanish feminisms in the 1960s and early 1970s was closely associated with the oppositional politics of the last years of the Franco regime. Partly as a consequence it was for a long time more explicitly politicized and, because its priorities lay elsewhere, less theorized than, for example, its US counter-part. Although a relatively small but dedicated group of feminist academics and activists have made up much of this theoretical ground in the last decade their wider impact so far has been limited, and forms of 'difference' feminism in particular remain a minority concern. This may help to explain why the sophisticated technological antihumanism of Haraway and others, and above all their psychoanalytically informed attempts to use cyberspace to expand women's repertoire of identifications, as yet barely resonate in Spanish women's Internet work. This does not mean that equality para-digms have been proof against key difference feminist claims – most notably the insistence on women's diversity. On the other hand, as is clear from institutional women's networks like Consell de Dones, it *has* helped to ensure that women's questions are not being worked out on the Internet exclusively at the level of the simulacrum.[3] As demonstrated by some of the sites discussed here, however, a focus on the construction of the social does not necessarily lead to reflection on the larger conceptual possibilities opened up by the new technological infrastructure. Nor on the crucial inter-face between virtual and non-virtual lives – on what remains of virtual empowerment, for example, when the computer is switched off.

Camps is right to suggest that the feminist discourse of the 1970s and 1980s needs a new register. This does not mean, however, that outstanding items on the feminist agenda (or, more properly and problematically, agen-das) simply need to be expressed via a medium or in a form accessible to younger women. For the realization of part of these agendas has, albeit unevenly, transformed the contexts from which they sprang. There are young women in Spain who accept, in whole or in part, an existing feminist agenda, many of them politicized in higher education at home or abroad. But films like *Hola, ¿estás sola?* flag up the fading of feminist history and of the aura of the 'feminist' mother for many other young women. The publi-cation by key feminist organizations of their own histories of second-wave feminism is motivated in part by a need to address this perceived 'amnesia' – to affirm what has been achieved, highlight what is felt to remain out-standing, and encourage younger women to see that they have a stake in this process (Instituto de la Mujer, 1994; Asociació de Dones, 1996). *Hola, ¿estás sola?*'s optimistic conclusion highlights why such publications seem necessary. Like some of the net users discussed, it registers the shift away from Enlightenment-informed notions of originary authority and linear progress towards more rhizomatic relations. And like them it obliquely promotes a more complex connectivity at the expense of cultural historic memory. Young women, it suggests, expect to be co-authors now, and for this they are prepared to take what they need from the resources available to them and to ignore the rest. For feminists whose agenda is inextricably embedded in the discourse that Camps seeks to renew, and who saw and see themselves as working for future generations of women, this may feel like a betrayal. Those who are working, consciously or otherwise, to produce new prototypes and cultural innovations for women may be readier to recognize it as one more reinscription of the pains and pleasures of (generational and other) change. But Camps is surely right that some version of feminism is needed in this new transition, to help ensure that key economic and cultural barriers do not prevent women from playing their part in the shaping of an increasingly technologized society. For as long as these barriers persist other voices will remain more audible, more seductive, and more authoritative.

Notes

1. We are thinking here primarily of the anti-feminist right-wing media. However, tensions between (institutional and other) left feminists and proponents of difference feminism in the 1970s and early 80s also had their effects (Brooksbank Jones, 1997).
2. The new space opened up by the Internet has been assimilated by some feminist theorists to the space that Luce Irigaray has sought to open up for the emergence of the new female subject. What Irigaray is not, and cannot be, clear about is what precisely might emerge to fill this space. Her early remotivation of the certain devalued figures (such as viscosity) to keep this theoretical space temporarily open has been extended by some antihumanist women Internet users (Schaffer, 1996). In practice, however, it remains unclear how these terms can be prevented from slipping back into the Symbolic binaries from which they emerged.
3. We are grateful to Catherine Davies for raising this question.

References

ASOCIACIO DE DONES 1996: *20 anys de feminisme a Catalunya*. Barcelona, Ajuntament de Barcelona, 223–38.
BROOKSBANK JONES, A. 1997: *Women in contemporary Spain*. Manchester: Manchester University Press.
CAMPS, V. 1998: *El tiempo de las mujeres*. Madrid, Cátedra.
CIBERDONES 1998a: *¿Qui som?* [online]. Available at: <http://members.xoom.com/ciberdones/qui.html> [accessed July 1998].
—— 1998b: *La plana de les Ciberdones* [online]. Available at: <http://members.xoom.com/ciberdones/qui.html> [accessed January 1999].
COL.LECTIU DE DONES JOVES DESOBEDIENCIA 1994: Mujeres jóvenes: iguales ¿en qué? Feministas ¿para qué? In Federación de Organizaciones Feministas del Estado Español, *Jornadas feministas: Juntas y a por todas*. Madrid: Dirección General de la Mujer, 223–38.
DONES PERIODISTES DE CATALUNYA 1997: *Més visibilitat a Internet* [online]. Available at: <http://www.adpc.org/2visible.html> [accessed July 1998].

ECHEVERRIA, J. 1996: Art in the telematic medium. In Lebrero Stals, J. (ed.), *Tecnología y disidencia cultural/ Technology and cultural dissidence*. Donostia: Gipuzkoaka Foru Aldunia/Kultura Eta Euskara Departamentua, 111–15.

ESPAI DE DONES 1998: *Espai de Dones/ Dones Intrepides* [online]. Available at: <http://www.pangea.org/dona> [accessed July 1998].

ESPAI DONES JOVES 1996: 'Feministes joves' in Associació de Dones per a la Celebració del 20 Anys de les I Jornades Catalanes de la Dona/Ajuntament de Barcelona, *20 anys de feminisme a Catalunya*, Barcelona, Ajuntament de Barcelona, pp. 74–7.

INSTITUT CATALÀ DE TECNOLOGIA 1997: *Mujeres en positivo hacia la tecnología: Acción 2. Examen de las actuaciones concretas de las mujeres con éxito profesional: 'El papel de la formación y las nuevas tecnologías'*. Barcelona: Institut Català de Tecnologia.

INSTITUTO DE LA MUJER 1994: *10 Años del Instituto de la Mujer*. Madrid: Instituto de la Mujer.

LEBRERO STALS, J. 1996: On the public domain, the net and art. In Lebrero Stals, J. (ed.), *Tecnología y disidencia cultural/ Technology and Cultural Dissidence*. Donostia: Gipuzkoaka Foru Aldunia/ Kultura Eta Euskara Departamentua, 108–10.

RIOT-GRRRLS 1998a: *Homepage* [online]. Available at: <http://regio7.com/ciber/1-980122.html> [accessed July 1998].

—— 1998b: *Homepage* [online]. Available at: <http://regio7.com/ciber/1-980122.html> [accessed November 1998].

SCHAFFER K. 1996: *The contested zone: cybernetics, feminism and representation* [online]. Available at: <http: www.lamp.ac.uk/oz/schaffer.html [accessed July 1998].

|22|

Laws of silence: homosexual identity and visibility in contemporary Spanish culture

ALBERTO MIRA

Who needs 'gay'?

In an unpublished interview with Armand de Fluvià, one of the key leaders of the Spanish gay movement in the 1970s, I asked him how far back gay activism in Spain went, as well as who, if any, he regarded as the movement's 'founding fathers'. His reply was a disheartening one: 'None.'[1] Elsewhere, homosexual traditions are key elements in building up the gay movement. Neither de Fluvià nor other post-Franco activists were aware of any tradition of homosexual politics, not to mention homosexual 'culture' in Spain: they felt they either had to do without it or import it from abroad. This is less surprising when one takes into account that most gay activists and intellectuals in Spain today show a clear reluctance to accept there is such a thing as a 'gay identity' or even, more problematically, a homosexual 'identity'. A clear distintion between 'gay' and 'homosexual' is not always made in gay writing (*see*, for instance, Sedgwick, 1990). In order to discuss the Spanish case, I feel such a distinction is not just useful but essential. 'Gay' is, strictly speaking, a model of homosexual identity born out of the Stonewall events, with a strong political element and with assimilationist agenda. 'Homosexual' will be used as an umbrella word covering all expressions of same-sex eroticism. This essay explores some of the consequences of such reluctance and sets anti-identity attitudes against the background of representations of homosexuality in Spain.[2]

One must start by saying that 'gay identity' is a far from clear-cut concept, and still the site of debate among gay academics both in Britain and the United States. Whilst accepted by some as a strategic way forward in the politics of homosexuality (Watney, 1987; Bersani, 1995), it is deeply mistrusted by some defenders of 'queer' sexualities as restrictive and risking essentialism (Simpson, 1996).[3] But Spanish intellectuals have remained unconcerned by the identity debate, making discussion of the issue almost impossible due to the lack of a common theoretical framework for dealing with it. Spanish academia in particular has been notoriously resistant to the wave of cultural studies, and popular writers and opinion-makers have never really caught up with the fresh approaches offered by this 'new' academic field. Post-colonialism and gender theory are pointedly dismissed by influential figures in the cultural landscape. Critic Miguel García-Posada, for example, who runs the literary section of the cultural supplement of *El País*, regularly expresses his contempt for 'multiculturalism' in a fierce assertion of cultural nationalism. All this is not necessarily a bad thing: the value of the revolution cultural studies has introduced into Anglo–American academia is still open to debate. Critics have pointed out its potential for strengthening hitherto weak or ineffective political identities, as well as the risk of superficial treatment or lack of coherence which accompanies the articulation of cultural issues from several different perspectives. In Spain, one consequence of the general mistrust of politically resonant accounts of textuality has been the lack of theoretical tools with which to approach the debate on sexual identity. The discussion of cultural expressions of sexuality thus takes place in a theoretical no man's land which unavoidably reduces the debate to questions of privacy and the individual's right to choose sexual partners.

Ever since 1969, Anglo–American culture has created and exported models of homosexual identity, most influentially that of 'gay' identity, readily recognizable and easy to insert into a new market. Gay identities risk being engulfed by capitalism, and subsumed into the very heterosexist matrix they are meant to oppose (Sinfield, 1998), a point repeatedly reiterated by some Spanish gay intellectuals. Juan Goytisolo would rather speak of practices than 'identities', arguing that he has nothing in common with other people with similar sexual practices; equally, Alberto Cardín, arguably the most influential Spanish homosexual intellectual, showed in many of his writings a disdain for any kind of organized gay identity (Cortés in Aliaga and Cortés, 1993, p. 173; Smith, 1996, p. 110).

Identity is constructed and activated in many ways. As Judith Butler (1990) has shown, there is seldom a stable essence behind sexual 'identities'. Identity is the result of first creating a common set of dreams and targets (even if such dreams are not based on any ultimate 'truth'), and then using it strategically to establish and justify social visibility (Hall and du Gay, 1996). Spanish activists have found it difficult to understand and embrace Butler's concept of 'strategic identity'. Debates on this subject invariably drift into the realm of 'what is true', rather than 'what is convenient', illustrating once again the resistance to postmodern theory among critics. Aliaga and Cortés's *Identidad y diferencia*, for example, ends with the transcription of a round table that included a wide range of Spanish gay intellectuals.

Identity is deemed by some as an 'impossible' target in the Spanish context, and by others as 'unnecessary'. There are few references to the need for cultural appropriation or finding a 'Spanish gay tradition' (1997, pp. 201–37).

In order to consider what basis, if any, there might be for a Spanish homosexual identity, two slightly divergent areas need to be taken into account: on the one hand, historical manifestations of homosexuality in Spanish culture; on the other, the basic notion of a 'Mediterranean homosexuality'.

Identity: history and politics

Any social minority group attempting to have a public voice will start by seeking its legitimization in history. Spanish intellectuals are not unaware of this strategy in other areas of the cultural landscape such as nationalist politics. With sexual politics, this has never happened. There is, however, a hitherto unexplored history of homosexuality in Spain, the manifestations and concerns of which could provide a culturally distinct framework which would render obsolete the need to take Anglo-American tradition as a point of reference. This 'hidden' history is waiting to be discovered by historians and cultural critics. Manifestations of a homosexual subculture at the turn of the century, for example, are rarely addressed by Spanish academics, although homophobic remarks were consistently used against members of the 'Modernismo' movement, and this was an issue we know concerned intellectuals at the time. Pío Baroja, for instance, expressed his disgust at homosexuals' attempts to justify their 'perversion'; others voiced concern for the use of Hellenism in poetry as an expression of homoeroticism. Such evident homophobia normally indicates a strong presence of homosexuals, as was the case in the literary circles of the time. A theoretically informed analysis of sexual dissidence within the 'Generación del 27' group of writers thus constitutes a major gap in Spanish literary and social history. Still further back, a wealth of information on articulations of homoeroticism in Spain can be discovered through the intellectuals of Al-Andalus, as Muslim Spain was known. Until now, such instances have remained outside the main flow of cultural tradition. Regarded at best as oddities, even if they seem to have had enormous symbolic importance at the time, their significance for cultural history has remained largely unexplored. This pact of non-discussion effectively takes homosexuality out of history, reducing it to a 'personality flaw' or individual choice. Silence cannot be converted into identity politics. The failure to produce homosexual visibility means that homophobic representations become the only way in which same-sex passion is discussed.

It could be argued that there are historical causes for such enforced silence. From the 1940s onwards an all-pervading censorship and keen mistrust for any kind of marginality (particularly where sexual dissidence was concerned) made the construction of homosexual identities virtually impossible. In Spain, however, the end of repression did not bring about – as it did in Germany or the United States – a co-ordinated (if slow) reconstruction of homosexuality as a politically relevant movement with important roots in cultural history.

This does not mean that the gay movement was non-existent. On the contrary. After Franco's death in 1975 there was a frantic battle to recover lost liberties, and the homosexual movement became part of that battle. In the unpublished interview mentioned above, Fluvià described large gay demonstrations and unconditional support from other democratic forces. Radical groups established short-lived alliances with other left-wing organizations that led to the repeal of homophobic laws in the early 1980s. Now Spain enjoys some of the most egalitarian legislation in Europe with regard to sexual orientation. And yet, not even at the peak of the gay liberation period, between 1977 and 1981, do we find a clear move to reclaim the past and provide a lasting social identity. Time has revealed that the gay rights struggle was a rather small and insignificant item in the larger agenda of opposing right-wing sexual conservatism. Once progress had been made, homosexuality became a non-issue, as its position had always been ancillary to the libertarian movement.

Mediterranean sexuality (and its discontents)

But there is a second reason why homosexuality has never worked as a political identity. History and politics are relatively flexible forms of cultural discourse, whereas the discourses regulating sexual practices are deeply embedded in a given culture's habits and self-perceptions, and therefore harder to reshape. Another issue underlying resistance to a political use of gay identity is the concept of 'Mediterranean homosexuality', a complex model differing significantly from the Anglo-American paradigm. Its proponents declare that homosexuality in Mediterranean (and, for that matter, Islamic) countries is frequently practised yet never discussed. Key figures such as Juan Goytisolo see merit in this delimitation. 'Sexual flexibility' is a basic trait of the model, as described by Giovanni Da'll Orto in Dynes's *Encyclopedia of Homosexuality* (Dynes, 1990, p. 780): sexual acts can vary at different stages of life, but personal identity does not depend on the biological sex of one's partner; practices can never determine identity in the traditional sense of the word. Homosexuality is not even used as a discriminatory label as long as the 'active' role in a relationship is adopted. This distinction between active and passive is key to any delimitation of sexual identities; virility depends on the role, and can be easily safeguarded. For those who defend the Mediterranean model of sexuality, this is having the best of both worlds: one's desire can be fulfilled without necessarily having to suffer social marginalization.

Of course, the price of the Mediterranean model is silence. Whereas men are allowed and encouraged to boast about their female sexual partners and even detail heterosexual encounters, homosexual encounters cannot be discussed; if they are, there is a tacit assumption that they were motivated by female deprivation rather than desire. For some, this is a small price to pay. For others, it becomes almost stifling since effeminacy and strong sexual interest between members of the same sex are still frowned upon. Given that the construction of a social identity is mostly about its expression, the Mediterranean model ensures homosexuality will never leave the closet – a special kind of cultural discourse, which is perfectly 'scripted', but remains unwritten. It is not difficult to see how this apparently liberating model makes the construction of a homosexual agenda based on 'coming out' and claiming right a difficult task.

Furthermore, the model itself is open to criticism: one might ask, for instance, whether the so-called 'Mediterranean' model is not merely a version of pre-identity models elsewhere in the world. Research about Elizabethan England and nineteenth-century America suggests that the features identified by Da'll Orto and others apply to these cultures as well. This would be a hard blow to those who defend the Mediterranean model on the grounds that it is an expression of cultural specificity.

Homosexuality and representation in Spain

Silence, then, is a central feature of perceptions and articulations of homosexuality in Spanish culture. It is not a total silence, but a strongly focused and discriminating one: representation of homosexuality is acceptable as long as the mode of the enunciation is not pro-homosexual. Treatments of homosexuality towards the end of the 1970s provide an illustration of the way in which such attitudes towards identity become something of a trap for Spanish gay people. The dizzy pace of social change in this fascinating period of Spanish history renewed the entire cultural landscape in less than a decade. Images in magazines, on television, in the movies, and the tenor of radio programmes and articles were transformed to reflect the making of a progressive country. As a consequence, social change became more shallow than it looked. The embedding of such a radical change in social attitudes would normally take several generations. Here, libertarianism was imposed rather than freely accepted, and new ideas did not have the time to settle.

Homosexuality was just one more taboo that had to be broken, so for a while it was fashionable to include references to homosexuality in popular and high culture. This often had very little to do with gay politics and was hardly more than a response to long years of sexual repression. Moreover these images and representations do not give the impression of gay men asserting their identity. There seemed no time to introduce a debate, much less admit that, given the chance to dissent, some people might find homosexuality offensive if it was more than a token presence. At the end of the 1970s everyone was assumed to be supportive of 'liberal causes' and, even in the mid-nineties, it was difficult to find Spanish individuals who would acknowledge they had racial, political, or sexual prejudices.

Depite this liberal agenda, little was actually done to render homosexuality political in mainstream texts. Its mere representation was taken as evidence of honoring liberal principles and emphasised as an act of courage. Imanol Uribe's 1984 film, *La muerte de Mikel*, for example, was generally discussed by the critics as a brave film about homosexuality. In fact homosexuality is featured in the film in a very confusing way. The protagonist (played by one of Spain's most promising stars at the time, Imanol Arias) is inititially in a heterosexual relationship but then, suddenly and for no apparent reason, starts visiting a cabaret where he meets a drag-queen performer with whom he has sex. The fact that the spectator does not know, for example, how Mikel feels about his sexual orientation may indicate an uncertainty, on the part of the film-maker, as to what the meaning of homosexuality should be. In the end, sexual orientation is subsumed into the problems of Basque nationalist politics, towards which there is a more critical attitude. Sexual dissidence was merely a device to spark discussion of other issues, and the film's condemnation is of reactionary attitudes in general, rather than of homophobia in particular. Other 'serious' films were similarly vague about 'what to do' with homosexuality once the 'brave' step of representation had been taken. At the opposite extreme of the representational spectrum, mainly in popular culture, homophobic stereotyping was frequent. Popular comedians resorted to facile clichés that made use of 'safe' notions of homosexuality – especially effeminacy and obsession with sex – and homophobic jokes were frequent in magazines and radio programmes. Libertarianism, it seems, meant that the topic could be freely mentioned, rather than that something progressive had to be done about it.

At the same time, it should be acknowledged that liberal attitudes became generalized in some areas of Spain's largest cities. A thriving culture based on sexual ambiguity and freedom spread quickly. The very loosely articulated movement known as *la movida* became something of a symbol of the new freedoms achieved and is perhaps most accurately described as a state of mind. Members of the *movida* met in certain bars and cafés, went out together and shared musical tastes. Some had artistic ambitions, but there was a clear mistrust of high culture. Even when most of the individuals associated with this movement proudly proclaimed sexual libertarianism, 'homosexuality' was not a word they felt comfortable with. 'I don't like labels' became one of their mantras, and this resistance to categorization cannot be dismissed too easily. There was a rejection of traditional political activism, and gay identity was regarded as dull and conservative. The notion of 'coming out of the closet', one of the central rhetorical strategies of Anglo-American gay activism, was regarded as irrelevant, as most people involved did not acknowledge they were in the closet to start with.[4]

This raises a number of issues which can only be briefly outlined here. First, despite claims to the contrary, closets did exist – constructed by denial or by silence – given that the default was always heterosexuality. Second, use of 'queer' identities to justify political laziness was based on ignorance and lack of sensibility: queer is significant especially in the context of saturation and glorification of a given assimilationist model that obviously was not working for many people. Without such saturation, *la movida* in Spain was just a way of not dealing with the issue. 'Queer' resisted identity definition by boasting publicly about unacceptable practices; *la movida* teasingly suggested these might be there, but then declared them off-limits for public discussion. The similarities between both models are very tenuous. Third, the claim that ambiguity and resistance to categories was the Spanish way to approach sexuality would later be questioned by the speed with which the gay market, mostly based on Anglo-American models, was accepted in Spain. Gay identity was resisted when it might have had political or cultural importance, but it became just too seductive or simply unstoppable when it was introduced as a marketable product.

Aids and the wages of invisibility

Maybe a devastating illustration of the consequences of this version of sexuality, unconcerned with the political, will help to reveal where the real problems lay.[5] Aids was one of the most important crises to affect homosexuals in the first world, certainly the turning point in post-Stonewall gay history. It became deeply unsettling both for the social achievements of homosexuals and for the individuals themselves, as they discovered the difficulty of facing a crisis without public support. After a few early years of tragic confusion, the gay movement managed to create strategies for survival, especially in the United States. 'Silence = Death' became one of the key slogans of the anti-Aids movement, an equation that was the expression of a ruthless logic. Fear to speak out was singled out as the main reason for political passivity; lack of positive discourses on Aids made homophobia the only discourse on homosexuality to be heard. Visibility meant strength; organization meant lives saved.

Media treatments of the issue in Spain were pathetically misguided and hardly visible. On the one hand there was reluctance to speak out for homosexuals; after all, they were people like everybody else and therefore tolerated. On the other hand there was ignorance of the issues in question: the fact that many people would resist association with a gay-identified disease, that misunderstanding of the way infection worked would play up homophobia and that implementation of safe sex would be difficult in an atmosphere where sexual practices were never publicly discussed. The debate that regarded Aids as a 'self-inflicted disease' and gave rise to aggressive activism in response to expressions of furious homophobia never reached Spain. It was never suggested with any degree of intensity that homosexuals were 'to blame' for Aids, but equally no voice was raised in their support. Public discourse on Aids dealt with it merely as a health issue, not recognizing its political implications. Such recognition would have meant an acknowledgement of homophobia and of the need to counteract it. The Spanish atmosphere of free-wheeling libertarianism made it difficult for individuals to accept their own prejudices.

As a result of this, in a vicious circle, homosexual men started to move away from anything that might reveal their sexuality, and whatever gay institutions existed at the time became even weaker. Campaigns came and went from 1987, and their effectivity was marred by inconstancy. Judging from media reports, Aids was something that, just like gay identity, only happened abroad. Magic Johnson and others were admirable in their restless struggle. No equivalents were found in Spain and, even if they had been, it is doubtful they would have enjoyed the same support from the media as their American counterparts.

Focus on prevention meant that no help was given to those already infected, no relief was provided to alleviate the new set of difficulties due to ignorance or intolerance. Finally, and most importantly, campaigns were seldom addressed to homosexual men, as sexuality was never an issue. There were health campaigns on using condoms targeting teenagers: a worthwhile endeavour, no doubt, but teenagers were never the most significant victims; they became problematic because it was felt that focus on adolescents was a result of a reluctance to make homosexuality public. Campaigns aimed at gay men were almost secretive and limited to some gay bars, therefore reinforcing the cliché that homosexuality is only something that happens in the dark and against the 'Mediterranean model', in the context of which men should not require institutions to meet. In media treatments of Aids, homosexuality became an embarrassment for commentators who either resorted to homophobic and simplistic notions of gay people as 'sexual compulsives' or chose to focus on drug-addicts, apparently more 'deserving' and safer to deal with as victims. As I pointed out at the time in my article on the subject, treatments of Aids became a kind of surreal rhetorical ballet to steer away from the dreaded 'h-word' (Mira in Aliaga and Cortés, 1993, p. 152).

The importance of gay identity in the effects of the Aids epidemic was missed both by well-intentioned commentators and by gays themselves. If sexuality is just a private affair – whereas homophobia seems unavoidably part of the social discourse – then Aids and political passivity are just a matter of bad luck and resignation is the only possible response. As a result, statistics show how, from 1987 onwards, Spain was among the European countries with the greatest number of Aids cases, and in 1992 it had the fastest growth rate of infection.

Arguably, the confusing treatment of Aids issues in the Spanish media is a direct consequence of Spanish culture's difficult relationship with homosexuality as a political identity. Whenever homosexuals are faced with criticism as a group – as happened again in what became known as the 'Caso Arny' (see Aliaga, 1997, pp. 39–50) – there is no common front to offer valid responses. Tolerance is seldom tested and therefore its limits are often blurred. A model of homosexuality based on 'Mediterranean' attitudes may be an act of resistance against identities created abroad in order to respond to a different set of problems, but it should not become an alibi for not establishing a framework within which homosexuality can be discussed. The Mediterranean model may, after all, be homophobic in its refusal to acknowledge sexual dissidence. Furthermore, in its acceptance of 'practices', it becomes aggressive towards those who want to go beyond practices into identities. The 'sensual' Mediterranean model punishes cruelly both the effeminate and those who fail to hide their sexual orientation, and this is difficult to accept from any liberal standpoint.

On the issue of the limitations imposed by labels, it must be remembered that it was not homosexuals who started labelling themselves: for centuries it was mostly a heterosexist strategy seeking to delegitimize any expression of sexual dissidence. Gay identity has to be regarded, in spite of any possible perversions, as a 'counter discourse' which is oppositional in nature. If homosexuals fail to work at creating the terms in which they want to be perceived, prevailing homophobic notions will remain the paradigm of homosexual representation.

Furthermore, as we observed earlier, the globalization of culture means that market-oriented 'gay identity' has become an integral part of Spanish perceptions of homosexuality – to the point that its influence cannot be disregarded in the construction of a Spanish gay identity. This shows that some kind of non-activist homosexual identities seem to be accepted by the system. Otherwise, what is put forward as a mistrust of conservative views of sexuality based on 'labels' may just be another name for the closet. The construction of a culturally specific Spanish gay identity needs more research into the way same-sex passion is articulated in Spain, rather than a refusal to acknowledge history.

Imaginative activism is a key element in the construction of social identity: maybe some points made by *la movida* about libertarianism and loose sexual categories were right, but their implications must be explored. It would help if same-sex love was acknowledged rather than merely taking refuge in some ambivalent 'omnisexuality' which fails to be transgressive because of its avoidance of really transgressive articulation in discourse. Freedom achieved through silence is necessarily double-edged – it certainly allows for greater personal self-realization, as *la movida* claimed, but also – and equally importantly – it fails to protect individuals when homophobia resurfaces. The fact that some members of the *movida* suffered the ravages of Aids (motivating some change of attitudes) is only a tragic reminder of this.

Notes

1. Author's unpublished interview with Fluvià in Barcelona, December 1997.
2. The arguments on this paper refer specifically to gay men and only marginally to lesbians. The reason is lack of documentation of the situation for lesbians in Spain.
3. For an excellent account of this debate, and an insightful discussion of possibilities for a way forward, see Sinfield, 1998.
4. This may help to explain film-maker Pedro Almodóvar's mysterious attitude towards homosexuality. He has often defiantly expressed his unwillingness to discuss homosexuality and even gay politics, and won't acknowledge some elements in his work (such as camp, taste for melodrama and retro pop, use of drag queens, religious imagery, etc.) are part of a 'gay culture'. Whereas he has been successfully apropriated as something of a gay icon in Britain and the United States (a role he may embrace for commercial reasons) he has been extremely reluctant to be understood in a gay context in his own country.
5. For a fuller account of media treatments of the Aids crisis in Spain around 1992, see my 'Esta noche ... sida. Comentarios a algunos tratamientos del sida en prensa y televisión', in Aliaga and Cortés (eds), 1993, pp. 145–62.

References

ALIAGA, J. V. 1997: *Bajo vientre. Representaciones de la sexualidad en la cultura y el arte contemporáneos*, Valencia: Generalitat Valenciana.

ALIAGA, J. V. and CORTÉS, J. M. G. 1993: *De amor y rabia: acerca del arte y del sida*. Valencia: Universidad Politécnica de Valencia.

ALIAGA, J. V. and CORTÉS, J. M. G. 1997: *Identidad y diferencia. Sobre la cultura gay en España*. Madrid: Egales.

BERSANI, L. 1995: *Homos*. Cambridge, Mass.: Harvard University Press.

BUTLER, J. 1990: *Gender trouble. Feminism and the subversion of identity*. New York: Routledge.

DYNES, W. (ED.) 1990: *Encyclopedia of homosexuality*. London: St. James.

HALL, S. and du GAY, P. (EDS) 1996: *Questions of cultural identity*. London: Sage.

SEDGWICK, E. K. 1990: *Epistemology of the closet*. Berkeley: University of California Press.

SIMPSON, M. (ED.) 1996: *Anti-gay*. London: Cassell.

SINFIELD, A. 1998: *Gay and after*. London: Serpent's Tail.

SMITH, P. J. 1996: *Vision machines. Cinema, literature and sexuality in Spain and Cuba, 1983–1993*. London: Verso.

WATNEY, S. 1987: *Policing desire: pornography, Aids and the media*. London: Methuen.

|23|

The politics and representation of disability in contemporary Spain

MADELINE CONWAY

Disability and Cultural Studies

Although the majority of work published to date on disability has been written from a political point of view, articles and books are starting to appear that study disability from a cultural angle, and the work of various theorists (e.g. Lacan, Foucault, Bakhtin) is now being used in relation to disability studies. Most of the small amount written about cultural representations of disability emanates from and deals specifically with the US and UK. However, some academics are now moving away from this Western-centred view, which seems to assume that all societies have one common attitude towards disability, and are examining how culture affects the lives of the physically and mentally impaired from a global, multicultural perspective (e.g. Ingstad and Reynolds White, 1995; Corker and French, 1999; Mitchell and Snyder, 1977).

It is therefore important, when considering disability within Spain, to remember that who is and is not considered 'disabled' is culturally variable – the word 'disability' does not have one meaning which is valid in every society. There are social, cultural, historical and educational differences that mean that the situation for disabled people in Spain is not the same as that in the UK or US. For example, because of the structure of the traditional Spanish family, a far higher proportion of elderly and disabled relatives is cared for at home.

Something else that should always to be taken into account is legislation governing the way in which people with disabilities are treated. Current legislation on disability in Spain is based on Article 49 of the Spanish Constitution of 1978 (Belmonte, 1979), which states:

The public authorities will carry out a policy of provision, treatment, rehabilitation and integration of the physically, sensorially and mentally disabled, who will be given the special attention and protection that they need in order to enjoy the rights to which all citizens are entitled.

This umbrella statement in the Constitution was subsequently clarified in far greater detail in the 'Ley de Integración Social de los Minusválidos' (Law on the Social Integration of Disabled People) – known as the 'Lismi' – 1982. This is a major piece of legislation, which covers, as one might expect, aspects such as the prevention, diagnosis and evaluation of disability, financial and social assistance, rehabilitation, work, mobility, physical access, etc. Several other pieces of legislation have since followed, which clarify or modify particular aspects of the Lismi, both at a national level (e.g. 'Real Decreto 28.4.95 de Ordenación de la educación de los alumnos con necesidades educativas especiales', which concretizes the rules regarding 'special education') and at a provincial level (e.g. legislation in the autonomous communities of Aragón, Canarias and Madrid regarding the improvement of access and the overcoming of architectural barriers).[1]

As space does not permit a detailed discussion of all the significant aspects of this legislation, I shall restrict myself to two specific areas: the question of who is disabled within Spanish society, and how they are educated.

Who is disabled?

The question 'Who is disabled?' is a fundamental one and, as stated above, the answer to it will vary culturally and historically. Article 7, part one of the Lismi states:

For the purpose of the current law, the word 'disabled' will be taken to encompass all those whose potential for educational, work, or social integration is diminished by a physical, mental or sensory deficiency, whether permanent or temporary, and congenital or otherwise.

I wish briefly to consider this in relation to the argument, which is central to disability politics, of the medical model (considered by activists in the disability lobby to be a negative way of looking at disability, where the 'condition' is looked upon as the problem) versus the social model (a more positive point of view, where the problem is not the 'condition' but rather that the disability is imposed by physical barriers and social attitudes). In other words: in Spanish disability legislation, is the problem portrayed as the condition or as the attitude of society?[2]

If we consider the wording of Article 7 of the Lismi, it becomes clear that this issue is a complex one. On the one hand, the law bases its decision as to whether or not somebody is considered to have a disability on 'una deficiencia' – a deficiency – which falls within the boundaries of the medical model. Moreover, this decision is to be taken by 'teams of professional assessors'. However, the situation is far from straightforward, for at the same time the law also sees the main issue as integration into society – i.e. society's (in)ability to accept a particular person. It seems, therefore, that the legislation is making an attempt to move away from the medical model (the doctor says there is something 'wrong' with you, and so you are labelled as 'disabled') to the social model. The emphasis of the Lismi is on integration. Moreover, it is emphasized that decisions should be made on an individual basis ('efectuado de manera personalizada') thereby judging each 'case' on its own merits. This emphasis on integration and individuality is apparent in this law's treatment of education.

Education: to integrate or not to integrate?

Article 24 of the Lismi states quite clearly the situation regarding education in Spain:

> One. The disabled person will be integrated into the mainstream educational system and receive help and resources as recognized by this Law.
>
> Two. Special Education will be provided temporarily or permanently for those people with disabilities for whom integration into the mainstream educational system proves impossible ...

The emphasis, therefore, is on the integration, whenever possible, of the disabled person into the general education system, with 'special education' as a last resort. In many ways, this is extremely positive, for it gives young disabled people the opportunity to integrate into 'normal' society from as young an age as possible and, moreover, gives 'normal' children exposure to people whose needs and problems are different from their own, thereby creating opportunities for greater understanding. It is interesting to note that the situation in the UK is the reverse, with people often having to fight to integrate disabled children into mainstream education.

The segregation inherent in systems of 'special education' is often considered detrimental to the representation of disability, due to the way it marks certain members of society as 'other'. However, not all so-called experts agree that educational integration – 'mainstreaming' – is the best way forward, and some believe that 'special education' can help to give the training and skills necessary for people with disabilities to adapt to society. It should also be remembered that segregation can lead to solidarity and politicization amongst those who have been segregated, by bringing them together (*see*, for example, Thomson, 1997; Johnstone, 1998).

Disabled rights

Despite the legislative emphasis on integration, Spain, in common with the rest of Europe, seems to lag behind the UK and US in response to disability politics. There is not the same strong, determined disability lobby fighting for disabled people's rights, nor the same situation of numerous respected charitable bodies funding research, raising awareness and providing assistance. In Spain, one enormous disability-related charity, the ONCE (National Organization for the Blind) is so powerful that other organizations dealing with the rights and welfare of people with disabilities seem to live in its shadow. This makes it much more difficult for other disability groups and organizations to achieve their aims.

The 'Lismi' established principles regarding normalization of services, integration and individualized attention with regards to people with disabilities. However, subsequent education-related legislation has been passed since 1982, in an attempt to keep up to date with social changes. This includes Real Decreto 334/1985 regarding special education; the Ley Orgánica 1/1990, which deals with the educational system in general; and the Real Decreto of April 1995, regarding the education of pupils with special needs. Legislation has also been implemented at a regional level. Although most of this legislation has involved little more than the fine-tuning of the principles laid down in the Lismi, significant progress has been made, both at regional and national level, with regard to the removal of physical barriers, which in turn assists eductional integration.

But is the legislation working? One of the ways to find out what is going on in Spain from the point of view of disability is to look at media coverage.

Media coverage

Articles dealing with various aspects of disability appear frequently in the Spanish press, both national and local – the articles that I am about to discuss all appeared during the first week of April 1998.[3] Disability is an issue that is increasing in importance, and Spanish television channels are also now starting to take seriously the need for signing and subtitling of their programmes. To give an example, Tele 5, a national commercial television channel, started to provide subtitling on some of its output on 14 January 1998. The number of hours of subtitling has gradually increased. In the last two weeks of January 1998, subtitling was provided on seven and a half hours of programmes. By March 1999 this had increased to an average of 25 hours per week. Clearly, there is a lot more work to be done before the situation can be considered satisfactory, but new digital technology is constantly improving the ways in which programmes can be made more accessible for the deaf and hard-of-hearing. A perusal of Spanish newspapers will reveal an interest in a variety of issues, especially access to public buildings and education.

As an example of the way in which legislation regarding university education is working, I should like to look at the recent case of María Auxiliadora Cabello, a 29-year-old with cerebral palsy who was attempting to enter Málaga University. An article about this case appeared in a local newspaper *El Correo de Andalucía* on 1 April 1998.[4] The facts were straightforward. A young woman wished to enrol at Málaga University, using one of the 3 per cent of places reserved for people with disabilities. This was denied her, due to the fact that her disability was 'only' 33 per cent, rather than the requisite 65 per cent (as established in the Real Decreto of 1992). This case brought into question the validity of the rule, for, ironically, somebody 65 per cent disabled by cerebral palsy would be unable to learn to read or write, never mind follow a university course.

The case was subsequently reported in the national newspaper *ABC* on 4 April.[5] This in itself is interesting, for *ABC* is not the kind of liberal publication that one expects to champion this type of cause. Moreover, *ABC* had not simply repeated information given in the original article in order to fill a few column inches, but had felt the subject important enough to warrant further investigation. It reported that María Auxiliadora's case had led to the Ministries of Education and Labour looking into the possibility of changing the legislation. Furthermore, it noted that the case had been taken up by the Federación Española de Atención a las Personas con Parálisis Cerebral (Aspace), an organization to help people with cerebral palsy. The appearance of such articles in the local and national press is obviously crucial in encouraging the public to treat, not only education, but further and higher education in particular, as the right of any citizen who has the capacity to benefit from it.

Interestingly, a small article appeared in *Gaceta de los Negocios* (a national daily business newspaper) on 3 April 1998, reporting on Anderson Consulting's computer program *Elegir carrera* ('Choose your degree'),[6] which is now accessible to people with both aural and visual impairments. The existence of such a program serves to emphasize that university education should be available for all. Unfortunately, however, the disabled person who overcomes obstacles to get into university will often be faced with insurmountable physical barriers. According to the press, various universities are attempting to remove architectural barriers, but whilst university authorities may wish to do this, their best intentions are often thwarted by a lack of funds.

So, media coverage clearly reveals that there are problems with the current legislation. What is positive in the press representations, however, is that nobody is calling into question the rights or ability of people with disabilities to benefit from as much education as possible. The social model seems to prevail here – the problem is portrayed in terms of the barriers imposed by society, and not the disabled person's condition.

Let's talk about sex ...

Sexual activity is a normal part of 'normal' life. However, there is a tendency to think that the idea of people with mental or physical disabilities having sex (either with other disabled people or – worse – with a 'normal' member of society) is 'wrong'. The concept of people with disabilities having sexual relations is an uncomfortable one for many people, and thus is seldom discussed. However, in order for full integration of all members of society to take place, it is must become acceptable for all members of that society to have the right to be sexually active (*see* Shakespeare *et al.*, 1996; Thomson, 1997).

Articles such as the following one, which appeared in *Hoy* (a regional publication covering Extremadura, Cáceres, Mérida, Plasencia and Badajoz), on 2 April 1998, must clearly have a positive influence.[7] Entitled 'El desarrollo sexual aumenta la integración de tetrapléjicos' ('Sexual development boosts the integration of tetraplegics'), this article emphasizes the importance of a satisfactory sex life, both for the paraplegic and his or her partner. The article suggests that sex should be fun, but at the same time it also stresses the importance of people with such disabilities having children. As the article says, 'Wheelchairs are not hereditary.'

It is also possible to see an increasing number of positive representations of people with disabilities in contemporary Spanish cultural texts. This is particularly the case with cinema, perhaps due to the visible nature of many of the physical differences that constitute 'disability'. An example of this can be seen in Almodóvar's film, *Carne trémula* (1997), in which the protagonist David is a wheelchair user with an active sex life. Javier Bardem is outstanding in the role of a paraplegic who not only satisfies his wife sexually, but plays sports. Moreover, the positive effect of the part Bardem played in the film extends beyond the screen: he was quoted in *Afim* (a disability magazine) in February 1998 as saying 'The paraplegic is someone full of life.'[8] Given that Bardem is known for his film roles as macho studs, this was inspired casting.

Staying with the medium of cinema, I shall conclude this article with a comparison between the freak show, a traditional form of visual entertainment featuring people with physical differences, and Alex de la Iglesia's 1992 film *Acción mutante* in which a group of physically disabled terrorists (Acción Mutante) takes violent revenge on the 'gente guapa' ('beautiful people') who control society.

Acción mutante: a modern-day freak show?

We human beings are, by nature, curious. For many centuries – first in Europe and later in United States – the abnormal ('monstrous') body was a valuable commodity (see Thomson, 1996 and 1997; Davis, 1997). 'Normal' people would part with their money in exchange for a look at 'abnormal' bodies, in a process that served to reassure the normal of their normality. What I wish to consider is whether or not Alex de la Iglesia's first feature film *Acción mutante* can be seen to function in the same way.

In traditional freak shows, the marketing of 'inhuman' commodities was of the utmost importance. They were sold through posters and flyers to an avid public. Similarly, in *Acción mutante* we see a group of disabled people being 'sold' to the public over the airwaves. Their bodily abnormalities are described in detail by a newsreader, supported by pictures, just as has always happened in the promotion of freak show exhibits to the public. Sensationalism of this type wins viewers and makes money.

When watching *Acción mutante*, do we, like visitors to a 'freak show', get pleasure and reassurance out of looking at others less 'normal' than ourselves? During the opening titles, the members of Acción Mutante pass across the screen, paraded in front of us like 'freaks' in a freak show. They, however, are not content just to be looked at. They look back, interact with the camera. M.A. (an enormously powerful deaf-mute with, we are told, an exceptionally low IQ) even bangs his head against the camera. We are not allowed to enjoy the dubious freak-show pleasure of looking at them in order to reinforce our feeling of normalcy. They remind us that although they may be physically different, they are nevertheless human. They are fighting back against 'normal' society's tendency to categorize them as non-human.

Acción Mutante's plan involves kidnapping wealthy, beautiful Patricia Orujo on her wedding day. They enter the party without difficulty, and none of the 'gente guapa' seem to notice anything strange about the group – there is no freak-show gawking. Their plan fails and, with Chepa the dwarf and M.A. dead, the remaining members of the group escape with Patricia Orujo, her father in hot pursuit. By the time their spacecraft crash-lands on the planet Axturias, only the leader Yarritu, Patricia, and Alex Abadie (dragging his dead Siamese twin, Juan, along with him) are still alive. As she is pulled around the rocky planet by her hair, Patricia starts to spout the kind of revolutionary arguments that one would expect a group such as Acción Mutante to use to further its cause. She has changed sides and joined the 'gente fea' ('ugly people').

Meanwhile, on another part of the planet, Alex Abadie is still dragging his dead, decomposing twin around with him. An attempt at taxidermy has been carried out on Juan, reminiscent of the way in which freaks were exhibited in shows even many years after their deaths (either embalmed or in photographic form). The showdown that ensues ensures that our sympathies remain on the side of Acción Mutante. The only concern of Patricia Orujo's father is that he should kill Yarritu, regardless of what happens to his daughter. Yarritu comes out best in the scene, for he is presented as fair and kind, and protects Patricia from her father. He even gives his own life to save Patricia, when she sets off her father's bomb by mistake. Yarritu is a hero, and the viewer therefore can empathize with the disabled 'other'.

Alex Abadie finally gets rid of his brother, ripping him off at the shoulder. This amputation has made him almost 'normal'. But Patricia has also lost an arm, thereby becoming a 'freak' physically as well as politically. She highlights the mutability of the body, and the fact that, potentially, we all face disability. Watching the 'freaks' in this film, therefore, does not reinforce our feelings of normalcy, as happened to the audience of the freak show, but rather breaks down the barrier between 'normal' and 'abnormal', 'able-bodied' and 'disabled'.

The way forward

Given the necessary limitations of my own research into the anthropology of disability and representations of physical disability in contemporary Spanish culture, there is ample scope for further investigation into disability in Spain. In particular, there is a need for both historical and sociological research to clarify the place of people with disabilities (physical and mental) in Spanish society in past centuries as well as the present. Critical study of disability-related legislation and of definitions of, and attitudes to, disability by insurance companies would also be valuable. In all of these cases, comparative studies between Spain and, for example, the UK or US, would be illuminating. Finally, an area which would be especially interesting at this time of increased public sensitivity and discussion of 'political correctness', is the way in which the language used in relation to disabilities is evolving: for example, the tendency to replace the earlier standard term 'minusválido' by the less offensive (but still problematic) 'discapacitado'. Cultural research of this type will hopefully prove beneficial to the experience of people who live with the kind of bodily differences which are currently treated as disabilities.

Notes

1. Further information on this legislation and on European disability law in general can be found in the volume edited by Muñoz Machado and de Lorenzo (1997).
2. Detailed discussion of the social and medical models can be found in Oliver, 1990, Pointon, 1997 and Johnstone, 1998.
3. These were obtained, via the Internet, from an information service provided by the ONCE (http://www.servimedia.es).

4. Maldonado, E. Una paralítica no tiene plaza univeritaria porque su minusvalía es sólo del 33 per cent. In *El Correo de Andalucía*, 1 April 1998.
5. A.E. El MEC estudiará un cambio en los criterios de admisión de los discapacitados en la Universidad. In *ABC*, 4 April 1998.
6. Programa informático para sordos. In *Gaceta de los Negocios*, 3 April 1998.
7. Fernández de Vega, E. El desarrollo sexual aumenta la integración de tetrapléjicos. In *Hoy*, 2 April 1998.
8. Entrevista con Javier Bardem. In *Afim*, February 1998, p. 32.

References

BELMONTE, J. 1979: *La Constitución. Texto y contexto*. Madrid: Editorial Prensa Española

CORKER, M. and FRENCH, S. (EDS) 1999: *Disability discourse*. Buckingham: Open University Press.

DAVIS, L. J. (ED.) 1997: *The disability studies reader*. London: Routledge.

JOHNSTONE, D. 1998: *An introduction to disability studies*. London: David Fulton Publishers.

INGSTAD, B. and REYNOLDS WHITE, S. 1995: *Disability and culture*. Berkeley, Calif.: University of California Press.

LEY DE INTEGRACIÓN SOCIAL DE LOS MINUSVÁLIDOS. BOE 103/1982, 11106–12.

MITCHELL, D. and SNYDER S. (EDS) 1997: *The body and physical difference: discourses of disability*. Michigan: University of Michegan Press.

MUÑOZ MACHADO, S. and DE LORENZO, R. (EDS) 1997: *European disability law*. Madrid: Escuela Libre Editorial.

OLIVER, M. 1990: *The politics of disablement*. London: Macmillan.

POINTON, A. (ED.) 1997: *Framed: interrogating disability in the media*. London: British Film Institute.

SHAKESPEARE, T. *et al.* (EDS) 1996: *The sexual politics of disability: untold desires*. London: Cassell.

THOMSON, R. G. 1997: *Extraordinary bodies: figuring physical disability in American culture and literature*. New York: Columbia University Press.

THOMSON, R. G. (ED.) 1996: *Freakery: cultural spectacles of the extraordinary body*. New York: New York University Press.

PART V

YOUTH AND POPULAR CULTURES

Introduction

The repressions, privations and denials imposed by a victorious Francoism on Spaniards after the Civil War became the perfect basis for Spain's largely uncritical assimilation of the new, mass consumerist culture when it finally arrived in the 1960s and 1970s. The new affluence, based on the notion of economic 'trickle down', was of course experienced highly differentially depending on class, regional location, gender, etc. and according to Spaniards' economic power to consume. While Francoist elites imported their American cars, urban working-class Spaniards had to put up with longer working hours, poor housing, poor sanitation and inferior education. Such conditions were hardly mitigated as yet by the meagre fruits of forced migration or the promise of a Seat 600 cc car. Though opportunities for greater material satisfaction grew significantly, this did not create the climate of political apathy the regime was anxious to foster. In fact, the reverse happened, with unmet rising consumer expectations combining with pressures for political freedoms and democratic change. All of this undermined the regime's quest for an 'end of history', post-conflict consumer society. Forms of mass culture did indeed establish themselves in Spain from the 1960s onwards (an expansion in ownership of cars, televisions, white goods, as well as publishing, protest song movements, etc.). This facilitated the rise of a new youth culture, which had an increasingly 'resistant', oppositional relationship to the regime, especially via student protest movements. And lacking appropriate outlets, such expressions of cultural dissent and unrest quickly became politicized.

Youth culture in Spain only really began to develop in the 1960s with economic development and the emergence of a gradually disaffected middle-class youth. But because of Francoism, Spain's experience of 'swinging' London and Woodstock would have to wait at least another decade. By the late 1970s, with Franco dead and all authoritarian taboos and prohibitions cast aside, starting in Madrid and spreading to other provincial capitals, young middle-class people (mostly students) began to spend their weekends drinking and chatting in bars and night clubs from dawn till dusk. This gave rise to a number of famous venues, with well-known clienteles, and conditions which saw modest instances of creative and artistic activity taking place (in writing, painting, posters, the plastic arts, as well as film). The increasingly fevered 'ambiente' of those years was well captured in Almodóvar's early full-length features. These were invariably garish, frenetic, frivolous, outrageous pieces, celebrations of bad taste and excess in all its forms. Such traits were also equated with the fun, frivolity and irresponsibilities seen as typical of Spain's 'take' on the postmodernist temperament.

Spain's post-Franco youth cultures thus arose out of the desublimations of the late 1970s, 'going mad' on what had been condemned and prohibited under Franco, fundamentally sex. And given Spain's relatively liberal attitudes to such indulgences, few people really cared or minded if kids were letting off steam. Unfortunately, such bohemian behaviour as well as official indifference and laxity, created the climate for the spread of other socially less acceptable indulgences, including the use of hard drugs and also the arrival of Aids. And yet, as some have argued over the last two decades, the alarming rise in the figures for the use of legal and illegal drugs, especially among the young, responds in some measure to Spain's rapid economic and social change and attempts by various groups of people to cope with the dizzying speed of such change.

If Francoism imposed a popular culture of escape and evasion, this has arguably been reinforced by one of excess and addiction. As some of the essays in this section show, Spaniards, like few other peoples, appear hopelessly addicted to football and to television; indeed the medium and the sport are virtually synonymous. As part of the entertainment and leisure industry, football in Spain is largely indistinguishable from other aspects of consumption activity, be it television serials and soaps or breakfast cereal and snacks promoted by major football stars, and advertised as wholesome, healthy family food. Indentification is the name of the game, as is the construction and reproduction of a sense of belonging through the purchase of club shirts, hats, bags, soap, toothpaste, and so on. By doing so, consumers of football seek to buy into that special, collective spirit of tribal loyalty, which both welds them together as fans but also (sometimes aggressively) differentiates them from rival tribes and teams. Moreover, the culture of contemporary Spanish football promotes deep attachments to place and locality, creating a nostalgia for 'imagined communities', when these have succumbed to economic imperatives and are long gone. This is especially so among the large Spanish clubs, where club loyalties and commitments to their fans are daily sacrificed on the altar of global media marketing pressures and the increasing commodification of the game. Such pressures and tensions are readily picked up and echoed in many of Spain's popular television serials and soaps, which seem dominated by story-lines involving generational conflicts and struggles between community and self-interested, individualist consumption. In short, whilst in the world of official Spanish politics, notions of community and collective resposibility appear increasingly marginalized given the current neo-liberal economic climate, paradoxically perhaps Spain's *telenovela* continues to provide spaces in which viewers can find a nostalgic outlet for other 'imagined communities'. Here, unlike the world of aggressive individualism and commodity fetishism, values of solidarity, respect, tolerance and community appear to survive and prosper.

|24|

The construction of youth in Spain in the 1980s and 1990s

MARK ALLINSON

Introduction

Youth culture in Spain in the 1980s and 1990s represents something of a paradox. It shares with many other youth cultures the characteristics of spontaneity, disrespect for authority, playfulness and erotic curiosity; and it also shares the social context of mass youth unemployment which conditions the predicament of youth across contemporary Europe. But Spanish youth culture is distinct in that its emergence from the heady excesses of a suddenly liberated post-Franco Spain deprives it of the social signification as deviance or resistance often associated with youth subcultures.[1] Thus, where other national youth subcultures, such as punk in the UK, are constructed as counter-hegemonic, Spanish youth culture has become 'the official image of Spain' (Graham and Labanyi, 1995, p. 312). In most societies, the construction of youth can be understood as a cyclical process where the adult population sees youth as a 'liminal phase' (Wulff, 1995, p. 1), and young people as incomplete adults, sometimes prone to unacceptable behaviour causing a wave of moral panic. The generational divide is then replicated when youth grows up. This cycle is interrupted in Spain, where the younger generation have not always been the radicals, and where the political and social context has created infra-generational divisions virtually corresponding to each decade from the 1940s to the 1990s. Despite the increasing disavowal of Franco's legacy by the young in Spain, the history of the dictatorship remains central to the formation of Spain's particular youth culture.

Pre-history

In the 1940s, youth in Spain was channelled into various falangist organizations, a strategy typical of Fascist control. By the post-autarky late

1950s, youth, and in particular the middle classes and students, were smuggling prohibited books into the country, and American culture was fashionable thanks to the pact with the USA. The 1960s were characterized by limited university protests, swiftly followed by the removal of radical professors like Enrique Tierno Galván (who would later become Madrid's most popular democratic mayor). But there was no 1968 in Spain, at least not until 1972 when student protest led to the closure of the University of Valladolid. After Franco's death in 1975, while the adult population cherished the new-found democracy, the youth of Spain preferred, unsurprisingly, to enjoy the social and personal freedoms of the new order. The late 1970s in Spain were characterised by apolitical hedonism, *pasotismo* (apathy) and an excess of 'sex, drugs and rock 'n' roll' among the youth population.[2] Nowhere is this generational divide better portrayed than in Pedro Almodóvar's first commercial feature film, *Pepi, Luci, Bom y otras chicas del montón* (*Pepi, Luci, Bom, and Other Girls on the Heap*, 1980), where the spectacle of democratic elections which gripped the adult community is parodied by the partying young in a drug and alcohol-enhanced competition, entitled 'erecciones generales' ('general erections'). The 1980s mark the beginning of Spain's full integration into European institutions and with it, the gradual alignment of Spanish youth culture and the 'youth problem' with the rest of Europe. The context of mass youth unemployment quickly dissipated the excitement of the early post-Franco years, and the hopes invested in the new Socialist government of 1982 was only partially vindicated by the following years of PSOE rule. The anxiousness, defensiveness and pragmatism of the individualist 1980s, tended to stabilize into widespread disaffection, sometimes delinquency or at the very least the cult of 'vivir al día' ('living for the day').

The evolution of a youth identity from the 1940s to the present has created a dangerous paradox for generational relations in today's Spain: an ideological consensus but no capacity to build a common future. Serrano and Velarde (1996, p. 23) describe this paradox: 'The only generation of parents since 1960 who have succeeded in making their children believe them, and accept the world of adults, have not been capable of offering them either a project or a place in that world.[3]

Unlike the familiar ideological generation divide, which tends to be deactivated as the young assume positions of responsibility, this situation (where generations agree but the young are deprived of their opportunity to inhabit the adult territory of responsibility) leads to frustrations which generate social problems. As Spain's youth population is, at 24.44 per cent of the total population, the highest, proportionately, in the EU, then the problems which affect the young are arguably the most serious facing the country. (Compare this to northern Europe where an ageing society and the demands this makes on the Welfare State constitutes a more serious problem.)

The 'youth problem'

Unemployment is at the root of almost all the problems affecting youth in Spain. The massive migration to the cities from the 1950s to the 1970s created the conditions for a consumption-led popular youth culture with a diet of music, television, sport and fashion, and for authentic youth subcultures. Urban life also allowed far greater access to education for the majority rather than for the privileged alone. The education of many young people up to university level created an expectation of similar access to appropriate employment which the 1980s and 1990s have spectacularly failed to deliver. This has forced many young people to live in the parental home much longer, extending the transition into adulthood, but also depriving many young people of the chance to live independent lives.[4] This problem is exacerbated by a disproportionate rise in housing costs in Spain over the last 10 years (Ross, 1997, p. 207). The housing problem has reached the point where the Comunidad de Madrid announced in September 1998 the building of 2400 subsidized flats with low rents for young people.

The response to the frustrations of the expectations of youth has been apathy and evasion. The vacuum created by the relative loss of a work ethic and associated respect for the educative value of the parental class has typically been filled by what Serrano and Velarde refer to as 'presentismo' ('living for the moment'), and 'endogamia' ('loyalty to peer groups') (1996, p. 24). Both these tendencies lead to increased consumption on the part of young people: the young are particularly susceptible to peer pressure 'to try new things'. These can take the form of fashion and music. But where they involve legal and illegal drugs further problems are created. Consumption of tobacco is falling in Spain, but none the less 50 per cent of 18–25-year-olds in Spain smoked according to a study in 1992.[5] And while Spain remains largely free from the binge drinking excesses of northern Europe, a 1993 survey showed that 50 per cent of 15–29-year-olds in Spain had consumed alcohol in the preceding week, and 28 per cent had either stopped drinking or had never tried. One significant feature is the widening gap between numbers who drink heavily and those who do not drink at all. The recent cult of the *litrona* (large plastic glasses of lager often consumed by the young on the streets) may well account for this increase in heavy drinking among a minority. The media response to increased alcohol consumption has been somewhat sensationalist, the slightest urban disturbance among the young being reported in detail. Among the headlines, however, is the fact, reported by the right-wing daily *ABC*, that drink-driving is the number one killer of 18–30-year-olds in Spain.[6]

A much greater problem is posed by drug-taking. Analysing the official figures, Hooper concludes that Spain's drug problem is significantly greater than that of the rest of the EU and comparable only to that of the USA (1995, p. 204). Spain has the highest rate of Aids of any European country, largely because of drug use, especially heroin (Truscott and García, 1998,

p. 266). One of the earliest measures of the PSOE government was to legal-
ize soft drugs for personal use in public and in private in 1982, and only in
1992 did the government prohibit public consumption. While for the governing class, drugs had been a sense-increasing experiment in the 1960s, for
the youth of the 1980s and 1990s, drugs were sense-numbing, a means of
opting out of the established community for an alternative (frequently
crime-ridden) marginal culture. But even for the many whose habits have
not led them to crime, drugs have represented the ultimate product, part of
a whole youth culture based on the consumption of nightlife, alcohol, music
and fashion.

1980s: music, politics and postmodernism

The proximity of youth culture to the market through consumption of popular music is not unique to Spain. And the appropriation of counter-
hegemonic subcultures by market forces is well argued by the likes of Dick
Hebdige (1979). What distinguishes the case of Spanish youth cultures/sub-
cultures from those of London's 'swinging sixties' or later punk, is the
extent to which large parts of society embraced this culture, including the
PSOE government. The phenomenon of the *movida madrileña* justifiably
dominates the (very limited) attention given to Spain's youth (sub-)culture
of the 1980s. The word '*movida*' originated from marginal Madrid drug
culture, which makes the establishment's espousal of the term all the more
astonishing. Paradoxically, the supportive political environment in which
the *movida* flourished may well have also been instrumental in its demise by
the mid-eighties, coupled with the more familiar commercial appropriation
of subcultures, and other local, national and international historical factors.

Madrid's *movida* was born out of the fortunate coincidence of internal
and external music and fashion styles. Emerging from the British trends of
punk and new wave as a response to the boredom of rock music, young
Spanish musicians and aspiring stars converged on Madrid and found
venues for their bands (however amateurish) and even record labels willing
to support them. The decade of the eighties was undoubtedly Spain's golden
age of pop music, firmly wedded to youth culture as indicated by the title of
Radio Futura's 1980 debut album, *Enamorado de la moda juvenil* (*In Love
with Youth Fashion*). The sudden explosion of both venues (El Pentagrama,
La Vía Láctea, El Escalón, El Sol, El Jardín, El marquee and Rock-Ola are
some of the most significant names) and new groups which included
Paraíso, Tos (later, Los Secretos), Nacha Pop, Mamá, Radio Futura, and
Alaska y Los Pegamoides, was matched by sponsoring record labels such as
Hispavox and Polydor, and friendly radio stations, especially Radio España
FM Onda 2. The excitement created by this new vigour in youthful, and
playfully transgressive popular music was self-perpetuating, and soon
attracted young groups from outside Madrid, including Loquillo, Rebeldes,

Siniestro Total and Derribos Arias. The seemingly limitless accessibility of this culture for anyone wishing to participate, create or perform became a magnet for those aspiring to produce things in other media. These included the designers Antonio Alvarado, Jesús del Pozo, Paco Casado, Francis Montesinos and Agata Ruiz de la Prada, the painters Ceesepe and las Costus, and the photographers García Alix, Miguel Trillo, Ouka Lele and Pablo Pérez Mínguez. The early films of Pedro Almodóvar are products of this artisan culture of production. (*Pepi, Luci, Bom y otras chicas del montón* was filmed over a year and a half with Almodóvar's friends acting without pay, and scraping together the money to buy further lengths of film.) But they are also a mirror of their times, portraying an era in which everyone had multiple creative projects, lots of free time, no responsibilities and few political convictions, as well as generous helpings of sex, alcohol and drugs.[7]

That the political establishment of 1980s Spain should lend its support to the frenzy which was *la movida* is perhaps not so surprising considering the previous years of social and political proscription. Indeed, given that there was no complete rupture with the Franco regime, but rather a transition in which many of the old political players remained, the permissive society allowing youth to run free represented something of a catharsis. For the PSOE, the emerging alternative youth culture was both popular internally and profitable for the selling of Spain's image abroad. Madrid's socialist mayor, Tierno Galván, who had been removed from his university post during the dictatorship, headed a City Council which organized rock concerts. At one such concert Tierno declared 'Todos al loro y el que no esté colocao que se coloque' ('Everyone on their toes and whoever isn't stoned yet better get stoned quick!'). A youth magazine from the suburb of Alcobendas with the name *Eyaculación precoz* (*Premature Ejaculation*) was financially supported by none other than Madrid's City Council. Tax-payers' money was also spent on subsidizing a San Isidro *fiesta* where the main act was a group called La Polla Record (Record Prick). (An equivalent in the UK would be the London Borough of Westminster subsidizing a Sex Pistols concert in Westminster Hall.) Madrid's beloved Mayor Tierno personally promoted the 1984 exhibition in the Centro Cultural de la Villa, entitled 'Madrid, Madrid, Madrid' and showcasing primarily the youth culture of the *movida*. But while politicians seemed limitlessly interested in youth culture, the youth of Spain were not similarly interested in politics. Few of the younger protagonists of this period had been active politically against the dictatorship in the way that many of their parents had been. Most were happy to let the older generation enjoy the excitement of political freedom while the young concentrated on the pursuits more natural to them. It is unlikely that the youth of older democracies would be labelled 'pasota' (apathetic) merely for not being interested in politics, but the adult population in Spain was apparently surprised at the apathy of the young. The lack of enthusiasm could be accounted for by the slow pace of change in the early days of democratic Spain. With the election of the PSOE government in

1982, expectations were raised among the young. But their espousal of largely free-market economics led Spain's youth into the same mass unemployment and associated problems which was affecting Europe as a whole. And on the only specific issue which has consistently mobilized young people, the definitive removal of Spain's hated military service for all young men, the Socialists were unable to deliver.

Apart from the gratuitous support of the political class, the *movida* found favour in its declared allegiance to postmodernism. The most emblematic magazine of the *movida* was *La luna de Madrid* which was founded in November 1983. The main feature of its very first edition was entitled 'Madrid 1984: ¿la posmodernidad?' and its contents were suitably eclectic and hybrid. There was the first instalment of the memoirs of pornography star Patty Diphusa (penned by Almodóvar), articles on punk, pop music, painting, photography, cinema (new and old), theatre, free radio, football, poetry, as well as a month-planner, an advert for Almodóvar's second film, *Laberinto de pasiones*, cardboard cut-outs of Madrid buildings and lyrics for songs like 'Sexo chungo' by playful punks Siniestro Total. Another feature compares Madrid with New York, commenting on the sheer quantity of cultural phenomena radiating from Madrid's youth culture. One month later, the second issue of *La Luna de Madrid* testifies to the transitory nature of the dizzying cultural wave that had hit the city, headlining the news that 'la posmodernidad ha muerto' ('postmodernity is dead'). As far as the *movida* is concerned, most interested parties signal its death between 1984 and 1985. In 1985, the city saw the closure of Rock-Ola, the most famous *movida* venue and a cultural crossroads for all kinds of products. The same year Spanish television decided to drop the most significant pop programme of the times, *La edad de oro* ('Golden Age'). But 1985 was also the year in which the 'happy consumption of drugs' (Memba, 1985, p. 639) began to turn into a serious problem of addiction, and the year in which Aids surfaced internationally. In any case, by this time, Spain was increasingly integrated into European and Western society and culture, the aspects of national culture most particular to Spain increasingly diluted by the internationalization of global consumer culture. Indeed, the late eighties and the decade of the nineties are marked by something of a deficit in national youth cultures at the expense of imported cultural products.

1990s: internationalization, pragmatism

Although the 1990s have seen something of a revival in the popularity of *cantautores* (singer-songwriters), among them Javier Alvarez, Pedro Guerra and Albert Plá, the music industry in Spain has come down from its 1980s cloud, with recession-hit record companies concentrating almost exclusively on the more profitable end of the pop spectrum. Only those capable of riding this commercial tide survived, and figures such as Alaska, Bonezzi, Miguel Bosé, Carlos Berlanga, Derribos Arias, Gabinete Caligari, Luz Casal, Mecano, Miguel Ríos, Nacha Pop, Radio Futura and Siniestro Total all had to make concessions to professional commercialism which they would not have considered during the heights of the DIY *movida*. While Spanish music has waned, international currents have become stronger than ever. The music of the nineties in Spain was *bakalao* (including house, techno, ambient, techno house – all imported styles). Nineties music festivals such as Espárrago Rock and Benicassim, have seen a representative mixture of international pop stars and Spanish artists, some of whom now call themselves 'indies' in the wake of the Britpop explosion. Unlike their *movida* predecessors, who imported the music of punk but not the English lyrics, these new indies (Australian Blonde is perhaps the most famous) sing in English, with their sights, doubtless, set on world markets.

Many of the artists of the generation of the *movida* are now consolidated mature professionals. Almodóvar's recent films are increasingly polished and their themes much less transgressive. Alaska is as famous as ever, but largely due to her many television appearances. But even the younger generation of creative talent in Spain appears much more mature and pragmatic than their equivalents 15–20 years ago. Young director Alejandro Amenábar whose 1995 film *Tesis* made him famous at only 26, speaks like a middle-aged film expert and knows who his market is and what they want.

The globalization of the media has also led to the diluting of Spanish youth culture. CD-ROMS, the Internet and satellite television offer a diet of international consumption in which the standard communicative mode for young people is the MTV style of spectacular, fast-moving, short-duration video clips. And the products promoted are also the same world-wide: a Doctor Marten fan in Spain, who is also into raves, piercing, fanzines, Beavis and Butthead and Tarantino, now has little to distinguish him (or her) from young people throughout the Western world. With notable exceptions such as the Barcelona-based *El Víbora*, even the popular Spanish form of the comic is now imported, largely from Japan.

By the mid-1990s, the lives of young people in Spain were in many respects indistinguishable from those of the young across the Western world. The 1980s had projected an image of frenzied creativity, irony, parody and postmodernism in the early films of Fernando Colomo (*¿Qué hace una chica como tú en un sitio como éste?*, *What's a girl like you doing in a place like this?*, 1978) and Almodóvar (*Pepi, Luci, Bom...*, 1980; *Laberinto de pasiones*, 1982). In the 1990s, the image of youth painted by José Angel Mañas in his 1994 novel, *Historias del Kronen*, (made into a successful film by Montxo Armendáriz) is much less entertaining, its culture hedonistic, escapist and lacking in creativity.[8] Mañas' protagonist Carlos refers to the eighties *movida* as 'la generación de los 80' (1994, p. 32), equating it firmly with the past. Nor is he interested in previous generations, rejecting, among other things, Buddhism because 'apesta a jipismo y a sesentayochismo' ('it stinks of hippies and 1968') (p. 35). Also 'out' are Antonio Machado's 'horribles poemas' (p. 42), old people, the Civil War and Europe. Carlos is a 21-year-old student from a prosperous family who lives in the comfortable Madrid suburb of la Moraleja. He lives for the night, especially for drugs, alcohol, dangerous driving and sex, all of which he shares with his friends and with various female casual sex partners. At home, he sleeps, eats, masturbates and takes money from his parents. He visits his sick grandfather, which only serves to convince him further that only the strong are worthy of respect. For Carlos, friendship is a sign of weakness. The spiral of drugs and alcohol-induced madness culminates in a party in which Carlos forces the diabetic host, Fierro, to drink whisky. Carlos reacts angrily when Fierro passes out. When they take him to hospital he dies. The scenario of Carlos' story is little different from Cohen's 1950s idea of juveniles as opposing sobriety and conformity with hedonism, defiance of authority and the quest for kicks.[9]

This rather desolate picture of youth is contrasted by certain more positive signs, such as the limited resurgence of Spanish grotesque humour among young creators, following the line that stretches from Quevedo, through Goya and Valle-Inclán to 1990s films such as *Justino, retrato de un asesino de la tercera edad (Justino, Pensioner Assassin*, 1994) by Cuadrilla, *Acción Mutante* (1992) and *El día de la bestia (The Day of the Beast*, 1995) by Alex de la Iglesia, and *Torrente, el brazo tonto de la ley (Torrente, the Stupid Arm of the Law*, 1997) by Santiago Segura. Though not a return to the excitement of the early *movida*, these films do reflect interesting currents in Spanish youth culture, and encouragingly, they have been helping to bring about renewed interest in home-produced cinema among the young.

It may well be too early to evaluate the 'youth product' of the 1990s in Spain. Youth-led phenomena like punk or the *movida* tend to be consolidated and theorized only after their demise. But at a time when the cultural boom of the 1980s in Spain is now almost venerated by critics and nostalgics, it remains difficult to foresee, 10 years from now, the same aura surrounding the youth culture of the 1990s.

Notes

1. See Helena Wulff's chapter, 'Introducing youth culture in its own right', in *Youth cultures. A cross-cultural perspective*, Amit-Talai, V. and Wulff, H. (eds), London: Routledge, 1995, p. 1.
2. There were politically active sections of the youth population of Spain, but these formed around issues (particularly the women's movement and peace protests) rather than institutionalized party-political activity.
3. Las únicas generaciones de padres desde 1960, que han conseguido que sus hijos y sus hijas les crean, y que acepten el mundo de los mayores, no han sido capaces de ofrecerles un proyecto ni un lugar en ese mundo.
4. According to Hooper, 1995, 70 per cent of Spanish 18–29 year-olds live in the parental home, p. 178.

5. Statistics are from an Instituto de la Juventud report, 'Youth and Drugs in the '90s', Madrid, January 1997, p. 8.
6. *ABC*, 21 February 1993, p.18.
7. There are clear parallels here between the *movida* and punk: the qualities of DIY and bricolage common to both periods, the links between music and fashion, the taboo contents of song lyrics, the debt both subcultures owe to the alternative press and fanzines, as well as the obvious aesthetic parallels. Many of these comparisons are made in *Sólo se vive una vez*, José Luis Gallero (ed.), Madrid 1991.
8. An alternative cinematic vision of Madrid's working-class suburban youth culture is represented by Fernando León de Aranoa's 1998 film *Barrio*. A very different picture, but of an equally relevant social phenomenon, the film depicts how boredom and petty crime lead to more serious crimes and eventually destruction.
9. Cohen's model is explained by Hebdige in *Subculture. The meaning of style*. London, 1979, p. 76.

References

GALLERO, J. L. (ED.) 1991: *Sólo se vive una vez*. Madrid: Ardora.

GRAHAM, H. and LABANYI, J. (EDS) 1995: *Spanish cultural studies. An introduction*. Oxford: Oxford University Press.

HEBDIGE, D. 1979: *Subculture. The meaning of style*. London: Routledge.

HOOPER, J. 1995: *The new Spaniards*. London: Penguin.

MAÑAS, J. A. 1994: *Historias del kronen*. Barcelona: Destino.

MEMBA, J. 1985: Bailando, me paso el día entero bailando ... ¿Qué fue aquello de la movida? *La Revista de El Mundo*, 634–48.

ROSS, C. J. 1997: *Contemporary Spain. A handbook*. London: Arnold.

SERRANO, M. M. and HERMIDA, O. V. 1996: *Informe. Juventud en España 96*. Madrid: Instituto de la Juventud.

TRUSCOTT, S. and GARCIA. M, 1998: *A dictionary of contemporary Spain*. London: Hodder and Stoughton.

WULF, H. 1995: Introducing youth culture in its own right. In Amit-Talai, V. and Wullf, H. (eds), *Youth cultures. A cross-cultural perspective*. London: Routledge, 1–18.

|25|

A *punk called Pedro*: la movida in the films of Pedro Almodóvar

NÚRIA TRIANA TORIBIO

In 1975, the *Sex Pistols* formed at Malcolm McLaren's shop in London and played their first gig in November. In Spain, that same month, Franco died. These seemingly unrelated circumstances, in fact, conspired to change Spanish popular culture beyond recognition. For most analysts, punk affected music most prominently, but it affected cinema in equal measure; indeed, it is almost impossible to explain the Almodóvar phenomenon without understanding the influence of punk. This essay will first contextualize briefly the phenomenon and then read Almodóvar as one of those urban youths absorbing punk as it came from the USA and Europe and supplementing it with autochthonous elements within that creative atmosphere.

Almodóvar was, in his origins, a punk film-maker who not only chronicled his times and collaborated with fellow scene members, but also adopted the representational strategies of the movement. Although the analysis here will concentrate on his early films *Pepi, Luci, Bom y otras chicas del montón* (1979–80) and *Laberinto de pasiones* (1982), even in his recent films we can see that he has not discarded these strategies entirely. How and why did Spanish youth come into contact with and adopt punk?

Franco's illness and other tell-tale signs of the weakening of the regime in the early 1970s (for example Carrero Blanco's assassination in 1973) inspired in Spain an atmosphere of preparation for a new, freer (and hopefully democratic) political future. The myths of the past were ripe for revision and even replacement. The already weakened barriers between Spanish and democratic European cultures were crumbling. This made the mid- and late 1970s a period in which news and cultural movements from outside could easily filter into Spain, while from the inside there was eagerness to adopt them. In the mid-1970s, punk was the subculture arising from youth cultures of the Anglo-Saxon world coming to terms with the conditions of late capitalism. This is the culture which, from the end of World War II, had set the trends that other youth cultures follow; and Spain's youth was no exception. There was a compelling reason for Spain's youngest generation, which had not been given access to institutional spaces, to adopt punk as a strategy to gain visibility; at that time, punk's strategies were being used effectively in order to attack other establishments, principally those of the UK and USA. As Borja Casani (García de León and Maldonado, 1989, p. 131), the editor of the cult avant-garde magazine of the time, *La Luna de Madrid* stated: 'La *movida* fue la aportación madrileña a la estética del punk' (the *movida* was Madrid's contribution to punk aesthetics).

Before we go any further in exploring the form that punk took in Spain, we must account for the *movida's* specificity, a specificity brought about by the mixture of an imported style with indigenous Spanish culture. At first sight, Spanish punk looks more inclusive of different epochs and styles and more celebratory than its counterparts in other European nations or in the USA. Spain had a lot of catching up to do, as far as adopting the trends and movements that had affected popular culture in the democratic nations after World War II. Perhaps for that reason, the sounds and clothing styles of American rock and roll of the 1950s and the sounds and fashions of 1960s pop were appropriated and mixed in with more 'orthodox' punk products and even autochthonous forms of popular culture.

Local socio-political circumstances shaped the movement in Spain differently. The expectant and less restrictive atmosphere inspired by the transition to democracy gave Spanish punk a less socially aggressive character than its counterparts in the UK and USA. (The increased availability of drugs, resulting from legislative changes affecting drugs, also had an impact on the character of the *movida*.) Socio-economic problems in Spain of the 1970s and early 1980s may have been different from those faced by American or British youth (unemployment for example), but the nihilism characteristic of punk, which mixed itself into the Spanish *desencanto* (apathy) was pervasive. Many young people did not expect democracy to effect any real change (Alas, 1989); after all, many of the democratic politicians were men of the regime's single political party, the *Movimiento*. Intriguingly, *Movida* and *Nueva Ola*, were the names given to Spanish punk; and *movida* is the one which has survived, perhaps because the name is a defiant, slangish pun on the Francoist *Movimiento*. The democratic times ahead would have a *movida* rather than a *Movimiento*.

Given that the punk explosion particularly targeted the music world, it will be illuminating here to survey briefly how the attack was mounted in the Spanish case. In the Spain of the 1970s, the hegemony of left-wing, oppositional political discourse made it the measure of everything else, effectively devaluing or excluding any cultural production that could not be integrated within it. The popular music scene of the opposition was dominated by the *rock con raíces* and singer-songwriters such as the members of the *Nova cançó*. These groups and soloists were advocating through their music social and political change. By virtue of their oppositional stance, they were under the scrutiny of censorship. Another important factor to take into account is the way Francoism had demonized all forms of rock music, mainly because rock was a form of expression of the urban working-class, as Jesús Ordovás (1989, p. 384) points out. Thus, rock was rarely seen live in concerts, infrequently shown on television, was marginalized by the radio stations and had no backing from record companies.

Once Franco died, *rock con raíces* and singer-songwriters became the popular-music establishment. However, a generation emerged into writing and listening to music in the mid-1970s who related to neither of the above. As Diego A. Manrique (1989, p. 478) put it: 'They were not marked indelibly by Francoism, they wanted an aesthetic break [with the past] and they wanted to enjoy immediately the political advantages of the new situation'.[1]

This meant that they chose not to address or listen to head-on political or social problems and they did not serve as mouthpieces for any of the emerging political associations. *Movida* members had been brought up listening to rock in English, or Spanish rock that revealed an Anglo-Saxon influence, and this was displayed in their compositions. There was a further distancing factor: class. Members of many of these *movida* groups were, in fact, sons and daughters of middle-class and upper-middle-class families (for example, Carlos G. Berlanga from *Kaka de Luxe* and *Alaska y los Pegamoides* – was the son of film-maker Luis G. Berlanga and had benefited from European travel; Santiago Auserón of *Radio Futura* was another, having studied in Paris and the USA).

The new musical establishment viewed this non-political attitude to music as an 'impostura' (not an acceptable attitude to take) (Manrique, 1989, p. 478) and did not encourage them. For this reason, *movida* musicians, at the dawn of democracy, did not benefit from the new resources that were being directed into popular music in general to correct the starvation of funds and venues effected by Francoism. In the face of indifference, the cultures of the new generation of young men and women went underground and unofficial: these Madrid *punks* found other vehicles of expression such as comics and music magazines (*Star, Disco-Expréss, Vibraciones*); fanzines and new music venues (bars and clubs such as *La Vía Láctea, Pentagrama* and *Rock-Ola*) sprang up, creating a 'scene' where fans and musicians, writers, film-makers and DJs could mix. Soon it was obvious to the media that there were many who identified with these attitudes, and from invisibility, the *movida* became the most popular movement of the late 1970s right up to the mid-1980s.

Enter Pedro Almodóvar

The punk ethos of the *movida* is crucial in accounting for Almodóvar the film-maker. The attitude to cultural representation within *movida* subculture affected much more than sounds and clothes styles. For example, punk encouraged anybody to try to cross the barrier between being a member of the public and a performer. Punk's philosophy, 'Anarchy is the key; do-it-yourself is the melody' and punk's minimalism (in other words, its denial that artistic competence, let alone excellence, was a prerequisite to access to the stage) meant that groups mushroomed in the early 1980s. Punk language often 'drew on discourses which not only had been previously absent from popular songs, but which had been excluded from the mainstream ... discourse of society as a whole: the area of "pornography" and "obscenity"', observed Laing (1985, p. 75). This strategy was adopted by Spanish punk too. Dick Hebdige's reading of punk (1979) points out another characteristic: old signifiers took on new meanings in the hands of punk, but, by the same token, not even those new meanings were 'permanently sacred'. Barriers between media were crossed, concerts became performance-art spectacles. This signified the beginning of a process that permanently undermined the validity of binary oppositions such as: artist/public, consumer/producer, present/past, authentic (from inside Spain or in Spanish)/non-authentic (from outside or not in Spanish) and political (lyrics that engage with the present situation) /non-political (escapist lyrics).

Almodóvar's involvement with this movement must be understood as more than a simple cinematic showcase for its groups and fashions. It is, in fact, an involvement which stems from a direct allegiance with it. He formed in 1983 *Almodóvar y McNamara*, a band whose performance strategies relied heavily on those of the 1960s New York Pop Style (of figures associated with Andy Warhol) and on those of the mid-1970s punk groups like the *New York Dolls*. As well as using this vehicle, Almodóvar also collaborated in publications which were vehicles of punk ideas such as the monthly music magazine *Vibraciones* and the Comics magazine *Star*. It is well known that, as Juan Arribas observes (1987), *Pepi, Luci, Bom ...* was first envisaged as a story about the punk scene in Madrid for *Star*.

Themes, genres and styles in Spanish cinema of the late 1970s, like those of music, were ripe for revision. Barry Jordan and Rikki Morgan-Tamosunas (1998) indicate that Spanish directors of the mid- to late 1970s, were obsessed predictably with film as political discourse. Those who, during Francoism, had been in the opposition (Saura, Bardem, Camus, Miró), with the coming of democracy, now formed part of the new establishment. They were the darlings of the film critics and the recipients of awards and grants, and they were expected to uncover and debunk the myths created by the Franco regime. Their favoured style, themes and genres became hegemonic. However, as in music, there were newcomers 'not marked indelibly by Francoism' who wanted cinema to make an aesthetic break with the past. They wanted to enjoy translating into images (and seeing) the new situation.

Almodóvar, the film-maker, started translating into a distinct film style a number of the punk strategies of the *movida*. First, this was done in order to access the public scene and, once that was achieved, in order to produce and promote the *movida's* new discourse with a new attitude to performance and representation, which became a challenge to the orthodox idea of artistic excellence. He also drew on the punk incorporation of themes previously absent from cinema. Finally in this essay, we will see how the 'absence of sacred signifiers' too became part of the Almodovarian discourse.

A new attitude to performance and representation

… every performance, however apocalyptic, offered palpable evidence that things could change, indeed were changing: that performance itself was a possibility no authentic punk should discount.

(Hebdige, 1979, p. 110)

As indicated above, *movida* members lacked institutional support. Their work was affected by lack of funds and venues and this generated frustration with the establishment. However, this frustration became productive and pushed them to adopt a 'do-it-yourself' attitude and a reliance on 'comrades in arms' rather than on the establishment. In Almodóvar's case this approach translated itself into using both an indirect route into and unorthodox methods of film-making.

Without time, money or places to learn and lacking the social capital that institutional training provides (Bourdieu, 1989, refers to social capital as those useful relations – social, political, cultural, etc. – built up by a person through family connections or career), Almodóvar started to use super-8 cameras and improvised screening spaces such as parties in university halls of residence and clubs (or at independent art houses like *Alphaville*) for his finished products. His early short films were first watched by a public that, normally, did not deem contemporary Spanish Cinema interesting, because of its political bias. Eventually, his films (and those of other experimental film-makers) gained some institutional space in the (few) showings of new talent at the *Filmoteca* (National Film Library/Archive). Nevertheless, Almodóvar became predominantly self-reliant and this would prove invaluable in order to survive in a culture too often dependent on government hand-outs. Ultimately, we could argue that the 'Do-it-yourself' discipline led to the creation of his production company (El Deseo S.A.) which has granted him unprecedented freedom and has served as an example to many younger directors.

Challenging the orthodoxy of artistic excellence

Punk musicians, designers, or film-makers have consistently acknowledged and flaunted their amateurism, their mercenary attitude to culture and their lack of virtuosity in order to demystify the process of representation. In the case of Almodóvar, as soon as his career started to attract critical attention, we learnt that he had a day job working for the Spanish Telephone Company (Telefónica). This job was as much flaunted by Almodóvar himself as a defiant banner as it was used against him by critics. For example, on the subject of breaking generic conventions, he declared: 'As I do not have any academic training these things are easier for me than for other directors'. ('Al no tener una formación académica este tipo de cosas me resultan más fáciles que a otros directores', Vidal, 1989, p. 183.) The specialized press in Spain decided to take issue with features which they viewed as detrimental to cinema as art and label Almodóvar's deliberate amateurism as incompetence. Almodóvar's alleged incompetence followed him until his international success in 1988 with *Mujeres al borde de un ataque de nervios*, after which the magazine *Fotogramas*, granted him the title of film director (Guarner, 1988, p. 10). In fact, this incompetence was, for the most part, cultivated. Although a certain degree of amateurism was imposed by the low-budget, self-financing, self-teaching conditions, this lack was instead capitalized on and turned into a style (trash aesthetics) which challenged hegemonic institutional cinema (Jordan and Morgan-Tamosunas, 1998, p. 82).

In the same way as censorship had concentrated the minds of oppositional directors and had given them a set of 'counter-guidelines', the high-production values characteristic of the new hegemonic style signalled for Almodóvar a way 'not to go'. Paul Julian Smith analyses the characteristics of this subsidized cinema and unravels the ideological intentions behind its aesthetics: 'The glossy production values ... are not thus merely the result of an individual director's artistic temperament; they also betray the ideological commitment of the Spanish government to the celebration of a certain cultural heritage' (Smith, 1996, p. 25).

While historical accounts or literary adaptations set in the past (Miró's *El crimen de Cuenca* and Camus' *Los santos inocentes* are two obvious examples) demanded naturalistic detail because 'they had to tell the truth', Almodóvar's themes and generic choices make other demands on the *mise-en-scène* and allow him the freedom to flaunt constructedness, playfulness, anachronistic collage techniques and melodramatic excess.

His *mise-en-scène* tends to portray urban exteriors, some of which were of particular significance for the *movida* subculture, but there is no attempt to empty this exterior of elements that are incongruous and anachronistic with the *movida* scenes that are staged in them. For example, *El Rastro*, the Sunday street market of Madrid, was an important showcase for all subcultures, but significantly for the *movida*, because of its unsanctioned and vaguely transgressive status. It was used as a meeting place and some stalls displayed their fanzines, records of emergent punk groups, etc. For this reason it is an apt setting for *Laberinto de pasiones* (1982), especially the opening scene where it becomes Sexilia's 'shopping area' for sex partners. However, the set is not emptied of observers, some of whom look directly into the camera and prevent the suspension of our disbelief.

Many of Almodóvar's urban interiors prominently feature public transport. In *Laberinto,* Sexilia takes a bus home after her first night with Riza, wearing her flamboyant cape and brightly-coloured plastic jewels. Whilst using public transport as a location was probably an economic necessity in these early films, it means, once more, that the director has little control over *mise-en-scène*, since the other passengers appear in the shot. However, these non-*movida* city people, dressed in drab colours and expressionless, provide a background against which Sexilia, in her colourful attire, is distanced from the Spain they conjure up.

We often see interiors and exteriors of clubs (*Rock-Ola*, especially in *Laberinto*) and bars. *Laberinto* includes an exuberant scene in *Bar La Bobia*, a hanging-out venue of the *movida*, in which Roxy (Fabio de Miguel) and a Punkette are drinking 'alcohol por un tubo' (a bucketful of alcohol) and sniffing 'an overdose' of nail varnish. Even shops are used as locations in imaginative and resourceful ways. A lamp shop in *Laberinto* provides the excessive background required for a photo-session. The group *Ellas* want 'to shine like jewels' on the cover of their record; the chandeliers on display provide the brilliance.

Also, while the commitment to verisimilitude, dictated by the political discourse of hegemonic, official cinema, demanded impeccable performances from its actors, Almodóvar used national punk-pop figures – Alaska (*Pepi* ...), Poch, Santiago Auserón, Fabio McNamara, etc. (*Laberinto* ...), McNamara (*What Have I Done to Deserve This?*) – who could not act. When professional actors were used, they were often cast against their usual types, in ground-breaking, imaginative ways, as in the case of Carmen Maura, as Pepi. Imanol Arias, Riza in *Laberinto,* was linked to the prestigious 'high art' theatre productions of Miguel Narros rather than to popular culture.

New strategies

Other strategies borrowed from punk found their way into Almodóvar's cinema: the incorporation of themes previously absent from popular cinematic representation and even excluded from mainstream media discourse effectively became a celebration of destabilization; for example the enjoyment by his characters of practices that clearly constitute antisocial behaviour. Punk was successful in making visible, for example, objects associated with pornography and sexual taboos (bondage trousers, chains, dog collars). In a similar manner, themes such as incest and scatology, hitherto largely absent from the mainstream Spanish cinema (although present in underground comics), were made visible by Almodóvar. In *Pepi, Luci, Bom* ... sado-masochistic practices form part of the film's narration and dialogue. Luci (Eva Siva) leaves her sadistic and fascist (*facha*) policeman husband to pursue an equally sadistic relationship with the lesbian punk singer Bom (Alaska). However, on discovering that there is more masochistic pleasure to be gained from her husband, Luci returns to him. Sado-masochism is made visible as a choice in sexuality. So is nymphomania in *Laberinto* ..., where incest is depicted as 'annoying' for the victim rather than 'disturbing'. Both problems are located in the plots simply for their own sake (and their shock potential). *Laberinto* ... also flaunts practices labelled as socially transgressive, especially in the scene where a photo-novel is being shot. A catalogue of deviant behaviour (including sexual masochism) is displayed with no function in the plot other than being a showcase for transgression.

The absence of sacred signifiers

The *movida* parodied its own components, and the texts it produced, as well as those of previous discourses. This self-appropriation or parody takes the form of an absence of 'permanently sacred signifiers'. As Hebdige observes, 'the forbidden is permitted, but by the same token, nothing, not even these forbidden signifiers (bondage, safety pins, chains, hair-dye, etc.) is sacred and fixed' (Hebdige, 1979, p. 115). The whole of Almodóvar's production illustrates this practice, but especially in his first two films. This is one of the reasons why sectors of the media and the academic establishment, with a more earnest attitude to cultural production, have consistently condemned Almodóvar. Paul Julian Smith (1994, p. 2) summarizes the attacks levelled:

> Thus Almodóvar is known as a 'woman's director' ... who has consistently placed woman centre frame in his cinema; yet he has been frequently accused of misogyny, of humiliating and fetishizing those same women. Secondly, he is often cited as the embodiment of post-Franco Spain, the representative of the new nation; yet his films studiously avoid debates such as those on regional independence ... . Finally he is known (outside Spain at least) as a gay-identified man, who appeals to queer-coded registers of kitsch or camp; yet, his filmic career can be read as a progressive disavowal of homosexuality, whether masculine or feminine.

This refusal to acknowledge 'sacred signifiers' or 'sacred values' connects with the *movida* intention not to address political or social political problems head-on, not to serve as a mouthpiece for any political discourse (and this includes gender politics, feminism, sexual politics, etc.). What was described as 'apoliticism' (wrongly as Smith explains, 1994, p. 2) is a distrust of right and left shared by most *movida* artists, which is induced by *desencanto* (apathy) and nihilism. It is significant that in *La flor de mi secreto* (1995) and *Carne trémula* (1997) Almodóvar has performed yet another 'defilement' of the expectations created by his earlier refusal to face politics. In the earlier film, a student demonstration against the Socialists is depicted.

However, characters deliver openly political lines at the end of the latter film. While many critics saw this concesion to political discourse as a new phase in Almodóvar, we should also think of the punk in him. Nothing, not even the expectations he has created in his public and the critics, is sacred or fixed.

Note

1. '[N]o estaban marcados decisivamente por el franquismo, asumían una ruptura estética y querían disfrutar inmediatamente de las ventajas políticas de la nueva situación.'

Filmography

ALMODÓVAR, P. 1979–80: *Pepi, Luci, Bom y otras chicas del montón.*
—— 1982: *Laberinto de Pasiones.*
—— 1983: *Entre tinieblas.*
—— 1984: *¿Qué he hecho yo para merecer esto?*
—— 1995: *La flor de mi secreto.*
—— 1997: *Carne trémula.*
CAMUS, M. 1984: *Los santos inocentes.*
MIRO, P. 1979: *El crimen de Cuenca.*

References

ALAS, L. 1989: ¿Quién engañó a Pedro Almodóvar? In Garcia de León, M. A. (ed.), *El cine de Pedro Almodóvar y su mundo.* Madrid: Universidad Complutense de Madrid, 63–75.
ARRIBAS, J. 1987: Por un cine nuevo: Pedro Almodóvar. *Reseña de literatura, arte y espectáculos* 175, 1–6.
BOURDIEU, P. 1989: *La noblesse d'état: grandes écoles et esprit de corps.* Paris: Minuit.
GARCIA DE LEON, M. A. and MALDONADO, T. 1989: *Pedro Almodóvar; La otra España cañí (sociología y crítica cinematográficas).* Ciudad Real: Biblioteca de Autores y Temas Manchegos.
GUARNER, J. L. 1988: Mujeres al borde de un ataque de nervios. *Fotogramas* 1748, 10.
HEBDIGE, D. 1979: *Subculture: the meaning of style.* London: Routledge.
JORDAN, B. and MORGAN-TAMOSUNAS, R. 1998: *Contemporary Spanish cinema.* Manchester: Manchester University Press.
LAING, D. 1985: *One chord wonders: power and meaning in Punk Rock.* Milton Keynes: Open University Press.
MANRIQUE, D. A. 1989: La trama de la conjura. In *Historia del Rock.* Madrid: Promotora de Informaciones, 477–8.
ORDOVAS, J. 1989: Hijos del Agobio. In *Historia del Rock.* Madrid: Promotora de Informaciones, 384–7.
SMITH, P. J. 1994: *Desire unlimited: the cinema of Pedro Almodóvar.* London: Verso.
SMITH, P. J. 1996: *Vision machines: cinema, literature and sexuality in Spain and Cuba, 1983–1993.* London: Verso.
VIDAL, N. 1989: *El cine de Pedro Almodóvar.* Madrid: Instituto de la Cinematografía y las Artes Visuales.

|26|

Femme foetal: the triple terror of the young Basque woman in Pasajes

RYAN PROUT

What it's about for these women is refusing to have a sense of humour and refusing to adapt to life as they find it. Simply put, they don't understand why the fuck their lives aren't better than they are.

(Daniel Calparsoro, in Heredero, 1998, p. 158)[1]

Made in 1996, *Pasajes* is the second in a trio of films set in the post-industrial landscape of the Basque Country. Together with Daniel Calparsoro's debut feature, *Salto al vacío* (1995) and his later film, *A Ciegas* (1997), *Pasajes* forms a triptych distinguished by an aesthetic of geographical disorientation, moral emptiness, and urban existentialism. *Pasajes* takes viewers into materially marginal spaces – corridors, lifts, subways, pedestrian walkways and the perimeters of depressed housing developments – which are populated by a makeshift family of young marginal characters who eke out an existence at the outer limits of capitalism's purview. Technically unemployed, they are far from idle. Rag-pickers adapted to a virtual environment, they are 'Millennial rogues who are forced to live by their wits in the face of an environment of economic collapse and material want' (El Deseo, 1996, p. 6).[2]

Manu and Butano, an aspiring impresario and boxer, live with Gabi and Gema, lesbian lovers and burglars, in the unintentionally minimalist accommodations of what seems to be an abandoned warehouse. Having received a tip-off from a colleague, Gabi and Gema raid the apartment of a Japanese architect. Gabi leaves behind her signature weapon – the fire extinguisher with which she stuns her victims. The obsessive police officer whose sole object in life is to apprehend Gabi says simply 'It's *her*' ('Es ella') when the extinguisher is discovered at the scene of the crime. In a quip attributed to

Jean Luc Goddard, it is said that 'All you need to make a film is a gun and a cigar'. If Gabi's penchant for fire extinguishers suggests a female reassertion of the phallic weapon so indispensable to movie-making, the substitution also shows a willingness on the part of the director to treat ironically the conventions and clichés of the thriller, and, in the process, to create a female persona who challenges gender stereotypes. This essay sets out to understand where Calparsoro's particular view of his millennial rogues comes from, and to situate this vision in a socio-political context informed by a cultural studies perspective. At the same time, by contrasting Gabi, Calparsoro's heroine, with her French counterpart, Luc Besson's Nikita, the essay sets out to examine how national and regional concerns make themselves felt in a contemporary Spanish film, one apparently focused on youth issues alone.

As the lesbian partners in crime try to make their getaway from the apartment building, the police are able to annihilate Gema with their guns. Gabi, the femme fatale, survives the attack. Just before Gema is killed, Gabi tells her that she is leaving her for another woman, one who wears marbled green shoes. She has not yet met this woman but says that she has thought of little else for several months: 'She's been trying to seduce me, but I'm not letting her' ('Quiere seducirme, pero no le dejo'). Not coincidentally, perhaps, it is just at the moment when Gabi articulates an amorphous protean sexual desire (something which is arguably more commonly perceived to be the preserve of men) that the forces of authority, in the shape of all-male paratrooper police squads, pursue her with every weapon at their disposal. Just before the shoot-out with the police, Gabi, already a thief, has stolen from the film's male protagonists what Laura Mulvey describes as cinema's controlling male gaze (1992, pp. 750–6). Her obsession with marbled green shoes makes her fetish for such items plain. Coupled with cross-cutting which attributes objects to Gabi's point of view, we know that it is her vision which searches out Gema's grungy sneakers, then a pair of hospital slippers, and later on, the high-heeled green shoes of alcoholic cleaning lady Carmina. The particular focus of Gabi's gaze is significant because, as Enzo Biffi Gentili (1994, pp. 25, 27–8) observes:

> In the charts of correspondences and analogies that have accumulated in the philosophy of magic over the centuries, the feet, one of the more shameful parts of the body, are linked to libido and rutting. The shoe is, therefore, both a shield against lust and a form of celebration of the wilder impulses. ... In the iconography of the virgin, Mary is shown crushing the proud head of the serpent with her heel, thus laying low the indecent seducer, the primordial temptation of the subconscious. And the wearing of snakeskin and crocodile-skin shoes by wealthy women refers back ... to that symbol of dominance over the lower and shadowy psyche.

From Buñuel's *Le Journal d'une femme de chambre*, where a lusty aristocrat drools over Jeanne Moreau's ankles, to Powell and Pressburger's *The Red Shoes*, where Anton Walbrook seeks to possess the mind and body of Moira Shearer through the control of her feet, the foot fetish has been coded in cinema as the preserve of the male gaze.[3] Gabi is an outlaw in every possible sense, then. Not only does she steal material property, but, through her gaze, she also reappropriates narrative and visual conventions for a central point of view to be read as female and lesbian. She likes women. She likes their shoes. She likes to look at their shoes. She wants to seduce a woman for the sheer heck of it. She is a tease. She is bad. She is the ultimate *femme fatale*, driving her male flat share to exasperation when she boasts 'I'm a liar: I like telling lies, tricking people, and being the leader of the pack. I'm a praying mantis. That's what our Gema said' ('Soy una mentirosa: me gusta mentir, engañar, y controlar a la basca. Soy una mantis. Eso decía la Gema').

Having seduced alcoholic cleaning lady Carmina, Gabi dumps her. Just for the sake of it, she seduces Manu too. He is left bleeding to death in another shoot-out with the police while Butano, already distraught over the death of his sister Gema, goes to pieces. Gabi, femme fatale to the last, walks out of the picture without a scratch.

Whilst *Salto al vacío* met with enthusiastic acclaim, the critical response to *Pasajes* was more muted and suggested a tendency to focus on the necessarily Spartan narrative at the expense of the more layered context. For example, E. Rodríguez Marchante (1996) complains that the film is marred by

> Too much fiction, too much story line, too much poetic ambition and too much of a desire to dress up the film in some kind of make-believe underworld. No doubt such a place exists somewhere, at least for Calparsoro, but it's not at all clear where this subculture is actually supposed to be located.[4]

To describe *Pasajes* as being set, at worst in a void, and at best in the personal imaginary of the director is bizarre since, as well as being a reference to the underworld of alley-ways and service ducts populated by thieves, the title also recalls the Spanish name for the Basque port town of Pasai Donibane and the surrounding district of Pasaia. Calparsoro makes it perfectly clear from a number of concise establishment shots that the action of his film unfolds in Pasajes the town as well as *pasajes* (passages), the margins. The film feeds into the town's history, from its rapid evolution as a hub of the Spanish fishing industry, to its post-industrial decay. An early edition of the Espasa-Calpe encyclopaedia could describe Pasajes simply as a 'Busy, picturesque, summer resort town' ('Punto de veraneo muy pintoresco y concurrido') (Anon., 1920, p. 456).

Subsequently, this summer resort town underwent rapid change. From 1926 until the 1960s, Pasajes was the base for PYSBE, the Pesquerías y Secadores de Bacalao de España (Salt Cod Fishermen and Driers of Spain).

Fishing and related industries became vital to the town, as Mark Kurlansky (1998, p. 212) notes in his history of cod fishing:

> In addition to fishermen and dockworkers, PYSBE had employed 500 workers in cleaning and drying alone. ... These workers were almost all women, earning very low wages and no benefits, spending their days simply removing the dark grey membrane that had been the organ cavity lining. It was thought to be unattractive and these workers cost the companies very little. ... With modern salaries and benefits, companies could not afford such huge payrolls. ... By 1990, only a very few old trawlers were rigged for cod fishing from Basque ports.

As a cultural studies perspective can show, then, as well as challenging presumptions and conventions about gender roles, Calparsoro's film also includes reference to the social history of the town where he has chosen to set the story about his post-industrial female rogue (*pícara*). Whilst Gabi may inhabit a void, that same void is not devoid of context. The emptiness of her surroundings is not simply the result of an aesthetic mannerism on the director's part but responds to the socio-cultural background of a real time and place. Once we know a little more about the history of Pasajes, we can see, for example, that it is no coincidence that Calparsoro chooses a fishery as the site/sight where Gabi initiates Carmina in the ways of theft. For a moment, the camera lingers on the skull of a dead fish as the film's narrative takes stock of its own context. In previous days, perhaps, a woman in Carmina's position could have found employment in Pasajes's thriving fishing industry. Fired from her cleaning job, now she has nothing to do. But under Gabi's tutelage, she steals back something from the past when the two of them make off with several crates of fish stolen from a processing plant (which would more than likely be one of those which nowadays treats salt cod imported to Spain from Iceland). When Gabi tips salt from the stolen fish over her shoulder, it is not merely a superstitious gesture, then, but a throw-back to the Basques' pioneering role in the development of food storage technology (Kurlansky, 1998, pp. 21–2). There is further irony in the fact that Gabi, described by the director as 'A capitalist of human relations' (quoted by Holland, 1996) should steal from a fishery, an enterprise extolled by Adam Smith in *The Wealth of Nations* as the ideal model of capitalistic endeavour (Kurlansky, 1998, p. 75). With cod along the Atlantic coast exploited close to extinction, what else is there to traffic in Pasajes, besides sentiment?

Another reason for the critical oversight of the film's clear social and geographical context may be that where films about the Basque Country are concerned, critics expect to find not Pasajes but *paisajes* (landscapes). Calparsoro has stressed his impatience with cinema's obsessive portrayal of the minor lifestyle problems of the middle classes and it may not be unreasonable to suppose that his decision to set a film in the marginal and run-down port town of Pasajes was also a response to the tendency within Spanish cinema to equate Basque identity with a bucolic landscape rather than with the problems posed by the post-industrial wasteland (Heredero, 1998, p. 157). As María Pilar Rodríguez argues, there is a current in Basque film-making (exemplified by Julio Medem's *Vacas* and *Tierra*) which tends to identify the Basques exclusively with an 'ancestral landscape of millenary trees and virginal beauty' (1997, p. 134). Arguably, the potential in this atavistic interest rooted in landscape for an historical enquiry is diminished by a collective amnesia, played out, for example, in Medem's *La ardilla roja* whose pretext is the loss of memory. By contrast, Calparsoro litters *Pasajes* with signs resonant of a recent past and invites viewers to recognize that his characters inhabit a real history as well as a mythological one. As Rodríguez goes on to argue, Calparsoro's cinema eschews the picture-postcard world of the typically remote Basque farmhouse (*caserío*) in favour of films 'about void, about sites of deprivation, about not having money, not having resources, not having love, not having sex, not having hopes for the future, not even having a life' (1997, p. 137). In place of the nationalized *locus amoenus*, Rodríguez suggests, Calparsoro substitutes 'A post-modern post-industrial vision of the nation at its limit [and] subverts the image of the Basque land as a magical, mystical, and mythological landscape by turning it into literal shit' (1997, p. 137–9).

In one of the film's most visually striking scenes we see Gabi from an underwater perspective as she douses herself in a sink brimming over with water (*see* Figure 26.1). It is a rare segment of beauty and colour stolen from

Figure 26.1 The lull after the storm: Gabi (Najwa Nimri) undergoes a baptism of fire
Used by permission of El Deseo S.A.

the drab grey milieu. Perhaps this scene is also a concession to the mythologized Basque identity described by Julio Caro Baroja where Basque fishermen were able to converse with mermaids and sirens. Momentarily Gabi becomes identified with an archetypal character in the mythologized national history. Once withdrawn from this aqueous womb of the past, however, Gabi quickly comes back to the reality of a dead girlfriend killed by a monomaniac police force more concerned with petty thieves than with drug dealers.

Although *Pasajes* carries the signature of the El Deseo production company, as the previous commentary illustrates, nothing could be further removed from the glamorous world of Pedro Almodóvar's cinema than the twentieth-century underworld (*hampa*) filmed by Calparsoro. Set in a town close to the border with France, stylistically *Pasajes* seems to owe more to the cinema of a director like Luc Besson than to Calparsoro's Spanish contemporaries. Despite Gabi's interest in high-heeled footwear, *Pasajes* has more in common with Besson's *Nikita* than it does with Almodóvar's *Tacones lejanos*. Like Besson, Calparsoro uses comic book characters – the obsessive policeman and the frustrated boxer – and occasionally seems to view the world from an underwater perspective, as when Gabi's face is shot from the point of view of a plughole (a scene which also echoes images from Hitchcock's *Psycho* and *Vertigo*). A further similarity in the work of the two directors is an interest in updating the femme fatale to an androgynous gamin assassin. Like Nikita, Gabi accentuates her femininity through concealment, hiding her eyes behind thick layers of mascara and her flaxen hair inside a hooded jacket. As Susan Hayward observes of Besson's films (1998, p. 127), they are marked by 'the regressive nature ... of all of his central protagonists. Characters retreat into a childlikeness and from there often encounter death'. Hayward also points to the structuring absence of the family in Besson's cinema. Similarly, both the regression of characters to a childlikeness and the structuring absence of the family are also important features of *Pasajes*. For instance, after Gema's murder, Gabi tells Manu:

> I'm gonna stay here and keep my head down for a while, okay? You know, just until I find someone to hang out with. I've been like the rolling stone that gathers no moss since I was twelve, but now I've had enough. I don't know how to read or write. But I'm no trouble. It just takes drawings, pictures, videos, anything that's colourful and pretty, to make me happy, you know, stuff like that. And I've no family, no ties. When I want something, I grab it and when I get bored with it, I chuck it.
>
> (Calparsoro, *Pasajes*, 1996)[5]

She talks about herself as if she were a pet putting herself up for adoption by a good home. Her constant companion is a pyjama-case teddy bear and when Carmina asks her how old she is, she seems not to know the answer or even to care about her age. She expresses herself in doodles, just like a toddler, and decorates the walls of Carmina's flat with vague scribbles.

Gabi's relationship with Charo López (the actress who plays the older woman, Carmina) is somewhat like Nikita's with Jeanne Moreau in Besson's film. In both cases, the director has made use of a glamorous middle-aged actress's curriculum vitae to establish the gulf between past and present models of femininity. However, whereas in *Nikita* it is Jeanne Moreau's task to tutor Nikita in the ways of a certain stylized femininity, in *Pasajes*, as so often in contemporary Spanish cinema, the roles are reversed and it seems to be the younger generation which has the task of making over iconic figures from the past. Thus, in *Pasajes*, it is Gabi who tells Carmina (and Charo López) how she should dress and behave if she is to achieve a desirable model of femininity. Gabi is detached from previous Spanish prescriptions of what it means to be a desirable woman as she is also from the norms supposed by an adherence to a conventional heterosexual routine. While the relationship between the older and younger woman in *Nikita* ultimately articulates a continuity between generations expressed through adherence to norms of gendered behaviour, in *Pasajes* this same relationship demonstrates the breakdown between generations divided by formative experiences gained during and after the regime. Gabi's desire to teach an older woman how to be a woman, rather than to become herself a student of a model derived from Francoist femininity, plays out the way in which resistance to gendered norms functions also as a slap in the face for the past.

Figure 26.2   Divided by a common gender: Gabi and Carmina break apart
Used by permission of El Deseo S.A.

Gabi and Carmina have their definitive falling out halfway across a bridge (*see* Figure 26.2). There seems to be no way in which the divide between their expectations can be sutured.

There are other important differences between *Nikita* and *Pasajes* which demonstrate the different formulations of the state in French and Spanish cinema. Arguably, in a state such as France, which is largely content with centralization, governmental machinery will be portrayed more benignly than in cultural productions from a nation like Spain, where the unitary national identity is contested from every direction. Correspondingly, although Besson portrays Nikita as a figure who must eventually erase herself from French visibility, he also repeats the concept of the state as a totalizing welfare device which can rehabilitate even the most wild of drug-addicted gun-toting women. Everywhere she goes, in the form of state surveillance, the male gaze follows Nikita to ensure her well-being, albeit if only to see to it that she survives long enough to perform further patriotic assassinations. When she wakes up from her persecution by the police, Nikita confuses the secret services' rehabilitation centre with paradise. Calparsoro's gamin assassin, on the other hand, is completely neglected by the Spanish state. Like Nikita, she is persecuted by the police but they have no redeeming function in mind for Gabi. Her vicious ways cannot be co-opted and put to good use by the machinery of state. Gabi's problem as a femme fatale is that she just keeps on surviving, only to find herself repeatedly abandoned. Authority in *Pasajes* exists only in the shape of the police and their homophobic, misogynist, death wish. In Calparsoro's vision, Spain is indifferent to Gabi's plight as an illiterate orphan. Equally useless to her is the brand of Basque nationalism anchored in the past. When she walks out of the frame at the end of the film, we know that there is no avuncular figure like Uncle Bob (Nikita's government benefactor) waiting to rescue Gabi from her disoriented life. Whereas in Besson's film the structuring absence is provided by a missing family, in *Pasajes* the structuring absence is provided by the double omission of both the family *and* the state.

Whilst a single film's portrayal of issues relating to the experience of a marginalized sector of Spain's young population can scarcely serve to provide general conclusions about the cinematic representation of youth, *Pasajes* (and the two other films on which Daniel Calparsoro and Najwa Nimri have collaborated) have been singled out by critics like Jesús Palacios as worthy of special attention. Palacios argues (1998, p. 127) that Spanish cinema featuring young people, and/or made by them, tends to regard youth as a malady which must be overcome by age, just as wealth is portrayed by cult directors like Alejandro Amenábar (in *Tesis*, for example) as a fault which rich kids pay for by becoming psychopaths: 'It's as if punishment and perversity were mandatory pay-back for physical beauty and wealth' (Palacios, 1998, p. 9).[6]

Palacios is equally disappointed by the apparent willingness of young directors to apologize for their youth by filming stories about older people.

He is unimpressed by the recently released *Barrio* and its depiction of three boys who are already world-weary by their teens. Roberto Cueto traces the reluctance to depict young people as transgressive agents of social change back to the regime. Franco's apologists, says Cueto (1998, p. 9), took pride in the absence within Spanish cinema of the young '"good-for-nothings and hooligans" ['indeseables y gamberros'] whose presence plagued the national cinemas of neighbouring states'. Both Cueto and Palacios (1998, pp. 129–30) suggest that a reticence in Spanish cinema to portray young people as rebels who revel in the polymorphous nature of their antagonism towards society is a feature that has been transferred into transitional and post-transitional cinema. Both writers point to Calparsoro's films as an exception to this tendency:

> Daniel Calparsoro is perhaps the only director who has been able to create a portrait, both coherent and fascinating, of rebellious and desperate, or just plain desperate, young people. Unlike his peers in Spain ... he has focused on Basque youths in all three of his feature length films. Recently returned from the United States and still brimming over with the positive effects of contact with New York's independent cinema, Calparsoro's first film takes us into a nightmarish world. His cinema affords us a dark fantasy about a group of young criminals who have a miserable lot in life and are submerged in a world of violence, shadows, and death.
>
> (Palacios, 1998, pp. 129–30)[7]

Where Palacios singles out Calparsoro for revelling in the belated misadventures of the rebels without a cause whose anger was suppressed during and after the regime, Cueto underlines the singularity which Calparsoro's depiction of marginalized young women lends his films:

> Even nowadays, when there's a whole wave of films being made by women, stories about women's marginalisation are thin on the ground. With the exception of the powerful and rounded female characters created by Daniel Calparsoro and Najwa Nimri, portrayals of women's specific alienation within the wider condition of alienation are scarce.
>
> (Cueto, 1998, p. 15)[8]

Thus, although Calparsoro's films may not be the last word on the depiction of youth in Spanish cinema, their unusual qualities, as singled out by Palacios and Cueto, serve to highlight the more common trends in the bulk of recent Spanish films which broach the subject of youth culture and marginalization. But whilst Calparsoro's portrayal of young women like Gabi in *Pasajes* may be progressive, it nevertheless presents problems when approached from the viewpoint of a feminist critique of the reappropriated female gaze in cinema, such as that expressed by Naomi Scheman. A tell-tale feature 'of the distinctively female, though only stuntedly feminist, gaze', Scheman argues, is 'the absence of mothers and maternity' (1995, p. 91). The validity of this argument is exemplified by the depiction in *Pasajes* of Calparsoro's two female protagonists: the one is a strong young female character who is at the same time an orphan and the other is an older woman who sets alarm bells ringing in a hospital's intensive care unit when she tries to comfort a baby in an incubator. The narrative does not allow these two women, Gabi and Carmina, to reconcile their desire for one another with Carmina's desire to have children. Gabi's anarchic attitude to life is punctured by the derision she heaps upon Carmina for the older woman's desire to be a mother. She is not a perfect anti-heroine, then. When she closes her heavily made-up eyes, they seem to be vacant sockets, the price she pays for stealing the male gaze. Even her gait is read as a masculine 'Max Wall walk' (Holland) and her inarticulate self-expression is characterized as the mantra of a witch: 'She is constantly muttering things to herself... like some kind of magic spells' ('murmurando constantemente... como si de fórmulas mágicas se tratese') (Palacios, 1998, p. 134). In spite of these provisos, however, it seems fair to say that Calparsoro breaks new ground in *Pasajes* in depicting an angry young woman whose antagonism, toward everything and nothing in particular, implicates the society and national identities of both Spain and Euskadi in a sweeping critique. Understood in its cultural context, Calparsoro's anthem for doomed youth is also, albeit perversely, a hymn to the formlessness of absolute freedom.

Acknowledgements

I am grateful to the Press Officers of the London Lesbian and Gay Film Festival for giving me the opportunity to see *Pasajes* before its general release on video and to Paz Sufrategui of El Deseo, S.A. for the generous provision of materials relating to the film's production, and to Peter Allmond of the Bodleian Library for tracking down other material unavailable in the UK. I also offer my thanks to Alberto Mira and María Donapetry for bibliographical references and for sharing with me their insights on *Pasajes*.

Notes

1. 'Lo que les ocurre a esas mujeres es que se niegan a tener sentido del humor y se niegan a conformarse con la vida que llevan: sencillamente, no entienden por qué coño no viven mejor.'
2. 'Pícaros milenarios que, en condiciones de ruina económica y de necesidad, se ven obligados a poner en práctica su ingenio para salir adelante.'
3. Of the relationship between shoes and desire in the cinema, Natalia Aspesi observes that 'Shoes made a stealthy entrance into the world of cinema as a minor

element, but they soon demonstrated that they were able to characterize not only an epoch but a personality, to build a star and create in the audience the desire to imitate, the desire to make themselves more important by wearing the same shoes as their screen idols' (1994, pp. 11–13). For a discussion of foot fetishism and shoes see O'Keefe (1996, 401–25) and Warhol (1997).
4. 'Demasiada ficción, demasiado cuento, demasiado afán poético y demasiada pretensión por rodearlo todo de 'mundo', o sea, el de Calparsoro, que sin duda existe aunque aún no esté del todo localizado.'
5. 'Me quedo aquí, quieta. Hasta encontrar alguien que me siga, ¿sabes? Llevo toda la vida a mi bola, rolando desde los doce años y ya, paso. No sé leer, ni escribir, no doy problemas. Me gustan los dibujos, las imágenes, los colores, los videos, ¿sabes?, lo bonito. Además, no tengo familia. No tengo cuelgas. Cuando quiero algo, lo cojo, y cuando me aburro, lo tiro.'
6. 'Parece como si la belleza física y el dinero llevaran implícitos por necesidad el castigo y la perversidad.'
7. 'Quizá el único director ... que ha sido capaz de trazar una poética coherente y hasta fascinante de la juventud desesperada y rebelde o, mejor dicho, desesperada a secas, sea Daniel Calparsoro. A diferencia de sus compatriotas ... ha dedicado sus tres largometrajes a la juventud vasca. Recién llegado de Estados Unidos, impregnado todavía de los efluvios benéficos del cine independiente neoyorquino, Calparsoro se estrena en ... una pesadilla, una fantasía oscura sobre un grupo de jóvenes criminales desgraciados, sumergidos en un mundo de violencia, tinieblas y muerte.'
8. 'Incluso hoy día, con toda una corriente de cine hecho por mujeres ... escasean las crónicas de la marginación femenina, de ese desarraigo dentro del propio desarraigo: con la excepción de los poderosos y rotundos personajes femeninos diseñados por el tándem Daniel Calparsoro/Najwa Nimri.'

References

ALMODÓVAR, P. 1991 (film): *Tacones lejanos.*
AMENABAR, A. 1996 (film): *Tesis.*
ANON. 1920: Article on town and district of Pasajes. In *Espasa-Calpe Enciclopedia Universal Ilustrada Europeo–Americana*, 43. Barcelona: Hijos de J. Espasa, 456–8.
ASPESI, N. 1994: Wandering between the stars. In Mazza, S. (foreword), *Cinderella's revenge*. San Francisco: Chronicle Books, 9–15.
BESSON, L. 1990 (film): *Nikita.*
BIFFI GENTILI, E. 1994: Shoe/obscure. In Mazza, S. (foreword), *Cinderella's revenge*. San Francisco: Chronicle Books, 25–31.
BUÑUEL, L. 1964 (film): *Le Journal d'une femme de chambre.*
CALPARSORO, D. 1995 (film): *Salto al vacío.*
—— 1996 (film): *Pasajes.*
—— 1997 (film): *A ciegas.*
CARO BAROJA, J. 1973: *Los vascos*. Madrid: Ediciones Istmo.
CUETO, R. 1998: Introducción: De los toros a la coca. In Cueto, R. (ed.), *Los desarraigados en el cine español*. Gijón: Festival Internacional de Cine de Gijón, 7–16.
EL DESEO, S. A. 1996: *Pasajes* press kit.
HAYWARD, S. 1998: *Luc Besson*. Manchester: Manchester University Press.
HEREDERO, C. F. 1998: Extracts from an interview with Daniel Calparsoro. In Cueto, R. (ed.), *Los desarraigados en el cine español*. Gijón: Festival Internacional de Cine de Gijón, 157–8.

HOLLAND, J. 1996: Review of *Pasajes* extracted for programme notes. 1998 London Lesbian and Gay Film Festival.

KURLANSKY, M. 1998: *Cod : A biography of the fish that changed the world.* London: Jonathan Cape.

LEON DE ARANAO, F. 1998 (film): *Barrio.*

MEDEM, J. 1991 (film): *Vacas.*
    1993 (film): *La ardilla roja.*
    1996 (film): *Tierra.*

MULVEY, L. 1992 [reprint of article published in *Screen* 16, 1975]: Visual Pleasure and Narrative Cinema. In Mast, G., Cohen, M. and Braudy, L. (eds), *Film theory and criticism.* Oxford: Oxford University Press, 746–57.

O'KEEFE, L. 1996: *Shoes: a celebration of pumps, sandals, slippers and more.* New York: Workman Publishing.

PALACIOS, J. 1998: Ni rebeldes ni causa: los años 90. In Cueto, R. (ed.), *Los desarraigados en el cine español.* Gijón: Festival Internacional de Cine de Gijón, 113–40.

POWELL, M., and PRESSBURGER, E. 1948 (film): *The red shoes.*

RODRIGUEZ MARCHANTE, E. 1996: *Pasajes*: Gran salto, pero vacío. Review published on Internet. 22 November, www.mat.upm.es/-jcm/marchante/51.html.

RODRIGUEZ, M. P. 1997: Dark memories, tragic lives: representations of the Basque nation in three contemporary films. *Anuario de Cine y Literatura en Español* 3, 129–44.

SCHEMAN, N. 1995: Missing mothers/desiring daughters: framing the sight of women. In Freeland, C. A. and Warterburg, T. E. (eds), *Philosophy and Film.* London: Routledge, 89–108.

WARHOL, A. 1997: *Shoes, shoes, shoes.* Boston: Bullfinch Press.

|27|

Media pleasures: reading the telenovela

HUGH O'DONNELL

Introduction

The *telenovela* – like its predecessor the *radionovela* – was originally a Latin American product, first appearing in Cuba in the 1950s. As a form of non-continuous serial, it is a close cousin, though by no means an identical twin, of the soap opera. The fundamental difference is that while a soap opera provides a narrative shell within which an endless series of overlapping stories can be told, the *telenovela* – as the name suggests (television novel) – takes the form of a single story which will eventually come to an end, usually after around 160 episodes. The export success of Latin American *telenovelas* has been and continues to be enormous, and, despite being virtually unknown in northern Europe, they are almost certainly, on a global scale, the most viewed television products of all time.

The first Latin American *telenovela* to arrive in Europe was *Gabriela,* a Brazilian production shown in Portugal in 1975, taking advantage of the new cultural spaces opened up there by the revolution of 1974. Spain had to wait another 10 years until the arrival of Mexican and Venezuelan productions such as *Los ricos también lloran* ('The Rich Also Cry') and *Cristal* in the late eighties. They were shown by the public service channel TVE1 during the time-slot known as the 'sobremesa', the mid-to-late-afternoon period which, due to Spaniards' different eating times, still constitutes a kind of secondary or even parallel prime-time. Their initial success was astonishing, with audiences at times exceeding 10 million, and they became part of the conversation of everyday life. As Villagrasa points out (1992, pp. 415–6):

> For the first time in the history of Spanish television, an afternoon soap was beating all the peak hour programmes. It also gained one of the most loyal followings among television programmes. *Cristal* and

its leading actors became something of a social phenomenon stretching into all walks of life, even into political speeches on the state of the country.

Their audience consisted overwhelmingly of women (Roura, 1993, p. 16), something which would earn them often vitriolic scorn from Spain's mostly male television critics.

With the arrival of the three new private television channels in 1990, it was only a question of time before one of them attempted to turn the tremendous popularity of this cultural form to its own advantage. The challenge was eventually taken up by Antena 3, which had set itself the objective of replacing TVE1 (now La Primera) as Spain's most-watched channel. Rather than produce its own *telenovelas,* however, it preferred to enter into co-production agreements with Venezuelan producers, thereby taking advantage of their already existing expertise. This was not a particularly successful strategy, however, with joint productions such as *El oro y el barro* ('Gold and Mud') achieving only very modest audience ratings, and the experiment was eventually abandoned.

Domestic Spanish *telenovelas* and soaps

Catalonia

The first truly domestic *telenovela* to appear in Spain was not in fact 'Spanish' – in the sense that it was not shown throughout Spain – but Catalan. Entitled *Poble Nou* ('New People'), it began in March 1994, its final episode being shown on Christmas Eve of the same year. It arose from the convergence of a wide range of factors. Among these was the emergence of 'regional' television stations in a number of Spain's Autonomous Communities in the 1980s. Catalonia had been among the first, launching its first channel, TV3, in 1983 and its second, Canal 33, in 1989, both of these broadcasting uniquely in Catalan. Of these, TV3 had set itself the target – seldom achieved prior to 1994 – of replacing La Primera as the most viewed channel among Catalans. A second and closely related factor was the on-going process of 'normalization' of the Catalan language which had been adopted as an official policy by the Catalan parliament, the Generalitat, in 1983 and had been pursued vigorously ever since: its aim was – and continues to be – to make Catalan the normal language of everyday life in Catalonia.

Poble Nou was also conceived and prepared in the period immediately following the Barcelona Olympics of 1992 when Catalan self-belief and self-confidence were riding high. And it also coincided with a period of much greater participation by the leading Catalan nationalist political party in central Spanish politics. Following the inconclusive results of the Spanish

General Elections of 1992, the governing Socialist Party PSOE had found itself obliged to enter into agreements with two nationalist parties: Convergència i Unió in Catalonia and the Partido Nacionalista Vasco in Euskadi. As a result, the Catalan President Jordi Pujol found himself thrust onto centre stage in all-Spanish politics, while his tactical support for the PSOE earned him bitter attacks from conservative sectors of the Madrid-based Spanish media, attacks often widened to include Catalonia as a whole. The period 1993–94 was, therefore, a period of heightened Catalan self-belief combined with a growing feeling of being under indiscriminate and unjustified attack, an aggression which also extended to attacks on the use of the Catalan language itself.

Poble Nou's main scriptwriter was Josep Maria Benet i Jornet, one of Catalonia's most admired dramatists, well-known for his generally left-of-centre views. He took a determined stance to avoid the melodramatic style and tone characteristic of the Venezuelan and particularly Mexican *telenovelas,* preferring to continue the more 'realist' style of earlier Catalan productions such as *La Granja* ('The Shop') and *Estació d'enllaç* (Main Station), and indeed of the English production *EastEnders* which, under the title *Gent del barri* ('The Locals'), was being shown in Catalonia (but not in the rest of Spain): in fact, *Poble Nou* would eventually take over its late-afternoon time slot. *Poble Nou* dealt with a largish group of people – mostly the Aiguader family and those around them – living in the district of Poblenou in Barcelona. In the first episode they win the lottery and use the money to set up a small supermarket, but ensuing episodes would revolve centrally around their conflict with Eduald Balcells, a corrupt municipal architect who offered them flats in the Olympic Village if they would give up their houses in Poblenou for redevelopment, but who then renegued on the deal. A vast range of secondary story-lines would also cluster around this central narrative.

The success of *Poble Nou* – set entirely in Barcelona and broadcast wholly in Catalan – exceeded all expectations. It was originally planned to run for 120 episodes, but so great was audience interest that the original ending was scrapped and a further 70 episodes were added, the final episode being watched by around 1.5 million people, making it the most viewed item of televisual fiction ever in Catalonia (such audiences are usually reserved for football matches between Barcelona and Real Madrid). It made *telenovela* viewing 'respectable' in Catalonia, particularly among the male audience – this process being much facilitated by its deliberately non-melodramatic style and its serious exploration of topical issues – with many men finally prepared to admit publicly that they did actually watch productions of this kind. In fact, the view was frequently expressed that not watching *Poble Nou* meant more or less automatic exclusion from social conversation. But as well as recounting the lives of the Aiguaders, *Poble Nou* set itself a progressive, modernizing mission as regards Catalan society as a whole. As Josep Maria Benet i Jornet put it in an article in the Catalan-language magazine *El Temps* (9 May 1994):

We have a progressive view of society and human relationships ... and we try to put these liberal values across through our characters' stories. We show a woman who is capable of living without having to depend on her husband, a homosexual couple who are not disapproved of and who behave like any other couple, a boy and a girl who go and live together without anyone making a fuss ... we are doing this deliberately.

The year after its completion *Poble Nou* was shown throughout Spain by Antena 3 under the title *Los mejores años* ('The Best Years'), dubbed into Spanish by the original actors. Its viewing figures in this guise were, however, very low. The 'context of reading' which had crystallized in Catalonia in 1994 – the growing political and cultural self-confidence, the sense of a community and a language under attack and in need of defending and even promoting – was not, indeed could not be, replicated elsewhere in Spain at the time, and the reading positions available to its Catalan audience could not be reproduced outside Catalonia. As a result, many of the meanings and pleasures which *Poble Nou* had generated for its primary Catalan audience remained invisible to audiences elsewhere in Spain.

Following the success of *Poble Nou*, TV3 has gone on to produce a further five *telenovelas: Secrets de família* ('Family Secrets') and *Rosa* in 1995; *Nissaga de poder* ('Lineage of Power'), which ran from early 1996 to mid-1998; *Laberint d'ombres* ('Labyrinth of Shadows'), which began in the Autumn season of 1998, and *Nissaga: l'herència* ('Lineage: the Legacy') – a spin-off from *Nissaga de poder* – beginning in May 1999. Unlike *Poble Nou*, most of these have usually featured at least one Castilian speaker, these invariably being shown in a very positive light.

Rosa was a direct spin-off from *Poble Nou*, centring on its main female character as she tries to build a new life for herself in Manresa. It went out on a once-a-week regime on Sundays and achieved audiences of around 800 000, a 33 per cent share. The others have all been aired on a five-days-a-week basis, and their audiences have levelled out at between 700 000 and 800 000, which now appears to be, after the runaway success of *Poble Nou*, the 'natural' audience for the domestic *telenovela* in Catalonia. Of these, the most remarkable was in many ways *Nissaga de poder*. Originally planned to run for one year, such was its popularity that it was extended for a second, and then for a third, finally exceeding 600 episodes. In fact it eventually crossed the border beyond which it ceased being a *telenovela* strictly speaking and in fact became a soap. In the end the producers seemed not to know what do with it, its final episode involving the two main characters sailing off in a boat and committing suicide, rigging the boat to blow up before they do so.

The range of issues raised by these productions has been immense, and at times pioneering and trail-blazing in nature. Thus *Poble Nou* dealt with drugs, rape, disability, teenage sex, homosexuality and Aids. *Secrets de família* included gambling and alcoholism, while *Nissaga de poder* featured a number of incestuous relationships (between a brother and sister, between an aunt and her grown-up nephew) and introduced what must have been one of the first lesbian relationships to appear in any domestic television production anywhere in Spain. The tone in relation to these issues is never automatically condemnatory, since the moral framework of these pro-grammes – like that of most European soaps – is structured along different lines, valuing community, consideration for others, tolerance of difference and sincerity. Condemnation would ensue only if the characters' motivations were judged to be abusive and self-seeking, and therefore to lie outside the programmes' moral consensus.

The Catalan *telenovelas* have continued to develop notions of Catalan national identity in various ways. First, they have explored the geographical extension of 'Catalan-ness' by being set in different locations: *Rosa* in Manresa, *Secrets de família* in Girona, *Nissaga de poder* in the vine-grow-ing area of Alt Penedès, and *Laberint d'ombres* in Sabadell. They have also introduced the notion of historical time, with *Secrets de família's* narrative beginning during the student riots at the end of Franco era, and *Nissaga de poder* featuring the land-owning Montsolís family whose genealogy stretches back to the eighteenth century, and involving characters whose spoken memories stretch back to the early years of the Franco dictatorship. Likewise, they have featured characters from a range of sectors of Catalan society, from the working-class couple who work in Antonio's supermarket in *Poble Nou,* to the wealthy land-owning Montsolís clan, to the family in *Laberint d'ombres* which is being torn apart by the father's unemployment, though their most emblematic characters – and the ones on whom moral protagonism is most clearly bestowed – belong (as is the case in the bulk of European soap operas) to the (lower-)middle class. This was again a delib-erate choice. As the Head of Drama of TV3 pointed out in relation to *Poble Nou:*

> It had to be a product for all ages, one which would bring together in front of the screen the grandmother and the grandson, who normally don't watch television together ... it had to try to identify with the majority of its audience by creating lower-middle-class characters as its starting point.

> *(El Temps,* 9 May 1994)

This is to some extent the key to the success of the Catalan *telenovelas.* They make best sense when viewed as a televisual contribution to 'con-vivència' – that commitment to living in harmony with and in ways sup-portive of the other members of your community which is widely seen in Catalonia as a key defining element of Catalan national identity (O'Donnell and León Solís, 1994). Characters who step outside this moral framework can expect to be roundly condemned within the *telenovela's* narrative world (indeed, many come to sticky and often violent ends), while those who practice 'convivència' will eventually see their trials and tribulations – of which there are, of course, many – eventually rewarded not necessarily by success, but at least with the respect and approval of their fellow citizens.

Though there is no reliable way of measuring the linguistic impact of productions such as these, there can be little doubt that they have been important elements in the process of normalization of Catalan, and there is some evidence of Castilian speakers learning Catalan in order to follow them better and participate in the discussions they evoke. Like virtually all soaps and *telenovelas* throughout Europe they eschew overtly political issues and references, but they do construct a society attempting to establish a model of inclusiveness rather than exclusiveness, open to all who accept its fundamental values of understanding and tolerance.

Euskadi

The Basque Country would follow Catalonia's lead with the launch in October 1994 of *Goenkale* (High Road), broadcast five times a week at 8 p.m. *Goenkale* was seen from the outset as a soap rather than a *telenovela* – and indeed is still running now in 1999, having clocked up in excess of 700 episodes – and is produced for the first Basque-language channel ETB1 by the independent production company Pausoka. Its popularity has been by any standards astonishing given the relatively small percentage of the population of Euskadi which is genuinely competent in Basque (perhaps around 25 per cent): it has attracted average audiences of around 400 000 – a 30 per cent share – and is by a long way the most watched Basque-language programme ever to be screened by ETB (in addition, a Castilian-language version was made available on ETB2 from September 1996).

Goenkale is set in the fictional fishing town of Arralde, and the emphasis is very firmly on community. The opening sequence shows the inhabitants of the street – mainly the Lasa family and those close to them – coming up a hill together in a large group. As time has gone on the focus of the programme has widened out to include issues facing the town as a whole – for example, should it keep its character as a fishing town or become a tourist resort with all that might mean for its traditional personality and values.

As in the case of the Catalan *telenovelas*, *Goenkale*'s aim is at least partly linguistic in that everyone speaks Basque (a relatively unlikely situation in a Basque town of any size). It not only ducks the dialectical conflicts which have bedevilled the standardization of the Basque language by having everyone speak standard Basque (Lasagabaster, 1995, pp. 354–50), but – like virtually all soaps everywhere – avoids raising political tensions directly in any way. Though this is an important element of soaps' celebration of community, the lack of any reference to ETA in *Goenkale* has been the subject of some comment. As the director of Pausoka put it in a rather uncomfortable interview in the magazine *Hika* (August 1995):

> We are making this product for – so to speak – a specific client, ETB, which has its own rules of conduct. Consequently, in order for this product to maintain its place in the schedules and not find itself in difficulties, it has, for example, to sideline the political element. We are writing in a society with powerful political conflicts and confrontations, but none of that can appear in *Goenkale.*

However, although this absence may be a cause for concern among commentators, it is not by and large perceived as such by *Goenkale*'s viewers (any more so than the absence of any reference to the IRA has been perceived as a lack by viewers of British soaps). *Telenovela* and soap-opera viewers are well aware of the limits of the genre, and have a subtle understanding of which topics can and cannot emerge within their narratives.

Goenkale has featured many of the issues which are now standard fare for soap operas throughout Europe – drugs, homosexuality, alcoholism – as well as a number which relate to its specific location in a fishing community, such as the effects of EU quota restrictions on the local anchovy catches.

Madrid – Andalusia

As news of the success of the Catalan and Basque serials spread, it was to some extent inevitable that other regional stations would also experiment with this particular kind of programme. The next *telenovela* to emerge, *Vidas cruzadas* ('Crossed Lives'), was a complex amalgam, being jointly financed and screened by Telemadrid (Madrid) and Canal Sur (Andalusia) and produced by the Zepellin company using Catalan scriptwriters, production expertise and even studios (the scenes set in Madrid were actually shot in the Esplugues studios in Barcelona). It revolved centrally around the conflict between two generations of the Ribera family: the older, extremely wealthy generation determined to cling to their wealth at all costs, and the younger generation consisting of two legitimate children and illegitimate twins who had each been adopted by different families, one in Madrid and one in Andalusia, all being brought together when the father commits suicide and his will is found to bequeath property to all four of his children.

Vidas Cruzadas – which was much more popular in Andalusia than in Madrid – clearly bestowed moral protagonism on the younger group, and used them not only to criticise the entrenched social prejudices of the older group, but also to argue (narratively, of course) for much greater tolerance regarding, for example, racism and homosexuality. A new Andalusian *telenovela* was to be screened in 1999.

Galicia

A Galician soap entitled *Aguas Bravas* ('Rough Waters') was launched by Televisión de Galicia in 1999. Set partly in La Coruña and partly in a small fishing village, it also raises themes of historical presence (its opening shot is of a map of the Kingdom of Galicia written in Latin) and of community based around language and transcending differences of location or class, as well as of the reconciliation of the pre-modern and the modern (the local bar in the village has a computer hooked up to the Internet). While it is too early to say where it is heading and what its uniquely Galician specificities might be (beyond the use of the Galician language), its broad similarities with the Basque and Catalan productions seem fairly obvious.

All-Spain soaps

Telecinco – the most 'down-market' of Spain's new commercial channels (though it has recently made considerable efforts to present itself as the pre-ferred channel of the new middle classes) – finally rose to the challenge of producing a soap-opera for the whole of Spain. Entitled *El súper: historias de todos los días* ('The Supermarket: Stories of Everyday Life'), it was launched in September 1996, and is produced by the same production company as *Vidas cruzadas* also using Catalan scriptwriters and expertise. It is a genuine soap, and has continued to run ever since. Shown in pre-prime time, it has attracted audiences of around 2.5 million, a 30 per cent share. According to Telecinco's own data, over a third of its audience are men.

El súper is based mainly on the Bernal family which owns a chain of supermarkets in Madrid. Though it does involve at least one visit to the supermarket every day, and the struggle for control of the chain between the unscrupulous Alfonso and the more enlightened Julia and Mayka (whose ecological products are part of a now widespread symbology of social aware-ness) has been a central on-going theme, *El súper* also deals with many other issues as well as the emotional entanglements of its wide range of characters.

In 1998 Telecinco also began screening a highly popular mid-afternoon soap aimed at a teenage audience: *Al salir de clase* ('School's Out').

Conclusion

A striking feature of the Spanish *telenovelas* and soaps taken as a whole is the frequency with which the theme of inheritance appears. It provided the opening drama of *Goenkale*, was absolutely central to *Nissaga de poder*, *El súper* and above all *Vidas cruzadas*, and also surfaced in important ways in both *Rosa* and *Secrets de família*. These constant clashes over the link between the past and the present, and the competing sets of values which swirl around them, are best seen as a narrative enactment of the struggle of Spain's younger generations to demand their rights to a modern and participatory society from a dictatorial and self-seeking past, part of which – the grasping and self-promoting part – is threatening to reappear in the neoliberal future. Indeed, the links between old-style paternalism and new-style neo-liberal individualism are clear in a number of these productions, nowhere more clearly than in *Nissaga de poder* where one of the main characters – the son of an abusive landowner whose relationship with his workers has strong Francoist overtones – quite explicitly brings neo-liberal ideas back with him from a stay in the United States.

The advance of neo-liberalism throughout Western Europe in the eighties and nineties has resulted in the widespread delegitimation in official political discourse of notions of community and solidarity, to be replaced by a heavy emphasis on individual consumption, individual entrepreneurship and individual success. It has also led to a widening gap between the largely working-class electorates of Western Europe ('working class' in the sense that they work for someone else for a living) and their official political representatives, of whatever colour. As notions of community have become more and more marginalized and even to some extent trivialized in official politics, soap operas and *telenovelas* have come, throughout Europe, to constitute a cultural space where such values are not only kept alive, but are even to some extent celebrated. They create imagined communities which, in a classic dialectic, are simultaneously conservative in their melting away of class barriers – in the Catalan, Basque and Galician cases to be replaced by linguistic unity – and their corresponding obfuscation of actual social relations, and progressive in their narrative defence of the social-democratic inheritance and its belief in the values of solidarity, mutual respect and sharing, and in their openness to and tolerance of difference. The Spanish productions carry, of course, all sorts of regional and historical baggage which is not replicated elsewhere in Europe, but their central function remains the same, and the pleasures they offer their viewers are amply attested by their large and faithful audiences.

References

IDOYAGA, P. 1995: *Goenkale*: Entrevista a Xabier Puerta. *Hika*, August.

LASAGABASTER, J. M. 1995: The promotion of cultural production in Basque. In H. Graham and J. Labanyi (eds), *Spanish cultural studies: an introduction*. Oxford: Oxford University Press, 351–5.

O'DONNELL, H. and LEON SOLÍS, F. 1994: The Catalan Janus: discourses of national identity in the Catalan press. Paper presented to the First Scottish Conference of Catalan Studies in Scotland, Strathclyde University.

ROURA, A. 1993: *Telenovelas: pasiones de mujer*. Barcelona: Gedisa.

VILLAGRASA, J. M. 1992: Spain: the emergence of commercial television. In Silj, A. (ed.), *The new television in Europe*. London: John Libbey, 337–426.

VOLTAS, E. 1994: 'Poble Nou': la vida en un 'súper'. In *El Temps*, 9 May 1994.

|28|

Football and fandom in Spain

LIZ CROLLEY

When analysing some of the features of football in Spain today, we are reminded of how complex the relationship is between sport and society. In many ways, football in Spain is a microcosm of Spanish society. Two features that have historically distinguished Spanish football as a cultural phenomenon are the combination of the close links between club and fan, and the close ties between football and the state. These distinguishing features have persisted into the 1990s where the interconnections between the media and consumerism have become increasingly significant in relation to questions of identity and nationalism in Spanish football.

The role of football during the Franco regime has been documented in detail elsewhere (Fernández Santander, 1990; Shaw, 1987; Duke and Crolley, 1996), but it is important to be aware of the crucial role of football during this time, as well as its roots in Spain at the start of the twentieth century. On the one hand, certain major football clubs in the *nacionalidades históricas* (that is, those regions granted autonomy under the Second Republic (1931–36)) such as F.C. Barcelona in Catalonia, and Athletic de Bilbao and Real Sociedad in the Basque Country, symbolized opposition to the Franco regime in an era when any demonstrations of opposition to centralist policies were severely repressed. Only at the football ground could Catalans or Basques wave their nationalist flags – the *senyeras* and *ikurriñas* respectively – and sing their own anthems. On the other hand, football, the catalyst for nationalist sentiment, was tightly controlled by the state. State intervention in the running of football was profound. Following a decision announced in 1938 by Moscardó, chairman of the National Sports Council (CND) – later to become the National Sports Delegation (DND) – chairmen of football clubs were all appointed by the state and positions of power were held by Francoists. Later, in 1946, this policy was seemingly relaxed when it was decided that football clubs could appoint their own *presidentes* (directors of Spanish football clubs who carry out the functions of chairmen), but that their choice must be approved by the DND. Football was highly politicized and exploited by Francoist manipulation to strengthen the notion of a single national Spanish identity. Real Madrid played the key role and was promoted as the pride not just of Madrid but of the nation of Spain, especially when it enjoyed the most successful period in the history of any European football club in the late 1950s and won five European Cups.

The Franco period served to reinforce and further deepen the divisions which already existed in Spanish football. Even at the start of the century when football as a sport in Spain was still in its infancy, rivalries and hostility existed between clubs such as Real Madrid and F.C. Barcelona, Español and F.C. Barcelona, whose roles were already clearly defined; Real Sociedad and Athletic de Bilbao were already seen as representatives of the Basque Country. The post-Civil War period exacerbated these tense relationships and fans chose their football club according to their political leanings.

It is against this highly politicized background that we have to look at the current situation of football fandom in Spain. In the post-Franco period, the process of democratization and subsequent cultural changes led to rapid developments in the notions of regional and national identities. Thus, in the *nacionalidades históricas*, football, while still an important symbol of nationhood, is no longer the sole vehicle for the expression of nationalism. Fans have other outlets where they can express their political views so the cultural and political role of the football club is less clearly defined.

The football club nevertheless continues to stand as a symbol of nationhood and national pride in some instances. Shaw claims that 'F.C. Barcelona is in effect Catalunya's "national team" and as such draws support from almost the whole of the region's six million inhabitants' (1987, p. 62). Indeed, F.C. Barcelona has a high profile as far as the promotion of Catalanism is concerned. The language employed at the club is Catalan. Its publications are also in Catalan and, through its many *peñas* (social/supporter clubs) within the *Comunidad Autónoma* (autonomous region), the club funds cultural events and activities which encourage the use of the Catalan language and knowledge of Catalan traditions. In the Basque Country both Real Sociedad and (more strictly) Athletic de Bilbao continue their policy of recruiting only Basque players. The clubs based in the *nacionalidades históricas* are still seen as important symbols of the nation, and also of 'anti-madridismo' (anti-Madrid sentiment) and so they attract support from people who share their political outlook but who live outside the cities in which the clubs are based.

In other *Comunidades Autónomas* such as Aragón and Andalusia, local attempts to foster feelings of identification with the newly established politico-administrative entities sometimes include promoting football as an expression of the identity of the population. In 1994–95, *Zaragozamanía* in Aragón, which culminated in their Cup Winners' Cup Final victory against Arsenal in May 1995, saw the number of *socios* (club members) at Zaragoza rise from 13 000 to 25 000. Significantly, many of the new fans came not from the city itself but from surrounding areas within the *Comunidad* of Aragón. Perhaps these fans were influenced by the local government campaign which claimed on every hoarding 'A victory for Zaragoza is a victory for Aragón', thus reinforcing a link between football club and *Comunidad*. The football club was hailed not only as the flagship of Zaragoza, but as representative of the whole *Comunidad*.

Increasingly, the football club is seen, then, in terms of the *Comunidad* it represents rather than just the city or town in which it is based. Local institutions benefit as local sentiments strengthen and the football clubs gain, not least of all financially, as their support base broadens into their hinterland. Just as F.C. Barcelona has drawn support from all over Catalonia ever since its formation in 1899, so now clubs increasingly have fans throughout their *Comunidad* (as we saw in Aragón) and the football club plays a significant role in the self-definition of the *Comunidad*. This is said to account, for example, for much of the increase in club members of Albacete when gates rose from an average of 8500 in 1994–95 to 10000 in the season 1995–96.[1]

A relatively recent phenomenon involves the role of football in youth culture and the rise of organized groups of supporters, something akin to *ultra* groups in Italy. Increasingly, popular youth movements in Spain are linked to football clubs. Football, it appears, is being used as a vehicle for extreme political groups, and the football grounds as the battlefields where members of these extreme right-wing groups or *cabezas rapadas* (youths characterized by their shaven heads) turn support into extreme nationalism. This trend is by no means exclusive to Spain but is present also in other European countries such as Germany and Italy – the *Liga Antidefamación* (Anti-Defamation League) claims to have identified around 70000 ultras across Europe.[2] It is perhaps ironic that the Europeanization of some aspects of football culture, as similar patterns of support and organization emerge more or less simultaneously in different countries, is taking the form of a rise in these nationalist, xenophobic and racist groups.

At present in Spain, some of the most violent groups are to be found among the *Celtarra* (Celta de Vigo), the *Riazor Blues* (Deportivo de la Coruña) and the *Ultra Boix* (Sporting de Gijón). According to the researchers from the *Comisión Antiviolencia*, the Commission against Violence run by the Home Office, there are now around 2000 *cabezas rapadas*, most affiliated to ultra groups or club *peñas* associated with a football team. It appears that the clubs themselves, in providing finance, for example, for ultras to travel to support the team when they play away from home, are indirectly supporting these groups. *Juntas Españolas*, an extreme right-wing group, even claims to have contacted Jesús Gil y Gil, *presidente* of Atlético de Madrid, to discuss the creation of a new 'national patriotic front'.

Not all ultra groups are violent. There are those who condemn violence and those who claim to use violence as a means of expression (such as the *Brigadas Blanquiazules* of Español, the *Ultras Norte* of Mallorca, the *Frente Atlético* of Atlético de Madrid, the *Ultrasur* of Real Madrid). While never experiencing a wave of hooliganism such as that in the UK in the early 1980s (best documented in Dunning *et al.*, 1988), Spanish football does suffer from a problem of organized violence. These ultra groups are usually responsible. The youths themselves blame society for violence in football and express views typical of neo-Fascists – that they are fighting for the good of the Spanish nation, that they only attack those who pose a threat to the unity or economic situation of Spain.[3]

Spain, however, maintains its unique status and ultra groups differ from those in other European countries in that some of these groups are characterized not only by their nationalist tendencies but by their separatist inclinations too. The first evidence of neo-Fascist *cabezas rapadas* was reported, and perhaps significantly, in 1985 after a match between F.C. Barcelona and Español when a Barcelona fan was stabbed by the *Brigadas Blanquiazules* of Español. Ever since it was established in 1900 as the *Sociedad Española de Football*, Español has been a club associated with support for centralist policies, although recent tensions exist between two sets of fans – those who continue to identify with 'Spanishness' (including most of the *Brigadas Blanquiazules*) and wave Spanish flags, and the Catalanists who take their *senyeras* to the football ground and chant in Catalan.

Many youths holding extreme right-wing beliefs have since joined forces in similar violent nationalist groups such as the *Boixos Nois* of Barcelona and the *Frente Atlético* of Atlético de Madrid. The *Ultrasur* of Real Madrid have been described as displaying 'evidence of a nationalism close to Francoism' (Broussard, 1990, p. 115) and some members (who occupy the area of the ground behind one of the goals) are still proud to adorn themselves with neo-Nazi paraphernalia. In interviews with these fans, it very quickly becomes clear that they particularly loath supporters of F.C. Barcelona and Athletic de Bilbao who claim to be Catalan and Basque rather than Spanish. They justify attacks on fans of F.C. Barcelona and Athletic de Bilbao by claiming that they are cleansing Spain of its impurities.[4]

These ultra groups can be highly structured and organized, sometimes forming powerful pressure groups and forcing even major clubs such as Real Madrid to take notice of their views. When Real Madrid hosted a friendly to raise the profile of anti-racist campaigns, the *Ultrasur* painted racist slogans on the walls of the stadium and boycotted the match. Media reports during Real Madrid's presidential elections in 1995 refer to the role of the *Ultrasur* in intimidating the candidates, reportedly vandalizing the campaign offices and even issuing death threats. That same year manager Jorge Valdano, criticized by some members of the *Ultrasur* for signing *sudacas* (a pejorative term for South Americans), raised publicly the issue of who was paying for all the *Ultrasur* flags which were demanding his resignation.[5] At neighbouring club Atlético de Madrid, when ultras of Atlético stabbed a black youth on the streets of Sevilla following a match in that city, club *presidente* Jesús Gil y Gil reportedly turned up at the police station where they were held to plead for their release.[6] Gil y Gil himself has been accused of racism on several occasions.[7]

Identity forms part of the packaging of football as a product. Since the state intervened in the running of football and, via the *Ley del Deporte* sports legislation of 1992, forced the conversion of all but four professional football clubs into *Sociedades Anónimas* (types of public limited companies), football clubs have been run increasingly as businesses and are obliged to balance their books. Failure to do so used to lead to automatic relegation from the *Primera Liga* to semi-professional *Segunda B* until the fiasco of summer 1995, known as the *guerra del fútbol* (football war), when two clubs, Sevilla and Celta de Vigo, failed to fulfil the criteria necessary to convince the Professional Football League (LFP) that their financial situation was in good order. The clubs were officially relegated, but subsequently appealed. Fans in Andalusia and Galicia took to the streets and, concerned with public order, the government intervened, reversing the LFP decision and modifying their regulations so that *presidente*s of clubs would be sanctioned rather than clubs being relegated.

The fact that the state continues in the 1990s to feel it necessary to become involved in football (and this was not the only recent instance, as we shall see later) indicates how seriously the role of sport is still regarded today in the Spanish political arena – not only because of notions of national/regional identities, but increasingly because of the financial power of football.

Attempts to repackage football as a product have been taking place all over Europe (for example, the *embourgeoisement* of football in England in the 1990s, as it loses its working-class image). Football clubs realise the importance of a large supporter base and want to broaden their catchment area beyond their local roots if possible. The larger, more successful clubs (typified by Real Madrid and F.C. Barcelona in Spain) can do this. The media play a key role in the new consumer society and the significance of their relationships with football cannot be understated. It is frequently via deals with media outlets that clubs invest in order to extend their merchandising operations. For example, in 1996, television station Canal Plus bought the rights not only to televise all matches played at Real Madrid's Bernabéu stadium, but also the right to sell club merchandise. In Spain, it is significant that those clubs who have enjoyed the greatest success in their marketing campaigns thus far have been precisely those with historically strong political connotations – that is, Real Madrid, F.C. Barcelona and Athletic de Bilbao.

Indeed, it can even be argued that Real Madrid and F.C. Barcelona exploit their historical and political heritage. By repeatedly reinforcing their respective representations of centralism versus decentralization (García Candau, 1996), they share the support of the whole of the population of Spain. In Spain, almost everyone supports either Real Madrid or F.C. Barcelona, often as well as their local team. Without their special status neither club would enjoy such wide support. Hence, the *presidentes* of both clubs (currently Núñez at F.C. Barcelona and Sanz at Real Madrid), frequently become involved in slanging matches. It is no coincidence that these disputes are public and well covered by the media (*see* Crolley, 1997, pp. 33–43). It would not be in the interests of either club if the historical factors which are 'constructed' as representing their very essence were to be forgotten. In fact, since the early 1980s, F.C. Barcelona have been actively marketing themselves as being 'més que un club' (more than a club). It is recognized, therefore, that notions of identity are central to the allegiances between football fans and clubs. In the 1990s, clubs are beginning to manipulate these relationships in new ways, marketing football by exploiting these identifications.

The notion of football as a commodity to be marketed is a relatively new one in Spain, as in the UK. Until the 1980s, football enjoyed a special status in society. It was rare for a football club to make money, and that was not its primary aim. It held an important position within a community, even when its players were not born and bred locally. It was with the introduction of satellite television that media tycoons realised the potential of football to help sell their products. Televised sport, and in particular football, was popular and to own or control the exclusive rights to televise the game would secure a guaranteed audience for a television station.

Since the mid-1990s, attempts to capture the exclusive rights to televise Spanish football have led to various heated debates (Calleja, 1997). As in the rest of Europe, wrangling between football clubs, their institutions and television stations are well documented in the media. In Spain, the coverage itself is highly politicized because of the high stakes the newspapers and TV stations themselves have acquired in the deals. The huge potential of football to help sell satellite and (later) digital television, with the enormous possibilities of 'pay per view', was realized in the late 1980s and the first serious attempts to obtain the exclusive rights to televise Spanish football came from Antena 3 TV in 1995, run by Antonio Asensio. Negotiations began in a highly controversial manner. Rather than negotiating with the LFP, who then controlled the rights to televise Spanish football League and Cup matches, Antena 3 approached individual clubs and put their offers on the table. Individual clubs then began making deals involving huge sums of money.

Canal Plus soon entered the fray and bought the rights to televise certain of Real Madrid's home matches ('friendlies' and European matches, excluding the Champions' League), along with the right to exploit the commercial side of the club for 8500 million pesetas.[8] Formal links between football clubs and the media (mainly television stations or newspapers) strengthened as football club board members also had their stake in a particular television station (e.g. Manuel Calvo, former *presidente* of Sporting de Gijón and Antena 3 TV; Antena 3 TV also controlled both Mallorca and Sevilla in the mid-1990s – even though the *Ley de Sociedades Anónimas Deportivas* (the decree which laid down how football clubs should convert to limited company status) prohibits any single body from owning more than one club. As television stations bought the exclusive rights to televise football, other media such as radio began to demand their right to be present at an event which they claimed was of public interest. The situation became legally complex, the LFP lost its credibility and hence its power, and the wrangling became so heated that the government intervened once again and declared that football was of 'public interest'. In 1997, it was agreed that terrestrial television should be allowed to televise one match per week.

In this media-dominated world, the relationship between fans and football clubs is largely forgotten, but without fan interest the pulling power of football would be vastly diminished. However, it is almost incidental to the central issues preoccupying clubs and media that such debates serve to fuel the interest of the reader, the viewer and ultimately the fan.

Ironically, attempts to capitalize on the special relationship that exists in football between the commodity (football) and the consumer (the fan) are beginning to dilute the very core of that special feeling of identification between club and fan. Successful marketing of the product and the expansion of the supporter base to capture a larger market, including a more affluent sector, mean that the clubs benefit by larger crowds, higher prices and increased income. Thus, a much healthier financial position than that prior to the *Ley del Deporte* in 1992 (when most clubs were suffering huge financial losses) is secured. However, at the same time, the link between the football club and its local community is weakening. Identification between fan and club is beginning to fade.

A further aspect of social change in the Spanish game in the 1990s which has hardly been explored by sociologists concerns gender issues. Much research has been carried out into the relationship between football and masculinity in England (see Dunning, 1986; Messner and Sabo, 1990; Duke and Crolley, 1996) and many of these theories can be transferred to the Spanish context where football has also been, traditionally, a game played by men, for men. In Spain, as in the UK, football has reinforced both ideological and biological gender roles. Men are praised if they are strong, competitive and aggressive, while these attributes are seen as 'unfeminine' in a woman. Yet, changes are taking place in Spanish football grounds that appear to mirror developments in the UK.

Media reports indicate an increase in female interest in football roughly dating back to the 1994 World Cup in the United States. Although there is now an established Women's Football League and a Women's Cup competition and female participation in playing football has enjoyed a relative boom period in Catalonia in particular, female interest in football has largely been as a spectator sport in Spain. Some of the 15 per cent rise in attendances at *Primera Liga* matches in the 1995–96 season was attributed to the rise in the number of females, particularly young women in the 16-25 age group, attending football. Women's magazines increasingly publish articles on football-related issues, reflecting this growing interest among women. Football is now fashionable among social groups which were traditionally excluded. Gender roles are changing and factors which define constructions of masculinity and femininity are by no means static. It will be a long time before women play any significant part in the running of football, but it appears that they are beginning to break into this male preserve.

The start of the new millennium, then, signifies an important period in the development of football in Spain. The relationship between football club and fan is changing from one which implied identification and allegiance to one of commodity and consumer. Football is rapidly becoming part of consumer society, although it will always be a rather special product in Spain and clubs will never be straightforward businesses. Football clubs are still important cultural symbols within the *Comunidades Autónomas* and also national symbols in the Basque Country and Catalonia, even though they are no longer as highly politicized as they once were.

Wider changes that are taking place in society are also being reflected in the world of football. Some of these changes reflect the globalization – or at least Europeanization – of Spanish football as patterns of support become more homogenous across Europe, youth movements exploit the football arena and women enter a 'football market', which is increasingly consumer-driven, globally produced and networked like any other cultural product. Yet, at the same time, the historical and contemporary links between football and the socio-political fabric of Spain remain complex and arguably ensure the survival and continuation of Spain's uniqueness, where the likes of F.C. Barcelona will doubtless remain *més que un club*.

Notes

1. *El País,* 29 August 1995.
2. *El País,* 29 July 1994.
3. *Interviú,* 23 December 1997.
4. *Interviú,* 26 August 1987.
5. *El País,* 17 October 1995.
6. *El País,* 3 May 1992.
7. For example, *El País,* 25 April 1995.
8. *ABC,* 9 January 1996.

References

BROUSSARD, P. 1990: *Génération Supporteur.* Paris: Laffont.
CALLEJA, B. 1997: *La guerra 'incivil' del fútbol.* Barcelona: Plaza y Janés Editores.
CROLLEY, L. 1997: Real Madrid v Barcelona: the State against a Nation? In *International Journal of Iberian Studies* 10 (1), 33–43.
DUKE, V. and CROLLEY, L. 1996: *Football, Nationality and the State.* Essex: Addison Wesley Longman.

DUNNING, E. 1986: Sport as a male preserve: notes on the social sources of masculine identity and its transformation. In *Theory, Culture and Society* 3 (1), 79–80.

DUNNING, E., MURPHY, P. and WILLIAMS, J. 1988: *The roots of football hooliganism: an historical and sociological study.* London: Routledge.

FERNANDEZ SANTANDER, C. 1990: *El fútbol durante la guerra civil y el franquismo.* Madrid: Editorial San Martín.

GARCIA CANDAU, M. 1996: *Madrid – Barça: historia de un desamor.* Madrid: El País Aguilar.

MESSNER, M. and SABO, D. (EDS) 1990: *Sport, men and the gender order.* Illinois: Human Kinetics Books.

SHAW, D. 1987: *Fútbol y franquismo.* Madrid: Alianza Editorial.

Glossary

abertzale	left-wing Basque nationalist
acoso sexual	sexual harassment
aperturismo	cautious liberalization (end of Franco era)
autonomías	autonomous regions
AVE (Alta Velocidad Española)	Spanish high-speed train
ayuntamiento	town council/town hall
Bachillerato	baccalaureate
bakalao	'house'/'techno' music
Barça	Barcelona Football Club
barrio/barrio viejo/barrio chino	neighbourhood/old quarter/red-light district
boixos nois	gang of football hooligans (who support Barça)
búnker	extreme right-wing, die-hard Francoists, opposed to reform
cabeza rapada	skinhead
cacique	local (political) party boss/fixer
cantautor	singer-songwriter
casa del pueblo	Socialist workers' meeting-house (local branches of the PSOE)
castellano	Castilian (i.e. *español* or Spanish)
catalán	Catalan (spoken in Cataluña, with regional variations in the Baleares (Mallorquín) and the Comunidad Valenciana (Valencía))
catalanisme/catalanitat	Catalan regionalism/'Catalan-ness'
caudillo	leader (title assumed by Franco)
charnego (xarnego)	derogatory term used by native Catalans to other Spaniards living in Catalonia, especially those from Andalusia and Murcia

clase obrera	working class
Cobi	mascot for the 1992 Oympics, designed by Javier Mariscal
Comisiones Obreras (CCOO)	Workers' Commissions (Communist Trade Union)
competencias	'powers' devolved to Spain's regions
Comunidad Autónoma	autonomous region
copla	popular song
Cortes	Spanish Parliament
costumbrismo	local/regional life and customs
cultura del pelotazo	'sleaze culture' (political corruption)
desencanto	political disillusionment (circa 1978–81)
destape	permissiveness/nudity (in press, magazines film, etc. post-1975)
Ertzainzta	Basque police force
españolada	romanticized archetypal folkloric (musical), often comedy
esperpento	theatrical form focusing on the grotesque (e.g. Valle-Suclán)
ETA	Euskadi Ta Askatasuna (Basque Homeland and Freedom)
etarra	member of ETA
Euskadi/Euskera	Basque Country/Basque language
Exposición Universal de Sevilla	Seville Expo (April to October 1992)
Falange Española	Spain's Fascist Party (under Franco)
familia numerosa	large family (with three or more children)
felipismo/felipista	leadership style of Felipe González/supporter of FG
Franco y Bahamonde (Francisco)	Spain's military dictator 1939–75
franquismo/Francoism	personalized political style attributed to Franco
fueros	ancient political rights and privileges (for the Basque Country and Navarre)
Gallego/galego	Galician: official language of Galicia
GAL (Grupos Antiterroristas de Liberación)	clandestine, anti-terrorist, mercenaries implicated in 'dirty war' against ETA, 1983–88
Generalitat	Catalan/Valencian regional government
golpismo/golpista	military inclination to mount coups/supporter of a military coup
HB	Herri Batasuna (People's Unity: political wing of ETA)
hispanidad	the essence of Hispanic identity (across the world)/'Spanishness'

ikurriña	Basque flag
Izquierda Unida	United Left (coalition party)
jota	traditional Aragonese song and dance
latifundio/a	large estate(s)
litrona	litre bottle (usually of beer)
macho/machismo	male/male chauvinism
madrileño(s)	people of/residents of Madrid
magrebí	North African
maketo	Basque term of abuse applied to Spaniards
milagro económico	economic miracle
minufundio	small-holding
minusvalía/minusválido	disability/disabled person
Movida (madrileña), la	Madrid's (youth culture) 'scene' in the early 1980s
Mossos d'Esquadre	Catalan police force
Movimiento Nacional	Franco's official political movement
Nacionalcatolicismo	Catholic nationalism
nacionalidad histórica	a region granted autonomy under the Second Republic 1931–36
Nou Camp	Barça's football stadium
nova cançó	(Catalan) protest song (1960s–70s)
ONCE (Organización Nacional de Ciegos Españoles)	National Organization for the Blind
Opus Dei	secret lay Catholic organization
patria/patria chica	native land/home town or local area
PCE (Partido Comunista de España)	Spanish Communist Party
PNV (Partido Nacional Vasco)	Basque Nationalist Party
poderes fácticos	'real' (de facto) centres of political power (such as the Army, Catholic Church, etc.)
posfranquismo	post-Francoism
PP (Partido Popular)	People's Party
PSOE (Partido Socialista Obrero Español)	Spanish Socialist Party
rastro	Madrid's flea market
RNE (Radio Nacional de España)	Spanish National Radio
RTVE (Radiotelevisión Española)	Spanish Broadcasting Authority
sainete	one-act play focusing on daily life
Santiago Bernabeu	Real Madrid's football stadium
sardana	Catalan national dance
SF (Sección Femenina)	Women's section of Falange
senyera, la	Catalan flag
sevillana	Andalusian folk dance

SIDA (Síndrome de Inmunodeficiencia Adquirida)	Aids
tablao	flamenco dance performance
telenovela	television serial
televisiones autonómicas	regional television stations
tejerazo	attempted military coup 23 February 1981, led by Lieutenant-Colonel Antonio Tejero Molina
transición democrática	democratic transition (1977–82)
TVE (Televisión Española)	Spanish Television Authority
UCD (Unión de Centro Democrático)	Democratic Centre Union
UGT (Unión General de Trabajadores)	General Workers Union
ultra	extremist/football hooligan
Ultrasur	gang of football hooligans (who support Real Madrid)
Vasco	Basque (language)
zarzuela	Spanish light opera/musical comedy

Further reading

ALIAGA, J. V. and CORTÉS, J. M. G. 1997: *Identidad y diferencia. Sobre la cultura gay en España*. Madrid: Egales.

BALCELLS, A. 1996: *Catalan nationalism. Past and present*. Trans. Jacqueline Hall. New York: St Martin's Press.

BOHIGAS, O., BUCHANAN, P. and LAMPUGNANI, V. 1991: *Barcelona, city and architecture 1980–1992*. Barcelona: Gustavo Gili.

BOLAÑOS, M. 1997: *Historia de los museos en España*. Asturias: Ediciones Trea.

BOYD, C. 1997: *Historia patria. Politics, history and national identity in Spain, 1975–1995*. Princeton N. J.: Princeton University Press.

BRENAN, G. 1950: *The face of Spain*. London: Turnstile Press.

BRENAN, G. 1990: *The Spanish labyrinth*. Cambridge: Cambridge University Press.

BROOKSBANK JONES, A. 1997: *Women in contemporary Spain*. Manchester: Manchester University Press.

BUTLER, C. 1980: *After the wake: an essay on the contemporary avant-garde*. Oxford: Clarendon Press.

CARR, R. 1980: *Modern Spain: 1875–1980*. Oxford: Oxford University Press.

CARR, R. and FUSI, J. P. 1979 (2nd edn. 1981): *Spain: dictatorship to democracy*. London: Allen and Unwin.

CASTELLS, M. 1997: *The power of identity*. Oxford: Blackwell.

COLE, J. 1997: *The new racism in Europe. A Sicilian ethnology*. Cambridge: Cambridge University Press.

CORNELIUS, W. A. 1994: Spain: the uneasy transition from labor exporter to labor importer. In Cornelius, W. A. *et al.* (eds), *Controlling immigration. A global perspective*. Calif.: Stanford University Press.

CROLLEY, L. 1997: Real Madrid v Barcelona: the state against a nation? The changing role of football in Spain. *International Journal of Iberian Studies* 10 (1), 33–43.

DEACON, P. 1994: *The Press as the mirror of the new Spain*. Bristol: Bristol University Press, Occasional Papers Series No. 15.

DIEZ MEDRANO, J. 1995: *Divided nations: class, politics and nationalism in the Basque Country and Catalonia.* Ithaca, N.Y.: Cornell University Press.

DUKE, V. and CROLLEY, L. 1996: *Football, nationality and the state.* Essex: Addison Wesley Longman.

EDLES, L. D. 1998: *Symbol and ritual in the new Spain. The transition to democracy after Franco.* Cambridge: Cambridge University Press.

ESENWEIN, G. and SHUBERT, A. 1995: *Spain at war. The Spanish Civil War in context 1931–39.* London and New York: Longman.

EVERETT, W. (ED.) 1996: *European identity in cinema.* Exeter, Intellect Books.

GILMOUR, D. 1992: *Cities of Spain.* London: John Murray

GIES, D.T. (ED.) 1999: *The Cambridge companion to modern Spanish culture.* Cambridge: Cambridge University Press.

GILLESPIE, R. *et al.* 1995: *Democratic Spain: reshaping relations in a changing world.* London: Routledge.

GRAHAM, H. and LABANYI, J. 1995: *Spanish cultural studies: an introduction.* Oxford: Oxford University Press.

GUNTHER, R. (ED.) 1993: *Politics, society and democracy: the case of Spain.* Boulder: Westview.

HANSEN, E. 1977: *Rural Catalonia under the Franco regime: the fate of regional culture since the Spanish Civil War.* Cambridge: Cambridge University Press.

HARRISON, J. 1993: *The Spanish economy. From the Civil War to the European Community.* London: Macmillan.

HEYWOOD, P. 1995: *The government and politics of Spain.* London: Macmillan.

HOLMAN, O. 1996: *Integrating southern Europe – EC expansion and the transnationalization of Spain.* London: Routledge.

HOOPER, J. 1995: *The new Spaniards.* Harmondsworth: Penguin.

JORDAN, B. 1990: *British Hispanism and the challenge of literary theory.* Warminster: Aris and Phillips.

JORDAN, B. 1990: *Writing and Politics in Franco's Spain.* London and New York: Routledge.

JORDAN, B. and MORGAN-TAMOSUNAS, R. 1998: *Contemporary Spanish cinema.* Manchester: Manchester University Press.

KINDER, M. 1993: *Blood cinema. The reconstruction of national identity in Spain.* Berkeley, Calif.: University of California Press.

KINDER, M. (ED.) 1997: *Refiguring Spain. Cinema/media/representation.* Durham and London: Duke University Press.

LIEBERMANN, S. 1982: *The contemporary Spanish economy. A historical perspective.* London: Allen and Unwin.

LONSDALE, S. 1990: *Women and disability: the experience of disability among women.* London: Macmillan.

MAR-MOLINERO, C. and SMITH, A. (EDS) 1996: *Nationalism and the nation in the Iberian Peninsula: competing and conflicting identities.* Oxford: Berg.

MAXWELL, R. 1995: *The spectacle of democracy: Spanish television, national-*

ism and political transition. Minneapolis, Minn.: University of Minnesota Press.

MONTERDE, J. E. 1993: *Veinte años de cine español (1973–1992). Un cine bajo la paradoja*. Barcelona: Ediciones Paidós.

MUSEO NACIONAL, CENTRO DE ARTE REINA SOFIA 1995: *Señales de video: aspectos de la videocreación española de los últimos años*. Madrid: Ministerio de Cultura.

NAVAJAS, G. 1996: *Más allá de la posmodernidad. Estética de la nueva novela y cine españoles*. Barcelona: EUB.

NEWTON, M. T. and DONAGHY, P. J. 1997: *Institutions of modern Spain: a political and economic guide*. Cambridge: Cambridge University Press.

O'DONNELL, H. 1996: Constructing the citizen-king: monarchy, media and myth in contemporary Spain. *International Journal of Iberian Studies* 9 (3), 143–54.

O'DONNELL, H. 1999: *Good times, bad times: soap operas and society in Western Europe*. London: Leicester University Press.

O'DONNELL, H. and BLAIN, N. 1994: Royalty, modernity and postmodernity: Monarchy in the British and Spanish presses. *ACIS Journal* 7 (1), 42–53.

PAYNE, S. 1984: *Spanish Catholicism: an historical overview*. Madison, Wis.: University of Wisconsin Press.

PAYNE, S. G. 1987: *The Franco Regime, 1936–1975*. Madison, Wis.: University of Wisconsin Press.

PEÑA-MARIN, C. and FABRETI, C. 1990: *La mujer en la publicidad*. Madrid: Ministerio de Asuntos Sociales: Instituto de la Mujer.

PRESTON, P. 1986: *The Spanish Civil War, 1936–39*. London: Weidenfeld and Nicholson.

PRESTON, P. 1986: *The Triumph of Democracy in Spain*. London: Methuen.

PRESTON, P. 1993: *Franco: a biography*. London: Fontana.

REY, J. 1994: *El hombre fingido: la representación de la masculinidad en el discurso publicitario*. Madrid: Fundamentos.

RINGROSE, D. R. 1996: *Spain, Europe and the 'Spanish Miracle' 1700–1900*. Cambridge: Cambridge University Press.

RODGERS, E. (ED.) 1999: *Encyclopedia of contemporary Spanish culture*. London: Routledge.

ROSS, C. J. 1997: *Contemporary Spain. A handbook*. London: Arnold.

RICHARDS, M. 1998: *A time of silence: Civil War and the culture of repression in Franco's Spain, 1936–1945*. Cambridge: Cambridge University Press.

SALMON, K. 1995: *The modern Spanish economy*. London: Pinter.

SERRALLER, F. C. 1988: *Del futuro al pasado: vanguardia y tradición en el arte español contemporáneo*. Madrid: Alianza Editorial.

SHUBERT, A. 1990: *A social history of modern Spain*. London and Boston, Mass.: Unwin Hyman.

SMITH, A. 1996: *A historical dictionary of Spain*. Lanham, Md.: Scarecrow Press.

SMITH, P. J. 1994: *Desire unlimited: the cinema of Pedro Almodóvar*. London: Verso.

SMITH, P. J. 1996: *Vision machines: cinema, literature and sexuality in Spain and Cuba, 1983–1993*. London: Verso.

SULLIVAN, J. 1988: *ETA and Basque nationalism: the fight for Euskadi, 1890–1986*. London: Routledge.

TORREGROSA, J. R. 1996: Spanish international orientations: between Europe and Iberoamerica. In Breakwell, G. and Lyons, E. *Changing European identities*. Oxford: Oxford University Press, 111–21.

TRUSCOTT, S. and GARCIA, M, 1998: A *dictionary of contemporary Spain*. London: Hodder and Stoughton.

WIARDA, H. 1996: *Iberia and Latin America. New democracies, new policies, new models*. Lanham, Md.: Rowman and Littlefield.

WRIGHT, A. 1977: *The Spanish economy. 1959–1976*. London: Macmillan.

Index